WAR CRIMES
AND
COLLECTIVE
WRONGDOING

D1501465

𝔹

For Devon and Nikola

WAR CRIMES

——— AND ———

COLLECTIVE WRONGDOING

A Reader

Edited by

Aleksandar Jokić

BLACKWELL *Publishers*

Copyright © Blackwell Publishers Ltd 2001

First published 2001

2 4 6 8 10 9 7 5 3 1

Blackwell Publishers Inc.
350 Main Street
Malden, Massachusetts 02148
USA

Blackwell Publishers Ltd
108 Cowley Road
Oxford OX4 1JF
UK

Library of Congress Cataloging-in-Publication Data

War crimes and collective wrongdoing: a reader / edited by Aleksandar Jokić.
    p. cm.
    Includes bibliographical references and index.
    ISBN 0–631–22504–8 (alk. paper)—ISBN 0–631–22505–6 (pb.: alk. paper)
    1. War crimes.   2. Genocide.   3. Nationalism.   I. Jokić, Aleksandar.

K5301 W368 2001
341.6′9—dc21

00–060792

British Library Cataloguing in Publication Data
A CIP catalogue record for this book is available from the British Library.

Typeset in Bembo 10.5 on 12.5pt
by Kolam Information Services Pvt Ltd Pondicherry, India
Printed in Great Britain by MPG Books, Bodmin, Cornwall

This book is printed on acid-free paper.

Contents

Contributors

Jovan Babic is Professor of Ethics, Chair of the Philosophy Department at the University of Belgrade, FR Yugoslavia, and Board Member at the Institute for European Studies (Belgrade). Professor Babic is co-founder of the International Law and Ethics Conference Series (organized every June at Belgrade University with follow-ups every October in the United States). He has published over 60 articles and essays in professional journals and collections, along with two books, *Kant and Scheler* (1986) and *Morality and Our Time* (1998).

David E. Cooper is Professor of Philosophy at the University of Durham. His several books include *Existentialism: A Reconstruction* (Blackwell Publishers, second edition 1999), *World Philosophies: An Historical Introduction* (Blackwell Publishers 1995), and *Heidegger* (1996). His many articles include several on the topic of collective responsibility.

J. Angelo Corlett is Professor of Philosophy at San Diego State University and Founding Editor-in-Chief of *The Journal of Ethics*. Professor Corlett has authored *Analyzing Social Knowledge* (1996), and numerous articles on moral, social, and political philosophy, including several on secession, political violence, rights, and justice. He is currently writing books on Racism and Reparations; Terrorism and Secession; and Responsibility and Punishment.

David A. Crocker is Senior Research Scholar at the Institute for Philosophy and Public Policy and the Maryland School of Public Affairs (MSPA) at the University of Maryland. He specializes in sociopolitical philosophy, international development ethics, and transitional justice. While Professor of Philosophy at Colorado State University (1966–93), Crocker wrote *Praxis and Democratic Socialism: The Critical Social Theory of Markovic and Stojanovic*

(1983). He has been a visiting professor at the University of Munich and twice a Fulbright Scholar at the University of Costa Rica. Since coming to the University of Maryland in 1993, Dr. Crocker has co-edited (with Toby Linden) *Ethics of Consumption: The Good Life, Justice, and Global Stewardship* (1998) and has written *Florecimiento humano y desarrollo internacional: La nueva ética de capacidades humanas* [Human Flourishing and International Development: The New Ethic of Human Capabilities] (1998). He is a founder and current president of the International Development Ethics Association.

Anthony Ellis was Senior Lecturer in Moral Philosophy and Chair of the Moral Philosophy Department in the University of St. Andrews, Scotland, before becoming Professor of Philosophy in Virginia Commonwealth University. He was also co-founder and first Academic Director of the Centre for Philosophy and Public Affairs at St. Andrews. He has published articles in a number of areas of philosophy, including Aesthetics, Philosophy of Mind, Philosophy of Religion, Philosophy of Law, Ethics and Wittgenstein. He now works mainly in the Philosophy of Law. He is the editor of *Ethics and International Relations* (1986) and of the journal *Philosophical Books*.

Richard Falk is Albert G. Milbank Professor of International Law and Practice at the Woodrow Wilson School, Princeton. He has authored more than a dozen books including *Law, Morality and War in the Contemporary World* (1984) and *Legal Order in a Violent World* (1968). He was counsel to the International Court of Justice; research director of the Coming Global Civilization project; and honorary Vice-President of the American Society of International Law.

Peter A. French is the Director of The Ethics Center and Chair of the Department of Philosophy of the University of South Florida. Before coming to the University of South Florida, he was the Lennox Distinguished Professor of the Humanities and Professor of Philosophy at Trinity University in San Antonio, Texas. Dr. French is the senior editor of *Midwest Studies in Philosophy*, editor of the *Journal of Social Philosophy*, and was general editor of the *Issues in Contemporary Ethics* series. He is the author of sixteen books including *Cowboy Metaphysics: Ethics and Death in Westerns* (1997), *Corporate Ethics* (1995), *Responsibility Matters* (1992), *Collective and Corporate Responsibility* (1984), *Ethics in Government* (1983), and *The Scope of Morality* (1979). He is currently writing a book on The Virtues of Vengeance.

Alan Gewirth is the Edward Carson Waller Distinguished Service Professor of Philosophy at the University of Chicago. He is the author of *Human Rights: Essays on Justification and Applications* (1982), *Reason and Morality*

(1982), *The Community of Rights* (1996), and *Self-Fulfillment* (1998). A pivotal figure in the twentieth-century Meta-Ethics and Theory of Justice, his work is the subject of *Gewirth's Ethical Rationalism: Critical Essays with a Reply by Alan Gewirth* (1984), and *Gewirth: Critical Essays on Action, Rationality, and Community* (1999). In *The Community of Rights* he extends his fundamental principle of equal and universal rights, the Principle of Generic Consistency, into the arena of Social and Political Philosophy.

Margaret Gilbert is Professor of Philosophy at the University of Connecticut, Storrs. She has held visiting Professorships at Princeton University, King's College London, and has been an Herodotus Fellow in the School of Historical Studies at the Institute for Advanced Study, Princeton. She lectures widely in the United States and Europe on topics in philosophical social theory and political philosophy. Her major publications include her books *On Social Facts* (1989), *Living Together: Rationality, Sociality, and Obligation* (1996), and *Sociality and Responsibility: New Essays in Plural Subject Theory* (2000).

Aleksander Jokić is Professor of Philosophy at Portland State University. Professor Jokić is Executive Director of the Center for Philosophical Education (at SBCC), founding Editor of *STOA – International Undergraduate Journal of Philosophy*, and co-founder of the International Law and Ethics Conference Series (organized every June at Belgrade University with follow-ups every October in the US). Author of *Aspects of Scientific Discovery* (1996), editor of forthcoming books: *From History to Justice*, and co-editor with Professor Quentin Smith of *Time, Tense and Reference* and *Consciousness and Mind/Body Problem*. His most recent published papers deal with the ethics of economic sanctions, fetal rights, Hegel on nationalism and state, and present rights of future individuals.

Richard W. Miller is Professor of Philosophy at Cornell University. Professor Miller joined the Sage School faculty in 1974. His interests include social and political philosophy, epistemology, philosophy of science, and ethics. His publications include: *Analyzing Marx: Morality, Power and History* (1984), "Ways of Moral Learning," *The Philosophical Review* (1985), *Fact and Method: Explanation, Confirmation and Reality in the Natural and the Social Sciences* (1987), *Moral Differences: Truth, Justice and Objectivity in a World of Conflict* (1992), "The Norms of Reason," *The Philosophical Review* (1995).

James W. Nickel is Professor of Philosophy at the University of Colorado, Boulder. He is the author of *Making Sense of Human Rights* (1987), and of many articles in ethics, political philosophy, and philosophy of law.

Alfred P. Rubin is Distinguished Professor of International Law at The Fletcher School of Law & Diplomacy, Tufts University. Since 1994 he has been President of the American Branch of the worldwide International Law Association. He is the author of about 94 articles on a wide variety of topics dealing with international law and the sole author of books, the latest of which is *Ethics and Authority in International Law* (1997), seriously critical of current efforts to establish an international criminal court.

Michael Slote is Professor of Philosophy at the University of Maryland, College Park, and the author of several books and many articles in ethics. A member of the Royal Irish Academy and former Tanner lecturer, his book *Morals From Motives* is being published in fall of 2000.

Burleigh T. Wilkins is Professor of Philosophy at the University of California, Santa Barbara. Professor Wilkins made substantial contribution to the analytic philosophy of history and the study of Burke's political philosophy. He is the author of *Terrorism and Collective Responsibility* (1992), *Hegel's Philosophy of History* (1974), and numerous journal articles including "A Third Principle of Justice," *Journal of Ethics* (1997).

Preface

The essays collected here are all associated with an ongoing project called "International Law and Ethics Conference Series." This unique endeavor, now in its fourth year, has used a dialogic-comparative model consisting of a conference each June at Belgrade University and a follow-up conference in the The United States. This two-part strategy has given leading moral, legal, and political philosophers – and increasingly, scholars from other disciplines – from the US and Western Europe the opportunity to meet with their Eastern European counterparts to discuss issues of global importance, many of which have been generated by events in the region.

This troubled region is hardly unique with respect to the need to analyze and understand the underlying causes of ethnic hatred and the need to discover ways of living together. Recent experiences in Lebanon, South Africa, Latin America, Northern Ireland, Spain's Basque region, Corsica, Cashmere, Rwanda, East Timor, Chechnya, and many other places around the world, demonstrate that sometimes there are real tensions between peace and justice. The goal of the essays is to examine conceptual and practical issues of war crimes, trials for war crimes, nationalism, collective responsibility, interethnic reconciliation, and transitional justice.

The central focus of this volume, however, is on war crimes and collective wrongdoing. The concept of war crimes is of major importance for international justice yet philosophers have hardly dealt with the issue of what to do about war crimes. The reason might be that in order to obtain a full understanding of this concept is required, interdisciplinary cooperation of the kind philosophers, until recently, were not likely to undertake. This is why the project that resulted in this book, and the corresponding conference series, was conceived as an opportunity to bring together philosophers and scholars from related disciplines to bear on puzzles regarding war crimes, collective wrongdoing, and a host of associated issues.

Most of the essays collected here were original contributions to the first pair of conferences in the series titled "War Crimes: Moral and Legal Issues." The conferences took place at Belgrade University on June 21–2, 1997 and at the University of California Santa Barbara on November 14–16, 1997. These are essays by Jovan Babic, Michael Slote, Burleigh Wilkins, Anthony Ellis, Richard Miller, James Nickel, Margaret Gilbert, Angelo Corlett, and David Crocker. It should be noted that Alan Gewirth and Peter French, while they were prevented from attending the conferences (in Belgrade and Santa Barbara respectively), still graciously produced papers for this purpose. The essays by Richard Falk and David E. Cooper come from the second pair of conferences titled "War, Collective Responsibility, and Interethnic Reconciliation." The conferences took place at Belgrade University on June 26–8, 1998 and at Santa Barbara City College on October 9–11, 1998. Finally, Alfred Rubin's article comes from what should have been the follow-up conference on "Secession, Transitional Justice, and Reconciliation" held at the University of San Francisco on October 29–31, 1999. Instead, it was the only conference in 1999, as the Belgrade June session had to be canceled due to NATO bombing of Yugoslavia.

As cofounder, with Jovan Babic, of the International Law and Ethics Conference Series and editor of this volume, I would like to express my gratitude for the opportunity afforded me to engage in this interesting, personally rewarding, ongoing, and, I hope, important as well as useful project. Thanks are due first of all to Peter MacDougal, President of Santa Barbara City College, who had the wisdom and courage to support the creation of the Center for Philosophical Education (CPE), housed within the Department of Philosophy at SBCC, which is the institution behind the entire endeavor while cooperating with many other organizations. I am also especially grateful to Joseph White and James Chesher for steering CPE in the right direction and keeping it afloat. Mark Juergensmeyer, Director of the UC, Santa Barbara Global Peace and Security Program, hosted the 1997 follow-up conference while Michael Torre and Abrol Fairweather provided a home for the 1999 conference. Burleigh Wilkins offered continuing advice and encouragement. Jovan Babic was the closest friend and ally every step of the way. Anthony Ellis took on the challenge to write a comprehensive Introduction intended to be particularly helpful to students and nonprofessionals while offering critical comments on some major issues that have not yet emerged clearly in discussions of war crimes and collective wrongs. Most of all, I thank my wife, Sharan, for her unwavering support, both intellectual and domestic.

A. J.
Portland, Oregon
March 2000

Acknowledgments

A version of "Collective Remorse" was previously published in *Sociality and Responsibility: New Essays in Plural Subject Theory*, by Margaret Gilbert, 2000. Reprinted with permission of Rowman and Littlefield.

"Transitional Justice and International Civil Society: Toward a Normative Framework" by David Crocker in *Constellations* (1998) Vol. 5:4, 492–517. Reprinted with permission of Blackwell Publishers Ltd.

A version of "Secession and Self-Determination; A Legal, Moral and Political Analysis" by Alfred Rubin was previously published by Stanford Journal of International Law, 2000. Reprinted with permission of Stanford University.

Introduction

Anthony Ellis

I

Are there really such things as "war crimes"? Certainly, terrible things are done in wars, things which, if done in any other context, would be crimes. But, done in the context of war, are they really crimes?

The question spans two different sorts of skepticism. One is a moral skepticism: the laws of morality, it may be said, do not apply to war, and so nothing that is done in pursuit of war aims can be immoral. Such a view is often, rightly or wrongly, attributed to Machiavelli, and is often known as Political Realism. But on reflection there seems little to be said for such a view. What, after all, is so special about war, that it should offer moral legitimation to anything that one does in pursuit of one's war aims?

One thought would perhaps be that morality applies only to the behavior of individuals, not to the behavior of states. But states perform actions only to the extent that individuals do, so what are we to make of the alleged contrast? Perhaps this: that when individuals act as representatives of states then they are not bound by moral considerations. But now, again, there seems little to be said for this view. It seems to be either an arbitrary linguistic stipulation, restricting the word "moral" to purely personal inter-actions, or a moral view whose unpleasantness is clear but whose motivation is obscure.

Another thought might be that of General Sherman: "War is cruelty, and you cannot refine it."[1] But going to war need not be an act of cruelty, nor need everything that is done in pursuit of a war. Nor is it true that war imposes circumstances in which it is impossible to constrain one's actions, at least to some degree, to what is morally required. Of course, moral atrocities are routinely carried out in wars, and that is not a coincidence. But it is dishonesty to think that this somehow legitimates one's own immoralities.

Perhaps there is nothing more to the thought than a confusion between two different claims. When Cicero said that laws are silent in a war[2] this could be taken to mean simply that, as a matter of fact, no-one does in fact obey moral rules during a war. But even if this were true, it should not be confused with the quite different claim that moral rules do not apply during a war; the fact that a rule is widely disobeyed does not mean that it does not apply. In any case, the first claim, though often asserted, is clearly false. People often obey moral rules during warfare, often to their, and their country's, detriment. Contrary to General Sherman, war has been "refined" considerably over the centuries by, for instance, codes of honor, standards of morality, self-interest, and international law.

The idea, for instance, that captured enemy soldiers may not be ill-treated is, in various forms, very ancient, and can be found in a number of different civilizations before the Christian era.[3] This is no surprise; like many moral rules, its general observance works to the benefit of all of those who partake in the activity that it governs. Its source in the notion of chivalry seems natural too: to take pride in one's profession is a natural human tendency, shared by soldiers as much as by others, and there seems little to take pride in in killing or mistreating the helpless.

In the Christian tradition St. Augustine and St. Thomas both addressed the issue of war, particularly the question of when it is morally permissible to go to war, and they were in no doubt that the decision to go to war is governed by stringent moral requirements. By the seventeenth century there was a substantial literature on this question, and, increasingly, on the question of what conduct is permissible in war. This literature is generally referred to as the "Just War" tradition, and the most notable part of it is Hugo Grotius's treatise *De Jure Belli ac Pacis*.[4] Grotius's writings did not seem to have much influence on the conduct of war for 300 years or so, but many of his basic ideas eventually found their way into international law and the military academies.[5]

The restrictions that were thought to govern the conduct of war (they are often referred to as the *jus in bello*) were not arbitrary; they derive in part from restrictions governing when it is permissible to go to war in the first place (the *jus ad bellum*, as it is known). Given that the death and destruction that war involves are terrible things, they need a strong justification; that justification must be that they are absolutely imperative for the achievement of a morally justified end. What morally justified end can war serve? The Just War tradition converged on the view that that end must relate to the defense of oneself or others against unjust aggression, the rectification of wrongs done by unjust aggression, or the punishment of aggressors in order to reform and deter. Grotius, for instance, says, "It has been shown before, and it is a truth founded upon historical fact, that wars are undertaken, as acts of punishment, and this motive, added to that of redress for injuries, is the source from which the duties of nations, relating to war, take their rise. . . . All punishment . . . must have in view either security against future aggressions, reparation for the injury done to national or private honour, or it must be used as an example of awful severity."[6] As for the conduct of war, justifying his view that rape "should not go unpunished in war any more than in peace," Grotius refers to "the fact that such acts do not contribute to safety or to punishment."[7]

We thus have two sets of moral rules, one set governing when it is justified for a nation to go to war, the other governing what it may do in the course of a justified war. The former correspond to the accusation, made against the Nazi leadership at Nuremberg, of "crimes against peace": "planning, preparation, initiation or waging a war of aggression, or a war in violation of international treaties."[8] The latter correspond to the accusation of "War Crimes": "Such violations shall include, but not be limited to, murder, ill-treatment or deportation to slave labor or for any other purpose of civilian population of or in occupied territory, murder or ill-treatment of prisoners of war or person on the seas, killing of hostages, plunder of public or private property, wanton destruction of cities, towns or villages, or devastation not justified by military necessity."

So there are moral rules, and those who break them act wrongly. And when we learn about particularly horrible war crimes, our natural attitude is one not simply of horror at what was done to the victims, but of condemnation, and not just condemnation of the actions but of the people who carried them out. Here, the Augustinian injunction to hate the sin but love the sinner is peculiarly hard to comply with. What our attitude should be to such people is the subject of Peter French's contribution.

It would perhaps be comforting to think that such people, when they commit appalling crimes, think that what they are doing is morally right. At least we could then attribute to them the virtue of conscientiousness.[9] It would also help us to retain the sense that a knowledge of morality is somehow an obstacle to doing what is wrong. French, however, suggests that there is little reason to think this. Bosnian war criminals who raped, tortured, multilated, and murdered defenseless women knew perfectly well in general what it is to believe that actions are morally right and wrong. And they knew that they were raping, torturing, multilating, and murdering. And "one cannot both know what it means to believe that some action is morally wrong and also believe that raping, torturing, multilating, and murdering defenseless women are not morally wrong" (pp. 36-7), because to know what such things are involves knowing that they are indeed wrong. We are then left with the alternative that such people knew that what they did was wrong, but did it anyway. A tradition of philosophy from Socrates onwards has denied that this is possible. French argues, on the contrary, that it is indeed possible, that it is just a fact that one can think that something is wrong, but care too little about that to refrain from doing it. "The average Bosnian war criminal . . . is the living moral monster, the possibility of whose existence has been denied by a legion of moral philosophers from ancient times to the present" (p. 39).

This having been said, there remains another question: should such people be held morally responsible? One answer, relying upon a certain interpretation of the principle that one can be morally responsible only for what one freely chooses, holds that they should not. Because they have been so enculturated with attitudes of hatred and contempt, they have no real capacity to control the actions in question and so no real choice about them. French rejects this view. He holds that we judge people morally responsible as part of the practice, amongst others, of blaming and praising, and that this practice has a point: morality is in large part our attempt to prevent evil, and one way in which we do that is by evaluating characters with the thought in mind that certain sorts of characters are ones that we ought not to have, and that we ought not to associate with others who do have them; for the purpose of such an evaluation it makes no difference how a character has been formed. We may thus say that war criminals are indeed morally responsible for what they do.

This is a moral judgment and, of itself, tells us nothing about whether it is appropriate to punish such people. That is a question that French does not take up. It takes us naturally into the second of the two sorts of skepticism that I mentioned at the beginning. When people speak of war crimes, the word "crimes" is usually intended to imply that, in some sense, the actions in question are offenses against the law, and therefore merit punishment. This skepticism has more substance than the first, the skepticism about whether actions taken in pursuit of war aims are subject to moral evaluation. It takes as its basis the maxim, *Nullum crimen sine leges*: without laws there is no crime. Where, it might be asked, is the law that defines what war crimes are?

Of course, nations have their own laws governing what their citizens may or may not do during wartime, and these laws typically include the behavior of soldiers during hostilities, occupation, and so on. There is little doubt that these laws are indeed law, and when people express dissatisfaction with the idea of war crimes, and their punishment, they are, of course, usually speaking of the "crimes" defined by international law. They may particularly have in mind the Nuremberg and Tokyo trials that were carried out after the Second World War. Those trials were found objectionable by many people for different, though connected, reasons: they were simply "victors' justice," they were revenge, or political policy, dressed up in legal garb, they exercised *ex post facto* lawmaking, and so on. But even the trials currently going on in The Hague and Arusha following the recent wars in the former republic of Yugoslavia and Rwanda have not met with universal approval. The inability to put on trial more than a handful of indicted individuals has been thought to show that, whatever the rhetoric of the United Nations, and whatever noble aspirations the trials may embody, there is really nothing of sufficient substance to suggest that, in this area at least, there is such a thing as international criminal law. One might think, adapting Maréchal Bosquet's famous remark about the charge of the Light Brigade at Crimea: "C'est magnifique, mais ce n'est pas le droit."

The conditions under which it can be said that a law exists are, of course, a matter of some dispute. And whether those conditions, whatever they may be, obtain in the case of international relations is a further matter of dispute. Gewirth, in his contribution to the volume, has no doubt that there is valid law covering the conduct of war. Like Grotius, he wishes to steer a middle course between those, on the one hand, who hold that all war is a crime, so that nothing one does in pursuit of a war is legitimate, and those, on the other hand, who hold that war is not governed by rules at all. The wrongs that are typically referred to as war crimes are violations of basic human rights. As such, according to Gewirth, they "can be appropriately classified as crimes regardless of whether they are encoded in positive laws" (p. 51). Some purpose is served by codifying crimes in positive law, for this serves to reduce uncertainty; but the wrongs in question are crimes whether or not a positive law says so. How can that be? How can something be a crime if no law has established it as such? Gewirth's reply is that "the ultimate criterion of criminality is moral rather than legal" (p. 51). If an action violates basic human rights then it is a crime, and what basic human rights there are "can be ascertained by objective rational methods of ethical analysis" (p. 51).[10]

On such a view, war crimes are, in a sense, just ordinary crimes, though they have an added dimension in that, as well as directly violating rights, they tend to destroy the respect for prohibitions which themselves are intended to mitigate the evils of war.

As to the content of the rules of war, Gewirth holds that they prohibit both aggressive war, war whose aim is the violation of basic human rights, and any conduct in a justified war which inflicts injury but is not justified by military necessity. Putting the latter point like this may suggest that the restrictions are nugatory, for, in the history of warfare the most horrendous actions have been regarded as militarily necessary. Gewirth, however, suggests that the qualification imposes a severe restriction: the means adopted to pursue an end must not themselves be antithetical to the end. In terms of warfare this means that, since war is justified only so long as it is the necessary means to protect human rights, it cannot use means which themselves violate human rights.[11]

Gewirth takes the view, a not uncontroversial one, that valid law must be grounded in morality. Jovan Babic, in his contribution, takes a view that sounds similar but is crucially different. In his view, law is not about what *ought* to be permissible but about what has been *decided to be* permissible. This means, according to Babic, that there can be no law without the state. And in that case there can be no such thing as "international law," at least not in "the fundamental sense of the word" (p. 63). This has important consequences for present practice, for the United Nations has long claimed the authority to put on trial those it alleges to have committed war crimes as defined by international law. As far as *jus in bello* is concerned, this could be accommodated, for, like Gewirth, Babic thinks that what the Nuremberg Tribunal called "War Crimes" – the ill-treatment of prisoners of war, and the like – are really just ordinary crimes that happen to take place within the context of war, and nations have the authority themselves to define and punish such crimes, an authority which they could also transmit to the international sphere on the basis of conventions and treaties. "Crimes against Peace," however, are a different matter. Once we say that "aggressive" war is a crime then it is determined in advance, so to speak, who is in the right and who is in the wrong. The group that is in the right is performing something similar to a police action. The group that is in the wrong, on the other hand, has no right to fight, even to defend itself. This might be acceptable if there were a world state, for then we could say that there is genuine law here. But in its absence there is no law, and war crimes trials, in Babic's view, are really only political actions masquerading as legal ones.

II

It may seem that nationalist aspirations have been the cause of many of the most awful conflicts of the latter half of the twentieth century. And some of the most awful aspects of them have been the atrocities – in particular the so-called "ethnic cleansing" – whose alleged perpetrators the United Nations is attempting to put on trial in the Hague and in Arusha.

And yet nationalism, and indeed various forms of particularism, have had growing support amongst influential philosophers and political theorists in the past 20 years or so.[12] In part this has no doubt reflected the dominance of conservative politics in Europe and the US in that period. But it has also been the result of a disenchantment with a conception of morality, found both in Kant and in utilitarianism, in which what is right and wrong is ultimately a matter of how things are when seen from an "impartial" point of view, whether the point of view of the Kantian rational agent, whose one imperative is to treat others, all others, as rational, autonomous agents rather than as means to his own ends, or the point of view of the utilitarian, a point of view in which persons are merely the bearers of utility, which is to be maximized without reference to which bearers are bearing it. From such perspectives, nationalism will not easily seem alluring. The utilitarian can, of course, have a provisional commitment to the values that nationalism espouses, for he can say that utility will be maximized by fostering a commitment to such values, and to the ways of life in which they are expressed. He can *say* this; but proving it is another matter, and in the light of the history of the latter half of the twentieth century, many would be skeptical. And, in any case, those who espouse nationalism do not normally do so because their doing so will be best for the world in general. Kantianism too will not find it easy to accommodate nationalist values. The Kantian, of course, need have no more objection to nationalism in itself than he need have to snooker, if we think of nationalism as merely a desire that some people have to live in certain cultural and governmental relations. But nationalists, those who think about such things anyway, typically think of their aspirations in a different way, as embodying values which ought to be respected. Thus it is much more difficult for the Kantian to accommodate; in the Kingdom of Ends, it may seem, there is but one Kingdom.

Despite its many excesses, nationalism – unlike some political movements – can be cast in a more attractive light than that thrown by the recent events in Rwanda and the former Yugoslavia. Many, probably most, of those whose political aspirations are for an independent Scotland in a European Union see this as desire for a state of affairs in which people will flourish "on both sides of the Tweed," and similar things could be said about most Irish nationalists, Quebecois nationalists, and many others. They regard their political aspirations as very important, but they would not be tempted to pursue them by means of the bullet or the bomb, let alone ethnic cleansing. And yet why not? What foundational ethical theory makes such a position possible? If the demand for, say, self-government is an important one that any reasonable person should accede to – presumably what most nationalists think – why should not deadly force be an acceptable strategy? One answer might be that deadly force is unlikely to be effective. Unhappily, that seems not to be true. Anyway, those who do accept such limits mostly think that there is a moral reason to do so, and not just a reason of expediency.

Richard Miller, in his contribution, outlines one ethical theory which can support nationalist sentiments whilst eschewing its worst excesses. It is a theory according to which whether an action is right or wrong is a matter of whether it would be part of an acceptable set of rules to govern society; and a set would be acceptable if any rational person choosing such a set could accept each rule as expressing his full and equal respect for all persons. Such a theory, Miller argues, supports nationalist aspirations. "[A] morality of respect for persons will accord great value to success in any life-project that is someone's intelligent way of pursuing what is of central importance to everyone who has full and equal respect for all. And all such people have a deep desire to participate in some collective process begun in past generations and handed on as the task to generations to come, in which their contributions express their identity and are valued by other participants in a way that confirms their sense of self-worth" (p. 149). And, "for many people, the collective affirmation of the self is, in large measure, a matter of joining with fellow-nationals in cultivating their nationality" (p. 149). A government, then, committed to equal respect for all will offer some support, if it is needed, to nationalist aspirations, even at some cost to those who do not support them. On the other hand, such a theory severely limits the nationalist aspirations which it thus supports, for it cannot require that those who do not support them make a sacrifice to promote that which is inconsistent with their own self-respect.

The theory is universalist, and its inspiration is Kantian. So the value of nationalist aspirations is not independent, but is simply a resultant of, on the one hand, a very general conception of what is right and wrong and, on the other, certain deep facts about human nature. Is it possible to have an acceptable nationalism which is not derivative in that way? Many humane nationalists seem to have an adequate basis for condemning such horrors as ethnic cleansing even though they reject the universal, impartial perspective at the heart of Miller's theory. While acknowledging the fundamental importance of full and equal respect for all, they hold that the very foundations of morality also include an independent principle of group loyalty. The question is whether such a hybrid theory can "tame the beast of particularism" (p. 144), whether it is a satisfactory means of establishing acceptable limits to the use of coercion in the interest of promoting nationalist goals. The proponents of such a theory can certainly lay down such limits, but they will be arbitrary, according to Miller, in need of a justification that the humane opponent of universalism cannot provide. Nationalist goals substantial enough to ground political duties will, he argues, conflict with equal respect for all in some cases. The importance that the humane, non-universalist nationalist does accord to equal respect makes it incumbent on him to explain why some departures from such treatment (for example, ethnic cleansing) are absolutely prohibited, while some are permissible. He cannot discharge this obligation by appealing to nationalist projects whose obvious moral stature cannot be derived from a requirement of equal respect for all – for this requirement does sustain all nationalist projects with obvious moral stature (or so Miller has argued.) By contrast, someone who accepts a nationalism based upon a universalist principle has a compelling justification of the extent and the limits of his nationalism. When those outside the favored nationality are required to make sacrifices for nationalist goals, this can be justified by reference to an argument which they can accept with self-respect; and when nationalists are denied the means, such as ethnic cleansing, without which they cannot wholly satisfy their nationalist longings, the same thing is true.

Miller takes it as given that "ethnic cleansing" is indeed morally unacceptable and, as that phrase is normally used, he is surely right to do so. The end to which it is an unacceptable means, however, need not be in itself unacceptable, or so many would think. James Nickel, in his contribution, points out that "getting rid of groups" in order to avoid having to live with them can have many different motivations; he lists six: "(1) to 'rectify' historic grievances; (2) to avoid living with a group that is believed to be inferior or depraved; (3) to acquire the territory or property occupied by another group; (4) to realize the nationalist ideal that every large ethnic group should have its own country in which it forms the overwhelming majority of the population; (5) to avoid ethnic conflict and civil war with another group by getting most of them out of the country; and (6) to create a strong military situation in light of actual or feared attacks by another group" (p. 164). In some circumstances, at least, some of these aims will be perfectly reasonable, and this raises the question whether there are any acceptable means to realizing them.

One way of eliminating a group of people with whom one does not want to live is by means of genocide. It needs little argument that genocide is morally illegitimate. The word was coined by Raphaël Lemkin in 1944 to describe the destruction of a nation or ethnic group.[13] When the UN in 1948 adopted a convention on genocide, which committed member countries to undertake "to prevent and to punish" it, it defined genocide as:

> any of the following acts committed with intent to destroy, in whole or in part, a national, ethnical, racial or religious group as such:
>
> (a) Killing members of the group;
> (b) Causing serious bodily or mental harm to members of the group;
> (c) Deliberately inflicting on the group conditions of life calculated to bring about its physical destruction in whole or in part;
> (d) Imposing measures intended to prevent births within the group;
> (e) Forcibly transferring children of the group to another group.

It is hard to imagine realistic circumstances in which any of these acts would be morally permissible if carried out with the specified intention.

"Ethnic cleansing" might seem different, for the bare words import no particular motive and no particular means. If we are merely referring to the forcible relocation of a population then, as Nickel points out, it is possible in principle to carry this out in such a way that harm and violations of rights are minimized; in such a case, it may be that a powerful goal – "creating ethnic boundaries conducive to stable peace in an area plagued by ethnic wars," for instance (p. 168) – might be sufficient to justify it. But, obviously, the word "cleansing" reflects the cynicism with which the phrase was coined, and it will in future always refer to the killing, terrorizing, and expelling of citizens which characterized the civil war in the former Yugoslavia. It is hard to imagine what could possibly justify that.

A third way in which one could eliminate a group is by what Nickel calls "forced assimilation": harsh measures may be used to force a community to give up the features of its life that give it its identity as a separate community. Here, no one need be killed or expelled; the people remain, though their character is changed. But this too is difficult to justify. We know that destroying established ways of life typically causes great harm: as religions, traditional ways of life, and traditional occupations disappear, many people find that they cannot cope, cannot adjust to new patterns of life with which they cannot adequately identify, and perhaps cannot even properly understand. Mental illness, suicide, crime, and drug-dependence are often the result. And, in any case, many people would think that we have a basic right to live our way of life in much the way that we have a basic right to practice our religion. That right may not normally be infringed even if it does not cause any independently specifiable harm. The upshot, according to Nickel, is that whilst a blanket prohibition on forced assimilation is not justified, the international community should prohibit, more specifically, the harshest means of achieving this.

A fourth way in which one could avoid living with a group does not involve moving the group in any way; instead one can move one's national boundaries so as to exclude the group: this is what Nickel calls "expulsive secession." This seems to be less objectionable than ethnic cleansing or forced relocation; those who have been expelled lose their citizenship, but they do not lose their land or their property. On the other hand, it is not without its problems. By definition, the expulsion is not desired by both sides, and this already brings in a moral dimension. In addition, there is not necessarily any guarantee that the expelled community can organize itself satisfactorily, either politically or economically. And, in addition to that, the expelled community may take up arms to resist the expulsion, causing yet further harm. Again, though there is no need for a blanket prohibition, expulsive secession should be bound by "substantial constraints that require careful evaluation of each particular case" (p. 174).

A more common way to avoid having to live with another group is, of course, ordinary secession. For whatever reason, a body of people may wish to leave an existing state and set up their own. Nationalist sentiment has been, on the surface at least, the most common reason, though often the desire to control important natural resources has gone along with this. If a body of people does desire to secede, do they have the right to do so? There are a number of different questions here, and Alfred Rubin distinguishes them in his contribution.

There is, first, a legal question: is there a legal right, in international law, to secede? Perhaps the most important source of international law lies in international conventions and treaties, and Article 1(2) of the United Nations Charter speaks of a "respect for . . . the self-determination of peoples"; this might suggest that there is indeed a legal right to secession.[14] But there is considerable agreement that this Article does not in fact give to minority populations the right to secede from a state to which they object. Decisions of the International Court of Justice are binding on members of the United Nations; could a population that desired to secede then take its dispute to the ICJ and get a legal right to secede? But, as Rubin points out, there is considerable legal dispute about the interpretation of the Articles that govern the ICJ. Consequently, he concludes, "arguments as to a 'legal' right to secession must be based on an interpretation of 'law' that is disputed," and so "there is no legal 'right' to secession" (p. 179).

(Conversely, of course, neither is secession *illegal* in international law; it is legally indeterminate.)

International custom may also be a source of legal rights, but the secessionist would not be well-advised to base his claim to a legal right here, for, as Rubin points out, it has not been the custom of the international community to support secessionist movements.

International law may also be based on "the general principles of law recognized by civilized nations."[15] If this phrase is intended to refer to what is traditionally called "the law of peoples" – a set of principles of justice underlying all systems of municipal law – then Rubin thinks that we should be skeptical about the existence of such a thing. If, on the other hand, it refers to "precedents and statements of government officials in the international arena as establishing 'general principles' that evidence a view of 'law' to be worked out in detail by the ICJ" (p. 181) then this is hard to distinguish from the preceding source, and thus gives no more sustenance to the idea of a right to secede.

If there is no legal right to secession, is there nonetheless a *moral* right? According to Rubin, this question must be settled separately in each case, by weighing the costs and the benefits of seceding; and since circumstances are so variable, there is no general rule that can be applied. Nor would we expect to find any great consensus about how to weight the costs and the benefits in a particular case, since there are numerous competing values that different agents will bring to bear upon the situation to be judged.

In Rubin's view, the only resolution possible when a population wishes to secede, and the state of which it is a part resists this, is a *political* resolution. And when a population successfully secedes "the international legal order must sooner or later accommodate itself to the new situation, with or without formal 'recognition'" (p. 186).

III

Wars invariably bring with them war crimes; what should be done about them when the conflict is over?

David Crocker, in his contribution, points out that our legitimate goals will be many and various. One thing we shall want to do is to prevent such crimes from occurring in the future, as far as possible. This may need changes in the law, and in the various arms of the government. We shall also want to do whatever we can towards reconciling the conflicting parties. Then too we shall need to take account of victims: they are entitled to a platform to tell their stories publicly, to a public acknowledgment that they have been wronged, and to compensation. But there are also the perpetrators; what is to be done about them?

One answer would be that summary justice should be meted out, by the victorious nation or others, to those who can be caught. Another would be that nothing should be done.

As is well known, many allied leaders in the Second World War, including Winston Churchill, initially favored a policy of arresting such Axis leaders as could be apprehended, and shooting them out of hand. But if "summary justice" is indeed supposed to be a form of justice then this idea is surely without merit. If someone is to be punished for his crimes, then it has to be determined that he actually committed those crimes; it also has to be determined what his level of culpability is. That is as important in the aftermath of a war as in more normal times – indeed it may be more important, since it can be very difficult to know much about what is going on within a country with which one is at war. That is particularly true, of course, of those relatively low in the chain of political and military command, but it can also be true of those who hold high office. Those who doubt this should consider the difficulties that the Nuremberg prosecutors had in understanding the structure of German political and military authority when they came to prosecute so-called criminal organizations;[16] they should also remember that not all of those who were put on trial at Nuremberg were found guilty, and that not all of those who were found guilty were sentenced to the executions that were generally expected.

The other alternative I mentioned was that nothing should be done. But this too is unappealing. As Rubin remarks, "[A]s a practical matter, to expect a person to resume normal intercourse with a neighbor who has tortured or killed relatives of the first is probably unrealistic" (p. 189). Rubin's view is that only time will solve this problem, and only full exposure and isolation of those who have committed atrocities will enable time to do this. This does not require criminal trials. The process of exposure can be institutionalized in "truth and reconciliation" commissions, for instance, as has been done in South Africa. Or it need not be institutionalized at all, but left to the news media and other informal channels.

Some will feel that more than this is sometimes required. In some cases, those who have committed awful crimes need to be prevented from doing so again, and informal exposure and isolation may not seem sufficient. This does not, of course, in itself require a judicial proceeding: the top Nazi leaders could have been caught and exiled in the way that Napoleon was. But we are still left with the imperative that those who are treated in this way had better be the people who actually present some future danger, and this will require some method of determining exactly who these people are, and there seems no acceptable alternative to something which will have the form of a judicial proceeding. We could, of course, simply ignore the imperative, but it is unclear why that imperative, which is an imperative of justice, should be ignored here when we do not ignore it in municipal law.

Even for the very limited goal of taking dangerous war criminals out of circulation, then, trials seem to be called for. But war crimes trials are usually not justified simply on this very restricted ground; reference is usually made to retribution and deterrence.

Gewirth appeals to retribution. Criminal "punishment, to be justified, must have as its end the restoration of an occurrent equality of human rights which has been disrupted by the criminal.... This requirement justifies a retributive basis for criminal punishment whereby only wrongdoers are punished, and in a way that is proportionate to their crimes.... [T]he human right to proportional distributive justice is violated by terrorist actions perpetrated against military personnel or innocent civilians. Human rights can thus be invoked to justify the punishment of such criminal agents" (p. 53). The notion of retribution is not a simple one, and can be articulated in a number of different ways, some of them very different from the way adopted by Gewirth. However, the idea that those who commit the most awful crimes deserve to suffer for them would strike a sympathetic chord with many people, and they would see punishment as appropriately serving this end.

Michael Slote, on the other hand, suggests in his contribution that the notion of desert is not the crucial one for deciding whether war criminals should be punished. He derives this view from a more general ethical framework, one which treats evaluations of *character* as the fundamental ethical judgments and derives judgments about whether *actions* are right or wrong from them. It is a framework often referred to as "virtue ethics," but Slote finds his closest historical antecedents not in Aristotle and his fol- lowers, but in the work of such eighteenth- and nineteenth-century thin- kers as Hutcheson, Hume, and Martineau. They based their ethics not on the abstract notion of *eudaimonia* – the good life for man – as Aristotle did, but on the moral goodness of certain natural dispositions, benevolence in particular. On this view, whether an act is morally good is a matter of whether it is motivated by benevolence. Translated into the political realm, we have the view that whether laws are just is a matter of whether they express or display sufficiently good motives on the part of the legislators. "If so, then the justice of legislation governing or refusing to deal with war crimes will depend on what a legislature is trying to do" (p. 81). If their desire is for the common good, then the legislation will be just; if not, it will not. And the demands of the common good will vary; sometimes, the need for reconciliation will best be served by prosecuting war criminals; in other circumstances it may be served by granting them amnesty.

Surprisingly, it may seem, Slote suggests that Nietzsche also provides grounds for thinking that the notion of desert is not the appropriate one for thinking about war criminals. Nietzsche held that it would be a mark of the genuinely powerful individual not to feel resentment towards those who unsuccessfully attack him, for such resentment is a sign of insecurity. Slote approves of such "inner strength,"[17] and thinks that "[a]pplied to war crimes, this implies that a society that tolerates, or at least that doesn't act angrily or punitively toward those who have committed such crimes may be in a sense nobler and more ethically attractive than one that displays the opposite attitude through its collective actions" (p. 83).

Burleigh Wilkins and Anthony Ellis in their contributions also make no reference to retributive aims. They think of punishment "as an institution ... designed to protect us from harm at the hands of others, and in this respect it is forward-looking" (p. 86). If punishment is forward-looking then the focus must be on reform, deterrence, and direct prevention. There seems little reason to think that punishment for war crimes is likely to have significant reformative effect, any more than for more ordinary crimes. In the case of top leaders, direct prevention is surely a consideration. The fact that they have indulged in aggressive attacks on their neighbors is surely some reason to think that they are likely to do so in the future; there is thus some reason, after due process, to remove them from harm's way. This leaves the remainder – ordinary soldiers, low-ranking bureaucrats, for instance – for whom such a course would be quite unrealistic. In their case, we are left with considerations of deterrence.

Wilkins, for his part, is skeptical about the deterrent effect of war crimes trials: "[I]t is, I think, abundantly clear that trials for war crimes have not had any effect whatsoever on the waging of wars or the manner in which wars have been conducted. So-called aggressive wars continue to be fought, often with great barbarity on both sides of the conflict" (p. 87).[18] The barbarity of the recent wars in Rwanda and the former Yugoslavia may seem to support this. Ellis, however, is more optimistic about the deterrent effect of punishment for war crimes – not in the sense that we should expect it to have considerable deterrent effect, for even punishment in municipal law cannot be shown to be so effective, but in the sense that it probably has sufficient deterrent effect to justify whatever costs it imposes. If punishment had no deterrent effect whatever, then it would be hard to understand human action at all. But we need not think that punishment must work by deterring the offender completely; it is enough, assuming that the costs of punishment are not incommensurate, that it should simply reduce somewhat the level of offenses by making it more difficult for the rational offender to commit them. There seems every reason to think that punishment has this effect in municipal law, and no reason to think that this effect is not reproduced in the case of international criminal law.

If we are to have war crimes trials, who should conduct them?

As Burleigh Wilkins points out in his contribution, there are three broad possibilities: "trials within a state jurisdiction in accordance with provisions of penal codes, military or civilian, which are already in place; trials conducted by ad hoc international tribunals; and trials conducted by [a] permanent international court" (p. 86). The Nuremberg Tribunal was an *ad hoc* tribunal, but it was not genuinely international because the judges were, not coincidentally, from only the four main allied powers. The tribunals responsible for trying indicted criminals from the wars in Rwanda and the former Yugoslavia, on the other hand, are genuinely international; they are also *ad hoc* tribunals for the UN has no permanent criminal court corresponding to the International Court of Justice.

In the flush of excitement following the Nuremberg and Tokyo trials – and embarrassment at the sense that there was something wrong with the allied powers trying axis leaders – there was a ground swell of opinion in favor of establishing a permanent, international criminal court. Despite support for this from many quarters, however, the international community did not have the will to bring it about. Perhaps, as Falk suggests in his contribution, it was always naïve to expect that "the Nuremberg precedent would bind states in the future, including the victorious parties" (p. 117). In part, he suggests, this is because there has continued to be no real alternative to self-help when a state's security is threatened except in those cases where upholding the norm of nonaggression has been anyway in the interest of the main political actors. He adds that a prevailing political realism which, if not as crude as the political realism I mentioned earlier, nonetheless gives priority to state interests and sees international law and morality as little more than propaganda instruments, has also made it hard for a conception of international justice to get a secure foothold. So powerful nations have thought that they had little to gain from an international criminal court – and much face to lose if their own leaders should be indicted and they then had to refuse to recognize the court (as the US did when its intervention in

Nicaragua in the 1980s was found in violation of international law by the International Court of Justice).

Recently, however, there has been renewed interest in the idea of an international criminal court, and in July of 1998, 120 nations signed a treaty agreeing to establish an international criminal court having jurisdiction over crimes of genocide, crimes against humanity, war crimes, and crimes of aggression. (The United States, having emasculated the treaty, then did not sign it.) As Falk points out, this renewed interest had a number of sources. One was undoubtedly the horrors that the world witnessed in the two major civil wars of the 1990s. There was also a general desire to deal more effectively with such threats to international order as international terrorism. There has also been pressure from "morally engaged sectors of civil society" (p. 123). And the end of the cold war has made it easier for allegations of criminality to be seen to be impartially grounded rather than cynical propaganda maneuvers. Falk, however, warns us that "the realist orientation toward the practice of geopolitics' is still dominant" (p. 118), and that "the realist gatekeepers of the international legal order will not accept comprehensive legal and moral restraints on the exercise of force as an instrument of foreign policy" (p. 131). Those who favor the establishment of an international criminal court, and all that it symbolizes for world order, should perhaps not yet be too optimistic.

As we saw earlier, Jovan Babic is skeptical about the idea of an international law governing war crimes; and this leads to a dissatisfaction with international war crimes trials. Burleigh Wilkins, in his contribution, is also skeptical about international war crimes trials. Unlike Babic, however, he is not skeptical about the notion of international law *per se*. His skepticism is rooted in what he thinks are deep facts about nations and international society, facts which, he thinks, will ensure that war crimes trials are problematic unless they are carried out voluntarily by a nation in regard to its own nationals. The Nuremberg trials already illustrate the problem, he thinks: despite the rhetoric of the Allies, what happened at Nuremberg was that the victors put the vanquished on trial. Allied forces, and indeed allied leaders, had done things which, prima facie seemed like war crimes – the bombing of Dresden, for instance – but none of them were put on trial; there was thus some justice in Hermann Goering's dismissive remark that the trials were merely "victors' justice."

The Nuremberg Tribunal was not, as I have said, a genuinely international body. But the situation is not likely to be better, according to Wilkins, if, as is the case with the present UN war crimes tribunals, the court can make out a claim to be genuinely international. In such cases, he argues, what we shall find is that only vanquished nations' alleged criminals will be put on trial, for victorious nations will refuse to hand over those of their own citizens – high-ranking ones especially – who are accused of war crimes.[19] That is because, however much we may wish that citizens should have a more cosmopolitan set of ideals, the ideal of the sovereignty of states, and nationalist sentiment, have been deeply rooted phenomena with which advocates of internationalism must compromise. International trials will thus be characterized by a pattern of discrimination, and so will violate the principle of equality before the law: "like cases have not been treated alike if losers in a war are solely or disproportionately singled out for trial" (p. 88).

Wilkins is not determinedly against war crimes trials, but thinks that, if they are to take place, then nations should try their own war criminals. This is for a number of reasons. For one thing, such trials are less likely, he thinks, to violate the principle of equality before the law. For another, the idea respects the sovereignty of states. But also, such trials are more likely to serve the end of reconciliation. For this end, it is important that a nation must face up to its past wrongs, to "internalize" the wrongness of them, and this is more likely to happen if the history of those wrongs be written by its own courts.

There are, on the other hand, those who think that the establishment of an international criminal court would be a significant step toward a fuller realization of a world order subject to law. That is the view of Ellis in his contribution. He thinks it doubtful, given the historical evidence, that national courts would do a good job of prosecuting their own war criminals. And whilst it is true that a nation must "internalize" the wrongs it has committed in a war, it is equally important, if there is to be any real reconciliation, that their opponents, and the rest of world, have access to a just and reliable accounting of those wrongs, an accounting which, within the bounds of human error, convicts the guilty and acquits the innocent with no partiality, nor the appearance of it. Ellis thinks that this is much more likely to be served by an international court.

David Crocker is also more sympathetic to the role of the international community, and in his contribution he explores the role that civil society, both national and international, may play in achieving the various goals that present themselves in the aftermath of a war. Despite some limitations, he believes, that "a nation's civil society is often well suited to prioritize the ends and implement the means of transitional justice" (p. 283), and that the role of international civil society, which includes, he suggests, the United Nations, can be indispensable.

IV

When a war is over, the nations involved need to live in peace and security again; and war crimes will make it harder to achieve the reconciliation that is necessary for this, for the memory of them may linger and fester. Particularly in the case of civil wars, those memories may become part of the stereotypes which the parties possess of each other, stereotypes which will be available to fan the flames of potential conflict. The civil war in the former Republic of Yugoslavia provides perhaps the most chilling modern example. But it is not confined to civil war; negative images of Germany were nourished in many quarters long after the end even of the Second World War by stories having their origin in the "Rape of Belgium" in 1914. Many people see punishment for war crimes as a necessary part of the antidote to this tendency. But punishment, by itself, will not achieve much. What is needed is that each nation must forgive the other any wrongs that it has committed.

The idea of forgiving a nation is not an easy one to understand. The most obvious problem is that not everyone in the nation to be forgiven will have committed the acts that require forgiveness, nor indeed been implicated in them in any significant way. This, of course, raises the problem of collective responsibility. But the problems go deeper; the bare notion of forgiveness itself is a difficult notion to understand. After all, recognizing that an act is wrong, how *can* we forgive it? But even if this question can be answered satisfactorily, a yet deeper problem remains, a problem that philosophers in recent years have called the problem of "moral luck."[20] We choose the actions that we do because of our characters; but we do not, and could not, wholly choose our characters, for this would involve a vicious infinite regress. We are, for the most part, the people that we are because of our genetic heritage and the circumstances of our upbringings. These things are, from our point of view, a matter of luck. Furthermore, it is a matter of luck what moral choices we have to face. Ordinary Americans or Britons did not have to face the agonizing dilemmas that confronted many ordinary, decent Germans who knew about, for instance, the Nazi death camps; had they done so, they would certainly have acted no differently. And yet we condemn those who failed the test we know that we ourselves would have failed. How can that be rational? But if it is not rational, then neither is forgiveness, for we can forgive only what we can condemn. These problems are the focus of David Cooper's contribution.

Cooper suggests that their solution is to be found in the reality of collective responsibility, an idea whose importance is confirmed by the phenomenon of moral luck. Collective responsibility "is not...the responsibility of each and every member of some collective....Rather it is a responsibility ascribed to the collective itself, as when, say, the tennis club *itself* is blamed for its closure or bankruptcy – irrespective of the blame, *if any*, attaching to individual members" (p. 206). Given this, we may condemn a group for wrongful actions whilst at the same time withholding condemnation of any of its members.

But if the phenomenon of moral luck leads us to withhold moral assessment of those who have done wrong, we do not expect the same detached attitude from the wrongdoers themselves. We expect that they should accept responsibility for what they have done. But accepting responsibility could not be a matter of simply accepting a judgment about themselves, for how could we consistently expect them to endorse a judgment that we ourselves withhold? What it requires is "an *act* – an apology, an expression of remorse, an owning to the harm they have done, an acknowledgement" (p. 213). And without this, there will be no possibility of them manifesting "a readiness to engage, once more, in a fellowship of human beings" (p. 214).

Cooper speaks of condemning the nation but withholding that attitude from many of its members. But we may want to speak of forgiving the nation too (which is not, of course, inconsistent with condemning it). Now the notion of forgiveness goes hand in hand with that of remorse, for, normally at least, we cannot forgive someone a wrong unless they feel remorse for what they have done. So if one nation is to forgive another for crimes it has committed in a war, then the guilty nation must feel remorse. But this may seem problematic. What can it mean to speak of a nation, or indeed of a group of people at all, as being remorseful? To be remorseful is surely to *feel* remorse, and it is by no means clear just what it would mean to speak of a group as *feeling* something. Margaret Gilbert, in her contribution, tries to explicate this idea.

One's first thought might be that it is for each of the members of the group in question to feel remorse for what he himself has done. No doubt such feelings would be appropriate; if particular individuals have committed war crimes, then they should feel remorse for what they have done. But such feelings, even if they were quite widespread, would seem to be a far cry from the *group's* feeling remorse. For one thing, it may be that most people in a war will themselves have done nothing to feel remorse about, and will know that; so it will make no sense to speak of them as feeling remorse for what they have done. The guilty minority, on the other hand, may feel remorse, but it seems odd to speak of a nation as feeling remorse if all that is true is that a minority of its members feel remorse. Secondly, war crimes need not be the isolated acts of individuals from which the rest of the nation can wholly distance itself. It was, for instance, Germany that invaded Poland in 1939, not just some individual soldiers ordered by politicians acting as private individuals (indeed, it is arguably a conceptual truth that invading a country is not something that ordinary individuals, as individuals, can do). This – of course – does not mean that every German was individually responsible for the invasion. What it means is that *Germany* was responsible for it. So it is Germany that should have felt remorse. Or so many people think. But it would not be true to say that Germany felt remorse if all that were true were that the Nazi leadership, those who were mainly responsible for the invasion, felt remorse for their individual parts in the invasion. Conversely, if most of them did not feel remorse, as seems to have been the case, this would not obviously prevent *Germany* from feeling remorse, and this suggests again that for a group to feel remorse is not a matter of its members feeling remorse for what they individually have done.

What is needed, it might seem, is that the members of the nation, or some sufficiently large and significant proportion of them, should feel remorse not for what they have done personally but for what their nation has done. But how is that possible? How would it have been possible, for instance, for a significant proportion of Germans after the war to feel remorse for the invasion of Poland when they played no significant role in it?

Gilbert sketches an account which, it is hoped, will explain how it is possible for a nation to feel remorse. At its center is the idea that group remorse requires that the group in question be "jointly committed to feeling remorse as a body." Conformity to this commitment will naturally lead the group to undertake certain actions, actions of the type which we think of as typically expressing remorse. So, for instance, a nation that has committed war crimes, and can correctly be said to feel remorse for them, would be expected to do things like offering compensation to victims, and under-taking any institutional or constitutional reforms that would make it difficult for such things to happen again.[21]

This account, of course, trades upon the idea of group action. For sure, this idea must, in some sense, be an acceptable one, for we speak in terms of group action all the time. It is, however, not an easy matter to explain in just what sense a group, as such, can act. According to Gilbert, a group performs an action, as a group, if the members are jointly committed to accepting the action's goal as a body, and act in the light of that commitment. Two people, for instance, acting as a group "must attempt as best they can to constitute as far as they can a four-handed, two-bodied person who (single-mindedly) has that goal" (p. 224). Importantly, members of a group "may be jointly committed to accepting a certain goal as a body without all knowing or even conceiving of the content of the commitment" (p. 225), for there may be a joint commitment to delegate to one member of the group the authority to make decisions for them. Thus, a government in offering compensation to victims may act for and on behalf of the nation as a whole, insofar as the relevant members of the nation have jointly committed themselves to regarding what their government does in their name as done by them.

Certainly, offering compensation would be a natural expression of remorse. But it will normally be required anyway, as part of the more general requirement of justice that any wrongs that may have been committed should, as far as possible, be put right. These wrongs will typically be of many different kinds, and rectifying them will normally be a difficult task. For instance, many people, particularly in a civil war, will have been imprisoned or otherwise interned; after the war, it may be no easy matter to distinguish those who have been wrongfully imprisoned from ordinary felons; it might be further difficult to distinguish those who were justifiably interned for security reasons from those whose internment was unjustified by any substantial concern for security and who are therefore owed compensation.[22] Again, those who have been wrongfully expelled from their homes should be allowed to return, with due compensation. This may not be easy to accomplish in the turmoil that usually follows a war. Yet again, those people who have had land, other resources, or private wealth more generally stolen from them, must have it returned. And, again, it can be difficult to determine the rights and wrongs here.

The last two sorts of case raise problems additional to the practical ones just mentioned. When property has been expropriated it may not be returned to its original owners, nor to their immediate descendants, but passed on down to the descendants of those who stole it. In such cases, an acute moral and legal problem can arise. Those now in possession of the land, let us say, may have had nothing to do with its expropriation, and may have only the dimmest sense – and perhaps no real sense at all – of how it came about that they are now in possession of it. What should be done if the descendants of the original owners can be found? On the one hand, it seems that it should be "returned" to them, on the principle that they would have possessed it if it had not been wrongfully taken from their ancestors. But things may not be so simple. For one thing, there is often little reason to believe the conditional embodied in the principle just stated.[23] If, for instance, people are driven from their land then it seems almost certain that this will have some effect on just which people are later born – eggs and sperm cells that would have come together had those lives not been disrupted will now, almost certainly, not come together, and different eggs and cells will come together to form different people. In that case, it may well be false for someone to say that if his great-grandparents had not been driven from their land then he would have inherited it; for if they had not been driven from their land it is unlikely that he would ever have come into existence.

There is also a further problem. Those who are now in possession of the land did not come by it through any of their own wrongdoing; and it may be disastrous for them if it is taken away (financially disastrous, primarily, though that is not the only consideration). Those to whom it is "returned," on the other hand, may have no serious need of it. In such circumstances, it seems likely that different moral and political principles will have different implications. Some will tell us simply to "return" the land to its "rightful" owners.[24] Others will tell us to determine the distribution on some quite different ground. Act-utilitarianism, for instance, will tell us to do what will produce the most utility now and in the future; what that is will depend upon the circumstances of the case, but it will not, save indirectly, depend upon whether the present distribution is the result of injustice. Other theories will have other results.

Angelo Corlett takes up some of these issues in connection with the question of reparations to Native Americans. The massive injustices done to Native Americans are a matter of historical record, and there is no serious dispute about them. What, if anything, should now be done about those injustices is another matter. There are those who think that, since the injustices were long in the past nothing need be done, for any claims that Native Americans had to land that was taken from them by early immigrants have now lapsed. Corlett, however, argues that rights cannot lapse simply with the passage of time, and that nothing has happened to take away the rights to land that Native Americans originally occupied. He therefore takes seriously the idea that Native Americans should be given adequate reparation. This would involve, he argues, complete restitution of lands that were taken from them by force or fraud, and compensation for personal injuries. In strict justice, this would involve a massive redistribution of land and resources, a distribution which, in fact, would spell economic ruin for the United States and indeed for a number of other countries. Less radically, a large tax (Corlett suggests a tax of 25% of each non-Native American's annual gross income plus a 5% state sales tax) could be levied for the purpose of making reparations and paying compensation. Even this, however, would require a considerable sacrifice on the part of those who themselves have, knowingly at any rate, done no wrong to Native Americans. Can they justifiably be required to make this sacrifice? They cannot mount any compliant, Corlett argues: they are occupying someone else's land, land to which they have no right. [25]

That judgment is, of course, highly controversial. But little is clear here, and all of the issues that I have touched on cry out urgently for clarification. There will, I assume, always be war and its attendant horrors, and the international community must try to hammer out a set of procedures for dealing with them, one which embodies a sound theoretical understanding of the moral and legal issues that they raise, and a sensitive appreciation of what it is practically possible to do about them. The papers that follow are a contribution to that endeavor.

Notes

1 Sherman, in reply to the Mayor of Atlanta, who had written to him protesting his intention to evacuate the city, wrote that "the hardships of war" are "inevitable." "War is cruelty and you cannot refine it." In fact, his earlier behavior in the war showed that war can indeed be "refined."

2 "Silent enim leges inter arma" (*Pro Milone*, iv. xi).

3 For some examples, see Leon Friedman, ed., *The Law of War. A Documentary History* (New York: Random House, 1972), vol. 1, pp. 3–6.

4 *De Jure Belli ac Pacis*, edited by A. C. Campbell (London: Dunne, 1901). For an assessment of the influence and contemporary importance of Grotius, see Hedley Bull, Benedict Kingsbury, and Adam Roberts, eds., *Hugo Grotius and International Relations* (Oxford: Clarendon Press, 1990).

5 This is not to say, of course, that Grotius's views are in keeping with modern international law; his account reflected, and was explicitly intended to do so, the practices of nations up to his own time.

6 *De Jure Belli ac Pacis*, Bk. II, Ch. 20, §§ xxxviii and xxxix. Cf. Samuel Pufendorf: "The just causes of engaging in war come down to the preservation and protection of our lives and property against unjust attack, or the collection of what is due to us from others but has been denied, or the procurement of reparations for wrong inflicted and of assurance for the future" (*De officio hominis et civis juxta legem naturalem libri duo* (1673), Bk. II, Ch. 16, § 2, ed. and trans. James Tully (Cambridge: Cambridge University Press, 1991)).

7 *De Jure Belli ac Pacis*, Bk. III, Ch. 4, § xix.

8 The Charter of the International Military Tribunal, Article VI(a).

9 However, from another perspective this might seem to make their behavior all the more chilling.

10 Gewirth has argued in detail for this view in *Reason and Morality* (Chicago: Chicago University Press, 1978), and elsewhere.

11 Consequentialists about ethics deny this, of course. On this issue see Samuel Scheffler, *The Rejection of Consequentialism* (Oxford: Oxford University Press, 1982).

12 Cf., for instance, Alasdair MacIntyre, *After Virtue* (London: Duckworth, 1981) and subsequent writings; Charles Taylor, "Atomism," in Taylor, *Philosophical Papers* vol. 2, pp. 187-210, and, more generally, *Sources of the Self* (Cambridge: Cambridge University Press, 1989); Michael Walzer, *Spheres of Justice: A Defence of Pluralism and Equality* (Oxford: Blackwell, 1983) and *On Toleration* (New Haven: Yale University Press, 1997); Michael Sandel, *Liberalism and the Limits of Justice* (Cambridge: Cambridge University Press, 1982—but Sandel seems to distance himself from the particularist understanding of his work in the second edition of the book (1998)).

13 Raphaël Lemkin, *Axis Rule in Occupied Europe* (Washington: Carnegie Endowment for International Peace, 1944).

14 Both the UN Covenant on Social and Political Rights and the UN Covenant on Economic, Social and Cultural Rights say: "All peoples have the right to self-determination. By virtue of that right they freely determine their political status . . ." (Article 1(1) in both cases). For a discussion of the idea of the self-determination of peoples, see Antonio Cassese, *Self-Determination of Peoples. A Legal Reappraisal* (Cambridge: Cambridge University Press, 1995).

15 Statute of the International Court of Justice, Article 38(1)(c).

16 See, for instance, Ann Tusa and John Tusa, *The Nuremberg Trial* (New York: Atheneum, 1984), ch. 16; and Telford Taylor, *The Anatomy of the Nuremberg Trials. A Personal Memoir* (New York: Alfred A. Knopf, 1992), ch. 16.

17 For a contrasting view, see Michael Moore, "The Moral Worth of Retribution," in Ferdinand Schoeman, ed., *Responsibility, Character and the Emotions* (Cambridge: Cambridge University Press, 1987), pp. 179–219.

18 Skepticism about the deterrent effect of war crimes trials is common. Cf., for instance, J. L. Brierly, "Do We Need an International Criminal Court?" *The British Yearbook of International Law*, vol. 8 (1927): 84; Richard, A. Falk, Gabriel Kolko, and Robert Jay Lifton, eds., *Crimes of War: A Legal, political-documentary, and psychological inquiry into the responsibility of leaders, citizens, and soldiers for criminal acts in war* (New York: Random House, 1971), p. 9.

19 This has perhaps been illustrated to some degree in the former Yugoslavia, where high-ranking leaders who have been indicated have, at the time of writing, so far eluded capture and prosecution.

20 See Bernard Williams and Thomas Nagel, "Moral Luck," *Proceedings of the Aristotelian Society, Supplementary Volume 50* (1976).

21 When British war veterans were offered an apology by Japan in January, 1998, they quickly responded that it wasn't enough; this could be taken for the

thought that, without adequate compensation, expressions of apology are not genuine expressions of remorse.

22 Japanese Americans were interned by the US government in the Second World War, as were, for a few months, German and Austrian Jews in the UK. The legality of the former internment was upheld by the US Supreme Court in *Korematsu v. U.S.* (1944). Later, however, the US government recognized that the internment had been unjustified and offered an apology and compensation.

23 Cf. Derek Parfit, *Reasons and Persons* (Oxford: Clarendon Press, 1984), ch. 16.

24 Cf., perhaps, Robert Nozick, *Anarchy, State, and Utopia* (New York: Basic Books, 1974), pp. 152–3; however, Nozick does not commit himself to any precise theory of rectification. For a discussion of Nozick and Native American claims to the return of tribal lands, see David Lyons, "The New Indian Claims and Original Rights to Land," *Social Theory and Practice* 4 (1977): 249–72.

25 In his book *Responsibility and Punishment* (Kluwer 2000) Corlett remarks that most US citizens would balk at even the hint of a *minimal* reparations tax (he suggests 1% of a US Citizen's gross national income) to cover the costs of arguably the worst evils perpetrated by a modern government. He regards this as the result of moral ineptitude.

Part One

<u>What are War Crimes?</u>

1

Unchosen Evil and Moral Responsibility

Peter A. French

During the ethnic conflicts in the former Yugoslavia, the news releases were regularly filled with reports of rape, torture, mutilation, and murder carried out by combatants on all sides in the name of "ethnic cleansing." War crimes' charges have been filed in the appropriate world court and the spectrum of legal and moral issues that dominated the aftermath of the Second World War in Europe again has been raised. I have no interest in examining any of the specific charges that have been leveled against groups and individuals in the Balkans. Rather, I am interested in trying to understand what sort of evil can be legitimately ascribed to typical perpetrators of war crimes such as those described in the reports of ethnic cleansing in Bosnia and Kosovo, and I am concerned with what our reaction to those who committed these atrocities should be, i.e., whether we should hold them morally responsible. I will concentrate on what I will call "average Balkan war criminals." By that I mean the ordinary folks, farmers, trades people, workers, etc., whose very characters, in fact, have been formed and nurtured in cultures that are utterly imbued with hatred, distrust, and suspicion of members of all other cultural or ethnic groups in their geographic region.

I

Aristotle, it may be remembered,[1] distinguishes three types of character that are to be avoided, that, at least in some extenuated sense, may be called evil: moral weakness, vice (or wickedness), and brutishness. Ronald Milo suggests that it is helpful to think of Aristotle's distinction between the first two in terms of "cases where the agent has good moral principles but fails to act on them and cases where the agent acts on bad moral principles."[2] The first type is typically described as a lacking of self-control or as a form of incontinence. The belief states of the agent, however, also are crucial to drawing the distinction between the morally weak and the wicked. The morally weak person believes that what he or she is doing is wrong. The wicked person, in Aristotle's view, believes incorrectly that what he or she is doing is right. The wicked person is ignorant of general moral principles that apply in his or her case and such ignorance is not exculpatory.

The picture of evil, however, is much more complicated than these distinctions suggest. Imagine that each of Aristotle's three types of evil character are subdivided in terms of the agent's belief states with respect to the rightness or wrongness of the actions undertaken. The result is at least six types of evil: (1) when the agent lacking self-control believes (wrongly) that what he or she is doing is the right thing to do; (2) when the agent lacking self-control believes that what he or she is doing is wrong; (3) when the agent acts on morally bad preferences or principles believing them to be morally good or right; (4) when the agent acts on morally bad principles or preferences believing them to be bad or wrong; (5) when one acts brutishly believing what one is doing is the right or the good thing to do; and (6) when one acts brutishly while believing that what one is doing is wrong or bad. Cases (1) and (2) are not especially relevant to the discussion of war crimes. I find it difficult to imagine that, for example, the war criminals of the recent Balkan conflicts were morally weak or merely morally negligent. It generally was not the case that they committed atrocities against those outside of their own ethnic backgrounds believing that what they were doing was wrong and wanting to alter their behavior, but that they were so weak of will that they could not do so. Admittedly, in the frenzy of killing, raping, and torturing that occurs in massacres during wartime, perpetrators can be so swept up in the carnage and the sheer exercise of violence against a hated enemy that it is difficult to identify their belief states or to make sense of the idea that their wills were too weak to resist what they believed to be wrong if, in fact, they did believe what they were doing was wrong. Nonetheless, brutishness and wickedness appear to be stronger candidates than weakness of will (akrasia) to account for their vicious actions. First consider brutishness.

Aristotle distinguishes between two types of brutishness,[3] but he says remarkably little on the subject. He tells us that brutishness is typically found in barbarians, where he attributes it to nature. Then he allows that civilized folk may be afflicted with brutishness as a result of habit. His example of the latter is startlingly modern: "when someone has been sexually abused from childhood."[4] The idea seems to be that if one is abused as a child, one may develop a brutish disposition that makes such behavior habitual. Aristotle is clear that those who are brutish by nature should not be categorized as morally weak, at least not in the standard sense he has given to that term. He adds that those who are brutish by habit are also not morally weak of will. It is, however, a morally praiseworthy accomplishment to master one's natural or habitual brutishness. Hence, it is a kind of moral weakness to be under the domination of either kind of brutishness, but it is not the same sort of moral weakness that Aristotle contrasts with wickedness (vice) and brutishness. He draws the distinction in the following way:

> It is, accordingly, clear that moral weakness and moral strength operate only in the same sphere as do self-indulgence and self-control, and that the moral weakness which operates in any other sphere is different in kind, and is called "moral weakness" only by extension, not in an unqualified sense.[5]

It seems reasonable to assume that those who are naturally brutish do not believe that what they are doing when behaving brutishly is wrong or bad. Perhaps they never think of what they are doing in moral terms. After all, they're brutes. They are natural amoralists. The habitually brutish do not care that what they are doing when behaving brutishly is not the morally right thing to do. Due to the experiences that ingrained the brutish habit, they are indifferent to the demands of morality, at least over some range of their behavior. Their weakness lies outside, as Aristotle might say, the "sphere of self-indulgence and self-control". It is not as if they are indulging themselves in some desired behavior over which they know or believe they should exercise control to prevent themselves from doing it. Brutes, whether natural or habitual, just do what they do.

The average Balkan war criminal, I feel safe in saying, is not brutish by nature. To my knowledge, there is no credible evidence that those who inhabit the former Yugoslavia possess some natural attribute of beastliness that most of the rest of the human race, thankfully, lacks. Those who committed the atrocities of Bosnia and Kosovo were not members of a pack of werewolves, driven by natural forces to rape, torture, multilate, and murder. Aristotle's examples of natural brutishness, however, are at least as vividly grotesque as the accounts of the behavior of the Serbian war criminals in Moslem villages in Bosnia and Kosovo. He, for example, talks of people who devour their children.[6] The sheer repulsiveness of an act, however, should never be confused with a trustworthy sign of its source in natural brutishness, nor in habitual brutishness, for that matter.

There might be some attraction to the notion that the average Balkan war criminals are brutish by habit. It might be suggested that, owing to a long history of past experiences in which they were brutalized, etc., they have become indifferent to the constraints of morality when they confront those they regard as their former oppressors. I do not want to give short shrift to the hypothesis that those who have been abused and oppressed may become habitually brutish and respond in kind when encountering their oppressors and abusers or act in similar ways to others when they are in dominant positions. I suspect there is some psychological/sociological evidence in its support. The problem with classifying the average Balkan war criminals in this way, however, is that, by and large, they do not come from the ethnic groups that were the most oppressed in Yugoslavia, and the Muslims who seemed to have suffered the most at the hands of, e.g., the Serbian war criminals, had not been oppressors. The habitually brutish, Aristotle suggests, might, if asked, respond that what they did was probably not the morally right thing to do, while evidencing an almost utter indifference to morality in the limited circumstances. If they believed that they were not doing the morally right thing, that belief was impotent with respect to altering their actions. Other facts about the situation impelled them, were far more powerful, and overshadowed moral constraints or common decency. Some of the average Balkan war criminals seem to fit such a description, but, I suspect, the majority did what they most wanted to do in the circumstances because that is exactly what they wanted to do and not because they were under the influence of past victimization that had been visited on them or on their families. In any event, the habitually brutish person, just as the naturally brutish person, is not incontinent, as Aristotle makes clear.

II

Wickedness takes quite a different description. Following the schema I have suggested above, a person of wicked character will be one who acts on morally bad principles and either believes that what he or she is doing is the right thing to do or believes that it is the wrong thing to do. Aristotle's account seems to require excluding the second type. For Aristotle, because the agent of the evil deed acts in accord with what he or she perversely believes to be good moral principles, he or she does not believe that what is being done is wrong, or immoral or evil. Ignorance (broadly and variously understood) of the right principles accounts for the perverse belief state. But, in so far as that ignorance is not excusable in the mature agent, as noted above, that type of agent is to be held responsible for his or her wicked deeds. Suppose we call this sort of Aristotelian wickedness (following Milo[7]) "perverse wickedness." Its description captures the sense of the Socratic dictum that no one does evil willingly. Plato writes: "Polus and I felt we had no choice but to conclude that no one wants to do wrong, and that every wrong act is done unwillingly."[8]

On one reading of "unwillingly" Aristotle may be taken as attacking this view because he maintains that "wickedness is voluntary."[9] By that he means that we are the sources of our own actions and so acting wickedly is not acting inadvertently or accidentally or the like. However, he does make it clear that "every wicked man is in a state of ignorance as to what he ought to do and what he should refrain from doing, and it is due to this kind of error that men become unjust and, in general, immoral."[10] Acting in ignorance, of course, is not acting involuntarily or not voluntarily, but it might be understood as unwilling, in that one turns out not to be doing what one believes one is willing oneself to do: the right thing. The ignorance of or mistake in moral principle leads one to do something one would not do if one were not ignorant or mistaken.

Milo notes that the other type of wickedness, the sort that Aristotle does not seem to admit, should be identified with the standard Christian conception of evil. For the Christian, "wickedness consists in knowingly doing what is morally wrong without any compunction or scruple."[11] Wickedness, on the Christian account, is preferential, or rather doing what is wicked is preferred to doing what is morally right, for any of a number of reasons that usually amount to pursuing some desired end where that end is incompatible with behaving in a manner that is consistent with good moral principles that the evildoer acknowledges and may even abide by in some part of his or her life.

Most media accounts of the average Balkan war criminals reflect an Aristotelian rather than the Christian conception of wickedness. The perpetrators come off as perversely, not preferentially, wicked. The reports make it appear that the perpetrators did what they did believing (albeit perversely) that it was the right thing to do. They imply that the war criminals were steadfastly convinced that mutilating, raping, torturing, and murdering those of other ethnic groups is morally demanded of them. Not infrequently, they are described as brimming with righteousness while carrying out the atrocities of ethnic cleansing. If the news stories are correct, the Balkan war criminals were notably different from the American soldiers of Charlie Company of the American Division in the village of My Lai 4 in

March of 1968. There is undoubtedly a wide range of accounts to be given with respect to the actions and belief states of those American soliders on that day, but very few, it appears, actually believed that what they were doing was morally right.[12]

Perverse wickedness is conceivable, as Milo notes,[13] from either a cognitivist or a noncognitivist perspective. Cognitivists will maintain that "the agent of a perversely wicked act does something that is morally wrong because he is ignorant that acts of this sort are morally wrong and falsely believes that such acts are right."[14] The noncognitivists will tell us that a perversely wicked act "consists in doing what is morally wrong because of one's acceptance of *bad* moral principles."[15] Nowell-Smith famously put forth such a position.[16]

One might be persuaded of the cogency of either of these accounts. Think of an average Balkan war criminal, a Serb, who, in a small mountain village, has raped Muslim women, tortured and mutilated them, and then murdered them. A noncognitivist would reject the notion that the Serb war criminal acted out of ignorance. For the noncognitivist, moral principles are not objects to be known or mistaken about or ignorant of. They are expressions of attitudes. So the noncognitivist will focus full attention on the sort of principles that the average Balkan war criminal holds most deeply. Those, by definition, are his moral principles. Among them we would expect to find some principle(s) that condones or encourages, perhaps even requires, him to rape, torture, mutilate, and murder Bosnian Muslim or Kosovar Albanian women. His wickedness is, then, perverse, but also, thereby, conscientious, and, on some formalist accounts that may be a mark of integrity.[17]

The cognitivist, defending the possibility of perverse wickedness, will focus on the Serb's ignorance. It is crucial that his ignorance is not what Aristotle would have called an ignorance of particulars.[18] It is not that the Serb is in the dark about some fact or facts of the matter concerning the Bosnian Muslim or Kosovar Albanian women in the village. Were that the case, his behavior might be, to some extent, excusable. Aristotle, for example, maintains that ignorance of the particulars (or at least some of them) may be involuntary and therefore pardonable: "A person who acts in ignorance of a particular circumstance acts involuntarily . . . especially if he is ignorant of the most important factors. The most important factors are the thing or person affected by the action and the result."[19] He does add the condition that "an action upon this kind of ignorance is called involuntary, provided that it brings also sorrow and regret in its train,"[20] and that, apparently, is not something that the average Balkan war criminal evidenced. Aristotle's point is that only factual ignorance whose cause is external to the agent is excusable. In the case of the Serb war criminal it is hard to imagine of which particular circumstances he may be ignorant due to forces external to himself. He surely knows who the persons are on whom he is acting and he knows the results his actions will produce. If he is ignorant of anything it must be moral principles. And that, Aristotle insists, is not pardonable. His perverse wickedness reflects a bad moral character.

Suppose that the average Balkan war criminal does have a bad moral character of the sort that Aristotle describes. Why should that render him ignorant of moral principles? Or as Milo asks the question: "If one adopts a purely cognitivist account of the nature of moral beliefs, i.e., if one holds that to believe that a certain act is wrong is to accept as true a proposition to this effect, then how does one explain why having a bad character... prevents a person from grasping the truth of this proposition?"[21] What blocks a person with a bad character from granting the truth of propositions to the effect that what he or she is doing is morally wrong? Aristotlelians might say that perversely wicked people are so morally sick that their intellectual capacities are impaired. They are afflicted with a cognitive blindness or, at least, cognitive myopia. There is something quite appealing in the imagery, but it really provides no insight into how perverse wickedness, bad character, produces ignorance of moral principles. If that cannot be explained, then it is conceivable that someone could have a preference for doing something while believing the proposition that the thing preferred is the morally wrong thing for one to do in the circumstances or under any circumstances. Some people, I am convinced, just do what they prefer doing regardless of the fact that they believe it to be morally wrong or improper to do it. And they are not displaying a weakness of will. They reveal what they care most about, and that is not doing what is morally right in those circumstances. Short of a demonstration that such people are not conceivable, the standard cognitivist line on perverse wickedness is not very persuasive.

As Milo notes,[22] the basic problem for a cognitivist's (and, it should be added, a noncognitivist's) conception of perverse wickedness links to the beliefs they ascribe to the wicked person. With regard to the Balkan war crimes, they must assign to the perpetrators beliefs to the effect that it is morally right to rape, torture, mutilate, and murder other human beings. The average Balkan war criminal must believe that committing such atrocities on women of another ethnic group is not morally wrong, but that it is morally permissible or, even, morally required. At first blush that sounds plausible. How else could he do it? How indeed! Of course, the average

Balkan war criminal believes that it is morally wrong to rape, torture, mutilate, and murder. It is just that he believes that what he is doing to women of another ethnic group is not really rape, torture, mutilation, and murder. It is ethnic cleansing. Nonsense!

To make accounts of this sort plausible, one must maintain that it is possible to believe that there are no kinds of acts such that if one knows what it is for an act to be morally wrong, one *must* believe that acts of that kind are morally wrong. For any act, it is possible to believe that it is either morally right or morally wrong.

Surely the average Balkan war criminal knew that he was committing forced sexual intercourse on, torturing, mutilating, and killing his victims. If you know what it is for an act to be morally wrong, one would think, at least, you should know that acts of that sort are prima facie morally wrong. It is hard to imagine that anyone who understands even the first thing about what it is for an act to be morally wrong would deny that the fact that what one is doing is an act of forced sexual intercourse, mutilation of another, or the killing of another is relevant to the moral status of the act. The further fact that these acts are being performed on defenseless noncombatants also cannot be ignored by anyone who understands what "morally wrong" means. The average Balkan war criminal is not a moron, nor a brute. He has, we may suppose, a perfectly adequate moral vocabulary. So I think it more closely mirrors the facts to say either that he does not care that he is acting in violation of moral principles, or that he cares more about performing acts of ethnic cleansing on the women of the Bosnian Muslim or Kosovar Albanian village than he does about acting in accord with moral principles that would forbid him from doing the very things he does to ethnically cleanse the village.

Aristotle departs from the defense of perverse wickedness because he cannot adopt the position that there are no kinds of acts such that, if one knows what it is for an act to be morally wrong, one *must* believe that those acts are morally wrong. He tells us that, for example, there are some types of actions "whose very names connote baseness, e.g., . . . adultery, theft, and murder. These and similar . . . actions imply by their very names that they are bad . . . It is, therefore, impossible ever to do right in performing them: to perform them is always to do wrong. In cases of this sort, let us say adultery, rightness and wrongness do not depend on committing it with the right woman at the right time and in the right manner, but the mere fact of committing such action at all is to do wrong."[23]

If Aristotle is correct, and I think he is, then one cannot both know what it means to believe that some action is morally wrong and also believe that raping, torturing, mutilating, and murdering defenseless women are not morally wrong. But this then should have profound effects on Aristotle's conception of wickedness and that of other cognitivists. It would seem that on Aristotle's account, where murder, adultery, and theft are concerned, one cannot be perversely wicked. If you know (or believe) you are committing (e.g.) adultery, you must know (or believe) it is wrong or bad to do it. Only those adulterers who do not know what adultery is and so do not know that what they are doing is adultery, can be perversely wicked. If you know it is adultery, you know it is wrong to do it. Then, if you do it, you are preferentially, not perversely wicked. But there are not supposed to be any preferentially wicked people.

Further, if you do not know what it means to believe that some action is morally wrong, you cannot have beliefs about the rightness or wrongness of what you are doing in the first place, so you cannot properly be described as perversely wicked. The most we could say about you is that you (sometimes) just prefer to do things that you should, but for some reason do not, know are morally wrong or bad. But that would make you preferentially wicked.

So perverse wickedness on a cognitivist's account, despite its original attraction to explain the behavior of people like average Balkan war criminals, loses its persuasive power. If the average Balkan war criminals are wicked, cognitivists may have to concede they are preferentially wicked and that seems to make them more reprehensible than when they were perversely wicked. Perhaps cognitivists will opt to shunt them off to Aristotle's habitual brutishness category. But that, I think, would reflect a certain moral spinelessness. A noncognitivist position might, however, preserve perverse wickedness to categorize the average Balkan war criminals. Then, at least, we can recognize in them the potential saving grace of conscientiousness and ascribe to them even a pitiable ignorance of the proper moral principles.

III

Noncognitivists hold that "believing an act to be morally wrong consists . . . in having a certain kind of con-attitude towards it."[24] The attitude or the disposition to choose one way rather than another is as far as the matter goes. So there is, as Milo points out, "nothing to be ignorant of or falsely believe."[25] One's moral principles simply are one's pro- or con-attitudes toward actions. For the noncognitivist, it may look as if preferential wickedness is not possible, at least as long as choice is determined by pro-attitudes. Only the degenerate or mentally disturbed would act counter to their pro-attitudes. Wickedness should always be perverse. Or so one might be led to think.

Nowell-Smith writes: "If a man consistently, and over a long course of years, tries to get the better of his fellows in all transactions of daily life or if he is never moved by the consequences of his actions for other people, we might say, colloquially, that 'he has no moral principles.' But this clearly means, not that he has no moral principles or that he has good ones and continually succumbs to temptation to act against them, but that he has bad moral principles."[26] Revelation of one's preferences is revelation of one's moral principles. And in some cases, one's moral principles are perverse, bad.

But an account like Nowell-Smith's overlooks equally acceptable alternative readings of the situation that are still within the scope of noncognitivism. Why should we describe the average Balkan war criminal as having bad moral principles rather than as having morally bad principles? (A point suggested by Milo.[27]) If we adopt the latter reading, then his wickedness is preferential, not perverse, for he is, after all, in either case acting on his preferences, his pro-attitudes. The noncognitivist, like Nowell-Smith, must call those preferences "his moral principles" and then judge them to be bad ones. But from what hat does the noncognitivist then pull the moral evaluative? Were we noncognitivists, however, we need not maintain that agents who are acting on their preferences, their pro-attitudes, must believe that they are doing what is morally right even if they are doing something so despicable as raping, torturing, mutilating, and murdering. They might prefer to promote their own ends, such as ethnic cleansing, by doing something they believe to be morally wrong, though not giving a damn that it is. Of course, if one's dominant pro-attitude is to ethnically cleanse one's neighborhood by raping, torturing, mutilating, and murdering women of different ethnic origins, it would seem fair to say that one has extraordinarily perverse preferences.

One might, I suspect, recognize the perversity of one's preferences, but still prefer them to doing the morally good thing in the circumstances. I seldom recycle cans. I guess that I just don't care that much about recycling. But my failure to recycle surely does not reveal a weakness of will on my part. It reveals only the importance I attach to recycling. It might even show a resoluteness in not recycling, though resoluteness is more likely to be associated with acting on what is really cared about rather than on what is not cared about much at all. You might criticize me, with justification, saying that I ought to care about recycling. You might try to persuade me to care. But persuading me to care and persuading me that it is morally wrong not to recycle cans are two rather different things. You may succeed in the latter and utterly fail in the former. And, if your attempts to get me to care are unsuccessful, it will be because that is just the sort of person I am: the sort that doesn't give a damn about recycling, a person who prefers other pursuits to taking the trouble to recycle cans, even though I am persuaded that recycling is the morally right thing to do. I just cannot be bothered when there are other things to be done that I care about more. I confess that where recycling cans is concerned, I am a preferentially, not a perversely, wicked person.

The noncognitivist's position, like that of the cognitivist, I have tried to suggest in the end collapses perverse wickedness into preferential wickedness. But a noncognitivist trying to rescue the category of perverse wickedness might maintain that a person who does evil deeds because of his or her dominant pro-attitude towards the pursuit of his or her own ends must believe that he or she is morally bound to do so and that failing to do so would be a moral failing. I cannot, however, find a compelling reason to adopt such an account. For example, that is not the way I see myself in the matter of can recycling. There is as much reason for a noncognitivist to maintain that the evildoer believes that what he or she is doing is morally wrong, while preferring to do it to all other possible actions in the circumstances. Why hang the belief that what he or she is doing is morally right around the neck of the wicked person? The noncognitivist's perverse wickedness amounts, it seems, to nothing more than the cognitivist's preferential wickedness, absent the knowledge element. Both have wicked people perversely preferring their own ends even when those ends conflict with such standard moral prohibitions as do not rape, torture, mutilate, or murder fellow human beings.

A pathetic naivete seems to afflict those who believe that if only the average Balkan war criminal could have been convinced that what he was doing was raping, torturing, mutilating, and murdering other human beings, he would have been caught up by the scruff of the neck by some moral invisible hand and just stop what he was doing. Nothing, I fear, is further from the truth. I am convinced that he knew full well he was raping, torturing, mutilating, and murdering. That is ethnic cleansing and that is what he preferred doing. He is not that morally ignorant. He is the living moral monster, the possibility of whose existence has been denied by a legion of moral philosophers from ancient times to the present. Yet our history books and newspapers and our newscasts are replete with accounts of him and his kind.

The preferentially wicked have no morally redeeming features of the sort that are typically associated with the perversely wicked: conscientiousness. They cannot claim that, had they known or believed that what they were doing was wrong, they would have refrained from doing it. They knew it was wrong, and they preferred it anyway. Normally they are treated as fully morally responsible for the evil they do. But should they be held morally responsible if their preferences for doing the evil things they do are the result of cultural inculcation over which they had no choice?

IV

The average Balkan war criminals did not choose to be racial and ethnic bigots. They were raised in a centuries-old culture of hatred, distrust, and conflict. In such a culture the preferences that form their characters were cemented. In so far as acting on those preferences, e.g., performing acts of ethnic cleansing instead of following moral principles is wicked, their wickedness, at an important level for moral evaluative purposes, was not chosen by them, even though it was preferential. Their preferential wickedness is what John Kekes calls "unchosen evil."[28] He writes, "The agents do not decide to cause evil, yet they do so as a regular by-product of their characters and actions."[29] Unchosen evil preferences may sound to some to have the peal of paradox. It should, however, ring no alarm bells. Preferences need not be chosen. They can, and typically are, habituated unconsciously.

From a cognitivist position, Kekes attempts to explain certain examples of unchosen evil as acting on mistaken moral principles, and thereby perversely wicked. In this, I think, he is wrong. It is not that those who flogged slaves, burned witches, treated infidels as vermin, tortured criminals before execution, or gassed Jews and Gypsies (all examples used by Kekes) acted on bad or mistaken moral principles while applying correct or good moral principles in their dealings with people of their own ethnic background. They believed, I think it fair to surmise, that moral principles did not take priority in their dealings with certain human beings or groups. Other things were more important, e.g., ethnically cleansing the area, exterminating threats to their superiority, punishing those on whom they have heaped the cause of their own misfortunes, etc. Still, Kekes is right that in most of the cases he cites, those doing the evil deeds *did not choose* the root cause of their actions: those inbred, ingrained preferences. "It often happens that people live in surroundings inhospitable to critical reflection ... Holding ... mistaken principles and acting according to them is an essential part of their form of life . . . Their identity and sense of belongingness to society, the respect they give and receive, . . . their own appraisals of themselves are all inseparably tied up with their pernicious principles."[30] If "preferences" is substituted for "principles" and "mistaken principles" I think Kekes correctly captures the situation. In other words, they did not (do not) have perverse moralities. They had (have) perverse preferences on which they felt (feel) compelled to act.

Suppose we grant, as I am prepared to do, that the vile actions of ethnic cleansing, by and large, are the products of vices or faults in character that were not chosen by the average Balkan war criminals. From the dominant point of view in moral philosophy, or what Kekes aptly calls "choice morality,"[31] such actions would not be ones for which the agent is to be held morally responsible, or at least not fully morally responsible. The type of people we are talking about cannot do other than they do, because they cannot have preferences other than the ones they have. "Ought implies can" – arguments, no doubt, will be trucked out to defend them.[32] If the average Balkan war criminals do not have the capacity to act in ways other than they did when confronted with the opportunity to ethnically cleanse their region, their behavior does not fit the typical criteria for chosen action.

Kekes, helpfully, catalogues those criteria in something like the following way: (1) the agent decides to bring about certain events; (2) believing that by doing certain specific things the desired events will likely occur; (3) the agent is not forced or coerced to try to bring about the events or to act in the specific way; (4) the agent has the cognitive, emotional, and volitional capacity to try to bring about other, quite different events and to perform the acts likely to do so; and (5) the agent appreciates the situation in which he or she acts.[33] J. L. Austin has important things to say about the last criterion,[34] telling us that a course in E. M. Forster would serve us well in grasping its significance. Though I think that the Bosnian war criminals might well suffer from an unchosen failure to properly appreciate the situations in which they act, the fourth criterion is most clearly unmet in their cases. They do not, I believe, have the capacities to try to bring about events that are radically different than, indeed, opposed to, those of ethnic cleansing. They are dominated by their ingrained, unchosen, ethnic bigotry. They are, if you will, possessed by it. It controls them, disposes them to act as they do in certain situations. It is who they are, their form of life, and they do not have the ability to dispossess themselves of it.

I am not saying that there is no possible world in which an average Balkan war criminal has a set of preferences different from the ones he actually has with respect to members of other ethnic groups. As a matter of fact, they do not have another set of preferences and they have the ones they do because that is the way they were raised. Had they been more independent in their thinking, had they questioned their upbringing, had they critically appraised their cultural traditions and heritage, they might have determined that their preferences are morally improper. But that is not the way they are. They are immersed in their culture of ethnic hatred, baptized in it from birth. It is an unquestioned, unexamined part of their lives. They know that what they are doing to those of other ethnic groups inflicts pain and harm on them, but they are convinced that doing so is to be preferred to acting in any other way toward those of the hated ethnic groups.

How can people become this way? That is a no-brainer. There are centuries of cases to examine and they all seem to share the characteristic that the members of prejudiced and bigoted communities, whether ethnic or racial or sexual, regularly reinforce those kinds of views in each other and over many generations. When the vast majority of the members of the community express a singular set of pernicious, perverse views and when they are incessantly echoed and enlarged upon by those in positions of authority, the scope of the questioning of the veracity and the morality of the dominant view narrows to a virtually invisible point. The perverse preferences of that form of life are among its essential features and they dominate the characters of those who share that form of life. They are the inescapable mark of belonging to those raised in that community and the individual members of the community have no effective control over their own adoption of those preferences. The preferences of that culture are learned by its members, but the process is predominantly one of "unconscious habituation" (Kekes' term), rather than rational reflective acquisition. It is unlikely that the members ever had an opportunity to alter the course of their character development, "since doing so would have required of them a sustained effort to act contrary to their own predisposition's and to the social context that favored their development in a particular direction."[35] The very virtues that might have stood them in good moral stead and withstood the pressures of their culture are exactly the ones that they lack because they were never encouraged or trained in them through the process of their enculturation. None of this, however, makes their raping, torturing, mutilating, and murdering those of other ethnic origins one iota less wicked, preferentially wicked.

The average Balkan war criminals did not sincerely believe, though falsely, that what they did to the women in the Bosnian Muslim or Kosovar Albanian village was "deserved punishment, a necessary corrective, justified self-defense, or only a way of instilling discipline."[36] They did not give a damn about any of that. Its moral status was of no consequence to them. They did it because they preferred to do it, purely and simply. That is their cultural heritage. They do not subscribe to a mistaken set of moral princip- les. When they are with their own kind they honor all of the standard moral principles. They just prefer what raping, torturing, mutilating and killing Bosnian Muslim or Kosovar Albanian women means to them: ethnic cleansing. The morally timid response that they must either (1) believe that Bosnian Muslim or Kosovar Albanian women are not members of the moral community and so fair game outside of the constraints of morality or (2) believe that what they are doing to the Bosnian Muslim or Kosovar Albanian women is not raping, torturing, mutilating, or murdering them, that it takes an entirely different and either morally neutral or commenda- tory description, has no foundation in the evidence, as I have noted above. There is little reason to not take the average Balkan war criminals and their evil actions at face value, other than, of course, to preserve an ancient dictum of moral psychology against the attack of reality. They are, quite frankly, preferentially wicked people whose bad characters were molded by unchosen habituation in an ethnically bigoted culture.

V

What then should be our response from the moral point of view to these average Balkan war criminals? Two sorts of responses will typically be registered. One will censure the raping, torturing, mutilating, and murder- ing perpetrated by the average Balkan war criminal, but it will excuse the perpetrator because his actions in these cases were unchosen by him. The excuse of unchosen evil will be treated as exculpatory. The perpetrator is not to be held morally responsible. This sort of response, Kekes calls it the "soft reaction,"[37] and I prefer to call it the "choice-based response," con- demns the actions but not the agent. "Their actions may be evil, but their actions do not reflect on them, because they have not chosen to perform them."[38]

The second type of response (Kekes calls it the "hard reaction"[39]) holds the perpetrator morally responsible for the evil regardless of whether it was chosen by him. As I feel strongly that the average Balkan war criminals are condemnably evil, and not that they just acted evilly,[40] I reject choice- basing as the sole justification of ascriptions of moral responsibility. Frank- furt-type cases,[41] around which a cottage industry of philosophical commentary has developed, provide grounds for holding that the principle of alternate possibilities that underlies choice-basing responsibility is false. I am not going to retravel those well-trod paths.[42] In fact, I believe that choice (the possibility of doing otherwise) is not even the primary basis of justifiable ascriptions of moral responsibility.

Suppose we ask, "what is the point of ascribing moral responsibility to an agent?" In *Responsibility Matters*[43] and following Pincoffs,[44] I maintain that there are at least three social practices that utilize and are codependent with responsibility ascription. One concerns the determination of who merits punishment, the second sets the targets for burden shifting, while the third identifies appropriate subjects of blame or praise. The third practice is fundamental to moral responsibility. Why identify proper subjects for blame (or praise)? Because morality is, in large measure, our attempt to prevent evil, to bring about a better community, the "Great Good Place."[45] One way, perhaps the dominant way, we do that within the moral sphere is to evaluate characters, ours and those of others, to ask ourselves what sort of people we ought to be and with whom we ought to associate. We express disapprobation[46] with regard to those who are not the sort of people that they ought to be if this is ever to become, or even approach, a truly moral, good, community.

When we make moral judgments reflective of our disapprobative attitudes, we do not focus, or we do not necessarily focus, on specific actions. Character traits typically draw our attention, and, without compunction, we regularly express disapproval of a person's character, regardless of how that person came to have such a character. What that means is that unchosen evil, at least when it arises from or reflects the character of the agent, warrants blaming the agent. Negative (that is blaming) moral responsibility ascriptions circumscribe those of bad character, whether or not we decide to punish them. What is important is not whether an agent chose to do what he or she did, but that what was done was evil. If morality is basically about preventing evil, then it must apprehend evil where it finds it.

The *New York Times* reported that Dr. Charles Epstein, one of the victims of the Unabomber, Theodore Kaczynski, after the Sacramento court case that ended in a plea bargain, said: "I looked at him in court and I came to the decision, this is a profoundly evil person. He is really the essence of evil."[47] When Epstein was asked if Kaczynski's mental illness affected his judgment of the man, he replied: "that doesn't take away for me from the fact that he is evil." In my view, Epstein has captured the essence of our moral blaming practice. Calling someone evil is to use our most severe term of moral censure. Importantly, it is not a choice-based term. Even, to

paraphrase Epstein, if Kaczynski's mental illness, which Epstein characterized as paranoid schizophrenia, determines the very preferences he has, that
he has no effective scope of choice when he is in its throes, he is no less evil,
"the essence of evil."

There is another side to moral responsibility that is worth noting: the
members of the moral community are expected to make identifications of
evil persons and to censure them, on pain of losing their own moral
standing. The condoning of evil is itself evil. The economy of moral
responsibility ascriptions is revealed in that in blaming one both identifies
the actions that were done as evil and one censures the actor. When I say
that an average Balkan war criminal is morally responsible for raping, and/or
torturing and/or mutilating and/or murdering women in a Muslim village, I
am both morally characterizing his actions as evil and animadverting him for
doing them. Morality requires this of me.

Holding him morally responsible, however, is not punishing him, nor
even threatening to punish him. It is to react to the central moral fact in the
situation: that evil was done, and, secondarily, that he did it. Moral appraisal
is dominated by those concerns and not with whether he could have chosen
not to do what he did or whether he should be punished for doing it. He is
identified as a horrible human specimen, an example of what we must all try
to avoid if we are to strive to make this a better place to live. We must
protect ourselves from him and his like. In effect, blaming him for his
actions does a great deal of important moral work. The point is that people
who do evil deserve to be treated as evil. They warrant our censure.

Does the fact that the evil was unchosen, the outcome of culturally
habituated preferences, alter the moral responsibility ascribed to the average
Balkan war criminal? I think not. In fact, it is one of the best reasons for
holding him morally responsible. He is dominated by, in that he is culturally
habituated to do, evil. Of course, the fact that he does not really choose to
do evil, if we are feeling merciful, may count with us as mitigatory when we
address questions of punishment. Kekes calls this the extenuating version of
the principle that "ought" implies "can."[48] Epstein, again, identifies the role
of moral responsibility ascription as contrasted to punishment. He is
reported in the *Times* as saying that he "would not have been unhappy if
Kaczynski had been executed. But other than the need to keep Kaczynski
away from society for the rest of his life, he had not concerned himself
greatly with the question of what penalty was appropriate."[49]

Kekes is right in emphasizing that choice plays only a subsidiary role in
moral responsibility. But he suggests that if we are convinced that the
evil was unchosen, we would treat that as a crucial factor in assessing

punishment. It is, he tells us "a civilizing force," a restraint on our "righteous indignation."[50] I am not so interested in mercy as Kekes may be. But he is right in reminding us that holding morally responsible and punishing are quite separable practices. The conditions we may impose on one are not necessarily the ones we apply to the other. Questions of efficacy and efficiency might play controlling roles in punishment decision-making and none in moral blaming.

My view, however, is that the average Balkan war criminals ought not to escape severe, indeed capital, punishment for the atrocities they committed. But that is another issue and beyond the scope of this chapter.

Notes

1   Aristotle, *Nicomachean Ethics*, trans. Martin Ostwald (Indianapolis, 1962), 1145a (hereafter cited as NE).
2   Ronald Milo, "Wickedness," *American Philosophical Quarterly* 20, 1 (January 1983): 69–79, p. 69.
3   NE 1148b.
4   Ibid.
5   NE 1149a.
6   Ibid.
7   Milo, "Wickedness," p. 70.
8   Plato, *Gorgias*, trans. Robin Waterfield (Oxford, 1994), 509e.
9   NE 1113b.
10 NE 1110b.
11 Milo, "Wickedness," p. 69.
12 See the BBC production, *My Lai Remembered*, for accounts by those who participated in the massacre.
13 Milo, "Wickedness," p. 70.
14 Ibid.
15 Ibid.
16 P. Nowell-Smith, *Ethics* (London, 1954).
17 See Owen Flanagan, *Varieties of Moral Personality* (Cambridge, MA, 1991), pp. 91–2.
18 NE 1111a.
19 Ibid.
20 Ibid.
21 Milo, "Wickedness," p. 71.
22 Ibid., p. 73.
23 NE 1107a.
24 Milo, "Wickedness," p. 72.

25 Ibid.
26 Nowell-Smith, *Ethics*, pp. 266–7.
27 Milo, "Wickedness," p. 73.
28 John Kekes, *Facing Evil* (Princeton, 1990), ch. 4.
29 Ibid., p. 70.
30 Ibid., p. 72.
31 Ibid., see especially ch. 5.
32 For example see Immanuel Kant, *Reason Within the Limits of Reason Alone*, trans. Greene and Hudson (New York, 1960), "When the moral law commands that we ought now to be better men, it follows inevitably that we must be able to be better men" (p. 46).
33 Kekes, *Facing Evil*, p. 67.
34 J. L. Austin, *Philosophical Papers* (Oxford, 1961), p. 194.
35 Kekes, *Facing Evil*, p. 75.
36 Ibid., p. 71.
37 Ibid., p. 85.
38 Ibid., p. 88.
39 Ibid., p. 86.
40 Peter Strawson, *Freedom and Resentment and Other Essays* (London, 1974), ch. 1.
41 See Harry Frankfurt, *The Importance of What We Care About* (Cambridge, 1988), ch. 1.
42 Peter French, *Responsibility Matters* (Lawrence, 1992), ch. 4.
43 Ibid., ch. 2.
44 Edmund Pincoffs, "Practices of Responsibility Ascription," *Proceedings and Addresses of the American Philosophical Association* 61, 5 (June 1988).
45 The term is borrowed from W. H. Auden, *The Dyer's Hand and Other Essays* (New York, 1962); see also French, ch. 18.
46 See Peter French, "Senses of Blame," *The Scope of Morality* (Minneapolis, 1979), pp. 163–78.
47 *New York Times* wire story carried in *St. Petersburg Times*, January 24, 1998, p. 1A and 8A.
48 Kekes, *Facing Evil*, p. 92.
49 *New York Times/St. Petersburg Times*, p. 8A.
50 Kekes, *Facing Evil*, p. 99.

2

War Crimes and Human Rights

Alan Gewirth

War crimes are crimes. As such, they are evil actions of murder, rape, torture, and other violations of basic human rights. Persons who commit, or order the perpetration of, such evils deserve severe punishment.

Such crimes occur outside war as well as within war. What difference does this make? This question is exacerbated by the fact that war itself involves many of the kinds of actions that are crimes. Patricipants in war try to kill or inflict intense physical injury on their opponents. It may be held, then, that all war is a crime, so that the phrase "war crime" is a pleonasm.

There are two bases for rejecting this idea, one deriving from the *jus ad bellum*, the other from the *jus in bello*. After all, war is a human activity, and concern for the human rights threatened or violated by war has led to an emphasis on various restrictions both as to the recourse to war and as to the ways it is conducted. These restrictions are designed in certain respects to "moralize" war or at least to mitigate its criminality. They indicate that even if all war, as such, is evil, there may be criteria, short of abolishing war itself, whereby some wars or acts of war may be morally justified or permitted if they do not transgress the restrictions. By these criteria, based on human rights, the criminality of war in general is at least modified or even completely removed, and this has corresponding effects on the guilt or responsibility of persons who engage in war.

From these considerations it follows that war crimes have a double relation to the morality of human rights. On the one hand, like crimes committed outside war, they are at least prima facie violations of morality. But on the other hand, unlike other crimes, war crimes have a further criminal status because they transgress restrictions that are designed to protect human rights with regard to the general context of war. To the extent that these restrictions are respected, the criminality of war is at least mitigated even if not completely removed.

It may be contended that the idea of "moralizing" war or making it "just" is an oxymoron; that all war is not only prima facie evil but is so conclusively evil that there is no way of rendering it moral or just. On this view, in its relation to the morality of human rights war is an all-or-nothing affair; any engagement in it is unmitigatedly evil. Just as murder and rape are evil as such, so too is war. On these grounds it may be held that only pacifism is justified.

Without wishing to blur the justified revulsion against war that underlies this position, I think it is important to note some of the constraints that serve to modify the criminality of war. One reason for emphasizing these constraints is that they can serve to uphold that very morality of human rights to which the pacifist opponents of war have also appealed. This upholding can operate in two ways, by providing moral criterial for the *jus ad bellum* and the *jus in bello*. Before considering each of these in turn, some linguistic clarifications are needed.

The phrase "war crimes" can be used in a broader or narrower sense. In the broader sense, it comprises violations both of the *jus ad bellum* and the *jus in bello*: that is, violations that consist both in resorting to war on wrongful grounds and in using wrongful practices within war itself. In the narrower sense only the latter kinds of violations are war crimes. Thus the Nuremberg Tribunal listed three kinds of crimes as "coming within the jurisdiction of the Tribunal": "crimes against peace," "war crimes," and "crimes against humanity." The first comprised "planning, preparation, initiation of a war of aggression, or a war in violation of international treatise"; the second ("war crimes") consisted in "violations of the laws or customs of war"; and the third included atrocities "committed against any civilian population, before or during the war."[1] Conceptually, it may seem possible for each of these three kinds of crime to occur independently of the other two. But, especially in the modern era when wars occur as expressions of extreme nationalist and ethnic hatreds, the three kinds of crimes are sufficiently commingled that the phrase "war crimes" can be used in a broader sense to comprise all three, and this is how I use it here.

In the reverse direction, however, it must also be noted that war crimes do not include all crimes that may occur in a theater of war. If, for example, a soldier commits a "crime of passion" against a fellow national, this is not a war crime unless it is directly bound up with the oppositions or conflicts involved in the war itself.

Let us now turn to the moral constraints that serve to modify the criminality of war. The primary basis for moralizing war in the *jus ad bellum* is that some wars are just, in that they are undertaken for morally justified purposes of protecting human rights. Let us first consider the purpose of repelling unjustified aggression. The killings in such a defensive war have a moral status similar to other means of self-defense. A partial analogue is found in the domestic criminal law. When a judge sentences a criminal to prison, he infringes the criminal's human right to freedom, but he does not violate that right insofar as the sentence is justified; on the contrary, the punishment he imposes is itself an expression and defense of the human right to basic well-being. In a parallel way, to kill or injure someone in self-defense does not violate the attacker's human right to life or physical integrity. So human rights, consisting in rights to freedom and well-being, are protected rather than violated when war is resorted to in order to repel aggression that aims to violate those rights.

The notion of self-defense calls attention to two different meanings of "aggression" and of "aggressive war." One meaning is primarily temporal; the other is primarily motivational. In the temporal meaning, aggressive war consists in the initiation of hostilities against an enemy. But the motivation for such initiation may itself be morally justified, as, for example, when a country that has been brutally subjugated by a dominating colonial power rises up to remove such subjugation, or when a "war of liberation" is engaged in by the oppressed domestic victims of a tyrannical regime.[2]

The moral opprobrium that attaches to "aggressive war" must, then, derive primarily from the motivating factor rather than from the temporal one. Aggressive war is morally wrong when the purpose or motivation of the government that wages it is to dominate other people, to subject them to the aggressor's will regardless of the victims' own needs or human rights. In this regard aggressive war is the antithesis of constitutional democracy, in contrast to aggressive wars that are initiated for the purpose of securing the human right to constitutional democracy by defeating rulers whose policies and motivations are themselves the antithesis of such democracy. The *jus ad bellum* in the latter kind of case, where the purpose is to secure human rights of political freedom or economic justice, serves to give a moral justification to such kinds of aggressive war.

On the other hand, to wage aggressive war in the motivational sense of aiming to subjugate others persons or groups is a crime: it is a wrong-doing in that it violates the basic human rights of the persons attacked. Here it must be emphasized that the crime consists not only in the motivation itself but also in the actions that proceed from that motivation. This judgment can be upheld regardless of the dictum *nullum crimen sinê lege* ("no crime without a law"). The development of international law, including the various covenants against wars of aggression, has been interpreted in different ways involving looser or stricter criteria of "law." But wrongful actions of the kinds cited above can be appropriately classified as crimes regardless of whether they are encoded in positive laws. What makes them crimes is that they are offenses against or violations of basic human rights. The criteria for the existence and contents of such rights and for their violations can be ascertained by objective rational methods of ethical analysis. These are quite independent of the enactments of positive statute laws.[3]

It is indeed true that to codify crimes in positive legal enactments can provide an important kind of security for the determination of criminality and the protection of human rights. Such positivity can serve to remove or reduce conflicting opinions about what actions are to be regarded as criminal. Nevertheless, there are objective rational standards for determining the contents of crimes as violating basic human rights, and positive laws to be justified must conform to these standards.

The need for such moral standards becomes especially important when positive laws are enacted that define as criminal actions that derive from, rather than violate, human rights. Obvious examples are legal prohibitions of speech that criticizes the government or that advocates help for the poor. In such cases it becomes especially important to keep in mind that the ultimate criterion of criminality is moral rather than legal.

The primary criminality of motivationally aggressive war aiming at violation of human rights pertains to the ruling groups who initiate such war. The subordinate soldiers and sailors who carry out their superiors' orders may not, as such, share their guilt. But insofar as the subordinates are aware of the wrongness of the war they are required to wage, a secondary kind of guilt attaches to them. If they can do so without undue cost to themselves, they should refuse to engage in the aggressive war. Because, however, the cost to themselves of their refusal may be great, their guilt for obeying the aggressors' order is correspondingly lessened. The complex problems that are involved here will be further considered below.

Distinct from the issue of war crimes as motivationally aggressive war is the issue of military conduct within war. This is the question of *jus in bello* as against *jus ad bellum*. Here, war crimes consist of inflictions of harm that go beyond military necessity. Rape and torture are prime examples, where the aims are to terrorize and humiliate one's victims and to gratify one's most bestial impulses.

The notion that war crimes are egregiously harmful actions that are "not justified by military necessity" was a central feature of the Nuremberg Tribunal's judgment.[4] This notion can be interpreted in two clearly related ways to try to refute the claim that such actions are crimes. One way is to deny that questions of moral justification are relevant to military actions. I have briefly dealt with this above in connection with the "moralizing" of war. The other way is to accept the relevance of justification but to assert that "military necessity" is so strong that it includes the murder, rape, and torture of civilians and hence excuses such harmful actions. This latter implies an appeal to means-end calculation: given the end of defeating one's military opponent, various modes of terrorism are justified as contributing to this end. The status of such means may be of at least two different kinds. On one view, the terrorizing actions may be upheld as efficient means to the end; on another view, they may be upheld also as indispensable for achieving the end. In all such cases, the appeal to justification by "military necessity" would be held to excuse and even to justify the various modes of terrorism.

The Kantian principle that "ought" implies "can" may also be invoked in this connection. If the waging of war cannot proceed successfully without such terrorizing of one's opponents, then it is not the case that the terrorism ought to be abstained from. And since human rights entail correlative strict "oughts," it follows that human rights are not applicable or relevant in the conduct of war.

Like all other empirical connections, the invocations of efficiency and indispensability are contingent, not necessary; they may be more or less sound as connecting means with their desired ends. Terrorism applied against civilian populations as well as against military personnel may serve to break the spirit of the victims and thereby lessen their willingness and ability to resist. But it may also serve to arouse and enrage the victimized populations, so that they resist the terrorizing aggressors ever more fiercely. Hence, the invocation of "necessity" in this context is far from decisive; and the invocation of the principle that "ought" implies "can" must be correspondingly modified.

What is universally decisive here, however, is the moral character both of the end itself and of the means. Even if "military necessity" can be shown to uphold the infliction of murder, rape, and other evils on civilians or military personnel, the basic question is whether a morally justified end can justify these evil means. If it cannot, then no amount of "military necessity" can succeed in such justification. We have here, then, a primary case of the continuum of means and ends. If the end is morally justified, such as to resist subjugation by forces bent on domination or to establish a constitutional democratic regime, then the means used cannot justifiably include actions that are antithetical to this end. Violations of basic human rights cannot justifiably be prevented by means that themselves violate these rights. Military necessity may here indeed include the use of force, including killing and wounding, to overcome the resistance of enemy soldiers. But it cannot, without violating its moral end, include the infliction of brutal harms like rape, torture, blinding, or cutting off of hands on civilians who are innocent bystanders or on military personnel.

An analogy to domestic criminal punishment may again be helpful here. Such punishment, to be justified, must have as its end the restoration of an occurrent equality of human rights which has been disrupted by the criminal. But in being thus instrumental to the end, the punishment must be *internally* instrumental in that it must embody the same distributive equality as is characteristic of the end itself, so that its features are constitutive of the end. This requirement justifies a retributive basis for criminal punishment whereby only wrongdoers are punished, and in a way that is proportionate to their crimes. This stands in contrast to an external instrumentality in which the end of proportional distribution has no effect on the means used to procure it or any other basis of punishment.[5] So again the human right to proportional distributive justice is violated by terrorist actions perpetrated against military personnel or innocent civilians. Human rights can thus be invoked to justify the punishment of such criminal agents.

In discussing military necessity as well as innocence, we must take note of what may be called the "totalizing" of these concepts. The appeal to "military necessity" may be extended to such an extreme that it subsumes under the end of "victory" myriad kinds of crimes that have either no causal connection with defeating the enemy or else the most tenuous kind of connection. Here the invocation of "military necessity" becomes a callous way of violating basic human rights. Such violation can be avoided only if two cautions are observed. First, the military end must be carefully specified; and, as we have seen, an end that involves the infliction or maintenance of subjugating the human rights of the victims cannot be justified. Second, the means to the end must also be carefully specified so that, in addition to the internal instrumentality indicated above, they do not go beyond what is required to attain the end. So human rights impose restrictions on both the ends and the means of war. Violations of these restrictions are war crimes.

It may be objected that war itself is such a totalizing relationship that the restrictions just upheld are incapable of application. Because "war is hell," it cannot be conducted like a game with carefully specified rules both about what constitutes winning and about the means to be used in winning. The brutality inherent in war involves not merely defeating the enemy but crushing and humiliating him, so that the restrictions upheld for the moralizing of war are inapplicable and irrelevant.

This view involves an essentialist view of war that removes it altogether from human control. It is indeed true that participants in war may be so carried away by hatred of the enemy that a kind of dehumanization takes place whereby the constraints of human rights and dignity are completely rejected. But this is not inevitable. War consists in voluntary actions, so that at important phases it is subject to the informed and unforced control of the participants. They can hence recognize the difference between a kind of "military necessity" in which no holds are barred and a different kind of "military necessity" in which defeat of the enemy can be secured without completely destroying or humiliating him.

The totalizing excesses that have been used to extend the idea of "military necessity" have also been applied to the concept of "innocence." One of the prime moral restrictions imposed by the *jus in bello* is that innocent persons or noncombatants must be kept immune from war's violence. This requirement is the antithesis of military necessity: since noncombatants are not engaged in waging war, there is no military necessity for waging war on them. But here a totalizing procedure has been applied, in the reverse direction from that of "military necessity." The scope of those who are "innocent," far from being extended beyond sound reason, is so restricted that almost no persons in the enemy country are deemed to be "innocent." A kind of pseudo-causal reasoning is again engaged in for the purpose of showing that all inhabitants of the enemy country are some how contributing to its war effort and are therefore not innocent.

So it may be held, to begin with, that persons who work in munitions factories are not innocent because of their direct contributions to the making of military weapons. But even in such an apparently clear case the question of innocence is complex. If the workers have been drafted into the factories, with refusal to work in them punished by death, then an important part of their *mens rea* is removed. Even if the principle of double effect does not apply here, in that, given their circumstances, what they directly intend is to make weapons whose foreseeable effect is the killing of enemy soldiers, still the workers may be confronted by a forced choice in which failure to comply leads, for them, to an even worse result. In addition, there is the question of whether aerial bombardment can succeed in destroying the factories without also killing large numbers of civilians who do not work in them.

The denial of innocence may be further extended to all the inhabitants of the enemy country, on the ground that they give aid and comfort to their family members or friends who are enemy soldiers. On this specious ground the most heinous acts of murder, rape, and torture, and indeed of genocide may be held to be justified, despite their obvious violations of human rights. The mass terrorization of indiscriminate aerial bombardment also belongs in this category. To hold that such actions are not crimes because their intended victims are not innocent is to ride roughshod over the whole concept of innocence. Indeed, the contention that whatever contributes to the opponent's war effort renders it noninnocent and hence subject to annihilation has been applied also to the nonhuman agricultural and animal environment that provides food and other necessaries for the "enemy" population.

In a related category, blockades of enemy countries that bring great suffering to their inhabitants who have not contributed to their government's motivationally aggressive violations of human rights are themselves violations of human rights. They cannot be excused on the specious grounds that the inhabitants are not innocent.

Guilt does attach to rulers who violate the *jus ad bellum* through initiating wars for evil purposes of self-aggrandizement by subjugating others. Soldiers who fight such wars may justifiably be killed if this is the only way of preventing their success in such wars. But if the prevention can be secured by means short of killing, the principle of human rights requires that such other means be employed. Guilt also attaches to the planners, the bureaucrats, and others who see to the details of the war's execution. In connection with the Holocaust a vast array of underlings cooperated in scheduling the death trains, procuring the lethal gas-oven equipment, and in other ways.[6] But there are degrees of responsibility here. They extend, for example, to the leaders of other nations who do not intervene when they know that war crimes are being committed. In all such cases the principle of human rights imposes on governments the duty to try to prevent these and other violations of human rights.

It must be emphasized that human rights are positive as well as negative: they entail not only noninterference with right-holders' having the objects of their rights but also active intervention to help provide these objects for persons who cannot attain them by their own efforts. So in the face of the kinds of war crimes represented by genocide and "ethnic cleansing," it is morally required that governments that have the means actively intervene to prevent such crimes and to punish the perpetrators. The development of the international law of human rights includes important steps in this direction.

War crimes, then, violate human rights in two main ways. One is when the motivation for waging war is to subjugate one's victims for purposes of governmental self-aggrandizement. The other is when, in the process of waging war, injuries are inflicted that go beyond military necessity. The totalizing interpretations of such necessity must be rejected. Both kinds of war crimes are violations of basic human rights, whose objects are the necessary goods of action and generally successful action. International law must be implemented so as to prevent and punish both kinds of violations of human rights. Such implementation is itself an application of human rights through its setting and enforcing moral requirements about the justified engagement in, and conduct of, war.

Notes

1   Excerpts from the Nuremberg Tribunal are conveniently reprinted in Richard A. Wasserstrom, ed., *War and Morality* (Belmont, CA: Wadsworth Publishing Co., 1970), p. 44.
2   On this point, see the essays by Elizabeth Anscombe and Richard A. Wasserstrom in Wasserstrom, ed., *War and Morality*, pp. 44, 88.
3   I have developed this thesis in considerable detail elsewhere. See Alan Gewirth, *Reason and Morality* (Chicago: University of Chicago Press, 1978), chs. 1–3; "The Epistemology of Human Rights," *Social Philosophy and Policy* 1, 2 (1984); 1–24.
4   This judgment is reprinted in Wasserstrom, ed., *War and Morality*, pp. 102–14.
5   I have developed this point more fully in *Reason and Morality*, p. 296.
6   I owe this point to David Cohen.

3

War Crimes: Moral, Legal, or Simply Political?

Jovan Babic

The notion of war crimes is a complex one. To the extent that it is about crimes, it belongs to the realm of legality, encompassing both national and international laws. To the extent that all aspects of law must be grounded in morality, war crimes also require such grounding. Given actual practices, however, I shall argue that the notion of war crimes is above all a political category. In this paper I explore these various aspects of war crimes in view of two main claims which I try to defend. First, describing an act by attributing to it the characterization "of war" forms no separate criterion of moral evaluation, nor does it represent an additional component of the criterion. Second, crimes against peace, consisting in the production of the causes of war, cannot be defined as just or unjust independently of the outcome of war; that is, they are amenable to moral assessment only in terms of the (military) defeat. Consequently, crimes against peace, while initially most interesting from the perspective of international law, in the final analysis turn out to be a political category and not a moral or legal one.

I The Notion of War Crimes as a Political Category

Morality and the crimes in war

Admittedly, one would find it awkward if, in the aftermath of a war, the defeated party were to speak of war crimes: speech acts, here as elsewhere, are determined by context. Talk of war crimes by the vanquished may strike us as a search for excuses, and thus be utterly unconvincing. Why should it be that we have this reaction? Does it mean that the matters of moral and legal justification are dependent on the outcome of war? Does it mean that the *wrong* side could never win a war, or that wars are not won by those with might, but by those who are in the right?

Let us look at two examples, a thought-experiment, the other a real case. First, the thought-experiment: imagine a rabbit that tries to lecture the hunter about the right to life. Given the context in which they occur, how credible or effective could the rabbit's arguments be? The second example is the bombardment of Dresden or Hiroshima during the Second World War. Although these bombings are arguably prime examples of war crimes, could anyone have realistically expected that they would ever come up for a trial like Nuremberg or Tokyo? A decisive factor in these matters, however, is not just who the victor is, but to an even larger extent it is the matter of who has greater power. For example, the US was defeated in Vietnam. Yet there was no tribunal that could rule, for instance, in favor of war-reparations owed to the victorious Vietnam. Nor that reparations at least to the victims of the war were in order; or even simply to the victims of war crimes, crimes which must have been rampant given the descriptions of the ease with which Americans operated with the notion of "tactical necessity."[1]

Our initial skepticism when the vanquished talk of war crimes is a moral reaction that tacitly assumes that the notion of war crimes is neither a moral nor a legal category, but a political one. I shall now try to substantiate this. Just as the depth of an abyss is measured by the same unit (meter, centimeter, kilometer), as, say, a road is, a measure of moral wrongness is always the same – only the actions and situations to which this measure is applied in our moral judgments are different. The fact that a wrong action takes place in the context of war does not serve to justify it morally. War is just a context within which certain sorts of actions occur, and these actions taken together constitute war. In other words, actions are right or wrong only as a result of their moral evaluation, regardless of whether they happen during war. Actions are evaluated by means of the very same yardstick that determines the rightness or wrongness of all actions – universalization. The moral requirement that the maxim of an action be universalizable is neither a mechanical abstract generalization, nor a utilitarian rule of the accumulation of general good, nor an abstract principle independent of its application; rather, it consists exactly in the procedure of the application of some rule, application that manifests itself as approval, adoption, and authorization of that rule, all carried through on the basis of universal respect. It is only in application that the demand for universalization gains its full meaning. For it is not simply a matter of projecting oneself, as one is, through the set of all people; rather, it involves placing oneself in their shoes, and so to speak trailing all of them through that position. This is why universalization is so difficult: I am not asking what I would do if I were in a particular agent's shoes, I am asking what it means to be him (or anybody else) in that place.

Looking at things this way, we see that the mere fact that an act occurs in the context of war cannot make it right, and of course it cannot make it wrong either, if the act isn't already judged as such. But, one might object: Doesn't war make killing acceptable? We could say that killing which occurs in wars is a possible consequence of the acceptance of the rules of this practice, or the institution we call "war." Similarly, breaking one's nose or knocking one's teeth out is a possible outcome of partaking in fist-fighting: if one takes part in a fight, it would be sheer nonsense to protest one's bloody nose or express shock that such a thing could happen. This doesn't mean that we ought to fight or start wars; it is just that we ought not to be surprised that in wars people get killed or that in fights noses get broken. It can happen, however, that a war (as opposed to, say, a fistfight) proves to be unavoidable, for war is a social category irreducible to contributions and decisions of people as (private) individuals. Collective decisions and collective actions can significantly restrict, in some situations even altogether eliminate, the possibility of free decision-making for individuals (and after a certain point of no return, this applies to groups as well).

Let us examine this more closely. We can agree that killing in self-defense is justified, that killing in self-defense isn't morally wrong. This is to say, of course, only under the constraint that there is a necessity for choosing just this means of self-defense. It is quite possible, however, for someone to take advantage of the situation by using self-defense as a cover for hitting harder than necessary and "finishing the job" (in the context of a situation in which successful self-defense doesn't require deadly force). In a situation like this, it may not be possible to establish beyond dispute whether the defender intended to hit harder than necessary, i.e., whether his self-defense was only a cover for murder. Hence, an act of killing isn't justified simply because it is committed in the context of self-defense. Rather, it is justified only when it satisfies the conditions of its permissibility, and this is the case when relevant values are so related that they provide justification for that act.

Such is the case with war as well. War is neither a part of nor a possible addendum to the criterion of morality. A "crime of war" is really a crime if the act in question is criminal, and the characterization "of war" is, morally speaking, superfluous, as it adds nothing to, nor does it take anything away from the characterization that the act is indeed criminal (if it is). This characterization only describes the occasion or situation (i.e., a "practice" or "institution") in the context of which the act was undertaken. The context of war provides an opportunity for many such acts to occur. But in order for each such act to happen, it must be carried out, it must be established as an action rather than a mere event. One must elect to perform the act in question, rather then for it to be a necessary effect of some cause; this is what moral responsibility is based on. War is a form of necessity, and for many acts carried out in the context of war agents escape responsibility because those acts are, just as in the case of self-defense, necessary. In order for crimes to occur, there must not be this sort of necessity, and this is why war, just as self-defense, cannot furnish any additional moral justification. If there were no necessity to act in a particular way, then the act would be free in a sense that all external conditions were only factual presuppositions for this act's execution (just as a murder with a gun might require that the gun be acquired first).

Actions done in war are permissible at the time they are carried out only if the conditions of their permissibility (that is, the universalizability of the maxim of the action) are also present. What is morally permissible in the context of war differs from other situations for human action only inasmuch as war, rather than peace, is the context in which the actions occur. Thus, it is only owing to a semantic confusion that an ordinarily impermissible act might be regarded as permissible in the context of war. This confusion in meaning results from an implicit assumption, based on a sort of arrogance and shallow optimism, that the concept of permissibility implies that what is permitted is in itself always some positive good. But we all know that conditions exist when it is permissible to cut human limbs off, to remove kidneys, eyes, or lungs. This is never a positive good, but only a negative one – a lesser of two evils. However, for this sort of action to be really permissible, the so-called normal situation must be drastically changed, as in the case of a serious illness. On that occasion, in a new set of circumstances, the same criterion provides an entirely new line of demarcation between what is permissible and what is not.

The fact that different ethical theories will provide different accounts of where exactly to place the demarcation line between what is permissible and what is not changes nothing in this evaluative logic: different theories will simply establish different criteria for evaluating the act under consideration. Thus, some actions will according to one criterion be permissible while according to another impermissible, but again not because the acts occur in war or peace, but because of the different ways these theories define values. Thus, the theory of the double effect – according to which the unintended although predictable consequences of some act can in good conscience be neglected by moral agents, since only what is intended counts – will rule as permissible many actions that the deontological theory would characterize as forbidden (for instance, massive bombardments if they are "successful"). This is so because all those unintended consequences are simply the "collateral damage," and they in no way count against the moral value of the original intent to achieve a just goal. Utilitarianism will assess as permissible even more. For example, revenge, intimidation, killing hostages, exemplary or collective punishment may in principle be permissible, or anything that is ultimately useful. Other theories, such as the natural rights theory, virtue ethics, or the human rights theory will each offer yet another set of answers. However, none of these theories, not even the most radical one, is capable of isolating any features specifically applicable to "crimes of war," just as they cannot do this with respect to, for example, the "crimes of passion."

Law and war crimes

When it comes to law, things are even more complicated. We suppose that the law is grounded in morality; most prominently, the presumption of legal innocence is an expression of the value of respect for rational autonomy. At the same time, law is not about what ought to be permissible, but about what has been decided to be permissible. This is why law requires the state and territory for its own validity. The state, of course, even when it is involved in war, cannot avoid its principal obligation of enforcing the law on all its citizens, which includes even the highest state officials together with those responsible for enforcing the law. If the law is not applicable equally to everyone it can provide security (and this is its basic role) for no one. It is another matter that laws can be violated and official posts abused. The opportunities for such abuses are much greater in wartime. Still, there is in principle no reason for crimes to go unpunished during war. If the state is well functioning, it will enforce its laws; if it isn't, crimes will go unpunished even in times of peace.

Of course, wars provide especially favorable conditions for a variety of wrongs (profiteering, looting, murder, massacre, etc.) – just as other, different, wrongs may be characteristic of business, medical, or legal practices. The state's criminal law determines which practices are wrong in these different contexts, assuming that the state actually has the genuine authority to enforce the law – that it isn't some private agency or a group of thugs who present their own will as legitimate power and the rule of law. Sovereign government always entails a code of laws, since the idea of a state without laws, in war or peace, proves practically impossible. A state without laws would have no legitimacy and could maintain itself only by sheer force, if it has adequate force, and only for as long as that force lasts.

In wartime as well as in peace, the state is torn between the demands of law, which require strict enforcement, and the demands of politics, which call for the efficient achievement of set goals. Yet any court that wishes to administer justice must have authority stemming from the legitimacy of the state, and this authority requires that no attention be paid to the state's own potential need to violate the law. The legal right of a court to administer justice presupposes this sort of authority which is itself based on tacit consent of the laws of a given state. These laws can be different in different states, and the states themselves can relate to one another in different ways, not only because of the conflict of interests, but also based on mutual perceptions of the quality and internal respect for the law in each of the states. These states may even wage wars among themselves. But what they cannot do is to stage trials for actions that are in the jurisdiction of the other state. In particular, they cannot make arrests in the territory of other states, try individuals (even in absentia) for deeds or crimes committed by citizens of another state in the territory of that other state.

Here we come closer to our problem: understanding what laws have the kind of sovereignty in virtue of which their being transgressed constitutes a "war crime." When an ordinary crime (to use this name in contrast to the term "war crimes) is committed in the context of war (as in the example above in which self-defense is used as a pretext for committing murder), it falls under the jurisdiction of the ruling authority, such that the difficulties in proving that the crime was committed are, as in other cases, of a factual nature. Crimes that can thus occur are violations of the demand for universal respect, and the fact that in the context of war the opportunity for such violations is dramatically increased is only a part of the description of war as an evil state of affairs. In principle, however, "war crimes" are crimes like any other, and do not constitute a separate category of their own. The right and the obligation that these crimes be prosecuted are in principle the same as for any other sort of crime. It is precisely this right and obligation, taken together, that empowers the proper courts with the authority to hear corresponding cases of alleged crimes.

Considering all this, the issue of war crimes should not present itself as a separate theoretical problem, apart from general philosophical and moral questions regarding law, punishment, crime, etc. What does present itself as a problem is war crime in the context of so-called international law, although it would be perhaps better to say multinational law. It appears to me that international law is not, and cannot be, law in the fundamental sense of the word. International law lacks the institutional structure (such as sovereign states have) necessary for its application, and instead appeals to the moral – and moralizing – sentiments[2] of those who are, or think they are, powerful enough to take their moral feelings at face value and transform their moral judgments into legal ones. What is more, the very phrase "international law" contains in itself a certain tension: it would really be a kind of law if a World State existed, and consequently it would not be "international." As we know, however, many states exist; hence this "law" cannot have at its disposal the kind of rule-governed institutions and practices required for a functioning court-system.[3] The existence of a plurality of states is a fact, and one may perhaps contend that this fact arises from freedom as a fundamental human characteristic, political freedom in particular as the freedom of association, which would be significantly hindered in a World State. It might be the case that as long as humankind remains unwilling to abdicate this freedom, there will be a plurality of states. And as long as there is a multitude of states there will be wars, as well as difficulties in prosecuting crimes committed in wars; and the demand will continue to be made that there be the institutions necessary for prosecuting alleged crimes. The need to successfully inflict punishment will remain as well as the desire to join in this process.

II Crimes Against Peace and the "Right to Victory"

This is where the problem lies. When we take a closer look at the classification of war crimes – they fall into three groups: crimes against peace, war crimes in the narrow sense, crimes against humanity – we can see that only the first category requires an international administration. However, I hope to show that a crime against peace is really a crime against defeat, and will substantiate the claim that this notion of "war crimes" is a political category in the legal domain as well. The remaining two types of war crimes may be placed in war law (*jus in bello*) and the "ethics of war" and then sanctioned, even internationally (on the basis of various conventions and international treaties), just as in the case of any other crime. Having no internal connection to the concept of war, they may be considered as just a special form of ordinary crimes. However, the notion of a "crime against peace" is complex and controversial: starting a war is, from the perspective of the *status quo ante*, always a violation of the established state and therefore a violation of international contract.

At this point we can consider the concept of aggression which is envisioned to play a decisive role in the context of international law. To begin with, we may note a distinctly negative normative meaning attached to the word "aggression" when it is contrasted with the term "attack." Initially, the concept of aggression seems quite promising, and the distinction "aggression *vs.* attack" can be quite useful. It has been helpful in distinguishing instances of military involvement deemed permissible from those that were not. As examples we might give the attacks of India against Pakistan in 1971, and Tanzania against Uganda in 1979, which were not characterized as aggressions.

However, the price for introducing the concept of aggression into international law is the complete abolition of the concept of war. In fact, it is actually the case with basic documents of the current world organization that they talk only of aggression and don't even mention war as such. This has the consequence that war is reduced to a kind of police raid in which it is predetermined which side of the conflict is in the right. The possibility of victory and defeat as an open question is thus effectively eliminated as the decisive feature of war. One side is denied the right to present its interests as legitimate ones (by being deemed the "aggressor"), which implies that it has no right even to defend itself, or even to flee. This would be the condition of a World Empire. Only under the assumption of an effective World State could it be determined unambiguously what the phrase "crime against peace" means. Without this assumption war, understood as a state of affairs in which there is conflict between two prima facie equally justified claims, remains, as it is in the real world, something which allows for the possibility of victory and defeat. According to the rules of war, the act of entering into war entails acceptance of whatever outcome might obtain as the just one. If the result is just, then the crimes against peace (and corresponding criminals) could exist only in case the one who plotted and started the war (that is, the aggressor, the insurgent, or the secessionist) is the defeated side. But this, if anything, is really just. For he who started the war is entirely responsible for his defeat, because his decision (to launch his attack or mount a rebellion) is one of the key causes of his defeat.

If the aggressor side is victorious in a war or the rebellion or succession is successful, the side which was attacked does not, merely by accepting defeat, become responsible for a "conspiracy against peace." The fact that the war occurred was not something of its own choosing; in defending the former state of affairs this side did not have to make any new decisions regarding what it wanted or did not want. The former state of affairs already existed, and it was either protected by the former peace among states (as a lawful state of affairs whose rules disallowed states to engage in mutual attacks) or by internal law (which forbids insurgency or secession). The side under attack had nothing to consider as a subject of its principled decision, except to evaluate whether or not there was a chance for a successful defense.

By contrast, decisions to mount a military attack, a rebellion, or a fight for secession constitute new causes. But the evaluation of one's chances for mounting a successful defense doesn't place one under an obligation in the moral or legal sense, but only in prudential sense: is it reasonable to opt for a hopeless defensive fight. However, the right to defense is not based on the probability of an effective defense. Rather it is grounded in the values of what is defended. By contrast, the "right to attack" (however it is construed) can be constituted only in relation to the likelihood of attaining victory. Without considerable probability that victory would be achieved, an attack, no matter how it might be justified, would be an irrational and irresponsible thing to do; thus, it constitutes nothing that could properly be claimed as a right.

Any putative right to attack, in this context, cannot be genuine. In war there can be no right to victory. Such a right would contradict the very concept of war. That is why the "right" to attack gets established as a right only after the victory, and has no retroactive force. Otherwise it would be possible to put on trial those who were attacked – for no other reason than that they defended themselves (not because of what proved to be their incorrect estimates regarding the likelihood of victory for their side, nor because of their defeat, but simply because they defended themselves).[4]

Such logic really exists in the case of a police raid, but a police raid does not involve an initial equilibrium of rights between the adversaries. This logic, when applied to the case of defenders in a war, raises the following question: *Who* would decide in advance which side is the aggressor? Who has the right to decide that putting up a defense constitutes an act of aggression? If there were an entity with such a right, then it would be endowed with the power to bestow the "right to victory." But if there were a body with this power, then it would also have the obligation to pre-announce the victorious side. This would in fact effectively preempt the war. If this power should fail to prevent the war in this way, then it would be itself responsible for the onset of the war. And if this power nevertheless goes on to confer the "right to victory" to either side, then it becomes the ultimate authority encompassing full sovereignty over the conflicting sides. But then war becomes just a police raid, an entirely different kind of practice which, unlike war, includes no rule that the victor's identity is to remain open until war ends. When the concept of aggression is introduced into international law,[5] this is exactly the result: arbitrarily and in advance the "right to victory" gets granted or denied. But such a right cannot exist. Raw power is its only possible source. The act of granting of this "right" a priori entirely nullifies any legal sense the "crime against peace" might have had.

But even when the victorious side remains unknown until the end of the conflict, this does not make crime against peace a moral or legal category. It remains a political category, even in the case when the defeated attackers or insurgents are put to trial. A trial of this sort would remain an entirely political act for the following reason. While victory will establish a new law, still victory (and defeat) are not ways of establishing that interests, which were present at the beginning of war, possessed (or failed to possess) compelling normative force. This is so because the nature of force, which decides who will be the victor, is such that it does not guarantee victory to the rightful or morally better party, but to whoever is stronger. For the moral and legal understanding of responsibility for war, the only relevant considerations are those that at the beginning could make victory appear as likely. However, there is no guarantee that a rebellion or initiation of an attack, no matter how promising it might appear at first, will in the end succeed. This is the risk would-be insurgents or attackers face. Those engaged in self-defense run the same risk with respect to the end result. But, should they suffer a defeat, they are protected from trials by the antecedently existing and established decision. This decision is comprised within the institutions that constitute the presupposition of peace, on the one hand, as internal law, which forbids insurgency, and, on the other, as international law, which forbids states to attack each other.

Consequently, while crimes against peace constitute in essence a political category, in the case of insurgency there is a preexisting set of legal sanctions. The case when a country attacks another is more complicated, but here too the introduction of the concept of a crime against peace into international law actually serves to eliminate the legal character of this offense and makes it purely a political one.[6] Now unless we are willing to ignore the usurpatory character of decisions made by intervening third parties, as in the decision to punish those who in the recent Yugoslav war attempted to defend the *status quo ante* (or in general those who merely try to defend themselves), and reward the rebellious seccessionists, then the concept of crimes against peace is shown to be essentially political in nature. This conclusion has very disturbing consequences for our estimation of the 1945 Nuremberg and Tokyo Trials, even though there we had on trial the defeated aggressors.[7]

III Conclusion

We may, therefore, conclude that out of the three types of crimes labeled as "war" crimes, only the "crime against peace" has characteristics setting it apart from other crimes that would make it a genuine war crime. That is, "war crime" in this sense indicates the production of causes leading to war. This defining feature sets war apart with respect to the application of the moral criterion. Everything else that transpires in war, be it evil or not, figures only in the description of acts to which this criterion is applied. However, this defining feature that sets "crimes against peace" apart from all other acts, also makes it unsuitable for legal regulation. The reason is that the determination of such acts as criminal is dependent on the outcome of war, and war is a human activity whose constitutive rule is temporary suspension of normal lawfulness. These rules ensure that war, or better to say its initiation, cannot be good or bad, with respect to either involved side, when it comes to the determination of the causes of war.

Considerations of whether the causes of war provide justification for war and similar questions have a definite answer only according to the final outcome of war: victory is what brings justification. It is victory, and not the justness of the goal, which justifies the initiation of war. If there is no chance for success, initiating a war is unjustified independently of how justifiable the cause leading to war had been. Defeat is a crime. There is, however, an important restriction here: defeat is really a crime only if the defeated side (whether a sovereign state or an insurrectionist group) is the one which started the war. If, however, the attacked side or the party that defended the *status quo ante* is defeated, then there is no crime. If this were not so, war would be a mere police raid. This, in turn, would presuppose that it is known in advance who is in the right, and independently of the final outcome, which in case of war is victory, i.e., one side would turn out to have a right to victory.

As far as morality is concerned, however, such a right could not exist, for if it did it would nullify the right to self-defense. It cannot exist in the legal sense either. Otherwise, the authority of a sovereign state to enforce its laws would be entirely wiped out by the alleged right to rebel with a guarantee to victory, or by the corresponding right to attack every time one has the right to victory. Consequently, the right to victory is reduced to absurdity in two important sense, moral and legal, since it implies the invalidation of the right to defense and the abdication of the possibility of establishing the authority to enforce the law. Since a consistent legal definition of war crime (in the variant of a crime against peace) is conceptually linked to the presumption of the right to victory, any attempt to understand war crime, in this sense, as a legal category leads to absurdity. Such an interpretation, it appears, is the result of a certain psychological characteristic of religious zealots, and gets naturally conjoined not only with paternalism, but also fanaticism and the escalation of violence and arbitrariness.

The act of punishing the defeated attackers or insurgents implies denying them the right to be one of the sides in the war. This is why trial and punishment even in a case in which there is a moral justification for an independent determination of a war crime – that is, in the case of defeated attackers or insurgents – in fact also amounts to a political act. (However, punishment of the defenders – because they engaged in defense – cannot be morally justified.) Thus, international prosecution of so-called war crimes, except according to conventions that states have freely signed on, is legally invalid. It represents a morally suspect paternalistic act, which can earn some sort of justification only as a political act, and only on the condition that real attackers and insurgents go to trial. Such a prosecution isn't then truly international; it's simply the court of the victorious side. On trial is the defeated side which started the war, and precisely because it is the vanquished that executed the suspension of law (this is in congruence with the internal law that by necessity forbids insurgency, or the international law which forbids states to attack each other). Thus, the victorious side, by an act of punishment, reinstitutes the lawful *status quo ante*. A nonparticipating third side (neither the victor nor the defeated) which is also present in the determination "international" has in fact no right to judge – not even the defeated. (It could, of course, join in like a vulture in the distribution of the prize.)[8] But if some international institution were to exist which had the right to distribute permits for war or insurgency in the form of licenses for victory, this would represent a negation of all lawfulness. Of course, the present world organization – and each era has had one – could fall prey (as happens anew every time) to the controls of some super power which can be expected to promote *its* goals as universal goals. While articulating an ideology of cosmopolitan impartiality and international justice, such a power will violate the principles it claims to promote and introduce exceptions to the order it promulgates. But precisely this is what is meant by saying that prosecuting war crimes is a political practice, even when it is described in legal and moral terms.

Notes

1 I shall offer one example in two parts. Part one: Lieutenant James Duffy storms a Vietnamese village and captures a man wearing an unmarked uniform who speaks no English. Before retreating, he asks his men if anyone wants to execute the prisoner. There are several volunteers, and the prisoner gets another night to live; the next day, the lieutenant selects one of the men, who kills the prisoner by shooting him in the head. The prisoner's only identification was an ID card which probably meant he was a former South Vietnamese soldier who, after being wounded, took the opportunity to desert the army and return to his family. At the trial it turned out, however, that the order was to take no prisoners (which could be interpreted differently) and that the military superiors "laid primary stress on the body count" – some sort of listing of "killed enemies," as if they were killed in combat. While all this was established by testimony, in the end Duffy was convicted of involuntary manslaughter! Part two of the example: Toward the end of the Second World War an American officer is wounded and taken prisoner by a German unit in retreat which becomes encircled and attempts to hide and pull itself out. Lieutenant Gunther Thiele commands this unit. The commander of the battalion, to which this unit belongs, Captain Shwaben sends an order to Lieutenant Thiele (an order motivated by the need to keep their position secret) to execute the prisoner. Lieutenant Thiele then orders the grenadier Steinert to perform the execution, which he does. All around them combat was in full motion, and Lieutenant Thiele's unit was encircled by the superior American troops. At the trial in 1947, the soliders who took part in the murder of the American prisoner were sentenced to death – the issue of tactical necessity wasn't taken into consideration at all. Eventually, the sentence was reduced to life imprisonment on the basis of "superior orders." Cf. Donald A. Peppers, "War Crimes and Induction: A Case for Selective Nonconscientious Objection," *Philosophy and Public Affairs*, 3, 2 (Winter, 1974): 153–4.

2 Let us grant for the moment that this is really the case and that nothing else is in the background.

3 Speaking in Kantian terms, international law lacks a *constitutive* rule of an institution such as provided by the state; instead, this "law" can have at its disposal only a kind of *regulative* rule insufficient to form courts and confer validity to trials that require institutional nature with constitutive rules.

4 It might, however, appear that some superpower could retroactively alter positions of aggression and defense. If you think you are superpowerful you might think that it is in your power to declare as aggressors those who you want to be so designated. You also may "manufacture" an aggressor from all those who are trying to prevent you from overpowering, conquering, enslaving, or crushing them, i.e., from those who are defending themselves. The logic of

power would in such a case appear to be developed to perfection: first you persuade one to organize a rebellion, then you ensure that side's victory, and finally from the victorious position declare that it was the defending side who won. In such a case, those who defended themselves become "aggressors," and, perhaps even "war criminals." However, such mechanical application of the logic of outcomes is oppressive and tyrannical. For in order for one to commit a crime against peace it is not sufficient that one be on the defeated side. Otherwise, force would have no internal boundaries and the distinction between force and violence would be completely obliterated. For the purpose of proper functioning of the reasons for actions it must be presupposed that force, as such, does not make all reasons for actions without exception "good." There must exist an independent and principled distinction between good and bad reasons.

5   As already mentioned, the international milieu is such that aggression is a concept to which the entire relevance of war is reduced, and this occurs in a way that detaches the concept of aggression from the institutional background of established rights, which constitute the *status quo ante*.

6   What follows from this is that it would be justified to put on trial only the organizers of failed rebellions, while in the case of unsuccessful external aggression the courts of the country which was the attacker and not of the one which successfully defended itself should conduct trials – although the country that successfully defended against the aggression has the right to demand that those responsible for plotting the aggression be put on trial.

7   This does not imply that the concept of war crimes, which falls outside the scope of international law, isn't complex and difficult. What we note first is the relativism with respect to the application. One of the most interesting examples where this relativism is evident is the case of execution of orders the outcome of which are war crimes in the narrow sense (breaking of laws and customs of war). If the execution of an order leads to a crime then that order itself ought to be illegal. In that case there would have to exist a right not to execute the order. This is easy to say. But when is an order illegal? Such orders might be a matter of administrative routine, a matter of general determination of goals or even a matter of concrete determinations of those goals – while the chosen or necessary means for their achievement are such that they lead to crimes. For example, the order might be to achieve a certain goal (without any specifications of the means), while among the means we might have the acquisition of some information that could most optimally be obtained by torturing prisoners. A massacre may play a similar role: it truly could achieve a strong discouraging effect on the enemy. (For example, massacres in Western Slavonia in May 1995 might have been a tactical prelude to the attack on Knin Krajina in August same year.) This implies that criminal activities might be simply ordinary and direct responses to standard orders. In this context a special role is played by the so-called tactical necessity (cf. note 1.) – according to this notion some act which is

in opposition to "law and customs of war" might be needed or even necessary precisely for achieving some concrete military goal in the field of operation. Courts, however, show unbelievable relativism in their approach to this concept. This might not appear so strange if we take in consideration: Who is the judge? And how this is done? Different courts use different legal standards: some courts will find one guilty if one executes the other if one refuses to execute an order. Thus it could happen that someone be tried simply for taking part in a war on a certain side – and that becomes "war crime" *strictu senso*: that act is determined only and exclusively by the war; nothing else enters in the determination of this crime. But what sort of trial is this? For the act for which one is tried must first be incriminated, and only then the sentence follows by subsuming the deed under the description: taking part in the war on the enemy side! But which order didn't he then execute? (On the other side he could be tried if he didn't take part, although to a description of such an act other characterizations may be added: breaking of the law by dissenting, the free-rider problem etc.) Formally speaking it is easier to argue if the transgression came about as a result of failing to execute an order. For when one is on trial for executing an order this brings in a package many immoral considerations. However, if one is on trial for failing to execute an order then he (or his defense) must prove that the order was irregular, which is a distortion of the principle concerning the presumption of innocence. If one is tried by an "international tribunal," this court could not have a valid authority; if he is tried by the enemy court there is no likelihood that the principle of impartiality could be ensured. If he was in the position to refuse to execute the order, he had to do it, but then the defense has to show that the order was unlawful. However, from the fact that he knew that the order was unlawful it does not follow that he knew that he could prove that. Furthermore, from the presumption that he could reject the order it is inferred that one knows when one must reject an order, which leaves him without defense – one way or another. For the fact that he could have rejected the order means that he was not forced to do it. However, he did not have to have had the knowledge that his rejection is legally valid, or, if he knew that, he did not have to have had the knowledge that he could prove this. And so on.

8   However, if a third party desires to punish the successful aggressor (because the side without the right to victory has won), it must first defeat this aggressor. But to do that it must become a party in the war, and thus no longer be a "third" party to the conflict. This can be done by forming *ad hoc* defensive alliances, as we have witnessed many times in history, but alliances may also be formed, as has been the case too, for aggressive purposes. Of course, we must keep in mind that victory, whether achieved as a result of successful defense or aggression, is a result of the ultimate balance of powers amongst which the military power is just one element, perhaps not even the crucial one.

Afterword to Part One

In Part One, Peter French, Alan Gewirth, and Jovan Babic endeavor to clarify the concept of war crimes. International and local law is widely disregarded during war, yet we do not consider it impossible to make moral judgments regarding much of the conduct that occurs in the context of war. We have come to distinguish three classes of events as "crimes of war"; crimes against peace, violations of customs of war, and crimes against humanity. What more precisely *are* the characteristics of acts we call "war crimes," and how is the evil attributed to the perpetrators to be conceived?

French is motivated to understand the nature of evil that can be ascribed to war criminals in cases of extreme ethnic strife, such as occurred in Rwanda and the Balkans. The war criminals French has in mind are those who are themselves products of cultures which are imbued with hatred for persons of other ethnic groups, simply because they *are* members of those groups. He employs an Aristotelian typography of evil to discuss the issue and focuses on two types of wickedness that may be identified as perverse and preferential. His position is that all wickedness is preferential. The average Rwandan or Balkan war criminals are, on this account, preferentially wicked. However, they did not choose to be bigoted. Although the evil they did may have been unchosen by them, this fact French contends, does not relieve them of moral responsibility. By arguing that the crucial point for moral philosophy is that choice is less important to justifiable ascriptions of moral responsibility than is typically held to be the case, French advances our understanding of the sense in which war criminals are to be held morally responsible.

Gewirth argues that human rights impose restrictions on both the ends and the means of war. War crimes are acts which violate basic human rights in two main ways. The first is when the motivation for making war is to subjugate one's victims for purposes of governmental self-aggrandizement.

The second is when, in the process of waging war, injuries are inflicted that go beyond military necessity. However, this qualification itself must be given an explication in terms of human rights, since war is only justified as a necessary means to protect human rights. With this end in mind, the means must similarly be restricted. Thus, he takes the view that relevant wrongs committed in the context of war are crimes whether or not this is encoded in positive law, for the ultimate criterion of criminality here is moral rather than legal.

Of the three usual categories of acts considered "war crimes," Babic claims, only crimes against peace have features that might qualify them as *genuine* war crimes. On the other hand, violations of the laws or customs of war and crimes against humanity are such *crimes* that the characterization *of war* adds nothing new to their moral or legal status, and hence their perpetrators ought to be tried in the same manner as all other criminals according to the demands of justice. Simply stated, they are just ordinary criminal acts; they neither gain nor lose anything because they occur in the context of war. There are problems, however, with the legal and moral status of the so-called crimes against peace. For only the defeated side in a war can ever be branded war criminals. Military victory *de facto* obliterates the guilt for initiating a war in the first place. Treating the crime against peace as the bona fide war crime (in a legal sense) leads to two absurdities. First, if victory absolves one from moral and legal responsibility for starting the war, then *defeat* would necessarily be criminal in nature. Hence, mounting an unsuccessful defense would also qualify as a criminal act. But, this contradicts the well-founded right to self-defense, justified through universalization. This conflict could be resolved only if there was a right to prosecute the defeated aggressors but not the defeated defenders. Second, war is by definition a practice in which victory is not predetermined. Hence, there is no right to victory. However, in order to bring charges for war crimes independently of the outcome of war, one side would have to be proclaimed as having the right to victory. This is absurd. On these grounds, Babic concludes, prosecution for crimes against peace is in order only when aggressors happen to be defeated. This, furthermore, implies that the practice of setting up courts and conducting trials is merely political and not legal procedure.

The issue of central importance, therefore, is the moral definition of war crimes, which stems perhaps from the appearance that these crimes are importantly different from all other crimes. This appearance may be due to the fact that war is a context of human action within which the application of the moral criterion is exceedingly difficult. War radically restricts (or eliminates) one's freedom, responsibility, and availability of choices in a way that makes normally impermissible acts into *de facto* permissible ones. However, the question is weather this is a consequence of a new moral criterion being introduced in the context of war or of the special restrictions placed on the old criterion. One way to resolve this is, as Gewirth does, by reference to the nature of a war: whether the war is just or not. The approach championed by French, that agents' unchosen evil still involves responsibility, implies the question of how far the responsibility in fact goes and whether responsibility might be even greater somewhere else. Babic insists on the constancy of moral criterion in all contexts, including war, and hopes to find the answer in the tense dialectic found in the concept of aggression. Views and arguments expressed here are far from uncontroversial, and they will surely inspire knew ideas and provoke counter-arguments.

Further Reading to Part One

Elizabeth Anscombe, "War and Murder," in her *Ethic's, Religion and Politics* (The Collected Philosophical Papers of G. E. M. Anscomb, volume three).

Michael Dockrill and Barrie Paskins, *The Ethics of War.*

Jean Bethke Elshtain (ed.), *Just War Theory* (Oxford: Blackwell, 1992).

W. B. Gallie: *Understanding War* (London: Routledge, 1991).

Terry Nardin (ed.), *The Ethics of War and Peace; Religious and Secular Perspectives* (Princeton University Press, 1998).

John Rawls, "Fifty years after Hiroshima," in his *Collected Papers* (Harvard University Press, 1999: originally published in *Dissent* (1995)), pp. 323–7.

Michael Walzer, *Just and Unjust Wars* (Harmondsworth: Penguin, 1980).

Part Two

Trials for War Crimes

4

War Crimes and Virtue Ethics

Michael Slote

In these pages I would like to sketch a possible ethical framework for thinking about war crimes. I am a virtue ethicist, but, unlike many of my confreres, the kind of virtue ethics I find most interesting and plausible is non-Aristotelian. It is a virtue ethics that finds its closest and most important historical antecedents, rather, in the moral sentimentalism of Hutcheson, Hume and Martineau, and in Nietzsche's philosophy of power. Both the latter ethical philosophies are forms of ethical naturalism, and by that I mean not some metaethical thesis *á la* G. E. Moore, but an approach that stresses natural sentiments in Hume's sense, sentiments and emotions and tendencies we have or can have independently of having moral views and self-conscious moral commitments. The benevolence and compassion stressed by the eighteenth- and nineteenth-century sentimentalists certainly stands opposed to Nietzsche's will to power, but all these psychological dispositions at least fulfill Hume's definition of naturalness; and in this talk I want to consider what one or another form of ethics based in such dispositions can say about war crimes and war criminals.

Now during the recent revival of virtue ethics, Aristotle has been the principal model and source of ideas, but lately people have been exploring other possibilities, and it is of two of those other possibilities that I want to speak to you here. The divergence from Aristotelianism is relevant to the topic of this conference, furthermore, because Aristotelian and neo-Aristotelian ethics would among other things stress issues about desert (about how or whether certain people deserve to be punished for what they have done to others), and the approaches I favor don't treat desert as the crucial element in talking about crime and punishment, and about justice and forgiveness (or toleration). (It is worth noting that certain other traditions in ethics, most notably contract theory and utilitarianism, also sometimes avoid the concept of desert in discussing issues of punishment and justice.)

I think Nietzsche's ethics and the ethics of sentimentalism are most forcefully deployed as (different) forms of virtue ethics, and let me now explain to you what kind of virtue ethics I have in mind. A virtue ethics can be called agent-based if it treats evaluations of character or motivation as ethically fundamental and derives evaluations of human actions from them. Aristotle's ethics isn't agent-based in this sense, because, according to how one interprets it, it either treats assumptions about the good life as basic to ethics and derives its moral understanding of both character and agent from what it has to say about *eudaimonia*, or else it involves intuitive assessments of the nobility or ignobility of actions that require no assumptions about an individual's overall character or motives.

By contrast, Francis Hutcheson's ethics comes quite close to being agent-based, because it treats universal/impartial benevolence as morally good apart from its consequences and in effect, therefore, regards that moral goodness as a ground-floor moral fact requiring no further anchoring in evaluative assumptions. Of course, Hutcheson goes on to adopt a version, arguably the first version, of the principle of utility, but there is a way of altering Hutcheson's view of how acts are to be assessed that turns it immediately into a form of agent-based virtue ethics. Instead of agreeing with Hutcheson that acts are good to the extent they achieve the good ends of universal benevolence, we can say that they are morally good to the extent they are *motivated* by such benevolence. The view we then end up with is agent-based in the above sense, and, moreover, and interestingly, it is also very close to the only historically actual form of agent-based virtue ethics I am acquainted with, James Martineau's views in *Types of Ethical Theory*. Martineau was just as much a naturalist (in Hume's sense) as Hutcheson and Hume were, and such naturalistic moral sentimentalism, gerrymandered in the way I have suggested, offers some very promising possibilities for contemporary virtue ethics.

However, there is another way one might move toward agent-basing, and that is from or out of Nietzsche's ideas about the will to power. At times, Nietzsche's views seem almost consequentialistic, and the criterion of the ethical seems to be whether some attitude or act *enhances* the power of the agent or the class of superior individuals. But at other times Nietzsche speaks more like an agent-based virtue ethicist, treating the will to power and all inner strength as admirable *per se* and without further argument and assessing any given action in terms of whether it expresses or displays or *is motivated by* inner power or strength.[1] In what follows I would like to see what such an agent-based version of Nietzsche has to say about the punishment of war crimes and war criminals, but first let us discuss how a sentimentalist-inspired virtue ethics would deal with the subject.

Moral sentimentalism first took off as a philosophical movement or phenomenon during the eighteenth century in Britain, but, as I have mentioned, we find its influence in the work of the later, nineteenth-century philosopher James Martineau, and I am not alone in thinking that the recent "feminine" ethic of caring also has affinities with the work of Hutcheson and Hume.[2] However, if we want to talk about the punishment of war crimes in sentimentalist-inspired virtue ethical terms, we cannot restrict ourselves to speaking of private motives and have to find a way of discerning the motives that lie behind laws and institutions. But this is not, in fact, so difficult to do. If private, apolitical, personal actions are to be morally judged in terms of the motives they express or display, why not say that laws and institutions are just and morally good only if they express or display sufficiently good *and relevantly public* motives?

Thus national legislators who pass a law may do so for many different possible reasons, but we might want to say that if they do so out of a desire for the public good, or the good of their country, then the law they pass is justly enacted and is a just law; whereas, if they act from greed or narrow sectionalism, then they don't act justly and the law they pass is tainted with that injustice. Notice too that just as an individual private action with accidentally good consequences can still be morally tainted if it was motivated by greed or malice, we can say that a law that accidentally has good consequences may still be morally criticizable on the basis of how it came into being; and once we agree to this, we can begin to see how an agent-based sentimentalist political morality can treat issues of war criminality.

Assume that a country has gone through internal strife or civil war and that in the aftermath of the conflict(s) a political decision has to be made about the prosecution of possible war crimes. Utilitarianism would tell us that that decision will be just which has optimal effects on the people of the country in question (assuming, for simplicity's sake that no other countries will be significantly affected by it), and a sentimentalist virtue ethics will also focus on the well-being of the people of the country in question. However, it will do so in a slightly different way, arguing that what makes a law governing war crimes just or unjust is not its actual (or even expectable) effects on people but rather what legislators and others responsible for the law were motivated or trying to do. If the legislators were seeking to advance the common good, were sincerely motivated by the desire to help the people of their country as best they could, then the law is just and moral, according to a virtue ethics based on benevolence or caring,[3] even if, for reasons beyond their ken or control, the law has bad effects. But of course once and if the legislators learn that the law is having bad effects, it will for the same reasons be unjust for them not to (try to) change it.

So a sentimentalist-inspired virtue ethics judges justice differently from utilitarianism and treats it more as a matter of the desire to produce good effects for people than as a question of actually producing such effects. But an objection arises from this fact that needs immediately to be answered, for it may be wondered whether our agent-based conception of just laws (and the same analysis applied to public institutions generally) doesn't allow legislatures in effect to get away with murder. For what if a legislature passes laws that lead to murder or other horrible results and yet pleads for the justice and moral approvability of what they have done on the grounds that they meant well, were doing the best they could for the country?

The answer to this difficulty emerges from considering the difference between two possible cases. If the legislature *hasn't done its homework*, if they pass laws in the mere hope or ignorant expectation of good effects, then, whether the good effects occur or don't, the legislature's claim to having genuine benevolent concern for the well-being of their compatriots is substantially undermined. In the private sphere, a person who has someone else's interests genuinely at heart can't just give to the latter impulsively and without thinking and learning about what that person really needs. To do so is to be proved *less* than fully or truly concerned with the good of the other, and the same point transposes to political examples in a most obvious way. Thus, if a legislature passes harmful legislation on the mere unresearched hope that doing so will be for the best, their claim to genuine concern for the welfare of their country is undercut and the legislation counts as unjust according to a sentimentalist virtue ethics.

On the other hand, if the legislature really does try to find out relevant facts and its laws are nonetheless harmful to the public weal, then the legislators can't be morally faulted for what they have done, and an agent-based view will say that their legislative acts, the laws they have passed, are also morally in order, despite any bad consequences they may unexpectably have. From a moral standpoint, then, those laws will be just (at least until their bad effects can be noticed), and since the idea of justice *is* a moral notion, that means we can say that the laws in question are, quite simply, just. So there is a real contrast here with utilitarianism, despite the common focus on human well-being, because sentimentalist virtue ethics makes well-being relevant to legal justice, not directly via a law's effects on such well-being, but rather indirectly and through the legislature's *desire* to pass laws that enhance people's well-being. And if we think (in a fashion reminiscent of Plato) that justice and morality generally are best or most nobly regarded as reflections of and on people's souls or character, then that favors virtue ethics over utilitarian thinking in this area.

If so, then the justice of legislation governing or refusing to deal with war crimes will depend on what a legislature is trying to do. If it responsibly determines that a moratorium on prosecutions or an amnesty will be best for the country, then legislation to that effect will be morally justified or just, but, of course, such a decision will invariably depend on facts or circumstances, as reflected in knowledge or efforts to know on the part of legislators. In one set of circumstances healing might be helped more by prosecuting war crimes than by ignoring or forgetting them, in another just the reverse, and so, relative to different presumed or putative facts, different decisions will be just and right. Just as utilitarianism declares the justice of a law to depend on factors that vary from historical circumstance to circumstance, a sentimentalist virtue ethics will also want to leave room for variation that depends not so much on actual facts as on what legislators (or others) learn or can reasonably learn about contingent facts.

It is worth noting one particular sort of problem, however. If people resent and wish to punish putative war criminals and would be less willing to accept a (new) political order if their crimes weren't prosecuted, then that may, according to the above, be a reason for legislators to pass legislation that mandates the prosecution of war crimes. Just as utilitarians have to take account of the prejudices and anti-utilitarian tendencies of others in deciding what to do, someone who accepts a sentimentalist virtue ethics based on the desire to help people may have to insist that legislators should take into account the contra-benevolent and punitive (and even the malicious) motives of some of their compatriots. To be sure, they may want to try to do away with such contra-benevolent motivation, but where that motivation cannot be done away with, it needs to be taken into account by just legislators, according to the view I am defending. But this is really not very paradoxical. A moral or rational person needs to take into account the immorality or irrationality of others, so why shouldn't benevolence have to adjust to the nonbenevolence of others?

In effect, then, a morality of war crimes based in sentimentalist virtue ethics will not decide issues of justice in terms of desert and in a backward-looking way. It will not say that so-and-so deserves to be punished, even if that makes it somewhat more difficult for a nation's wounds to heal, but rather, in determining what is just, it will look to what *people (notably but not exclusively legislators) are trying to do with a nation's future*. It will worry about the healing of wounds, but it will also recognize that in many cases the prosecution of war crimes may make it easier for people harboring under-standable resentments to accept a new political order. The cathartic effects of punishing those one resents is a perhaps unfortunate but arguably inevit-able fact of life, so a sentimentalist virtue ethics will not say that certain criminals deserve to be and must be punished, but neither will it discount – or ignore as *undeserving of our consideration* – what it by its own lights must consider to be the morally deplorable or unfortunate *ressentiment* of those who want, at almost any cost, to see war crimes punished. But how all this theoretical apparatus affects the particular debate about what to do in the former Yugoslavia or in South Africa I leave, as I say, to those better acquainted with facts on the ground.[4]

Having said as much, I would like to explore the other possible virtue-ethical approach to justice and war crimes that I spoke of earlier, namely, Nietzsche's philosophy of inner strength or the will to power conceived in agent-based terms. Of course, at a first glance the whole idea of Nietzschean justice seems like a nonstarter, for Nietzsche is frequently regarded as an egoist (he sometimes says this of himself), and a purely egoistic view of justice is entirely beyond the ethical pale as far as most of us nowadays are concerned. But Nietzsche is in fact not an egoist, and let me begin our discussion of him by briefly saying why.

Nietzsche certainly thinks that those who give to others out of con-science, guilt, or pity are acting from weakness, and, assuming that he holds an agent-based view of ethics, this is tantamount to a condemnation of benevolence *that is motivated in certain ways*. But Nietzsche also holds that it is possible to give to others out of an overflowing sense of superabundance, and such giving, he thinks, comes from strength rather than from weakness. To that extent, Nietzsche offers a justification for certain acts of benevol-ence and even of altruism, and I use this latter term deliberately. When one gives out of sense of superabundance or power, one isn't giving now in order to receive benefits later and thereby enhance one's well-being. One gives *out of* a sense of well-being, but not necessarily *in order to promote* that well-being, so the kinds of actions Nietzsche is here recommending or praising really are altruistic, given a standard philosophical understanding of the term. (At the deepest level, Nietzsche arguably thinks that his ethics is beyond the egoism–altruism distinction, but let me for present purposes simplify.)

However, even if Nietzsche can justify certain forms of altruism, I don't think his philosophy can justify all the forms of giving and other-concern most of us find ethically compelling or attractive. Nor are we going to suddenly discover that Nietzsche's views surprisingly lead to a vindication of democratic institutions. But in the area of war crimes and justice, Nietzsche's philosophy may have something important to teach us, and in fact, as we shall shortly see, that something somewhat resembles what sentimentalist virtue ethics tells us about this subject.

Nietzsche says that a really powerful individual or society of such will not act vindictively toward those who unsuccessfully attack him/it and will even, to some extent, *tolerate* (and be amused by) the attackers. And one can understand this attitude in Nietzschean terms as a form of inner strength. To feel vindictive toward those who attack one is a sign, he thinks, that one feels threatened, that one isn't confident of one's (hold on) power, and that is arguably a form of weakness. If the person who gives money or benefits out of a sense that he has a superabundance of such things demonstrates a kind of inner strength, then clearly, and by intuitive analogy, someone who brushes aside or ignores attacks out of a superabundant confidence in his own (hold on) power also manifests strength. And so Nietzsche in effect gives us another argument for the conclusion that sentimentalist ethics also leads to, the conclusion that the *lex talionis* is not an ethically acceptable way to understand punishment and justice. Applied to war crimes this implies that a society that tolerates, or at least that doesn't act angrily or punitively toward, those who have committed such crimes may in a sense be nobler and more ethically attractive than one that displays the opposite attitude through its collective actions.

But although this argument in a way dovetails with sentimentalist virtue ethics, one may well wonder whether the Nietzschean reason for not displaying retributive tendencies is nearly as convincing as the sentimentalist justification for not doing so. In the end, that depends on what one thinks of inner strength and on whether one really agrees that it takes a certain (admirable) strength to ignore attacks on oneself. Someone might hold, for example, that far from displaying strength, the attitude of someone who ignores attacks is simply feckless or morally insensitive, and though I am inclined to agree here with Nietzsche rather than the just-mentioned potential critic, I don't know how to *prove* this point. Certainly, I think that when we think of something as genuinely a form of strength, we are already, in effect, regarding it as ethically admirable, and I am thus inclined to believe that a certain kind or degree of toleration of those who attack society *is* admirable (it is a form of magnanimity, isn't it?).

But, then, even if magnanimity is admirable, it may not be admirable to ignore attacks *when they threaten the fabric of society or when ignoring, rather than punishing, the attacks will itself put society in jeopardy*. I take it that in that measure concerns about social well-being have some sort of intuitive

precedence over Nietzschean ideals of superabundant magnanimity, but I
am not absolutely sure that this is something even Nietzsche would wish to
disagree with. At any rate, agent-based virtue ethics offers us (at least) two
possible motives by which we can judge the ethical advisability or justice of
pursuing, trying, and punishing putative war criminals, and the ethical
criteria thus offered are not only different from those familiar from traditional philosophical discussions of the subject, but (I hope I have shown)
have an interest and plausibility of their own.

Notes

1 Actually, Nietzsche sometimes exhibits both tendencies on a single page: e.g.,
   p. 1 of his *The Anti-Christ*.
2 Both Annette Baier and Larry Blum have pointed out this similarity.
3 It isn't obvious that an ethic of caring should in this way favor caring about the
   public good over particularized caring for individuals one knows, but I have
   tried to establish the point in my forthcoming "The Justice of Caring," *Social
   Philosophy and Policy* 15 (1998).
4 However, where enough of the people of a given country are resentful and
   contra-benevolent enough (toward enough people), the country itself, as
   opposed to any given act of legislation, is unjust. As I see the matter, a country
   or society is just only if enough of its people have motivation that is close
   enough to the desire for the common (the country's) good. But even if the
   society isn't just, a legislature that recognizes that fact (or the badness of people's
   motivations) will show itself just and pass just legislation if *it* is motivated by the
   desire for the good of the country (remember, we are ignoring effects on other
   countries). For the rationale behind this distinction, see "The Justice of Caring."

5

Whose Trials? Whose Reconciliation?

Burleigh T. Wilkins

War crimes fall into three categories: crimes of planning and waging wars, crimes committed during a war, and crimes against humanity including but not restricted to genocide. Although there are important differences among these three categories, I shall speak of war crimes in a general way as involving crimes in any or all of these categories. Whatever the history of the concept of war crimes may reveal, the idea that there are war crimes is at least as old as the just war tradition. Crimes of planning and waging aggressive wars appear, at least initially, to violate the just war tradition, which affirms that wars must not be fought for unjust reasons, and crimes committed during a war appear to violate the requirement that a war, whether just or not, be fought in a manner that does not violate certain moral constraints, and what we have come to call crimes against humanity would perhaps be considered especially egregious violations of constraints governing warfare. What is a fairly new idea is the proposal that violations of the just war tradition be considered legally punishable offenses and that trials for such offenses be conducted by international tribunals. After the Second World War there were the Nuremberg Trials in which high ranking German officials were tried and convicted by an Allied Military Tribunal, and afterwards there were trials of lesser officials and participants in war crimes either by the Allies or by German courts. And there were also the Toyko Trials in which high-ranking Japanese officials were tried by the Allies. However, although these trials were generally considered morally defensible, their legality was suspect: there were charges that such prosecutions involved serious violations of the rights of the accused and that they depended heavily upon ex post facto laws. To avoid such charges where future trials were concerned, it was proposed that there be a permanent international court for the trials of war criminals, but this proposal languished until fairly recently. Civil wars in Bosnia and Rwanda, and the

United Nations involvement in the prosecution of alleged war crimes in these countries, has led to a renewal of the proposal that prosecutions for war crimes should take place before a permanent international court. Where trials for war crimes are concerned there are three possibilities: trials within a state jurisdiction in accordance with provisions of penal codes, military or civilian, which are already in place; trials conducted by *ad hoc* international tribunals; and trials conducted by the proposed permanent international court. In what follows I shall be highly critical of trials conducted by either *ad hoc* or permanent international tribunals, and although I express some reservations about a state's ability to try its own nationals I believe that if we must have trials for war crimes such trials are best left in the hands of individual states.

Trials for individuals accused of war crimes must be understood in the context of punishment considered as a rule-governed institution. Punishment as an institution is designed to protect us from harm at the hands of others, and in this respect it is forward-looking. However, in one fundamental respect it is backward-looking as well: only individuals who have harmed or tried to harm others may be punished. The punishment of such individuals is designed to protect us from further harm by the accused and by others who might be tempted to commit similar harms. Most philosophers would, I think, agree with what I have just said, but now serious difficulties begin to emerge. Is the fact that someone has harmed, or tried to harm, another person a sufficient condition for punishing him, or is it only a necessary condition? Here the debate about the death penalty in America may be relevant. It has been argued that the establishment of culpability for some forms of homicide is sufficient for imposing the death penalty, but some philosophers and moralists have expressed concern over a clearly documented pattern of discrimination in the application of the death penalty, so that a disproportionate number of those sentenced to death are black and poor while a rich white man is never sentenced to death. Also, there is the fact that in those jurisdictions which have the death penalty a majority of the individuals now on "death row" are to be found in Texas, Georgia, and Florida. The reply to this has been that all punishment is selective since not all crimes can be punished, but this argument, although true, ignores the reasons why some individuals are sentenced to death but others are not. Racial and economic factors are clearly involved, and this seems to violate some of our basic intuitions about fairness and equality before the law: a man may be to blame for committing a crime, but he is not to blame for being black and poor. Thus, it is argued that if a man is to be punished he must be punished for the right reason, and the right reason must now be read as having two components: he must be guilty of the crime with which he is charged, and factors such as race or economic status should not enter into the reasons why he is punished.[1] It is, I believe, fairly easy to see how the above considerations apply to trials for war crimes.

While the evidence that the death penalty has helped to prevent some homicides is ambiguous and hotly debated, it is, I think, abundantly clear that trials for war crimes have not had any effect whatsoever on the waging of wars or the manner in which wars have been conducted. So-called aggressive wars continue to be fought, often with great barbarity on both sides of the conflict. It is true that war among the major powers has not broken out since the Second World War, but this seems to have been due mainly to the fear of nuclear warfare and not at all to any fears of punishment for war crimes. Other lesser wars have, of course, frequently occurred, with or without the encouragement of the major powers, and some of the major powers have sometimes been directly involved in wars with some of the lesser powers; none of these has been affected by any fear of punishment for war crimes, although clearly war crimes were committed in all of these conflicts. Trials for war crimes, starting with the Nuremberg and Toyko Trials have, correctly in my judgment, been stigmatized as "show trials," "victor's justice," and even "legal lynchings." Such trials have systematically ignored the basic question posed by Telford Taylor in his reflections on the Vietnam War: *What is the common practice?* I believe Taylor's question should be applied with equal stringency to both victors and losers in a war. But no British personnel were tried for the bombing of Dresden and no Americans were tried for bombing Hiroshima or Nagasaki. Beginning, perhaps with the German use of submarines in the First World War, participants in armed conflicts have tended more and more to conflate "military necessity" and "military usefulness" with the result that moral and legal constraints on the conduct of war have been increasingly ignored; this may explain the urgency of renewed interest in trials for war crimes, but it does not settle the issue of whether such trials might help restore even a modicum of civility to armed conflicts.

Given the way the world is, it is highly unlikely that any state would voluntarily surrender its political leadership or military personnel to an international tribunal to be tried for war crimes. John Rawls in his "The Law of Peoples" has argued that, in the Original Position where we are seeking principles to inform the relations among states, sovereignty, especially the absolute sovereignty of states, is not a given, not a datum of experience, but only a datum of our experience of the last two hundred years or so, and he has maintained that we can in the Original Position limit sovereignty as we see fit.[2] Where the selection of principles of justice is concerned I concur with Rawls, but in our historical experience national sovereignty has been (if I may borrow a phrase John Noonan used in the abortion debate) "a nearly absolute value" with which advocates of international law have had to live as best they can. Intellectuals have, by and large, failed to appreciate the force of nationalist sentiments and aspirations. Perhaps the classic example of this failure lies in the First World War, where socialists were surprised and dismayed by the enthusiasm with which workers in one state chose to participate in a war against workers in another state: what had become of the solidarity of workers worldwide and their antagonism toward all capitalist states? Following the collapse of the Soviet Union we have once again been surprised by the resurgence of nationalist sentiments when perhaps we should best see this as a continuation of the anticolonialism which emerged at the end of the Second World War. The relevance of the above bit of history to the issue of trials for war crimes is that it helps explain the reluctance of a national state to allow its nationals to be tried for war crimes if it can possibly avoid doing so. Only the nationals of a state that has lost a war are likely to be surrendered, and even if they are guilty of committing war crimes one suspects that their prosecution will be tainted by the fact that they were on the losing side of an armed conflict. Here the analogy with the application of the death penalty in America is obvious: even if the trial proceedings themselves were somehow scrupulously fair, equality before the law has been violated, e.g., like cases have not been treated alike if losers in a war are solely or disproportionately singled out for trial.

What I have been saying above about national sovereignty is perhaps best described as a point about what might be called common sense political science, and as such it is, I hope, helpful in our efforts to understand what is now possible where international law is concerned. However, although it is dangerous to speak as if world opinion is monolithic or unanimous in its judgments, world opinion has shown an increased tendency to regard war crimes as punishable, and this is, of course, reflected in various resolutions of the United Nations and in the international war crimes trials in The Hague and in Rwanda. Thus, it may be that the difficulty I have called attention to may not prove permanent. Certainly, the principle that war crimes are punishable could be treated as a principle of international law without this showing that principles respecting state sovereignty and nonintervention in the internal affairs of states are no longer viable. But this in turn involves a point about what principles of law, international or national, are all about. Principles, unlike rules, are not all or nothing affairs, as Ronald Dworkin has pointed out in his reflections on Anglo-American law. If Dworkin is correct, the difference between rules and principles is that principles of law must be weighed, as more than one principle may apply to a given case: there simply is no automatic decision procedure telling us how this should be done. Questions of "fit" must be answered, and this involves complicated questions as to how a given decision will relate to the law as a whole.[3] This is a Herculean task where municipal law is concerned and presumably it is even more so if our field of inquiry includes both municipal law and the body of international law. The minimal upshot of all this is, of course, that in both municipal and international law no principle can be said to prevail absolutely. On my interpretation, the fact that a given application of principle may be controversial or unpopular cannot be allowed to determine our judgment, but, if what some American jurists have called "evolving moral standards" also apply to international law and affect our answers to questions of "fit," so too must the facts of strong nationalist sentiment be taken into account, no matter how atavistic they may seem to some of us.

In his important book *Law, Morality and the Relations of States*, Terry Nardin has argued persuasively that the principles of national sovereignty and nonintervention in the affairs of sovereign states will not necessarily collapse if we add a principle protecting human rights,[4] but in the real world, the principles of national sovereignty and nonintervention would in all likelihood be impacted negatively. Indeed, if any weight is given to the principle that human rights must be protected this might involve intervention in the affairs of sovereign states if all other means of obtaining protection fail and if the violations of human rights are sufficiently grave. If we transpose this to the problem of war crimes and argue that the principle that war crimes ought to be prosecuted should be seen as a principle of international law, it must be acknowledged that, in some circumstances, this principle might be allowed to override the principles of national sovereignty and noninvolvement. In the real world, however, this seems to be a principle that we would be extremely reluctant to see applied where our own national sovereignty is concerned. Indeed, where American law is concerned, experts generally agree that US treaty obligations cannot override provisions of the American Constitution. I am only what the British call "a sea lawyer," but to me it seems arguable that even if the United States has signed a treaty obligating us to turn over indicted Americans to an international tribunal, we cannot legally do this unless that tribunal affords to the accused the same protections American constitutional law provides. This seems highly unlikely because we lead the world in the safeguards our law provides those accused of criminal offenses.

Trials for war crimes have continued from the Nuremberg era onward, but they have been trials conducted by sovereign states and the accused have been citizens of the state conducting the trial. Of course, the capture and trial of Adolph Eichmann by the state of Israel is a notable exception, but the circumstances of his capture in Argentina and his trial by a state which did not exist at the time he committed the atrocities with which he was charged gave rise to serious legal and moral questions. It would, perhaps, have been better had Eichmann been turned over to German authorities who could, and undoubtedly would, have prosecuted him under German law. Indeed, where issues of law and morality are concerned, it seems to me appropriate for a state to conduct trials of its own nationals, as this can be viewed as part of a country's coming to grips with its past. The Germans even have a word for this: *vergangenheitsbewaeltigung*. Even when such trials are delayed by decades, as in the case of certain post-Second World War trials in France, it is perhaps better to have justice delayed than to have justice done by an international tribunal. Where France was concerned it took a long time for France to surrender a long-cherished picture of noble Frenchmen participating in the Resistance movement and to replace this with a more complex picture in which some Frenchmen eagerly assisted their German captors in the persecution of Jews, but this was worth the wait since the trials, when they did occur, reflected not merely the guilt of individuals but the relation of these individuals to French society. The trials of war criminals in France, and also in Germany, have apparently been of therapeutic value, since the cliche that moral health and denial are incompatible seems applicable here.

In recent years, however, war trials by international tribunals established by the United Nations have resumed, and I have misgivings about this and where it might eventually lead. The trials in question have concerned so-called civil wars in Bosnia, and in Rwanda; in Rwanda the situation is complicated by the fact that two separate sets of trials are proceeding, one under the jurisdiction of the United Nations and the other under the jurisdiction of Rwanda. Literally, questions of life and death for the defendants arise here since Rwanda recognizes the death penalty while the United Nations tribunal does not. The idea of extending trials for war crimes to cover civil wars has complications of several sorts. First, there is the moral question of whether, if there are to be such trials, should they be conducted by international or national tribunals. Here cosmopolitanism and nationalism collide head on. Initially, cosmopolitanism would seem to prevail: civil war crimes are violations of human rights which are universal in nature and which accordingly would seem to merit international protection, but there are considerations which point in the other direction. Also, there is the fact that, while wars between states usually turn upon territorial disputes, civil wars may or may not be wars of territorial secession, and their motivation may accordingly be more complex than we find in wars between states. Then, there is the conceptual problem of how to mark off a civil war from a revolution, a *coup d'etat*, ethnic and religious strife, and civil unrest. But none of these difficulties has stopped the demand that international tribunals intervene in the affairs of individual states. Cambodia seems next on the list, and who is to say where it will all end since there are no agreed upon criteria as to when domestic strife or violence will be judged an appropriate object for trials conducted by international tribunals. The United Nations has claimed that civil wars which pose a threat to international peace and security warrant the use of international tribunals, but this is vague; and it is arguable that neither the civil wars in Bosnia nor Rwanda posed a significant threat to international peace and security.

The moral rhetoric in support of international trials for civil war crimes seems inflated, especially when other serious human rights violations by sovereign states go unchallenged. China, for example, does not seem likely to be tried for anything, or even to be condemned by the United Nations Human Rights Commission, an omission which seems linked to the presence of Cuba, Iran, and Libya on this Commission. (Here one can raise an alarming possibility: what if jurists from Cuba, Iran, Libya, and China come to serve on either *ad hoc* international tribunals or a permanent international court?) Advocates of trials for civil war crimes insist that such trials are indispensable for the achievement of certain laudable objectives. More specifically, supporters of such trials stress the importance of "individualizing guilt," which they see as a necessary means to "reconciliation" between warring parties. I believe this way of thinking is dangerous: dangerous because guilt in such circumstances is rarely if ever "individual" in the relevant sense, and because the contribution that the trials of individuals can make to reconciliation seems minuscule or even negative. At the very best, treated as a causal hypothesis, the idea that such trials can contribute to reconciliation remains untested, and some common-sense reflections on history cast doubt upon its value. As a thought experiment, take any civil war in recent history, the American Civil War, for example, and ask whether international trials for war crimes would have helped or hindered reconciliation between the warring parties.

The idea of "individualizing guilt" has a pedigree at least as old as the Nuremberg Trials and the Allied decision to try a few top German leaders; and it is important more in terms of what it omits, namely the idea of collective responsibility, than in terms of what it includes. Some people believe that there is no such thing as collective responsibility and that, indeed, the idea of collective responsibility is subversive of individual responsibility and thus of morality, while others see it as being merely a form of strict liability which, at its best, serves some limited social policy function, and which, at its worst, is simply a device helpful for lazy prosecutors unwilling or unable to bring prosecutions pinpointing the responsibilities of particular individuals. In contrast I see collective responsibility as a form of strict liability but one aimed not merely at increasing social utility but at protecting the rights of individual persons and groups. Strict liability laws may, for example, be seen as protecting consumers from harmful products made by companies which have neglected public safety. In moral and political terms, ascriptions of collective responsibility may be used to hold a state or a group within a state responsible for harms done on its behalf; and it is arguable that if there are going to be international trials for civil war crimes there may be circumstances in which the indictment of a state or an organized group within a state would be appropriate. There are various models of collective responsibility, but the one which seems most applicable in the present context is one where a harm has been done by some but not all the members of a state or a group within a state against the members of some group within that state because of their membership in that group, and the harm has been done by agents or representatives of the state or of the group intent upon perpetrating the harm. In *Terrorism and Collective Responsibility*,[5] I argued that terrorism by the oppressed against a state may, under some circumstances, be justified, and for purposes of modeling I used business corporations as examples of organized groups which are sometimes held to be collectively responsible for harms done by their officers or employees. There are perhaps some useful analogies between the question of who should be tried for crimes by a business corporation and the question of who should be tried for war crimes. In business ethics some philosophers and moralists have taken the position that only individual officers or employees of corporations should be held responsible for harms done on behalf of a corporation, while others believe that only corporate entities should be held liable (chances are that the individual actors were only "doing their job" as they saw it). Here it should be noted that ascriptions of collective responsibility differ from ascriptions of individual responsibility in one crucial respect: what Joel Feinberg has called the contributory fault condition is weakened or absent. An individual may be liable to sanctions for actions with harmful results when these actions are done on behalf of a group to which he belongs, even if he is not the actor who performed or authorized the actions in question. I believe that the idea of collective responsibility is compatible with the idea of searching out and punishing the actor(s) who did perform or authorize the actions in question. But the argument continues: if we can find who committed or authorized the harmful actions, why go further?

The answer depends in part upon the question of what it is that we are seeking to accomplish. In the case of trials for civil war crimes we are told that the objective is "reconciliation" among the warring parties. While we have at least an intuitive grasp of the conditions which will help individuals, friends and lovers for example, to reconcile when they have been at odds and some understanding of what will count as a successful reconciliation, it is less clear what will be helpful where the reconciliation of groups is concerned or even what will count as a successful reconciliation. Accordingly, what I have to say about reconciliation will be somewhat tentative. Since the odds are high that war crimes will have been committed by virtually all the groups involved in a civil war, reconciliation cannot, I believe, go forward until this painful fact is acknowledged by the groups in question. Of course, some states and some organized groups within a state may have "clean hands," and others may be implicated only to the extent that "loose cannons" among their forces have acted wrongly, but in all likelihood they will be the exception. In all other cases a state and organized groups within a state must acknowledge that their agents or representatives have at times acted wrongly on their behalf, although obviously it does not follow from the fact that a state and organized groups within a state are blameworthy but that they are equally blameworthy. Explanations of why civil wars and civil war crimes have occurred may vary, but at least, in some cases, "a way of life" or institutional deficiencies may be cited. In those cases institutional changes or other reforms may be deemed appropriate remedies if steps toward reconciliation are to be effective and lasting.

Part of the trouble with focusing exclusively on individual actors in trials for war crimes is that this may represent an incomplete and superficial step toward reconciliation. Individuals come and go but states and organized groups within states tend to remain in some form or other. Of course, as a methodological individualist, I see states and organized groups within states as consisting of individuals but individuals bound together by a common or shared acceptance of a set of rules, traditions, or principles. We change the behavior of such individuals, not by punishing a handful of leaders or followers but by changing the rules, etc., which govern their behavior and bind them together. The punishment of individual actors may help bring about such changes, but it may hinder them as well. A state or an organized group within a state may blame only its leaders, or those who were indicted, for what went wrong, and may fail to see how the criminal activity of a "few" related to the political or social structure of institutions and how this structure in turn related to the moral life of individuals.

I find it difficult to see how trials for war crimes can be relied upon to further reconciliation. A war is over, perhaps the time has come to forgive and forget as best we can, but, as in individual relationships, constant reminders and recriminations may delay or prevent rather than hasten reconciliation. A prolonged dredging up of the past may prove counter-productive. Resentments may flourish on both sides, especially as new allegations and revelations occur; and when only a handful of individuals are held responsible a state or a group within a state may simply breathe a collective sigh of relief and go about its business morally untouched. The ugly truth about any war, whether international or civil, is that it brings out the worst in us. One man's war criminal is another man's war hero, and the punishment of individuals may do nothing to alter this. In the final analysis, reconciliation is not achieved by courts of law and adversarial proceedings but only by institutional reforms and ultimately a change of heart, and prolonged legal proceedings may be an impediment to both. Since the idea of a change of heart may bring to mind religious beliefs and traditions not shared by all, let me note briefly that for purposes of living together without bloodshed and with some measure of civic harmony, the minimum that may be required for reconciliation is that we somehow move from what Rawls has called an unstable *modus vivendi* within a state to a moral commitment to fair rules of social cooperation. In states held together artificially by pressures from the international community even the achieve-ment of the most modest *modus vivendi* may be extremely difficult, and any eventual reconciliation will depend upon many variables, including, of course, the severity and intensity of the animosities that led to the conflict in the first place. Other things being equal, a war of territorial secession may pose fewer difficulties for reconciliation than a war involving ethnic and religious animosity. Even in the simplest cases the process of reconciliation may be long and difficult, and in some cases reconciliation may not be possible no matter what we do.

In the above remarks I have distinguished sharply, perhaps too sharply, between trials for war crimes conducted by international tribunals and trials conducted by an individual state, and I must confess that my own feelings about the propriety of trials conducted by an individual state are somewhat mixed. Trials by either international or national tribunals may be politicized, trials of a few individuals may be superficial and fail to get at the roots of a conflict, and such trials may fail to further reconciliation. Why then have these trials at all? Why not simply have truth commissions like those in El Salvador and South Africa where amnesty may be granted in exchange for full confessions by accused individuals? These are valid questions, but here I must be content simply to suggest that if we must have trials for war crimes, it is probably better that such trials be conducted by individual states. There are two separate but related reasons why I believe this is so. First, it respects the autonomy of sovereign states, which is of practical and moral significance. It avoids the hurt feelings and moral outrage which may well accompany the decision of an international tribunal to pluck a citizen from a state for trial, and it may be helpful for all citizens to know that the rights of accused parties within the jurisdiction of their own state will be respected. It also enables a state to make the painful decisions as to which of its citizens to try in the light of the history and the practices of that state. The possibilities of abuse by authorities within a state are legion, e.g., getting back at an old political enemy, but I believe that it is important for an accused party to be tried before a jury of his peers and that an individual state can accommodate this principle in ways that an international tribunal could not. Second, I believe that reconciliation among groups within a state requires that the groups in question must face up to their own past, even if this involves delays in judicial procedures which would otherwise be unconscionable. There is an old adage that history is written by victors, which rankles because it contains so much truth. Part of the idea is that history is written from the outside, by parties victorious in an international conflict. I think it is important that justice not be written, or determined, from the outside, where trials for civil war crimes are concerned. Justice, to be effective, should come from the inside in two respects: first, a state must decide which of its citizens are guilty of committing war crimes; second, citizens of a state must "internalize" the verdicts in question, or in other words must come to see the moral rightness of these verdicts. The "internalization of the law" must be taken to include the internalization of the verdicts of the law if trials for civil wars crimes are to further reconciliation.

Notes

1   I am indebted to Anthony Ellis for pointing out that "punished for the right reason" is ambiguous. Perhaps the distinction made by Justice William Douglas in *Furman v. Georgia* between the motives that lead to the imposition of the death penalty and a law which in practice leads to unfair or disproportionate

sentencings will prove helpful here. Even if the motive is not to discriminate in
the application of the death penalty, the practice may yield effects which are
discriminatory. Thus, "right reason" would require that on both the level of
motive and outcome a just punishment must not be discriminatory.

2 "The Law of Peoples," *Oxford Amnesty Lectures* (New York, 1993), pp. 41–82.
3 The most succinct formulation of Dworkin's position is perhaps to be found in
   "Natural Law Revisited," *University of Florida Law Review* 34 (1982): 165–88.
4 *Law, Morality, and the Relations of States* (Princeton, 1989), pp. 272–9.
5 *Terrorism and Collective Responsibility* (London, 1992), pp. 102–49.

6

What Should We Do With War Criminals?

Anthony Ellis

I

That alleged war criminals should be put on trial and, if found guilty, punished has a long lineage. In 1625, for instance, Grotius held that this was appropriate in the case of those who had violated the law of nature. In 1792, the French National Assembly enacted a law requiring in part that "all cruel acts, violence or insults committed against a prisoner of war shall be punished as if committed against a French citizen."[1] After the American Civil War, Henry Wirz was tried and punished by the US government for maltreatment of prisoners of war in the Andersonville concentration camp. There were strenuous demands during the First World War that war criminals, including the Kaiser, should be tried and punished. And, of course, most famously, there were numerous war crimes trials after the Second World War.

Despite this, many people remain skeptical about the morality, the legality, and the viability of war crimes trials, particularly when conducted by an international body. What, then, should we do with war criminals? The question is a difficult one, and it is likely that there will be no wholly satisfactory answer.[2] But I shall suggest that, at least in many cases, they should be tried by an international court, or under its supervision, and, if found guilty, punished; and that this would be done better by a permanent court rather than by *ad hoc* tribunals such as those in Nuremberg and Tokyo after the Second World War and those following the civil wars in Rwanda and the former Yugoslavia. We should thus welcome the renewed interest, on the part of most nations (but not, apparently, the US) in establishing a permanent international criminal court.

II

War crimes trials are often castigated with the rhetoric of "victors' justice." Many have thought that the Nuremberg trials, for instance, were simply the victorious meting out their own conception of justice – or revenge – to the vanquished. As such, they did not even rise to the level of *legal* proceedings, let alone *defensible* legal proceedings.

But, stated simply like this, the point is confused. The victors did not, at Nuremberg, put on trial the vanquished. The victors and vanquished in a war are *nations*, but no nation was put on trial at Nuremberg; only individuals were tried. Of course, it is true that members of the vanquished nation were put on trial by members of the victorious nations; but that is not, of itself, problematic, since the individuals who were put on trial were not only members of the German nation: they were also members of international society and subject to its laws, and it is in that capacity that they were tried. Equally, there is nothing necessarily improper about the fact that the judges at the trials were members of the victorious nations. One might think this a less than ideal situation, and it has to some extent been rectified in later war crimes trials. The establishment of a permanent international criminal court might serve to give a yet greater appearance of impartial justice, though it is hard to imagine a state of affairs in which there would be no suspicion of partiality. But the relevant question is always in the end whether applicable law is interpreted and administered impartially; in the case of the Nuremberg and Tokyo trials, that question is not answered merely by adverting to the fact that the judges were members of the victorious nations, and indeed, those who were put on trial were given trials as fair as those that are routinely administered in the municipal law of the best jurisdictions.[3]

But, when this has been said, there may remain a cause for disquiet. War crimes trials are inevitably selective, for only a small percentage of those who commit war crimes can be found and punished. This, again, is not in itself particularly problematic, since the operation of any law is bound to be selective in that way, and it is unfortunate, but not because it violates anyone's rights or runs counter to any constraint that the legal order should operate under. Burleigh Wilkins, however, draws a parallel with a "clearly documented pattern of discrimination" which, he says, characterizes the death penalty in America: "a disproportionate number of those sentenced to death are black and poor," and "factors such as race or economic status should not enter into the reasons why" someone is punished (this volume,

p. 86). If they do, this violates "some of our basic intuitions about fairness and equality before the law" (p. 86). In a parallel way, there is an aspect to the selectivity of war crimes trials that is not merely random: it is the vanquished who are put on trial and not the victors. "[E]quality before the law has been violated, e.g., like cases have not been treated alike if losers in a war are solely or disproportionately singled out for trial" (p. 88). And so long as the sovereignty of states is as entrenched in the world order as it is, this will remain so – "Given the way the world is, it is highly unlikely that any state would voluntarily surrender its political leadership or military personnel to be tried for war crimes" (p. 87).

To assess this argument, let us first remind ourselves of what we mean by talking of equality before the law. As we normally think of it, it has two parts. First, there is what I shall call the formal guarantee: the considerations upon which decisions about prosecution, guilt, and sentencing are based are to be applied impartially. This by itself would allow that such factors as race might be taken into account, so long as this were done impartially. Second, however, there is what I shall call the substantive guarantee: certain considerations, such as race, are to be precluded even if their use were quite general and impartial. The preclusion is not arbitrary; it has its roots in the idea that legal decisions should, apart from blameworthiness, not be based upon considerations which disadvantage some but not others. (I do not say that this substantive element is without its philosophical problems.)

The formal guarantee is breached in the criminal law when considerations are taken into account in one case but not in another which is relevantly identical. If, say, race is taken into account in deciding whether to prosecute in one case but not in another, then normally, though not necessarily, that guarantee will have been breached. This is entirely a matter of individual justice; one of the individuals – indeed, each of them, in principle – will have an individual complaint against the state, which has failed to honor its guarantee to treat him as it treats others.

The substantive guarantee will normally be breached if race is taken into account at all, however impartially, for, if it is, some individuals will have been disadvantaged on the basis of a consideration that should be regarded as irrelevant. Again, this is entirely a matter of individual justice.

I have emphasized that breaches of the guarantee of equality before the law are individual injustices, to be decided on a case-by-case basis. This does not mean that patterns of selectivity, such as those mentioned by Wilkins, have no importance, but their importance is simply evidential. If we find that blacks are disproportionately sentenced to death in America then there is a natural, though rebuttable, presumption that this is the expression of a lingering oppression of one group by another. And that presumption carries through to a presumption that *this individual* black person's conviction and sentence have been based in part upon considerations that are not taken into account universally, and indeed should not be taken into account at all.

The guarantee is not breached merely because one offender is prosecuted and other, similar offenders are not. That will depend upon the circumstances of the particular case. And not just any pattern of selectivity will provide evidence that the guarantee of equality before the law has been breached. It is perfectly clear that the poor, for instance, are more likely to be executed in the US than are the rich; but here the issues are complex. If the fact that someone is poor were to be taken into account in the decisions leading to his punishment when this was not the usual practice, then this would violate the formal guarantee; and it would violate the substantive guarantee even if it were impartially taken into account, for it would disadvantage the poor without reference to blameworthiness. But, as is familiar, there are other possibilities. One is that the poor are more likely to be executed because they cannot afford the best legal representation. Here – assuming that the distribution of resources which leads to this result is itself a just one – there is no injustice, and there is no violation of the requirement of equality before the law. The guarantee of equality before the law does not entail the guarantee that all defendants shall have equally good representation; it guarantees only that, with the exception of blameworthiness, their treatment will not be based upon factors which disadvantage some but not others.

We can illustrate all of this by thinking for a moment of the Nuremberg trials. Does the fact that allied leaders were not tried violate the guarantee of equality before the law (assuming for a moment that they could plausibly be accused of war crimes)?

I think not. There was no violation of the substantive guarantee. Irrelevant considerations were not taken into account in determining how to deal with those on trial.[4] It was mainly a matter of retribution and deterrence. Here we must be careful how we speak: Wilkins says that "factors such as race or economic status should not enter into the reasons why" someone is punished (p. 87). Nor should the fact that they have been vanquished in a war. But the fact that the Nazi leaders were members of the vanquished nation was not a consideration that was taken into account when their punishment was decided upon, nor when it was decided to prosecute them. That they were the losers was, of course, one of the "reasons why" they were tried and punished – but only in a quite different, and quite anodyne, sense. If you relate the historical sequence of events leading to their punishment then you will include their having lost the war. That is, in one sense, the "reason why" they were punished, but that does not violate the requirement of equality before the law. It *would* violate that requirement if, when you were to relate the *justification* available for punishing them, you should need to mention this. But, as I have said, that is not necessary.

But what about the *pattern* of selectivity? Can that play the evidentiary role that many people think is played by the pattern of black executions in the US? It might suggest, for instance, that motives of revenge and hatred were present, assuming that this is the usual attitude of victors to vanquished. No doubt such motives were present, and this might create a presumption that such irrelevant considerations were the basis of the decision to punish. If so, the presumption, taken in the relevant sense, is easily rebutted. The question is whether a satisfactory justification can be made out that makes no reference to such irrelevant considerations. I think it can; it would be satisfactory to refer to retribution and deterrence, so long as it was reasonable, if not necessarily correct, to expect these two goals to be promoted by the trials; and that was indeed a reasonable expectation. The actual motives of the instigators of the trials are irrelevant, just as the motives of a District Attorney in bringing someone to trial are, in themselves, irrelevant to the question of the justice of so doing.

What of the guarantee of formal equality? That guarantee is breached when legal proceedings take into account considerations that are not given weight in other, similar, cases. Did this happen at Nuremberg? It is often said, for instance, that Churchill and Truman should both have been indicted for deliberately killing civilians by aerial bombardment; but the Tribunal was given jurisdiction only over Axis war criminals. So relevantly like cases were not treated alike.

As far as the motives of some of the historical agents is concerned, there is little reason to doubt this, for many were motivated not by a concern for justice but merely out of a desire for revenge. However, that is not the relevant question at the moment. The relevant question is whether there was a reasonable justification for prosecuting the Axis leaders but not Allied ones. I think there probably was. In municipal law, prosecutors are normally required to prosecute only when it is in the public interest to do so, and this is a practice which makes good sense.[5] The requirement of equal treatment before the law must be read in the light of that requirement. So if one offender is prosecuted and another, identical, offender is not, this does not entail that there has not been equality before the law, for the public interest considerations might have been different. Public interest considerations are very various, ranging from considerations of the likelihood of a conviction to questions of fairness, mercy, and a concern for national and international security.[6] Now, would it have been in the public interest for the Allied leaders to have set up the war crimes tribunal with jurisdiction over their own actions? It is hard to imagine so. To start with, there would have been virtually no public support for this at any level; Congress and Parliament, for instance, would certainly not have agreed to support such trials, even if the President and Prime Minister had done so. And if, by some bizarre turn of events, they had done so, it is inconceivable that the court would have indicted Churchill or Truman. For one thing, there would have been no serious possibility of a conviction. That is not merely for political reasons: international law on aerial bombardment was unclear. But the political reasons should not be treated too lightly either. If Churchill, say, had been found guilty of crimes against humanity and sentenced to be hanged, the results would have been catastrophic beyond imagining, and it would have been quite improper for any court to have invited them. There is no breach of the guarantee in taking all of this into account, so long as it is done impartially. No doubt that was lucky for Churchill and the others, who, at the very least, skated close to legal thin ice in bombing civilian populations. But that is often the way in the law, and it does not impugn the impartiality of the tribunal itself or of its proceedings.

One may still feel that, in an ideal world, those who ordered the bombing of Dresden, Cologne, Hiroshima, and Nagasaki should have been tried. But the law operates in the actual world, not an ideal one, and it does not guarantee the realization of ideals.

War crimes trials, to repeat, will inevitably be selective. But they need be no more problematically so than in municipal law.

III

To show that war crimes trials need violate no ethical or legal requirements is not, of course, to show that they are justified. That will depend upon what their point is, and whether they can achieve it to a satisfactory degree.

One thing that war crimes trials do is to ascertain and publicize facts that might otherwise be kept hidden. That is a great benefit, but – if we are really talking of inquiries which take the form of criminal prosecutions – then it is a side-benefit; for if that were our sole aim then criminal prosecutions would not be the most appropriate means. The point of war crimes trials is fundamentally to determine punishment. Their general legitimacy, there-fore, depends upon the ability of punishment to achieve its ends in this sphere.

The alleged aims of punishment are many and various, but I shall simply assert, and not argue, that the only legitimate aims of punishment must be forward looking; and that the only realistic aims are deterrence and incapa-citation.[7] We are thus pushed back to the question of whether punishment for war crimes has sufficient such effects to justify it.

IV

The goal of incapacitation is that of preventing the offender from re-offending, temporarily at least. One might think of such a goal most naturally, perhaps, when one is thinking of burglars, or persistent violent offenders, but it has its analog in war crimes trials. Incapacitation was not much mentioned as an aim of the Nuremberg and Tokyo trials; but it was certainly in the instigators' minds, particularly concerning such charismatic figures as Goering. It is quite clear that Goering, and others like him, had they been let free, would eventually have tried to resurrect the Nazi party or something like it. What success they would have had is hard to know, but it was surely not a risk that the allies could legitimately take; one way or another, such people must be removed from circulation.

Here, of course, a much-discussed moral question arises. It is one thing to punish people for what they have done in the past; it is quite another to regard what they have done in the past as mere evidence for what they may do in the future and "punish" them in order to prevent them from doing these things. I shall not discuss that issue, but assume that in some circum-stances it is indeed legitimate to confine people who pose a danger to others. But, of course, the application of such a dangerous principle must be constrained by procedural safeguards, and that is as true in the case of alleged war criminals as in the case of ordinary criminals. That is one function of war crimes trials.

There seems little reason to doubt that the incapacitative function of punishment can be achieved by confining, or killing, war criminals. The matter is otherwise with deterrence, however, and many people entertain serious doubts about whether this aim can be achieved to any significant degree. Richard Falk, for instance, says, "Surely, there is no evidence that the punishments imposed at Nuremberg helped to deter future war crimes,"[8] and it would be easy to cite more examples.[9]

The view may seem an appealing one in the light of the political history of the last half-century – the two hundred or so armed conflicts that have taken place since Nuremberg have routinely involved war crimes. But, on reflection, this seems poor reason to think that war crimes trials have had no deterrent effect, just as the frequency of burglary is a poor reason to think that threatening punishment for burglary has no deterrent effect, and an even poorer reason to think – what would be more to the point – that doing so has too little effect to justify its costs. In both cases it seems likely that the threat of punishment does indeed have real deterrent effect. The argument for this is not simply empirical, and has something in common with a familiar common-sense justification for the idea that punishment deters; but it is easy to misunderstand that common-sense justification – both how it works and what it proves.[10]

Let us think for a moment about deterrence in municipal law. Does punishment deter there?[11] Certainly it does. I know from my own experience that I am deterred from committing some offenses – speeding on the highway, for instance – by the desire to avoid punishment. It would be perverse to deny that this must be very generally true, for it is a priori that we could have no grasp of human motivation unless we assumed that the threat of punishment, in some circumstances, had some deterrent effect – circumstances in which the expected utility of an action is insufficient to motivate it when the prospect of punishment is factored in; and, though it is not a priori, it is surely obvious that such circumstances are found in all sorts of everyday situations. Of course, no threat of punishment will deter all potential offenders in all circumstances. But that is not to the point; all that matters is that a deterrent threat be sufficiently effective to justify its costs. That condition is surely met routinely in municipal law.

It might be though that this, though true, is not at present relevant. Even if what I have said is true of speeding offenses and the like, the situation is different, it may be thought, with serious violent crime. Most people are not routinely deterred from, for instance, rape and murder by the threat of punishment, because these are things which they have no routine desire to commit; so the threat of punishment is largely ineffective so far as they are concerned. On the occasions when they do commit such offenses, they are probably not motivated to any significant extent by rational considerations; in such circumstances we have again little reason to believe that deterrent threats have much effect. And as for those who do, routinely, have such desires, they fall outside of the psychological norm and it is not perverse to question whether punishment has any deterrent effect on them. We may be left, then, with little reason to think that, for offenses of this sort, punishment has any significant deterrent effect at all. And if that argument is correct, it may seem to apply in the case of war crimes. War crimes are typically much more like offenses such as rape and murder than exceeding the speed limit. Further, it may be said, in the heat of war, motivations are abnormal, and we should not extrapolate from the case of respectable citizens driving on the highway to the behavior of soldiers in battle.

But none of this argument is correct.

The first thing to be said about the a priori argument for the effectiveness of deterrence is that it does not just apply to average citizens and their behavior when driving. It applies universally, so long as we understand what it proves. It is surely perverse to think that even the most obsessive serial killer is not deterred in any way at all from his activities by the threat of punishment, for even obsessive people necessarily share normal patterns of motivation to some extent. Ted Bundy, for instance, killed a lot of women, but there seems little reason to think that he would not have killed many more had he had a legal *carte blanche* to do so. Punishment works, here as elsewhere, by curtailing the circumstances in which the offense can be rationally committed, and that is a major way in which it reduces the level of such crime.[12] It is, of course, merely one social constraint amongst others, in particular self-protection and revenge. They work, structurally, in the same way as the law: in some cases, fear of them will wholly deter someone from committing an offense; but when someone is determined to commit the offense, then they will make it more difficult to do so, and thus will still have some effect. The law simply adds a *further* deterrent, and one which, insofar as it is effective, reduces the relatively high costs imposed by the others. I speed when I can do so with safety and impunity; that is not as often as I would like. Bank robbers steal when they can do so with impunity; presumably that is not as often as they would like, either.

We should not expect things to be radically different in the case of war crime. There will always be those who commit war crimes, just as there will always be those who commit other sorts of crime; but there is little reason to think that the threat of punishment will not be one of the motivating factors in their behavior, reducing their crimes to some significant degree.[13] Certainly the claims I mentioned a moment ago about motivation in war time provide little reason. War crimes are not typically committed in the heat of battle, when soldiers are under great strain and their judgment and self-discipline have been savaged. The recent wars in Bosnia and Rwanda illustrate this clearly, and one could give many more examples. They are, of course, sometimes carried out under superior orders; but that is, in its

own way, often true of municipal crime too. And, again, they are carried
out in circumstances in which the prospect of eventual punishment is
slight;[14] but, again, that is largely true of municipal law too for many sorts
of offense. Soldiers typically act in circumstances no more inimical to the
deterrent effect of punishment than do ordinary criminals.

I have spoken so far, of course, about ordinary soldiers and the crimes that
they commit. But what of the leaders who initiate aggressive war in the first
place? Is it perhaps unrealistic to think that the threat of punishment will
deter *them*? The question here is more complex, for a number of reasons.
But why should it be unrealistic to expect punishment to have *some*
deterrent effect? Obviously, those who have actually waged aggressive
wars have not been deterred by the threat of punishment; presumably,
they typically thought that they would be the victors and therefore, as
things tend to go, would not be punished. But, so far, this is no different
from the case of ordinary criminals again, most of whom presumably think
that they will get away with their crimes and not be punished.[15] But we
assume that there is, in addition to the class of offenses actually committed, a
class of cases in which potential criminals are deterred, temporarily at least,
by the threat of punishment, from committing offenses which they would
otherwise commit. It is not clear why, if there were a permanent threat of
judicial punishment for those who initiate war, this would have insufficient
deterrent effect to justify its costs.

A common thought is that political leaders who wage aggressive wars are
the sort of people who, for some reason, do not fear punishment, or at least
not punishment in the circumstances we are discussing. That is doubtless
true of some cases; but the leaders of nations that wage aggressive wars are
not always, nor even typically, like this. After all, most of the high-ranking
Nazis fled after the war precisely in order to avoid punishment. And the
Nazi leaders put on trial at Nuremberg chose, for the most part, to defend
themselves. In some cases they regarded their trials as an opportunity for an
aggressive announcement to the world that they did not accept the justice of
the trials; but in most cases it was a genuine attempt to avoid, or mitigate,
punishment. They did not choose martyrdom, but sought to avoid it. They
feared punishment as much as anyone else. There seems little reason to think
that punishment has *no* deterrent value against initiating wars of aggression.
The only question is whether such deterrent value as it possesses is worth
the costs it imposes; I myself should think that an easier question than the
parallel question about deterrence in municipal law.

Of course, the effectiveness of a deterrent threat is in part a function of
the likelihood of its being carried out, and carried out reliably. For that

reason, it is important that war crimes should, in general, be punished whenever they justly can be. In the present state of things, it is extremely difficult to arrest and try war criminals, high-ranking ones especially. That is in part a result of the woefully inadequate machinery for this purpose, but it is not just that; there will often be complex political problems involved, and sometimes they will be insoluble. But, again, this is not so very different from the municipal law; we cannot put on trial all of those whom we think guilty, and this for all sorts of reasons. The question is, again, simply whether we can achieve enough to make the undertaking worthwhile. Presumably we can; there is little reason to think things different in the area of war crimes.

V

It is often said that war crimes trials should serve the end of helping to reconcile the warring parties. People sometimes speak in this way about municipal criminal law too. But, in this latter case, apart from one or two special cases it seems wholly inappropriate. It is a way of talking whose natural home lies in the idea that criminal offenses are *disputes*, that in "constructing" them as crimes, we falsify them, and that the proper aim of the law should be a satisfactory resolution of the dispute. Such a view, once common amongst criminologists, is no longer popular; and justly not so. A rape is not, save trivially, a dispute, and it does not demand reconciliation; we should not preclude that if both parties want it, of course, but we should not expect the criminal law system to provide much help. What rape demands is *prevention* (and retribution, if one believes in that) and that is the only thing that it is realistic to expect the criminal law to do to any significant extent.

The same is true of war crimes. A war may sometimes be simply a dispute, but a war crime is not; it is a wrong done by one party to another and calls for prevention. Of course, the warring parties will eventually have to be reconciled, but there is little reason to expect war crimes trials to be very much help in achieving that goal.

Indeed, they can, in some circumstances, actually make reconciliation harder.[16] Then we have to weigh the expected benefits against the expected losses, as we often do in municipal law, and decide whether it is wise to go ahead with them. And, more generally, we need a format for such trials that will minimize this danger. One thing that this will require is, of course, the appearance, as well as the reality, of impartiality. And that raises the

following question: if there are to be war crimes trials, who should conduct
them? There are a number of possibilities.

VI

One possibility is that nations should be expected to try and punish their
own war criminals.

On the face of things, this would not seem like a promising suggestion.
Why, after all, should we expect a nation to have the resources of impartiality and political courage that would be necessary to put on trial and punish
those who had fought for it? And surely the historical record provides some
basis for this skepticism? Think of two famous cases. Germany was required
to try many of its nationals for war crimes after the First World War. The
trials were few and perfunctory, many of them transparently having no other
purpose than to foreclose the possibility of those offenders being tried under
other jurisdictions which would have taken the matter more seriously.[17]
More recently, literally thousands of war crimes were committed by both
sides in Vietnam, but there were virtually no trials for them. There was, of
course, the famous trial of Lieutenant William Calley for the massacre at Son
My. Lieutenant Calley was charged with the murder of 109 people. He was,
however, widely fêted as a hero, and when he was found guilty President
Nixon declared that he would personally review the transcript of the trial.
He was sentenced to ten years in prison, but served three and a half years of
house arrest and was freed.

And the danger is not simply that war criminals will be treated too
leniently by their fellow citizens; it may go the other way, as events
following the Nuremberg trials illustrated. Those who were acquitted at
Nuremberg could not initially leave the building because they were afraid of
arrest, and possible lynching, by those who saw them as the ultimate cause of
the terrible disaster that had befallen Germany. And despite being acquitted
at Nuremberg, all were subsequently tried by German courts, and given
substantial sentences which were later overturned or reduced.[18]

None of this is to deny that nations can, and often do, try their own war
criminals (a sense of military honor has often led to this). But it is expecting
too much of a nation routinely to deal justly with its own war criminals.
The alternative, then, is some sort of international court.

The trials of those accused of war crimes in Rwanda and the former
Yugoslavia are being held before *ad hoc* tribunals. However, in Rome in
July of 1998, 120 nations signed a treaty agreeing to set up an international

criminal court with jurisdiction with respect to genocide, crimes against humanity, war crimes, and aggression; it will come into effect when 60 nations ratify it. Though the court was considerably weakened by resistance from the US (which, along with six other nations, did not sign the treaty) its establishment should be supported as a step toward the goal of an international society governed more fully by law than it is at present.

There are those who object to the notion of a permanent international criminal court on the ground that it offends against "the sovereignty of states."[19] But the sovereignty of states is a modern phenomenon, and one which had a rationale in a certain historical context. Nation-states need some guarantee against intervention from other nation-states in a world in which order is based wholly upon the relations between them. But that is not the world we live in any longer. The emergence of two major non-state jurisdictions has changed things, and will continue to do so. I speak, of course, of the United Nations and the European Union. It is common, especially in the US, to speak slightingly of such bodies, partly because of the political realism which governed American political science for so long (and partly for less admirable reasons). But from one perspective their contribution to recent history has surely been phenomenal. Indeed, it may be no exaggeration to suggest that world order is moving towards what Hedley Bull described as neo-Mediaeval order.[20]

Think, for a moment of the European Union, a grouping of 15 nations (and perhaps as many as 26 within a few years) all subject to a common set of legal principles and institutions. Of course, those nations have not given up the claim to national sovereignty. Many in the UK, to take the most obvious example, have fought strenuously against recognizing the validity of European law in the UK, and as little as 20 years ago it would have been inconceivable that UK labor law, for instance, would be subject to dictates from Brussels. But it has been, for the most part, a losing battle. The UK generally follows European law when it has spoken (in all sorts of matters, criminal ones included), and all the evidence is that it will do so more and more.[21] And this should be welcomed; it is no accident that when the UK has found itself condemned by EU law it is generally the UK that has been in the wrong. So too with the United Nations. It has not yet lived up to the hopes of those who created the League of Nations; but the decisions of its International Court of Justice are generally followed.

Another problem with an international court is that it will often be difficult to arrest indicted criminals. If a nation will not hand them over – and we can be sure that this will happen often enough in the foreseeable future – then there is little that the UN can do (though we should not forget the arrest of Adolf Eichmann by the Israelis; the Argentineans, after sputtering with rage, later declared the incident closed). But the problem should not be overestimated. After all, however dissatisfied some may feel with the progress of the war crimes trials following the war in the former Yugoslavia, there have been trials and convictions which would otherwise not have taken place. In any case, the fact that nations will often not hand over their criminals for trial is not in itself much of an argument against having a permanent court; after all, a nation that will not hand its criminals over to the UN will generally not try them itself either.

Notes

1   Leon Friedman, ed., *The Law of War. A Documentary History*, vol. 1, p. 12.
2   Cf. J. L. Brierly, "Do We Need an International Criminal Court" (*The British Yearbook of International Law*, 1927), p. 83.
3   I am assuming that those who were found guilty of waging aggressive war were not illegitimately tried under *ex post facto* law; there is, of course, room for more than one view about this matter. I am also assuming that, even in the best jurisdictions, there is often unfairness in criminal proceedings.
4   More precisely: some people no doubt did have irrelevant considerations in mind, such as naked revenge. But the justification can be mounted without referring to any such irrelevant considerations.
5   Even in systems like the German and Austrian, where prosecution is in principle compulsory when there is sufficient evidence, numerous exceptions have introduced considerable scope for discretion. See J. Herrmann, "The Rule of Compulsory Prosecution and the Scope of Prosecutorial Discretion in Germany," *University of Chicago Law Review* 16 (1974): pp. 468–505, esp. pp. 475ff.
6   See, for instance, the UK *Code for Crown Prosecutors* (Crown Prosecution Service, 1994).
7   Incapacitation can, of course, be achieved only by certain sorts of punishment.
8   Falk, Richard A. Gabriel Kolko, and Robert Jay Lifton (eds.), *Crimes of War. A Legal, political-documentary, and psychological inquiry into the responsibility of leaders, citizens, and soldiers for criminal acts in war* (Random House, 1971), p. 9.
9   Cf., for instance, J. L. Brierly, "Do We Need an International Criminal Court," p. 84; and Burleigh T. Wilkins, this volume, p. 87.
10 For brief surveys of the empirical evidence, see, for instance, James Q. Wilson, *Thinking About Crime* (revised edition, Basic Books, 1983), ch. 7, and Nigel Walker, *Why Punish* (Oxford University Press, 1991), ch. 2.
11 For brevity, I shall put it in this way. But if it is deterrence that we are speaking of then it is really the *threat* of punishment that deters.

12 At least one victim of the serial killer Peter Sutcliffe was saved from death by the accidental proximity of a policeman; that is one life that can be credited to the threat of punishment for murder. And Peter Sutcliffe seems to have been rational in only the most minimal sense.

13 In fact, we have seen something like this in operation. Think of the behavior of many of those who operated Nazi concentration camps and extermination camps as allied victory approached them; their behavior was very obviously motivated by a fear of retaliation, and this saved a considerable number of lives. That was not fear of legal punishment, of course, but the psychology is the same.

14 J. L. Brierly, "Do We Need an International Criminal Court," p. 83.

15 That is to say: most of whom think that the expected utility of committing the offense is greater than of not doing so; this of course brings in more than the likelihood of being caught.

16 Cf. Wilkins, this volume, p. 91. There was always considerable resentment in Japan about the Tokyo trials. Resentment grew in Germany until 1949, when Konrad Adenauer tried to have the continuing war crimes trials stopped (in fact they carried on into the 1960s).

17 Almost 900 individuals were accused of war crimes; there were eventually 13 trials. For an account of the debate, and the eventual unsatisfactory trials, see James F. Willis, *Prologue to Nuremberg. The Politics and Diplomacy of Punishing War Criminals of the First World War* (Westport, CT: Greenwood Press, 1982).

18 Hans Fritzsche was sentenced to 9 years at hard labor and pardoned in 1950. Hjalmar Schacht was sentenced to 8 years and acquitted after an appeal. Franz von Papen was sentenced to 10 years in a labor camp; in 1949 his sentence was reduced, and he was set free.

19 Cf. Wilkins, this volume, p. 88.

20 In 1977, Bull wrote as follows:

We might imagine, for example, that the government of the United Kingdom had to share its authority on the one hand with authorities in Scotland, Wales, Wessex and elsewhere, and on the other hand with a European authority in Brussels and world authorities in New York and Geneva, to such an extent that the notion of its supremacy over the territory and people of the United Kingdom had no force. We might image that the authorities in Scotland and Wales, as well as those in Brussels, New York and Geneva enjoyed standing as actors in world politics, recognized as having rights and duties in world law, conducting negotiations and perhaps able to command armed forces. We might imagine that the political loyalties of the inhabitants of, say, Glasgow, were so uncertain as between the authorities in Edinburgh, London, Brussels and New York that the government of the United Kingdom could not be assumed to enjoy any kind of primacy over the others, such as it possesses now. If such a state of affairs prevailed all over the globe, this is what we may call, for want of a better a term, a neo-mediaeval order. (*The Anarchical Society. A Study of Order in World Politics* (2nd edn., Columbia University Press, 1995), p. 246)

That is still imagination. But in 1997 Scotland and Wales voted to have their own elected assemblies. Other regions of the United Kingdom saw this as a precedent, and were encouraged to do so by Mr. Blair, the Prime Minister. And the persistent demand for Scottish independence in a federal Europe will not go away – a reminder, incidentally, that the aspirations of nationalism do not require the sovereignty of states.

21   Times have changed since Harold Wilson, then Prime Minister in the UK, scoffed threats from the European Common Market, whose regulations Britain was in breach of: What could the EEC do, he asked a television interviewer with a smirk; it wouldn't just be a matter of sending across "a couple of gendarmes" and arresting him, he remarked.

7

Accountability for War Crimes and the Legacy of Nuremberg

Richard Falk

Today, "Nuremberg" is both what actually happened there and what people think happened, and the second is more important than the first... it is not the bare record but the ethos of Nuremberg that we must reckon today.
Telford Taylor, *Nuremberg and Vietnam: An American Tragedy*[1]

We must never forget that the record on which we judge these defendants is the record on which history will judge us tomorrow. To pass these defendants a poisoned chalice is to put it to our lips as well.
Justice Robert H. Jackson, Opening Statement, Nuremberg Trials, 1945

In keeping with Telford Taylor's admonition, the focus of this chapter is upon "the ethos of Nuremberg" rather than upon a reconstruction of the historical record yet again.[2] And this ethos is itself shaped by a series of recent developments that have revived widespread public interest in this matter of holding political and military leaders internationally accountable as individuals for violations of international law. The interpretation of the Nuremberg ethos is at the present juncture very much caught up in the global atmosphere brought about by the end of the cold war. It is especially being shaped by the 1993 decision of the United Nations Security Council to convene an *ad hoc* tribunal at The Hague to indict and prosecute individuals accused of war crimes arising out of the breakup of former Yugoslavia, especially in relation to the war in Bosnia, as well as the later analogous initiative undertaken as a response to genocidal events occurring in Rwanda during 1994.[3]

This current interest in Nuremberg is also fueled by the recent campaign to establish an international criminal court that would function as part of a structure of global governance for international society. A major intergovernmental conference was held at Rome in 1998. As a result, a treaty has been tabled and rather widely endorsed, but also significantly resisted by the United States and several other major states.[4]

A further related set of concerns has been associated with transitions from oppressive rule in the last two decades, posing alleged tradeoffs between "peace and justice." Often the approach taken included a bargain involving impunity for offenders in exchange for their participation in a formalized, public, truth-telling process. Such an arrangement was challenged internationally in late 1998 when a Spanish court issued a request for the extradition of Augusto Pinochet who was temporarily in London for medical treatment. The British legal system at its upper reaches has been wrestling ever since with the question of how to respond, whether to grant extradition or accede to the request of the Chilean Government for Pinochet's release.

From the outset, the Nuremberg enterprise has been controversial, as has been each major occasion of its reenactment and invocation. For some, Nuremberg was a great step forward in the struggle for justice in international relations. For others, it was and remains an exercise in hypocrisy and geopolitical convenience that cannot be otherwise given the character of international society.[5]

There exists another matter of fundamental interpretation. It has been natural until quite recently to view the narrative of international law as one expression of the optimistic western idea of linear history. In this sense, Nuremberg is both an event and a process. This process that is often interpreted teleologically as containing an assured promise of future justice, one dimension of which will be a reliable framework within which to establish the accountability of leaders for severe violations of international law. According to such thinking, it is merely a matter of patience, allowing political evolution to run its course, until a fully articulated international legal order emerges that is global in scope, evenhanded in application, and effective in operation. A useful contribution of the critical side of postmodernism has been to cast severe doubt upon any and all such "meta-narratives," suggesting that what purports to be an objective account of an unfolding reality is more properly understood as a self-serving rationale of power by the powerful that is closer to the biases of ideology than to the course of history. The West has been, and remains, particularly proficient at mythologizing its experience as the foundation for a beneficial order and destiny for the whole of humanity.[6]

Taking seriously this deconstructive insight clarifies the scope of this inquiry. The prospects for an effective legal framework for the accountability, under international law, of leaders, are dependent on the outcome of a complex social struggle currently underway in many distinct arenas. Whatever the result, it will reflect a contingent *social construction* by prevailing political tendencies rather than manifest a pattern expressive of historical inevitability. At the same time there are predisposing elements that are animating and shaping the struggle, and seemingly inclining the process toward greater regularity, and possibly achieving a degree of institutionalization. It is, above all, the interconnectedness of life on the planet, due to technological innovation, economic integration, and global media that exerts pressure to generate common norms and their consistent implementation, especially in extreme cases. This dynamic also generates much speculation about the decline of the state as the exclusively effective ordering instrument on a global level, and a growing receptivity to alternative accounts.[7] Among those alternative accounts that are being taken seriously are those concerned with "global governance" and "cosmopolitan democracy."[8] It seems more natural in a globally framed world than it did in a statist world to posit accountability of leaders as an essential attribute of a more globalized world order.[9] At the same time, the persistence of geopolitics should not be underestimated. The US Government, although formally in favor of a general and vague effort to institutionalize accountability and supportive of the *ad hoc* moves against former Yugoslavia and Rwanda, opposes the Rome treaty and related efforts to create an independent tribunal. This geopolitical caution has been described as an approach to accountability with the following feature – "everybody but us."[10] Indeed, the "us" is broader, including close allies as well.

Finally, it is important to appreciate the special role of the United States in relation to this range of concerns. As with so many elements of the normative (ethical and legal) side of international relations, the standpoint of the United States is crucial, contradictory, and in the end, highly ambivalent. During the Vietnam era the behavior of American leaders, and their refusal to accept the relevance of Nuremberg to their own challenged behavior, retrospectively strengthened the hand of both those who had all along condemned the process as self-serving and opportunistic from the outset, and those who opposed the war, pointing out the discrepancy between the earlier stand on German and Japanese leaders and the refusal to heed such standards of accountability as applicable to its policies.

It also affected those with more positive expectations at Nuremberg, as was certainly the case with Justice Jackson despite his image of the poisoned chalice, or Telford Taylor, who in light of Nuremberg found it necessary to regard Vietnam as "an American tragedy."[11] Both of these important actors on the stage at Nuremberg had repudiated the taunt made by the Nuremberg defendants that the whole proceeding was from start to finish "a kangaroo court" or a spectacle of "victors' justice." They genuinely endorsed the idealistic expectation that Nuremberg would be a precedent that would be respected by the governments of those leaders and their citizenry who had sat in judgment of the leaders defeated in the Second World War.[12] The United States remains the principal originator and champion of the Nuremberg ethos. It is now more salient in its identity as the lion that appears to be blocking the path to the more consistent application of ideas of accountability, and of respect for the norms of international law, whose acute violation engages the issue of responsibility.

It is also true that Americans have done the most to keep the spirit of Nuremberg alive during the last half-century, mainly as a consequence of its citizens of conscience acting vividly within the spaces of civil society. This double relationship toward normative achievement is a feature of the overall contradictory connection of the United States to virtually the whole agenda of international normative concerns, starting of course with Woodrow Wilson's extraordinary crusade to establish the League of Nations after the First World War that culminated in the Senate's refusal to ratify the Versailles Peace Treaty that established the organization.[13] The interpretative perspective of an American, regardless of her particular slant, also exerts a major influence on what issues need to be discussed, and how the Nuremberg experience is to be regarded.[14]

There is some risk that the American role is overstated at the expense of the overall orientation of policy-making elites around the world. The US in this regard is a normal state that is no more "realist" than other state actors, but because of its power and leadership role its pronouncements are most noticed and given greater attention. Indeed, what most distinguishes the US approach is that it professes a moral orientation, and thus cannot comfortably embrace an overtly realist posture. As a result, its own elite is often confused and its citizenry divided over such issues as to whether and to what extent the government should uphold international law in the conduct of its foreign policy.

If a more structural/ideological interpretation is emphasized, then it seems evident that there is an encounter between the sovereignty orientation of leading governments and the global village outlook of transnational activists.

Against the background of this introductory note on the Nuremberg ethos, a short discussion of the historical roots and contemporary context is set forth. This is followed by a more focused consideration of the

Nuremberg approach in the period between 1945 and 1999, with reference to the distinctive US role during that period. On these bases, the chapter concludes with an assessment of Nuremberg as it relates to present concerns and future challenges.

I The Nuremberg Idea up against World Order

Throughout this century, mainly in reaction to the devastation caused by the two world wars, there have been a series of reformist steps taken that challenge statist logic. These involve efforts to restrain the state legally and institutionally in relation to its discretion to use force as a discretionary instrument of policy. It is outside the scope of this article to evaluate the overall success of these various efforts, except to suggest that the record is, at best, mixed.[15] The central effort is associated with the fundamental undertaking of the UN Charter to prohibit aggressive force and to offer the collective capabilities of international society to a victim of aggression. It was this commitment that was also at the heart of the Nuremberg experience, especially if considered *textually* in view of the stress placed in the Judgment on Crimes Against Peace. If considered *contextually*, then the Nuremberg stress on criminalizing severe abuses of people, of which genocide offers the most extreme instance, is also a part of the Nuremberg core as associated with Crimes Against Humanity.

The idea that the Nuremberg precedent would bind states in the future, including the victorious parties, is what seems in retrospect to be so naïve. It is naïve because there continued to be no alternatives to self-help to uphold the security of the state, except in those rare situations where upholding the anti-aggression norm coincides with geopolitical interests of the main political actors. This happened in response to the 1990 attack and annexation of Kuwait by Iraq, even prompting the American president at the time to put forward the prospect of "a new world order" in which the UN would finally fulfill its Charter commitment to make the world unsafe for aggression. But, just as with Nuremberg, once Kuwaiti sovereignty was restored, and geopolitical priorities again pointed to a reliance on self-help in the form of unilateral force, the discourse of a new world order was eliminated from the language of diplomacy.

It is important not to become irresponsibly cynical in light of these disappointments, but it is also equally important to take account of prevailing ideas about security among governmental elites and the patterns of international practice in recent decades. Realism tends to be the prevailing orientation toward the formation of policy by the leadership of most states. It puts state interests at the top, and tends to regard respect for international law and morality as instruments of propaganda rather than as providing policy guidelines that clarify national interests. Such realism, especially as an ideological orientation of elites in the American setting since 1945, view the restraining claims on behalf of a Nuremberg worldview as "legalistic" or "moralistic," as misplaced and dangerously sentimental given the structure of international society. The complacency of liberal democracies in the face of the rise of Hitler gave the realist assessment great leverage in the process of learning "the lessons of Munich." American realists are a divergent lot, ranging from Henry Kissinger on the one side to George Kennan on the other side, but they share the fundamental view that interests, not rules or values, are the ground of policy for a state in its external relations.[16]

Realist opponents of the Vietnam War invariably argued that it was an imprudent war due to its high costs relative to the calculus of expected gains.[17] To insinuate Nuremberg considerations into the debate over Vietnam policy was completely alien to the realist discourse for critics and apologists alike, and it remains so to this day. Hedley Bull provided an early non-American realist set of arguments for not moving in a Nuremberg direction, resting on his belief that the quality of international order needed to be premised on continuing respect for the sanctity of sovereign rights and an ethos of noninterventionism.[18] In Bull's view, international society lacked sufficient solidarity to impose on individuals acting on behalf of their states "a higher law" than that of their domestic political circumstances. The Nuremberg idea was structurally unsound.

Such an argument is persuasive so long as the structure of world order is more or less exclusively shaped by sovereign states, with the more powerful states assuming special prerogatives. What such a realist perspective overlooks, however, is the emergence in the last several decades of a series of world order challenges, and especially, those associated with regionalism, globalization, and civic transnationalism. Along with such changes in world order structure, there have also been important ideological challenges mounted to realism, at least in its hardest edge forms. Among these challenges, the most subversive of all might be connected with human rights and ideas related to a legal entitlement to democratic governance.[19] These factors combine to produce a political climate in which the promotion of the Nuremberg idea is a feasible political project, but only to the extent that it is no longer conceived to be an intergovernmental undertaking.

In my reading of Taylor (and Jackson for that matter), their expectations about Nuremberg are linked to tacit assumptions about the receptivity of liberal democratic governments to moral and legal pedagogy. Such assumptions lead to the view that a legal precedent can by its own force overcome contrary pressures, and it also incorporates, without being explicit, the belief that moral and legal progress in relation to international behavior is the natural course of history. Taylor, to be fair, at the end of his *Nuremberg and Vietnam*, is himself "a realist" when it comes to the role of domestic courts in the United States with respect to the continuation of the Vietnam War. As usual, Taylor's formulation is worthy of quotation: "There is no simple way to end the Vietnam tragedy, for the Supreme Court is not a *deus ex machina*. This war, and the agony and rancor that are its product, have been the work of the President and the Congress – the people's elected agents – and the war can be ended only by action of the national will, exerted through political, not judicial, channels."[20] But again to express a disagreement, the role of judicial action would be to embed international law in the constitutional structure of democratic governance. It would thereby give civil society an instrument by which to challenge a wayward national will, a prerogative of especial importance with respect to the actions of the US Government that involve protecting a wide range of global interests, the frequent recourse to force, and a range of undertakings that affect the well-being of persons with no access to processes of decision within the United States.[21] For Taylor to accept this realist account internally, but ignore it externally, seems to invite both an underestimation of the role of civil society in implementing the Nuremberg idea and an overestimation of the willingness and capacity of governments operating in a realist mode to adhere to the Nuremberg idea if it runs counter to perceptions of interest. Without a world order perspective it is almost impossible to assess either the potential or the limitations associated with the original Nuremberg experience.

II The Agency of "Geopolitical Convenience"

An essential feature of the Westphalian state system of world order that is often overlooked, or simply not discussed, concerns the managerial role played by leading or dominant states, what used to be called in the colonial era, "Great Powers." It is a problematic feature because it does not fit comfortably into the juridical logic of equality among states that is integral to the idea of sovereignty. If a political entity qualifies as a "state," enters into diplomatic relations with other states, and participates as a member of international institutions, then it enjoys a *juridical* equality of status with all other states (that structures most formal activities in organized international political life). The United Nations broke to a limited extent with this logic of equality by conferring permanent membership and a veto power on five major countries that were most prominently associated with the outcome of the Second World War.[22] The Bretton Woods institutions also rest on inequality to the degree that they incorporate weighted voting based on levels of contribution into their operations.[23]

But far more important than these formal encroachments on the idea of sovereign equality are those aspects of international life that exhibit inequalities of power, size, wealth, and diplomatic ambition. Especially in relation to the war/peace agenda, these inequalities exert a decisive influence on the character of international relations and have done so since the rise of the sovereign territorial state as political actor on the global stage. In the absence of strong central institutions of regional and global governance, dominant states have assumed leadership roles in a variety of settings with more or less approbation.[24] In this century, particularly since the end of the First World War, it has been the United States more than any other country that has played this role, and especially with respect to the politics of global reform. To varying degrees this role has been shared with other states, either as alliance partners or adversaries, making a full rendering of global leadership rather complicated because of variations over time not central to this inquiry into the Nuremberg legacy.

In focusing on the relevance of inequality to Nuremberg and its legacy, it is of special importance to take note of the priorities of dominant states. It is these priorities that gives coherence to the idea of "geopolitics," a shorthand for those dimensions of international relations that are primarily shaped by assertions of political power. It is only by being attentive to geopolitics that we can begin to grasp the puzzling pattern of achievements and disappointments that have flowed from the Nuremberg idea since its inception, and in relation to its principal antecedents.[25]

In a fundamental sense, as with human rights, it is difficult to comprehend why sovereign states should have been ever willing to validate such a subversive idea as that of international criminal accountability of leaders for war crimes. It goes directly against the spirit and ideology of sovereignty. It only makes sense from a statist perspective if the imposition of accountability is understood to be a *particular* advantageous response to a given geopolitical challenge, whose wider implications can be avoided. For this reason the Nuremberg promise of Justice Jackson, later reinforced by Taylor as indicated above, is so revealing. By insisting that what was done at Nuremberg would become a general framework in the future, Jackson was implicitly accepting limits on the use of power by states and their leaders that would, if implemented, transform the practice of geopolitics as it had developed over the centuries. Generalizing such accountability, particularly if accompanied by effective institutional mechanisms, would represent a *radical* change in the functioning of the state system involving the elevation of law above the will of the sovereign. But without this insistence Nuremberg would, in retrospect, certainly seem to support the most cynical appraisals to the effect that "it was nothing more than victors' justice," and as such, profoundly hypocritical.

Taylor bravely recognized that the Vietnam War was a decisive test of the Nuremberg Promise. But his intergovernmental orientation and inherent conservatism led him to view the failure of the US Government to follow through on Nuremberg as "an American tragedy."[26] The problem with such an assessment is that it does not recognize the degree to which Nuremberg was an exceptional circumstance that allowed geopolitical forces to coalesce around the idea of a criminal prosecution of surviving leaders. Among the factors that can be mentioned are the following: the claim of the victorious powers that the losing side embodied an evil ideology; the public pressure for some sort of punitive action against those believed responsible for waging such a devastating war; the consensus among leaders that Germany (and Japan) must not be held collectively responsible in the manner of the peace settlement after the First World War (what might be called "the lesson of Versailles"); the closely related geopolitical idea in the West that the defeated enemy states might soon become valued allies in the next phase of geopolitical rivalry; the guilty conscience in the West that not enough had been done to protect the victims of Nazi persecution before and during the war itself (for example, the refusal of liberal democracies to accept Jewish refugees; the failure to bomb the railroad tracks leading to Auschwitz), and the overall sense that the reconstruction of world order around moderate lines would be helped by a dignified trial of German defendants as opposed to the impression created by a vengeful process of summary execution. In addition, there were those, such as Jackson and Taylor, who believed that Nuremberg represented a solemn commitment by the convening governments to submit to the rule of law in their international activities, and that such submission might help to prevent the recurrence of major wars in the future. And there were those who went further, viewing Nuremberg as a desirable and necessary step toward realizing a far wider program of global reform. In this latter view only some form of world government, accompanied by disarmament at the level of the state, could save the human species from extinction given the prospect of the next world war being fought with nuclear weaponry.[27]

Despite agreeing with Taylor's invocation of Nuremberg during the Vietnam War, my expectations of compliance were not disappointed. I never expected the Nuremberg Promise to be kept by leaders confronted by geopolitical challenges that could not be met within the four corners of the United Nations Charter, especially its anti-aggression norm.[28] To this day I disagree with the geopolitical calculus that prevails in realist circles, which accords such a low priority in the form of national interest to respect for the Rule of Law in the setting of security policy. But it seems to me impossible to deny the existence of such a realist calculus and its virtually unchallenged control over foreign policy. The consensus is so strong in the United States that the question of using force has been generally backed by overwhelming bipartisan, as was the case in relation to Vietnam for many years, and the role of international law is mainly one of rationalization. Only when the war began to be perceived as too costly for the interests at stake, as occurred after the Tet Offensive in early 1968, did some concerns about the restraints of international law become evident, and then in the form of halfhearted self-enforcement at low command levels as occurred in response to media disclosures of the Mylai Massacre.[29]

My point here is that Nuremberg occurred only for opportunistic reasons within the specific historical setting of the ending of the Second World War, and that far deeper than the normative impulses associated with imposing criminal liability on the individuals responsible were the currents of opinion that stressed the vital importance of moving toward unabashed realism in terms of American participation in the world. This outlook included warnings to avoid taking the UN too seriously as a basis for collective security, and the corresponding importance of peacetime military vigilance at the level of the state. The main realist contention being that countervailing power, and the credibility associated with its potential use, could both keep the peace and avoid aggressive attacks on the established territorial and political order. The requirements for such security were shaped by both the existence and developments of nuclear weaponry and the character of the expansionist threat posed by the Soviet Union. Ideas of "containment" and "deterrence" reflected such thinking, and their implementation as in Vietnam were not very much affected by the relevance of legal factor. As the American debate developed, it was mainly conducted among realists, with anti-war realists such as Hans Morgenthau, George Kennan, and George Ball arguing against the war on pragmatic grounds associated with foreign policy priorities and opportunity costs.[30]

If such "a reading" of Nuremberg is made, how then can one explain its resurfacing in the 1990s? There are at least four lines of explanation. First of all, the end of the cold war meant that allegations of criminality would not be perceived as mainly an exercise in hostile propaganda that dangerously inflamed efforts to sustain what had come to be called "peaceful co-existence." Secondly, to be discussed in the next section, that to an extent not even imagined at Nuremberg, the Nuremberg Promise was taken seriously by morally engaged sectors of civil society. Thirdly, the war in Bosnia with its genocidal features, especially "ethnic cleansing," again challenged the liberal democracies to show that they cared about the victims, a pressure intensified by "the CNN factor."[31] And fourthly, there was a geopolitical incentive to create some sort of international criminal tribunal to cope with the security threats to the established order posed by international terrorism, the drug trade, and the revival of piracy at sea. These international factors led to the reemergence of a circumstance where the revival of Nuremberg was again, almost 50 years later, a matter of "geopo-litical convenience."[32] It also generated a campaign to establish an interna-tional criminal court that has so far culminated in a draft treaty agreed upon in Rome last year.

Despite these developments, the idea of criminal accountability remains in my view subordinate to the realist orientation toward the practice of geopolitics. This subordination is especially manifest in the American reluct-ance to endorse the rather feeble proposal for an international criminal court agreed upon at Rome. It was also evident in relation to the American reluctance to support UN humanitarian peacekeeping efforts with a will and commitment of resources required for effectiveness, a pattern especially pronounced since the 1993 Somalia experience resulted in American casual-ties. This American reluctance was decisive in relation to the failure of the UN to provide timely protection to the Tutsi minority in Rwanda in 1994 when it was confronted by Hutu genocidal threats, and its efforts to block moves to protect refugees threatened by warfare in Zaire. Given the degree of American leadership in relation to UN peacekeeping, this reluctance reinforced the view that realist geopolitics was still in command of the policymaking process, and that recourse to Nuremberg would remain confined to situations in which it was geopolitically convenient for leading states. Such a reassessment is bolstered by consideration of American policy toward Iraq and its behavior generally in the Gulf region where major strategic concerns (including nonproliferation, oil reserves, containment of political Islam, and security for Israel) are clearly at issue. In the Gulf context, there is no reluctance to have recourse to high magnitudes of destructive force, although the objectives and approach also express the overriding effort to avoid American casualties.[33]

The geopolitical convenience that led to the Nuremberg trials was in the setting of defeat and occupation of the country whose individuals were being accused of criminality. It also involved relying on important documentary archives that had been developed by the Nazi regime, and functioned as an invaluable source of evidence for the prosecution, particularly as contained so many admissions against interest. This setting was not available for Bosnia, and not entirely in relation to Rwanda. As a result, it has been difficult to obtain custody over the most prominent perpetrators of criminality in the former Yugoslavia, with two of the prime suspected culprits remaining not only unindicted, but retaining positions of formal authority (that is, Slobadan Milosevic and Tudjman).[34] Also at large are the main architects of ethnic cleansing in Bosnia, Karadsic, and Mladic. Although the momentum in support of the Hague Tribunal has led to more impressive results than seemed likely at the outset, there is still present the impact of geopolitical concerns that go *against* holding the maximum leaders responsible for what they have done. Part of the geopolitical pressure is to stabilize the internal situation in Bosnia and elsewhere in former Yugoslavia so that the transition to "peace" can proceed, thereby making viable the Dayton Agreement. It is in this sense that widening the arc of personal responsibility to encompass the top Serb leaders allegedly might provoke a Serbian backlash that could either lead to a resumption of the war or, at the very least, prompt terrorist attacks on the NATO presence. The other geopolitical pressure involved the incentive to work with Milosevic and Tudjman so as to produce and sustain a diplomatic settlement. A further geopolitical pressure that has emerged subsequently to Dayton concerns the western response to claims for self-determination in the form of independent statehood for Kosovo. European and American diplomatic initiatives have proceeded on the dubious assumption that the Kosovar case for self-determination should be legally, politically, and morally rejected in favor of support for an autonomy arrangement.[35]

In summary, it can be concluded that the Nuremberg idea remains alive on an *intergovernmental* level, but that its enactment is highly selective, and depends upon an international context that supports implementation due to the balance of geopolitical considerations at stake. Whether this pattern of implementation can be made less selective will be determined by two sets of other considerations: the degree to which the endorsement of the Nuremberg idea by transnational civil society can mount a successful challenge to the influence of geopolitical realists in the shaping of governmental policy, particularly in the United States; and the extent to which the application of international standards relating to the punishment of those accused of crimes of state can be addressed by judicial bodies internal to the state.

III   The Relevance of Global Civil Society[36]

Little of the vast corpus of literature on Nuremberg gives attention to the role of civil society as an agency of implementation, and yet it is primarily through the efforts of individuals and small groups that Nuremberg persisted as a challenge to political elites in the decades since 1946. Of course, the potency of these civic initiatives is greatly enhanced in settings where the political elite finds itself divided, as was the case in the United States in the latter stages of the Vietnam War and, less dramatically, with respect to forming a response to the terrible ordeal of Bosnia in the period 1992–5. At some point, the energies of civil society are sufficient to alter the international climate in a manner that places geopolitical realism on the defensive, or isolates its adherents. Arguably, this has happened to a limited extent with respect to antipersonnel land mines, the status under international law of nuclear weapons, and the institutionalization of criminal accountability.[37] Transnational civic forces have been able to mobilize widespread grassroots support and media interest, and have enlisted many governments in the effort that shaped their policy on a basis that is less responsive to geopolitical realism, and more in line with legal/moral factors, and a genuine commitment of global humane governance as a long-term goal. In each instance, the United States as undisputed geopolitical leader has been able to block serious implementation and cast a shadow over these projects, at least for the present.

It seems most important to acknowledge the unexpected, yet vital, role that civil society has played in keeping the Nuremberg idea alive during the cold war era. The two substantive concerns that contributed most explicitly to this process were opposition within the United States to the Vietnam War and concerns within Europe and the US with respect to nuclear weaponry. Also, closely related was the surprising emergence of human rights as an active dimension of public policy debate and as an instrument of foreign policy.[38] It becomes more evident that if governments assume the legal responsibility for upholding international standards with respect to human rights, then it is less of a leap to expect adherence to the Nuremberg Principles, especially as Crimes Against Humanity overlaps to a considerable extent with the imperatives of human rights. Put differently, by accepting limited international accountability for severe violations of human rights, states have themselves already compromised their claims to be "sovereign."

The contributions of civil society are too numerous and scattered to be recited comprehensively here even if the focus is limited to the Nuremberg idea. What can be mentioned in a summary form is the degree to which anti-Vietnam and antinuclear protesters who broke "the law" consistently relied on the Nuremberg argument to uphold their claims of legal innocence in domestic courts. Such claims were bolstered by international law specialists who testified as expert witnesses, essentially arguing that it was reasonable for individuals to believe that the war in Vietnam was a Crime Against Peace in the Nuremberg sense and violated the anti-aggression norm in the UN Charter.[39] Similar lines of legal defense were put forward in antinuclear settings, alleging either that nuclear weapons were intrinsically illegal, mounting a threat that if carried out would be necessarily a Crime Against Humanity even if in self-defense, or that particular weapons systems or doctrines of use were illegal (for example, neutron bomb, Trident submarines, cruise missiles, first-strike).

Some dramatic instances can be mentioned. Daniel and Philip Berrigan both defended their recourse to nonviolent resistance by an appeal to Nuremberg (and to religious authority), as did James Douglass.[40] Their activities covered a range of resistance moves, such as burning and pouring blood on draft cards of young Americans, entering nuclear weapons facilities and damaging warheads, trespassing to prevent trains from carrying nuclear warheads to submarine bases. Another prominent instance of a civic initiative occurred when Daniel Ellsberg explained that his decision to release The Pentagon Papers (that contained a vast repository of internal, classified documents under Pentagon control) was based on a reading of the Nuremberg Judgment, and on his belief that when the American people were exposed to the truth about how Vietnam War policy had been made, they would rise up to reject the war itself. As with Taylor, Ellsberg's expectations were too optimistic, underestimating the degree to which the American citizenry entrusts its fate in foreign policy to its elected leaders and bureaucratic appointees, and it not seriously committed to legality and morality beyond territorial limits. In other words, such initiatives overlook the extent to which the political identity of civil society is itself predominantly concerned with prospects of winning and losing, and the strategic stakes of conflict relative to the costs. Nevertheless, the appeal to Nuremberg was important in challenging war policy, if only to ground the actions of opponents on a basis believed to be legally and morally grounded, and in keeping the Nuremberg flame at least as a flicker.

With the cold war over and the resurfacing of Nuremberg on the intergovernmental level with a measure of geopolitical support, the transnational effort moved in a different direction. It formed a campaign to pressure governments to support the establishment of an international criminal court that could operate as an internal element in any viable scheme for global governance. This lobbying campaign was waged both at the level of grassroots opinion, but mainly in relation to the official policy of governments, resulting in a quite formidable coalition between a large number of governments and representatives of global civil society.

IV   The Transition to Democracy Problem and the Pinochet Incident

The collapse of militarist rule in the Southern Cone countries of Latin America revived the Nuremberg ethos in a series of distinct political settings that shared the need to solve "the transition to democracy problem" within the confines of state/society relations.[41] In essence, the problem was one of negotiating the voluntary renunciation of power by a previous authoritarian political leadership. Such a negotiation was complicated and influenced by the extent to which the oppressive elite retained great influence in the security sectors of the state bureaucracy, namely, the military, police, and intelligence sectors. It was also complicated by the anger and resentment in civil society, which in large part regarded these former leaders as responsible for unforgivable crimes against the people. Even before power was relinquished, there was speculation that militarist rule persisted longer than otherwise because "the ghosts of Nuremberg" were lurking in the background, inhibiting beneficial political changes out of fear of exposure to criminal prosecution in relation to policies pursued during the period of governmental tenure.[42]

On the one side, the memory of Nuremberg served to reinforce claims in civil society for justice and the rectification and documentation of past evils, especially among those who had been directly affected and their political allies. There was a need to have some sort of closure in relation to the past, particularly for families that had experienced the loss of a close relative due to "disappearance" or through torture and execution. On the other side, was the strong political will to negotiate a peaceful and irreversible transition that would emancipate a country from its prior reign of terror, and succeed in restoring constitutional moderation and successful economic development. Such a process required some meeting of the minds between the old and new leadership, compromises on both sides, and was carried on subject to the scrutiny of global society.

This process produced what has been derisively called "the culture of impunity," as it restricted greatly the option of indicting and prosecuting individuals placed high in the former government, that is, it effectively granted immunity to individuals who were comparable to the defendants at Nuremberg (and Tokyo). Part of the wider compromise was to establish an array of truth and reconciliation commissions at the level of the state that took on the job of documenting the crimes of the past, providing an accounting for past wrongs, but detached its findings from any application of the ethos of individual responsibility. The degree of success achieved by these commissions varied from country to country, and depended on how they were perceived by the citizenry in relation to their stated objectives of "truth" and "reconciliation." It remains a matter of controversy as to whether the bargains struck were reasonable under the circumstances, or even more, the best result that could be achieved in circumstances where the oppressive elite has not surrendered, but voluntarily gives up political power, thereby avoiding a longer period of abuse for the population and achieving a nonviolent transition to constitutional democracy.

The dramatic detention of Augusto Pinochet in Britain in the Fall of 1998 brought this issue before the court of world opinion in a vivid manner, thereby bringing to the surface the contradictory priorities at stake, including the usual exclusion of external sources of authority from the decision-making process on these matters. Pinochet was detained in response to a request for extradition from a Spanish criminal court that was prepared to hear evidence against him relating to Crimes Against Humanity (rape, torture, disappearances, massacres, murders) in which Spanish nationals had been the victim. The issue now resolved in Britain had been treated in the media as mainly posing the legal issue of whether diplomatic immunity should be given to Pinochet because he was head of state during the period when the alleged crimes were committed.

In my view, the more fundamental issue at state is whether the immunity arrangement negotiated in Chile with Pinochet, while he was still dictator, should be respected at an *international* level under circumstances where the democratic government in Chile that reached the agreement requests his release and return to Chile. The encounter can be understood as between the implementation of universal standards and the encouragement and maintenance of past and future peaceful transitions to democracy. How should this encounter be resolved? By deference to the Government of Chile that currently represents the Chilean people, and presumably weighs the pro and contra arguments on the basis of its assessment of well-being in Chile (an assessment itself controversial within the country)? Or, in a judicial arena external to Chile, should the dominant consideration become the maximum possible implementation of international law enforcement, putting aside claims that holding Pinochet accountable before a Spanish court of law would hurt diplomatic relations between Chile and Spain, and Chile and Britain, as well as threaten the sustainability, or at least the serenity, of the transition of democracy in Chile.[43]

It is a dilemma with no obvious answers. Jurisprudentially, it seems most flexibly handled by a contextual approach. Account needs to be taken of whether the government objecting to extradition is a democratic political entity, of the nature of the agreement that it reached with the military regime, of the severity of the crimes committed, of the degree to which a fair trial could be anticipated in the country requesting extradition, and many other considerations. Diplomatic immunity, however, does not seem relevant if the Nuremberg Principles are treated as expressive of positive international law at this point, which should be the case.[44] The difficulty arises in balancing the desirability of prosecuting someone accused of unforgivable crimes of great number against the importance of not disrupting the fragile transition process underway in the very society that has collectively suffered from a pattern of criminality.

Also in the picture is the highly speculative impact of the outcome on either deterring future crimes of state by punishing perpetrators wherever and whenever caught or, to the contrary, on deterring dictators from giving up their power without a violent struggle since an immunity bargain is not binding beyond the borders of the country where it is struck. Without any clear empirical guidelines, the best approach would seem to support a presumption of extradictability and subsequent criminal jurisdiction that could only be overcome by a convincing showing that the implementation of international law would constitute a "clear and present danger" for the country of the objecting government. What seems clear is that Pinochet has no valid personal claim of immunity or exemption from prosecution, regardless of the bargain struck earlier within Chile.

Whatever our thoughts now on the Pinochet incident, it has been a momentous event in the struggle to extend the Nuremberg Idea. It has given unprecedented salience to the question of the international accountability of a head of state for Crimes Against Humanity. It has suggested a possible major role for domestic courts in extending the reach of the

Nuremberg Principles. And it has added to the momentum in civil society to press forward with its campaign to establish an international criminal court along the lines agreed upon in Rome.

V Conclusion

The legacy of Nuremberg remains complex and controversial, but the 1990s saw the revival of a serious effort on several fronts to push forward with the central effort to hold perpetrators of crimes of state individually accountable. In this respect, also, Telford Taylor's underlying commitment to treat the Nuremberg Judgment as the foundation for future accountability seems somewhat closer to realization than during the cold war, but with still a long path ahead littered with obstacles. One of the most formidable of these obstacles is the reluctance of major states, especially the United States and China, to participate in this process if it includes the risk that their leaders might stand accused at some future point, as would be the case if an international criminal court, freed from the constraints of Security Council vetoes, were allowed to come into existence. International experience to date suggests that an international tribunal of the Nuremberg type will only be brought into being if it is geopolitically convenient for the governments of the leading states, an observation that casts some shadows across the current efforts at The Hague and in Arusha.

There is also the possibility of empowering domestic courts to hear charges against those accused of crimes of state. Israel initiated this possibility when it abducted Adolph Eichmann in Argentina, and put him on trial in Israel for crimes committed before the country existed and outside its territory.[45] In such circumstances, vividly evident in relation to the 1999 Turkish capture in Kenya of PKK leader, Abdulla Ocalan, there is a serious concern as to whether minimal conditions of fairness to an accused defendant can be met in the inflamed setting that prevails. As with piracy, there exists universal jurisdiction for such crimes of state, and a large potential implementation and enforcement role for domestic courts around the world. The Pinochet incident and Ocalan seizure underscores these possibilities, but also the difficulties, especially when prosecution proceeds in the face of an earlier negotiated bargain that gave perpetrators a promise of immunity from prosecution in exchange for letting go of the reins of power, or involves overseas abduction and prosecution of a revolutionary leader at war with the prosecuting state. Whether such a bargain is entitled to extraterritorial application is one question that remains unresolved at this point, as does the related question of the legal status of extraterritorial paramilitary seizure and trial.

It seems evident that individual accountability for crimes of state is an integral part of any adequate conception of a *just* world order.[46] But it seems equally evident that the realist gatekeepers of the international legal order will not accept comprehensive legal and moral restraints on the exercise of force as an instrument of foreign policy.[47] In this regard, Taylor's notion that America made "a tragic mistake" in Vietnam by contradicting the standards it had established at Nuremberg missed the central point that American leadership was never prepared to accept such a framework of restraint as seriously applicable to *its* future diplomacy. In fact, the country was all along mainly led by realists in the Machiavellian tradition that believed that the security interests of the state were paramount, especially in light of "the lessons of Munich," and found discussions of limits imposed by international law diversionary unless used as propaganda tools for castigating enemies or rationalizing contested moves in foreign policy.

The prospects for subordinating geopolitics to an ethos of individual responsibility subject to third-party implementation in a court of law remain remote at this point. To bring Taylor's bright hopes for the legacy of Nuremberg to fruition will depend on a major push from transnational civil society. Pinochet's detention and Ocalan's seizure suggest that this matter of accountability is "a hot issue" for many persons around the world, as does the ongoing campaign to bring the international criminal court into being. But the resistance to genuine judicial independence for this subject-matter is likely to be insurmountable in the near future. At least the struggle is underway, and rooted in the core aspirations of global civil society. It is a confusing, controversial struggle, polarizing support and opposition in relation to dramatic contexts of policy choice on both state and global levels of decision. At present, imposing account-ability on leaders depends on geopolitical convenience and the physical control over the accused. As a result, the pattern of implementation is selective, and strikes many as arbitrary. Such a circumstance is likely to persist so long as political life is shaped by nonaccountable geopolitical forces.

Notes

1   Telford Taylor, *Nuremberg and Vietnam: An American Tragedy* (Chicago: Quad-rangle, 1970), pp. 13–14.

2 With a certain irony, it is Taylor himself who gave us the most compelling historical account. See his *The Anatomy of the Nuremberg Trials* (New York: Knopf, 1970) (hereinafter referred to as *The Anatomy*); but there is, as well, an enormous secondary literature. One useful overview is Joseph E. Conot, *Justice at Nuremberg* (New York: Harper & Row, 1975).

3 For diverse perspectives and background see Roger S. Clark and Madeleine Swain, eds., *The Prosecution of International Crimes: A Critical Study of the International Tribunal for the Former Yugoslavia* (New Brunswick, NJ: Transaction, 1996); see also conference proceedings "War Crimes Tribunals: the Record and the Prospects," *American University International Law Review* 13: i–xi, 1383–1584 (1998).

4 For a useful assessment of the Rome Conference, and the controversial aspects of the proposed treaty see Leila Sadat Wexler, "The Establishment of the International Criminal Court: From The Hague to Rome and Back Again," Washington University School of Law, Working Paper No. 99-01-1, 1–36, Jan. 1999.

5 E.g. see review of *The Anatomy* by Istvan Deak, "Misjudgment at Nuremberg," *New York Review of Books*, Oct. 7, 1993, 46–53; Eugene Davidson, *The Trial of the Germans* (New York: Macmillan, 1967); also, H. Bull, "The Grotian Tradition," in *Diplomatic Investigations: Essays in the Theory of International Politics* (1966), pp. 51–73.

6 Among recent prominent instances one thinks immediately of Fukuyama's claims set forth under the rubric "The End of History" and Huntington's strident anticipation of "a clash of civilizations." Both perspectives concern the effort by the West to shape the future in its image, and by force if necessary. Francis Fukuyama, *The End of History and the Last Man* (New York: Simon & Schuster, 1996). For an excellent overall assessment of Fukuyama and Huntington, as well as other scholarly projections of western ideas about the world see Jacinta O'Hagan, "Conceptions of the West in International Relations Thought: From Oswald Spengler to Edward Said," a dissertation for Ph.D. degree at Australia National University, July 1998.

7 On the decline of the state see Joseph A. Camilleri and Jim Falk, *The End of Sovereignty? The Politics of a Shrinking and Fragmenting World* (Hants: Edward Elgar, 1992); Kenichi Ohmae, *The End of the Nation State: The Rise of Regional Economies* (New York: Free Press, 1995). See also the array of accounts in a stimulating collection of essays. Karen T. Litfin, ed., *The Greening of Sovereignty in World Politics* (Cambridge, MA: MIT Press, 1998).

8 See Report of the Commission on Global Governance, *Our Global Neighborhood* (New York: Oxford, 1995); Daniele Archibugi and David Held, eds., *Cosmopolitan Democracy* (Cambridge: Polity, 1995); on the wider consequences for international relations see James N. Rosenau, *Global Politics in a Turbulent World* (Princeton, NJ: Princeton University Press, 1990); on the sharply contested implications for citizenship and political identity see Martha Nussbaum et al., *For Love of Country* (Boston: Beacon, 1998).

9   For a world order perspective on this changing reality see Richard Falk, *Law in an Emerging Global Village* (Ardsley, NY: Transnational, 1998), and below in section I.

10 For this ambivalence see statement by Ambassador David Sheffer, the main government official representing the US Government, on these matters at the American University conference. See note 3, 1389–1400, and comments in response by M. Cherif Bassiouni, 1400–1406, and Tina Rosenberg, 1406–1410.

11 The subtitle of Taylor's book is a reference to the tension between what was decided at Nuremberg and what was being done in Vietnam.

12 See also the assessment of Nuremberg along similar lines by a famous philosopher, but from the perspective of its legitimacy for German society. Karl Jaspers, *The Question of German War Guilt* (Westport, CT: Greenwood, E.B. Ashton, trans., 1978); also Jaspers, *The Future of Mankind* (Chicago: University of Chicago Press, E. B. Ashton, trans., 1958).

13 See Thomas J. Knock, *To End All Wars: Woodrow Wilson and the Quest for a New World Order* (New York: Oxford, 1992).

14 It is helpful to recall that the Tokyo Tribunal was constituted on a broader basis than Nuremberg, and produced a far wider range of views on the fundamental issues of priority. The most vigorous dissent was written by an Indian judge, R. B. Pal, who sees the whole of the Second World War from an interpretative perspective located in the South, and refuses to exempt the behavior of the victorious powers from critical scrutiny, including their role in pushing Japan toward "aggression" and expansionism. For partial text of Justice Pal's dissenting judgment see *II The Law of War: A Documentary History* (New York: Random House, 2 vols., 1972), pp. 1159–83.

15 The Nuremberg condemnation of aggressive war was only one aspect of the effort by international law to impose strict limits on the right of states to use force. For generally skeptical assessments of this undertaking see Anthony Clark Arend and Robert J. Beck, *International Law and the Use of Force* (New York: Routledge, 1993); A. Mark Weisburd, *Use of Force: The Practice of States Since World War II* (University Park, PA: Pennsylvania State University Press, 1997).

16 Realism is also dominant, and divergent, in academic circles. For useful surveys see Robert O. Keohane, ed., *NeoRealism and Its Critics* (New York: Columbia University Press, 1986); Michael Joseph Smith, *Realist Thought from Weber to Kissinger* (Baton Rouge, LA: LSU Press, 1986).

17 See George F. Kennan, *On Dealing with the Communist World* (New York: Harper & Row, 1964); Kennan, *Democracy and the Student Left* (1968); Hans Morgenthau, *A New Foreign Policy for the United States* (New York: Praeger, 1969).

18 Bull develops such a position in Bull, "The Grotian Conception of International Society," in Herbert Butterfield and Martin Wight, eds., *Diplomatic*

Investigations (Cambridge, MA: Harvard University Press, 1966), pp. 51–73; also Hedley Bull, *The Anarchical Society: A Study of Order in World Politics* (New York: Columbia University Press, 1977).

19 The emerging right to democratic governance has been given prominence by Professor Franck. See Franck, "The Emerging Right to Democratic Governance," *American Journal of International Law* 86: 63 (1992); on the subversive tendency of human rights norms see Falk, "The Quest for Human Rights in an Era of Globalization," in Michael G. Schechter, ed., *Future Multilateralism: The Political and Social Framework* (London and New York: Macmillan Press Ltd. and St. Martin's Press, Inc., 1999), pp. 153–78.

20 T. Taylor, *The Anatomy of the Nuremberg Trials*, p. 121.

21 See Falk, "The Extension of Law to Foreign Policy: The Next Constitutional Challenge," in Alan S. Rosenbaum, ed., *Constitutionalism: The Philosophical Dimension* (Westport, CT: Greenwood Press, 1988), pp. 205–21.

22 It is also true that during the cold war when the Security Council was generally gridlocked, and attention shifted to the General Assembly, that attacks were made on the legitimacy of its recommendations because a coalition of states representing only a small percentage of the world's population or of annual dues paid to the UN, could must a voting majority.

23 Such inequality has also been criticized for its failure to give sufficient weight to the views of economically disadvantaged states. Divergent views as to the *appropriate* criteria of inequality have so far prevented the selection of additional permanent members of the Security Council despite the widespread acknowledgment that was done in 1945 needs to take account of immense changes in world order, especially reflecting the impact of decolonization and globalization.

24 Bull has most influentially theorized this role in *The Anarchical Society*, n. 18.

25 On pre-Nuremberg antecedents see especially *The Anatomy*, pp. 14–20.

26 It is notable that each of the four victorious powers that sat in judgment at Nuremberg subsequently embraced policies and practices that appear to be in flagrant violation of the Nuremberg Principles. As a result there is "a British tragedy," "a French tragedy," and "a Soviet tragedy," as well as an American tragedy.

27 See Jonathan Schell, *The Fate of the Earth* (New York: Knopf, 1982) and Schell, *The Gift of Time: The Case for Abolishing Nuclear Weapons Now* (New York: Henry Holt, 1998).

28 For varying views see Thomas M. Franck, "Who Killed Article 2(4) or: Changing Norms Governing the Use of Force by States," *American Journal of International Law* 64: 809 (1970); W. Michael Reisman, "Criteria for the Lawful Use of Force in International Law," *Yale Journal of International Law* 10: 279 (1985); Oscar Schachter, "The Lawful Resort to Unilateral Use of Force," *Yale Journal of International Law* 10: 291 (1985); Oscar Schachter, "The Right of States to Use Armed Force," *Michigan Law Review* 82: 1620 (1984);

see generally Myres S. McDougal and Florentino P. Feliciano, *Law and Minimum World Public Order* (New Haven, CT: Yale University Press, 1962); A. Mark Weisburd, see note 15.

29 See *Nuremberg and Vietnam*, pp. 122–53.

30 For representative works see George F. Kennan, *The Cloud of Danger: Current Realities of American Foreign Policy* (Boston: Atlantic-Little Brown, 1977) and Kennan, *Democracy and the Student Left* (Boston: Atlantic-Little Brown, 1968); Hans J. Morgenthau, see note 17; George Ball, *Past Has Another Pattern: Memoirs* (New York: Norton, 1982), esp. pp. 360–423.

31 Also in the background was the so-called "transition to democracy" problem affecting a series of important states in Latin America, as well as those in East Europe and South Africa. For representative writing see Neil J. Kritz, ed., *Transitional Justice: How Emerging Democracies Reckon with Former Regimes* (Herndon, VA: US Institute of Peace, 3 vols., 1995); Naomi Roht-Arriaza, ed., *Impunity and Human Rights in International Law and Practice* (New York: Oxford, 1995). See also discussion in section IV.

32 See literature on the establishment of the Hague Tribunal. Useful is "Prosecuting War Criminals in the Former Yugoslavia," Report of Lawyers Committee for Human Rights, May 1995, 80 pp.; "A Critical Study of the International Tribunal for Former Yugoslavia," *Criminal Law Reform* 5: 223 (1994).

33 Comprehensive sanctions, of the sort applied against such countries as Iraq and Cuba need to be subsumed under the category of force directed at civilian society. The result of such a combination of considerations is lethal destructiveness so far as the adversary is concerned, but with virtually no human risks, a one-sidedness of outcomes that raises its own problems of morality and law. When military force is used in such a one-sided way, the structure of violence resembles torture, as the torturer decides how to inflict pain in controlled conditions in which the victim is helpless to retaliate or even to defend. For profound reflections on the role of violence in different settings see Elaine Scarry, *The Body in Pain: The Making and Unmaking of the World* (New York: Oxford, 1985); also John Keane, *Reflections on Violence* (London: Verso, 1996).

34 See criticism of Hague in comparison to Nuremberg along these lines in Deak, *The Anatomy*, p. 46.

35 The assumption as of 1999 is dubious given the uncontested, overwhelming wish of the people in Kosovar for secession, and the record of brutal Serbian oppressive rule over a long period.

36 On the terminology see Falk, "Global Civil Society: Perspectives, Initiatives, Movements," *Oxford Development Studies* 26 (1998): 99.

37 See generally, Falk, "The Nuclear Weapons Advisory Opinion and the New Jurisprudence of Global Civil Society," *Transnational Law and Contemporary Society* 7 (1997): 333.

38 For discussion on this, see Falk, "A Half Century of Human Rights," *Australian Journal of International Affairs* 52 (1998): 255 (1998).

39   See Francis Boyle for the most sustained argument from a legal perspective in this direction. Boyle, *Defending Civil Resistance Under International Law* (Dobbs Ferry, NY: Transnational, 1987).

40   Daniel Berrigan, *The Trial of the Catonsville Nine* (1972); Francine du Plessix, *Divine Disobedience* (New York: Knopf, 1970); James Douglass, *The Nonviolent Coming of God* (Maryknoll, NY: Orbis, 1991).

41   Subsequently, comparable problems have surfaced in many other regions, including other parts of Latin America, Africa, Eastern Europe and the former Soviet Union, and parts of Asia.

42   The phrase is that of Jacopo Timmerman, Argentinian journalist and human rights activist, while living in exile during a conversation in Princeton in the late 1970s.

43   For supportive view of extradition see Peter Kornbluh, "Prisoner Pinochet: The Dictator and the Quest for Justice," *The Nation*, Dec. 21, 1998, 11–24; Grahame Russell, "Pinochet and the Law," *Third World Network Features*, undated, #1838/98, 4 pp.; for a more skeptical view of prosecution see editorial "Pinochet's Paradox," *Wall Street Journal*, Dec. 9, 1998, A22 and George Melloan, "Pinochet, Ocalan, and the Hypocrisy of the Left," Dec. 1, 1998.

44   For the text of Nuremberg Principles see Burns H. Weston et al., *Supplement of Basic Documents to International Law and World Order* (St. Paul, MN: West, 3rd edn., 1997), 193–200.

45   For important assessment see Hannah Arendt, *Eichmann in Jerusalem: A Report on the Banality of Evil* (New York: Viking, 1963).

46   See Falk, "The Pursuit of International Justice: An Imagined Future and Present Dilemmas," *Journal of International Affairs*, forthcoming.

47   There is an encouraging official disposition to confine recourse to force to military targets, but such disposition seems eroded by the indiscriminate nature with which sanctions are used even in the face of sustained and massive suffering and death for the civilian population, as has occurred in Iraq since the ceasefire in 1991.

Afterword to Part Two

Unlike the first half of the twentieth century, which was marked by international violence in two World Wars, the most dreadful conflicts in the later part of the century were characterized by excessively bloody interethnic slaughter. Such was the case in the former Soviet Union, the Balkans, Indonesia, central Africa, and elsewhere. The most horrendous aspect of these conflicts has been *atrocities*. And consequently, we face the issue of what to do with the alleged perpetrators of these atrocities.

From Michael Slote we learn that virtue ethics offers some new ways to conceive the ethics of war crimes. Aristotelian virtue ethics would focus on desert, but the more motive-centered or "agent-based" virtue ethics that one can develop out of Nietzsche's philosophy and out of the moral sentimentalism of Hutcheson and Hume has distinctive things to say about what we should do about war crimes. Moral sentimentalism stresses warm and humane motives like benevolence and compassion, and a philosophy of justice calls for the prosecution of war crimes only if doing so will express a concern for a nation's good (or the good of the community of nations). Still, some people in a nation that has suffered war crimes will be unforgiving, and their feelings cannot be left out of account by those who wish to do what is best on the whole, to heal a given nation and allow it to flourish into the future. Nietzsche's stress on power and strength also lends itself to a virtue ethical account of the ethics of war crimes. If the magnanimous person shows strength, then there may be reason not to punish certain crimes. But where the failure to punish threatens the ability of a society to heal its wounds and prosper, concern for the public good à la moral sentimentalism may in virtue ethical terms take precedence over the magnanimity and strength.

Where trials for war crimes may be in order, what is the morally appropriate way of conducting them? Such trials can, in principle, be held in an *ad hoc* international tribunal for the crimes committed, in a permanent international tribunal for the war crimes, or within the legal system of the country whose citizens have committed the crimes. Burleigh Wilkins brings forward the ethical and the legal reasons in favor of the third option. The following two reasons are primary: (1) using the legal system of the offending country, the autonomy of the sovereign state is observed, and this has both practical as well as moral significance; (2) the need for reconciliation between warring parties demands that members of the conflicted groups themselves face their own past. The implementation of justice from the international tribunals makes it very hard, if not impossible, for the citizens of such a country to appreciate some tribunal decisions.

Anthony Ellis, for his part, defends war crimes trials against the charge that, being so selective, they violate the requirements of equal treatment before the law. The central function of a criminal court is to decide upon guilt and punishment. It is justifiable to punish war criminals, according to Ellis, in order to remove them from circulation and give some deterrence to other, potential war criminals. Admittedly, war crimes trials can make little contribution toward reconciliation between warring parties; but that is not their central function, any more than it is the central function of criminal courts in municipal law to reconcile the offender and his victim. The legitimate aims of war crimes trials, Ellis contends, would be best served if they were conducted by an international criminal court.

Richard Falk, in his article, seeks to revisit the ideas contained in the Nuremberg Judgment of 1945 in light of intervening developments in international society. At Nuremberg, the victorious states in the Second Word War had promised that in the future the principles of individual criminal accountability would be applied to all countries, and not just reserved for the surviving leaders of defeated states. The intervening international experience supports the view that this promise has been broken, casting doubt on war crimes prosecutions. It is possible that the movement to establish a permanent criminal tribunal, which produced the Rome Treaty in 1998, will restore the Nuremberg Idea by establishing a tribunal with authority to prosecute individuals from any state in the event of indictment, but it is too soon to tell whether such an initiative can succeed, given the geopolitical realities of political power in the world.

Views presented here show that the values of peace and justice often seem irreconcilable in concrete cases, and much attention to details of specific circumstance and care at every step are needed for a desirable outcome. The approaches adopted in these essays have different ethical theories as their guiding principles: virtue-theory (Slote), utilitarianism (Ellis), a sort of humanistic pragmatism or realism (Falk), common-sense or almost Kantian theory (Wilkins). The complexities of a difficult balancing act are well explored in these articles and they offer much material for further consideration.

Further Reading to Part Two

Charles Beitz, *Political Theory and International Relations* (1979).
—— et al. (eds.), *International Ethics* (1985).
Donnelly, "Human Rights, Humanitarian Intervention and American Foreign Policy. Law, Morality and Politics" *Journal of International Affairs*, vol. 302 (1984).
Gerald Doppelt, "Statism without Foundations," *Philosophy & Public Affairs* 9 (1980).
Gerald Elfstrom, "On Dilemmas of Intervention," *Ethics* 93 (1983).
——, *Ethics in International Relations: A Constitutive Theory* (1996).
Mervyn Frost, *Towards a Normative Theory of International Relations* (1986).
David Luban, "The Romance of the Nation-State," *Philosophy & Public Affairs* 9 (1980).
Thomas Pogge, "Cosmopolitanism and Sovereignty" *Ethics* 103 (1992).
W. Michael Reisman, "Sovereignty and Human Rights in Contemporary International Law," *American Journal of International Law* 84 (1990).
Michael Walzer, "The Moral Standing of State," *Philosophy & Public Affairs* 9 (1978–9).
Christopher Wellman, "Secession," *Philosophy & Public Affairs* 24 (1995).

Part Three

Nationalism and Collective Wrongdoing

8

Nationalist Morality and Crimes Against Humanity

Richard W. Miller

The atrocities of ethnic cleansing in the former Yugoslavia might seem to reveal the moral absurdity of nationalism, showing that nationalists lack an adequate basis for condemning acts that any morally decent person must condemn. After all, ethnic cleansing is a plausible means of pursuing standard nationalist goals. If I want the government that dominates my life to celebrate and perpetuate the practices and historical outlook of my nationality and to treat fellow-nationals as specially worthy of concern, then the presence of large numbers of outsiders is an obstacle. As voters, they are apt to interfere with the use of government to cultivate my group's distinctive practices. (To illustrate this from the standpoint of just one of the many nationalisms whose moral integrity is at issue: Muslims and Croats will hardly want the Serbian Orthodox Church to have a unique, officially sanctioned status in politics and education.) The public expression of the outsiders' distinctive practices makes my local public spaces less effective in expressing and perpetuating my nationality's common ties. (An Orthodox church makes a town square less Croatian.) Intermarriage makes it less likely that a proud and thriving national community will sustain my nationality for centuries to come. So the presence of large numbers of outsiders threatens these familiar nationalist goals. And outsiders whose families have dwelled among us for centuries are not apt to leave voluntarily. Terror may be needed to remove these obstacles – terror which, for most Americans, is epitomized in the massacre of Muslims by Serbian nationalists at Srebrenica, but which was inflicted just as cruelly on Serbs and Croats who were obstacles to other nationalisms.

I believe that the claim that ethnic cleansing is a *reductio ad absurdum* of nationalism is half true. It is half false because there are nationalists whose commitment to their nationality is regulated by a universalist morality. In their view, some perspective of equal concern or respect for everyone everywhere is the sole and decisive basis, in the final analysis, for resolving questions of right and wrong. Any duty to advance the interests of one's nationality and any permission to do so in ways that hurt others must be derived from a perspective of universal regard in which there are no outsiders. One of my goals is to show how certain universalist moral foundations can sustain a version of nationalism – a version that will differ from many other nationalisms in its demands, strategies, and hopes, and that will prohibit ethnic cleansing decisively and nonarbitrarily.

However, the moral absurdity of ethnic cleansing does undermine another, more fundamental sort of nationalism. I have in mind a nationalism based not on a universalist foundation, but on a particularism which makes some principle of group loyalty part of the foundations of morality, denying that any perspective of equal concern or respect resolves all questions of right and wrong. Such a fundamentally nationalist morality might explicitly take the extreme position that no injury to outsiders, however grave, could be an overriding reason to oppose any measure that advances the interests of one's fellow-nationals or perpetuates their common culture. I have nothing useful to say about this appalling extreme: its self-conscious partisans will not regard ethnic cleansing as unacceptable. My target is the moral particularism of many humane nationalists, who introduce an independent principle of group loyalty into the foundations of morality and, then, try to tame the beast, limiting permissible harms to outsiders through appeals to other parts of the foundations, which require overriding concern for limited universal rights. After grounding certain nationalisms on universalist foundations, I hope to show that the beast of group loyalty cannot be tamed, once it is included in the foundations of morality. Making an exclusive group loyalty, which is relevant to nationalism, morally fundamental creates a dilemma for humane particularists: either allow group loyalty to override universal respect for all, making an absolute prohibition of ethnic cleansing arbitrary, or subordinate group loyalty so completely to universal respect that too little is left to constitute a plausible independent basis for moral duties.

If I am right, then reflection on recent crimes against humanity helps to resolve an intellectual conflict that has engulfed Anglo-American political philosophy. Starting around 1980, Charles Taylor and Alasdair MacIntyre began constructing a case for a morality in which group loyalty, independent of universalist principles, plays a fundamental role, capable of sustaining nationalist commitments. Theirs were lonely voices at the time, but they have now been joined by many others, including David Miller, whose arguments about social justice within a nation-state have often allied him with liberal universalists, and Michael Walzer, who eloquently supports multicultural tolerance in his own American setting. Even Ronald Dworkin, whose rights-based liberalism had earlier seemed profoundly individualist, has resourcefully defended the independence of certain communal obligations from duties of justice, fairness, or concern that might hold among strangers. Far from expressing callousness toward outsiders, the critique of universalism has often been part of an effort to do justice to the claims of other people's nationalisms; indeed, some of the richest critiques are an effort by the Anglophone Canadian, Charles Taylor, to do justice to the pursuit of Francophone cultural survival in Quebec. In aspiration, this philosophical movement is light years away from acceptance of ethnic cleansing as a legitimate policy. Since rejection of such atrocities is a fixed point in the moral universe of the leaders of this trend, I hope that my argument will contribute to its decline.[1]

I The Indictment

Here is the indictment of nationalism for licensing ethnic cleansing. Like most perfectly adequate indictments, it relies on some controversial claims that the defense might reasonably challenge. It will take plenty of further arguments by the prosecution to show that these rebuttals do not work unless they ground nationalist endeavors on a universalist morality.

Nationalists (the indictment begins) regard the promotion of national community as a great political goal, capable of justifying the bloodshed of nationalist insurrection and the day-to-day exercise of state-sanctioned coercion by officials of a nationalist state. So a nationalist cannot, in all consistency, condemn ethnic cleansing just because it uses deadly force, on a large scale, to advance nationalist goals. Rather, atrocities of ethnic cleansing would have to be ruled out on the ground that their violence is directed at relevantly innocent people or at relevantly innocent aspects of their lives. But nationalist goals deprive the victims of ethnic cleansing of relevant innocence. To see why, consider the larger projects of Bosnian Muslim civilians massacred at Srebrenica (and, *mutatis mutandis*, Serbs massacred at Gospic and Croats at Vukovar.) Of course, at the time of the massacre, they were doing nothing that threatened Serbian nationalist goals. But the same can be said of a sleeping enemy soldier killed when a military base is bombarded. In the activities leading up to the massacre, most of the victims were engaged in a collective project of maintaining a continuing Muslim presence in the midst of the so-called "Serbian Republic." They were joined with many thousands of Bosnian Muslims in mutual aid directed at

maintaining a culturally visible presence over the long run, a project that
was an obstacle to Serbian nationalist goals. From a nationalist perspective,
their project of presence was a sufficiently aggressive enterprise, blocking
important political goals that are to be advanced, as needed, by coercive
means. Massacring some and terrifying the others may well have been the
only feasible counter-offensive. Perhaps commitment to goals implemented
through ethnic cleansing is still compatible with imposing some moral
limits, say, the sparing of young children, since the children had no opportunity to choose whether to join the project of persistent presence. Perhaps
ethnic cleansing by massacre must be avoided when ethnic cleansing by
mass deportation is feasible. Still, such limits fall far short of what moral
decency requires.

How can a humane nationalist respond to this indictment? Before sur-
veying the available defenses, I must say something about much disputed
questions of definition, the meaning of "nationality" and "nationalism."
The following definition of ties of nationality seems to capture the commonalities to which nationalisms are addressed. Fellow-members of a
nationality are people who share common cultural practices, practices
typically acquired in the course of early upbringing, taken to descend, in
this familial way, from people who once lived together, and much more
easily cultivated if the culture-sharers live together; finally, many of those
sharing in these practices must find it vitally important to cultivate them,
wishing that others would, as well, and take the sharing of these practices to
be a source of special obligations of mutual aid which they want other
sharers to acknowledge.[2]

What is nationalism, then? It is a politics of loyalty to a nationality. A
nationalist is someone who supports a political program directed at the
cultivation of the practices constituting her nationality or the special interests of those who share these practices, and who thinks that her fellow-
nationals ought (all else being equal) to join her in active support because
they are members of this nationality. By the cultivation of the national ways,
I mean their celebration, inculcation, and preservation for generations to
come, as vital ingredients in a thriving cultural and political life. Depending
on her circumstances and her larger morality, a nationalist might support
political means to these ends that are as mild as tax-supported community
centers or as harsh as ethnic cleansing. But it ought to be a matter of
definition that a nationalist thinks a state, which pursues her goals of
nationality as its special mission, should be realized if this is not too harmful,
that she thinks revolution could, in some circumstances, be an appropriate
means of achieving goals of nationality, and that she does not regard it as an

insuperable moral objection to these coercive endeavors that a significant number of people in the potential territory of the national state do not care about the crucial ties of nationality. A weaker commitment would not constitute a nationalist political attitude, as opposed to a mere strong inclination to hang out with some people rather than others.

II   Universalist Nationalism

Someone could embrace a political program of nationalism on universalist grounds. And such a nationalist could adequately respond to the indictment, given a universalist morality of the right kind.

The restriction to the right kind of universalism is extremely important. For example, the abuse of minorities is a very effective *reductio* of certain forms of utilitarianism, in which the increased enjoyments of many nationalist Croats could, in principle, outweigh the loss of future enjoyment of a few massacred Serbs. A universalist morality that excludes intolerable oppression of minorities while coping with the unavoidable conflicts of interest that make politics necessary must, I think, be based on an ultimate attitude of full and equal respect for all persons everywhere. According to this universalism, a choice is wrong just in case it is incompatible with any total set of rules such that the chooser could, rationally, express his or her full and equal respect for all persons in wanting everyone to live by those rules. I do not think this morality can be further specified in a single, reductive axiom, the individual terms of which require no moral judgment for their application. Rather, those who continue Kant's project of basing morality on respect for persons should also follow his practice (in spite of certain reductive illusions) and give substance to their morality through alternative general equivalent formulations, each of which includes some morally-loaded terms. I will appeal to three.

1   One avoids moral wrongness just in case one conforms to the least demanding rules by which one could express one's regarding everyone's life as equally valuable. (Note that I can regard people's lives as equally valuable without being equally concerned to help them. I am not willing to do as much for the girl who lives down the block as for my daughter, but I certainly regard her life as equally valuable.)
2   One avoids moral wrongness by conforming to a moral code under which everyone is fully, fairly committed to an ideal of universal harmony in which everyone fully enjoys the pursuit of goals with

which she intelligently identifies. (Of course, one can be fully, fairly
committed to an ideal without making every sacrifice that advances the
world the least bit toward it.)
3   A choice is wrong just in case it violates every set of shared rules of
    conduct to which everyone could be freely and rationally committed,
    without anyone's violating his or her own self-respect. (Contentment
    with oneself, which may be nothing more or less than a defense against
    painful frustration, is not sufficient for self-respect. Otherwise Uncle
    Tom would have been been self-respecting.)

From this standpoint, atrocities of ethnic cleansing are not just wrong, but
obviously wrong, condemned by all the equivalent, fundamental principles.
In accepting rules of conduct that permit the killing of some who want to
live in peace and at home, killing them so that others can feel more
culturally at home, I hardly express full and equal respect for all. I could
not accept such trade-offs if I regarded the lives of all concerned as equally
valuable. Someone engaging in such a massacre would hardly be loyal to the
ideal of universal harmonious living. Rules permitting killing someone on
account of ethnicity could not be freely upheld by a vulnerable member of
an ethnic minority who was self-respecting.

If such a universalist morality can sustain certain versions of nationalism,
these versions are not guilty as charged in the indictment, since their
underlying justification requires condemnation of ethnic cleansing. I think
that a morality of full and equal respect for all does sustain certain forms of
nationalism. However, through its universalist constraints, it traces a highly
restrictive blueprint for humane nationalism, limiting bias and exclusivity,
requiring acceptance of diverse attitudes toward nationality, and producing a
close resemblance between duties of loyalty to one's own nationality and
outsiders' duties of sympathetic support.

One universalist source of nationalism is the connection between equal
respect and an interest in people's life-prospects, i.e., their chances of
succeeding in their lives given willingness to sacrifice for success. In general,
to ascribe the same value to my life as to yours, you need only be concerned
that my choice to make an effort have as serious an impact on my success as
equally strenuous choices of yours have on your success. To help me
regardless of what I choose to do is not just to regard your life and mine
as equally valuable, but to identify my good with yours; this is more than
your fair share in world-improvement requires and more than sensitivity to
my self-respect demands. Although a moral code expressing the equal
valuing of everyone's life must include a prima facie duty to support equality

of life-prospects, this duty is limited by a variety of legitimate excuses, involving the burdens of helping the disadvantaged. Still, a morality of respect for persons can require political support for more equal life-prospects. For example, if I take part in the political life of my society and the laws that I help to create and enforce burden others with inferior life-prospects, I must be willing to support changes in the direction of equality if the consequent losses to me are less than the consequent gains to the disadvantaged. Any other moral code for civic conduct would permit domination that a disadvantaged person could not freely uphold without loss of self-respect.

None of this would have anything to do with legitimating nationalism if the relevant successes, gains, and losses had to consist of income, wealth, or some other all-purpose resources for even the crassest individualist. But a morality of respect for persons will accord great value to success in any life-project that is someone's intelligent way of pursuing what is of central importance to everyone who has full and equal respect for all. And all such people have a deep desire to participate in some collective process, begun in past generations and handed on as the task of generations to come, in which their contributions express their identity and are valued by other participants in a way that confirms their sense of self-worth. Indeed, it is hard to imagine how any human could become and remain moral, for-swearing any benefit from practices that self-respecting others could not freely uphold, unless she wanted to engage in practices in which contributions expressing her own identity were valued by others as advancing a common good, a project of past generations and a task for future generations.

Some ways of pursuing this good are cosmopolitan, for example, a university intellectual's contribution to the ongoing collective project of political philosophy or a Japanese musician's contribution to the ongoing collective project of Italian opera. However, for many people, such collective self-affirmation is, in large measure, a matter of joining with fellow-nationals in cultivating their nationality. So, it is just as legitimate for the national to assert their interest in the thriving of their Serbian (or Mexican–American) nationality as it is for the musical to assert their interest in Italian opera, in deliberations over government aid.

Not only can someone's commitment to a large historical mission be a commitment to cultivate her nationality, the thriving of a nationality of which one is a member is (as Kymlicka has emphasized) almost always a precondition for the meaningful commitments (national or not) that make successful living possible.[3] Life-projects with which one intelligently identifies must grow out of values, expectations, and preferences among which one is at home. As the dead metaphor of at-homeness suggests, this background for meaningful choice is typically acquired in early upbringing, with a core passed down from parent to child. Although background attitudes worthy of cultivation must be compatible with full and equal respect for all, a background confined to moral values that are the common ground of those who display full and equal respect will hardly be rich enough to nourish the development of a successful life. To be prepared to live a life that is interesting and self-expressive, one has to identify securely with diverse nonmoral conceptions of how to live, approved by others whom one respects, diverse enough to guide the life-choices of a mature person and receptive to deliberative scrutiny and exhilarating cultural expression. At least in modern times, such an inherited background almost always includes a nationality. On my broad understanding of the term, many of us are members of more than one nationality, and it is not predetermined that our most exclusive club is the most important. Still, people cannot simply take off an identity, when it is threadbare, and put on something plusher. Life-prospects can be threatened at their very core by the impoverishment of a nationality whose thriving happens to be a condition for the meaningfulness, intelligence, and interest of one's own choices and the choices of those one loves.

In sum, intense interests in the thriving of one's nationality are common among those who have full and equal respect for all; indeed, they are, to some extent, inherent in the self-respect which a morality of full and equal respect must accommodate. Still, the mere existence of these interests (like all other legitimate interests) is not enough to reconcile their governmental promotion with full and equal respect for all. In such a political program, outsiders and those who do not care about the nationality in question are forced to contribute to its promotion. This political process of forcing some to help others advance these others' interests must be capable of support by all without violating anyone's self-respect (and without anyone's doing more than her fair share in world-improvement). In a morality of respect for all, this entry of nationality into politics can be created by special burdens making it specially hard for people with some national identities to cultivate the nationality on which their personal thriving depends. Without political intervention, Mexican–Americans with a central interest in cultivating their nationality may lack financial resources for its effective pursuit. Quebecois may be unable to resist the cultural solvent of the ocean of English that surrounds them. In the most extreme cases, the national project of collective confirmation of self-worth is blocked by government interventions showing active contempt for one's nationality, the contempt that Albanians have protested in Kosovo and Palestinians in Israel. In all these cases, the universalist nationalist seeks special attention to the needs of her nationality, but special attention regulated by a goal of greater equality of life-prospects among compatriots of all nationalities.

So far, a morality of full and equal respect has come to the aid of nationalities that are in peril. However, such a universalism can also sustain policies in the interest of dominant nationalities which genuinely imperil minorities. Speaking a language which is a medium of important politics, commerce, and high culture in one's territory, and having customs within the range that children are expected to observe in public schools is a virtual prerequisite of cultural thriving. But it is not feasible to grant this status to more than a very few languages or to customs outside a narrow range. Through their policies, governments, in effect, ration access to public grounding, this scarce resource for projects of nationality. At an even more elementary level of social life, political choices concerning secession, autonomy, education, and immigration determine the routine local cultural expectations that make it easier for some than for others to display and enjoy social grace (to joke with salespeople or customers, to be polite but not deferential, and so on through the hard currency of being at home in one's society.) A universalist need not be ashamed of such rationing, when it serves the interests of her dominant nationality. But she will be concerned to support it by appeal to some principled basis for neglect that everyone can accept without lacking self-respect, for example, "If all interests at least as acute as yours, shared by groups at least as numerous as yours and important to people in these groups for similar reasons received the political attention you seek, what most people would lose through the resulting fragmentation of public life would be more serious than what you would gain."

Apart from these various considerations of distributive justice, a universalist will also be concerned with the integrity of political life as a whole, and this concern may, independently, require the political cultivation of a nationality. Just as everyone committed to full and equal respect for all wants to be part of ongoing projects of mutual cultural affirmation, every such person wants her own political life to be characterized by mutual respectful appeals to principles, sufficiently congruent, that principled consensus plays an important role in the passage of laws and people whose political views do not now carry the day need not regard their outlook as permanently incapable of providing effective principled arguments. For such a person, a political life based solely on competition among interest groups to see who can finance the most effective sound-bites or inspire the greatest fear of disruption or reprisal is a great loss in itself. If someone did not have this deep desire that politics express trust and respect through appeal to common ground, it is hard to see how she could have an adequate motivation for an unconditional commitment to live by rules that everyone could uphold without loss of self-respect. Willingness to give up any benefit incompatible with rules that all self-respecting people could freely support does not rationally cohere with indifference to whether one advances one's interests by means of political interactions in which people respectfully seek common ground. However, such a political practice requires an actual consensus in politically relevant concerns. So, to advance a goal of everyone who equally respects all persons, people may seek a local homogeneity of culture and interests favoring their nationality.[4] Prior to Slovenian secession, a Slovenian's desire for political life based on the principled pursuit of common ground was certainly frustrated by constant bickering over inter-regional transfers and the turmoil of rancorous conflicts among nationalities other than her own. Secession may have been legitimate simply because this cost was too great.

Still, even if she supports political measures enhancing her nationality's dominance of a territory, a universalist's attitude toward homogeneity will be suffused with equal respect for all. Someone committed to equal respect for all must have an interest in empathic appreciation of a variety of ways of life. And diversity often does not interfere with a politics of mutual respect and trust. So a nationalist ultimately committed to equal respect for all will seek to avoid more homogenization than mutually respectful politics requires. A similar search for balance will affect her thinking about all favoritism toward insiders. For example, because of the corrosive effects of local economic inequality on local respect and trust, she will want there to be a substantial bias toward compatriots in tax-financed aid to the needy, even if she lives in a per-capita rich country. But she will take the local cost in social trust to be nothing more than a legitimate excuse for avoiding evenhanded provision for the disadvantaged in the world at large, an excuse whose scope must not be exaggerated as people pursue their ultimate moral commitment, a full and fair share in world-improvement.

Even if full and equal respect for all is compatible with support for familiar nationalist goals, such universalism might seem to conflict with the exclusivity of nationalist movements, as they pursue these goals. Nationalists, after all, appeal to fellow-nationals to be active participants in the movement advancing *their* nationality, a movement in which non-nationals are usually asked to be no more than sympathetic fellow-travelers and are virtually never called on to help direct the movement. (Although Charles Taylor can support the Quebecois nationalist goal of cultural survival, "*le survivance*," he cannot call it "*notre survivance*," so he could not become a Quebecois nationalist.)

In fact, the universalist rationales for certain nationalist goals also provide a justification for this much exclusivity in the movement. The cultural vitality of a nationality and the principled appeal to shared political values will hardly be sustained by a movement whose leadership and energy come from outsiders. Still, even here, universalist exclusivity is limited by its underlying rationale. For there is much less room than many nationalists want there to be for group-based duty and group-based betrayal. A universalist nationalist will want there to be a vital national movement in which her fellow-nationals actively participate, and she will take such participation to be one good way for any fellow-national to discharge everyone's duty to help improve the world. But in normal times, she will not propose that every fellow-national has a duty, all told, to invest his energies in this project (beyond the mere passive support which is often the duty of non-nationals as well). If other projects of cultural development or mutual aid better express someone's personality, there is usually no good reason why he should cultivate his tenuous attachment to his nationality. Sensible Norwegian nationalists do not propose that Norwegian musicians who hate Grieg's music have a duty to play it. Indeed, a universalist nationalist is keenly aware that active engagement in nationalist movements can endanger full and equal respect for all by reducing empathy or exaggerating fears. So she will *want* other fellow-nationals (though not all fellow-nationals) to pursue cosmopolitan projects.

The exception to this tolerance is the sort of crisis of oppression in which the unified attention of all is needed to defend vulnerable fellow-nationals from stultification, brutality, or pervasive disrespect. But note that in these cases, non-nationals also have a duty to give aid. A Serb in Milosevic-controlled Kosovo had a duty to do something to oppose anti-Albanian racism (if the personal costs of this opposition were not too great). When a duty of national loyalty binds all insiders, a duty of active support binds outsiders, as well. Ultimately, the only moral betrayal is the betrayal of humanity.

Finally, if she seeks a government which, as a whole, favors her nationality, a universalist nationalist will disagree with many nationalists of other kinds in how she wants this nationality to be defined. Commonalities rich enough to express a substantial part of people's identities, command serious cultural interest, sustain social grace, and provide common grounds for political choice are, inevitably, exclusive. Such rich ties will not encompass some people within the nation-state, and most people outside the nation-state (which may include poor people who would like to get in). Any nationalist worthy of the name is willing to accept some losses to those not bound by these ties in order to use state power to cultivate her nationality or promote special interests of her fellow-nationals. But a universalist nationalist will actively regret the inevitable harms of exclusivity. So a universalist nationalist will encourage their fellow-nationals to adopt the most welcoming conditions for membership in the national community that are compatible with the goals that justify her nationalist activities. Ideally, the enduring project that someone must join to enter the state-sponsored nationality will be a specific historical process, no doubt imperfectly conducted so far, of improving justice, doing good, and contributing to charm and beauty – a mission that people are welcome to join, regardless of ethnicity.

III   The Beast of Particularism

I have tried to derive the legitimacy of certain nationalist commitments and the duty, in some circumstances, to support certain nationalist goals from a universalist morality that ultimately expresses full and equal respect for all. In the alternative, particularist approach to the morality of nationalism, a principle of group-loyalty that is an independent part of the foundations of morality is supposed to be capable of justifying nationalist activities, even when they impose significant costs on outsiders. The crucial principle lays down some obligation of special concern for interests or practices of those who are in an unchosen special relation to oneself; an obligation that directly entails a special interest in fellow-nationals and their ways, at least in modern circumstances. Often, this principle might naturally be stated as a go-for-it imperative, for example: if one has an opportunity to cooperate with others who share inherited practices that are sufficiently comprehensive and territorially dominant to be the basis of politics and high culture, cooperating with them in using government to cultivate those practices or to express special mutual concern, go for it. Purely for convenience, without presupposing any specific form or content, I will call the independent, fundamental, nonuniversalist, nationality-sustaining principle "the principle of nationality."

So long as it admits that universalist principles are also part of the foundations, this particularist nationalism is an attractive way of connecting the demands of morality with important motivations for self-sacrifice. But it should be rejected, for it cannot adequately account for the wrongness of ethnic cleansing.

Very likely, there are nationalities whose national ways require the avoidance of ethnic cleansing. (Maybe there is now an American nationality of this kind, though I'm sure that many Cherokees would have interesting comments on this hypothesis.) Still, the existence of benign nationalities would not sustain an adequate particularist condemnation, since the wrongness of ethnic cleansing hardly depends on what happens to be the content of the potential cleansers' national practices. In light of my previous arguments about the productive role that ethnic cleansing can play in promoting the collective interests of a nationality, appropriate condemnation must appeal to some across-the-board limitation on the assertion of group-loyalty. This limitation cannot be adequately grounded, once a nationalism-sustaining independent principle of group loyalty is made part of the foundations. This beast cannot be tamed.

I am not proposing that the stipulation of a sufficiently powerful prohibition makes the whole particularist nationalist package self-contradictory. Without self-contradiction, the particularist can lay it down that terrorizing people who only seek peacefully to continue their culturally visible presence in conditions of self-respect is never permissible. However, once a nationalist insists that a principle of nationality accompanies the demand for full and equal respect as an independent principle, resting on no deeper moral standard, then that across-the-board prohibition of ethnic cleansing becomes arbitrary, in need of justification that the nationalist cannot provide. Particularist nationalism subjects the condemnation of ethnic cleansing to legitimate justificatory challenges that cannot be met, unless particularist nationalism is abandoned.[5]

The indictment noted that someone who takes standard goals of nationalism to be great political goals, legitimately sustainable by deadly force as such goals are, will have to countenance ethnic cleansing if he happens to be part of certain nationalities in certain circumstances. In light of further definitions, these goals would seem to be the cultivation of the distinctive ways of one's nationality and special concern for fellow-nationals. A humane particularist nationalist might respond to the indictment in either of two ways. He might claim that the political goals that the principle of nationality independently imposes on a member of a nationality, over and above the requirements of equal respect, are not sufficiently morally important to justify the violence of ethnic cleansing. Or he might seek a further specification of the principle of nationality, restricting it to good kinds of nationalism, so that troubling conflicts with the politics of equal respect will not arise. But neither strategy succeeds. The first, "No big deal" response cannot be reconciled with the moral seriousness of the burden imposed when a government implements the principle of nationality through a measure that cannot be justified as a dictate of equal respect. On the other hand, the second, "Only the good kinds" response must, in the end, accord so much moral authority to universalist principles that further preferences for goals of nationality will lack the moral force ascribed in the principle of nationality.

An extreme version of the "No big deal" response would reduce particularist nationalism to the claim that opportunities to promote one's nationality are to be seized, prima facie, i.e., in the absence of reasons to the contrary. But this is too modest a commitment to constitute a nationalism worthy of the name. For nationalism always encounters reasons not to pursue its political goals. After all, nationalism forces those outside the dominant nationality (or nationalities) to conform to arrangements that do not advance their interests – a negative consideration from any humane point of view.

Instead, the most promising version of the "No big deal" strategy factors out the independent contribution of the principle of nationality, and offers a modest appraisal of its importance: this principle justifies some institutional arrangements which would not be justified in an exclusively universalist framework, but what the *extra* measures add to political life is not so important as to justify implementation by such means as ethnic cleansing. This might seem an apt expression of the common sense of moderate nationalists. Many Quebec nationalists want commercial signs in English to be prohibited, but would adamantly oppose the ethnic cleansing of Westmount (the main English-speaking neighborhood of Montreal) as a means of ending Anglophone resort to English store signs.

However, the description of what sensible, moderate people believe can hardly resolve our question of logical priority, which requires scrutinizing alternative justifications, to see what belongs in the foundations of morality. The piecemeal demands of moderate nationalists, such as the Quebec language laws or the perpetuation of the Church of England, may or may not have a justification on the basis of full and equal respect for all. Suppose such a measure lacks such a justification. Then someone born and raised in a territory, fully prepared to take part in democratic citizenship on a basis of full and equal respect for all, is forced to bear some cost to sustain an arrangement that she could not actively support without violating her self-respect. The baker in Westmount is prevented from putting "Cakes a Speciality" on his sign, even if this is *not* part of a means of preventing

French–Canadian culture from dissolving in the surrounding sea of English. The Jewish Englishperson is required to pay taxes to support the Church of England in the absence of an argument locating this collective provision in a specific historical mission of creating goodness and beauty that he can, in good conscience, join. Forcing people to obey such measures in the absence of full and equal respect is, of course, much less harmful than massacring people or destroying their homes. Still, if a morality of full and equal respect is the universalist part of morality, these are important harms. Having to put "*Specialites de gateaux*" above the door is no big deal in itself, but it is a major harm to be subjected to laws based on rationales that one could not embrace without losing self-respect, rationales expressing a lesser valuation of one's own life than of others'. This will be the toll of any politics that imposes costs which are not ultimately justifiable as part of the implementation of full and equal respect for all.

If a goal is sufficiently important to justify such harm, it is a big deal indeed. If nationalist goals justify such harms, why don't they justify ethnic cleansing? In response, the humane particularist can only stamp his foot, insisting that some expressions of disrespect go too far. His humaneness is arbitrary. The universalist's is not.

It might seem that I have just graded the rival positions for neatness, when more substantial, moral virtues are at issue. To the contrary, the arbitrariness of this humane particularism is a crucial moral disadvantage, if I have succeeded in grounding the most morally compelling nationalist projects on full and equal respect for all. A strong desire that choices which harm others be justifiable on the basis of underlying principles is not a preference for neatness, but an expression of equal respect: one wants the harm to be justifiable to a self-respecting victim as based on a general rule that she can accept in spite of its outcome in the case at hand; one wants to reconcile the harming with a moral personality that one can respect in oneself. Imagine the baker in Westmount asking, "What makes forcing me not to post an English sign all right, if deportation is wrong?" It is not just a desire for intellectual neatness that presses a humane nationalist to find an answer. Note, too, that in dealing with politically active fellow–citizens, as in dealing with government officials, the more choices reflect case-by-case discretion, the less secure is trust; yet anyone who equally respects all will seek political unity based on secure mutual trust.

Admittedly, the goal of avoiding arbitrariness through a deeper justification is not necessarily overriding. There could be a rivalry between fundamental independent principles in which the obvious conscientious preference sometimes goes to one, sometimes to the other, in the absence of a deeper principle regulating the rivalry. But if my universalist case for many forms of nationalist activity is valid, the residue of nationalist projects that would conflict with full and equal respect for all do not have the obvious, overriding moral authority that could command reluctant assent to arbitrariness on the part of someone with a strong desire to base conduct on principle. And this is a strong desire that the humane particularist shares. She, too, has a strong (if not an absolute) commitment to equal respect. Ironically, the partial falsehood of the charge that ethnic cleansing exposes the illegitimacy of nationalism is an important ingredient in the case for its partial truth: the fact that a universalist morality of equal respect can legitimate certain nationalisms helps to establish the conclusion that the condemnation of ethnic cleansing cannot adequately be justified once a nationalism-sustaining duty of group-loyalty is made an independent part of the foundations of morality.

In fact, since humane particularist nationalists typically regard certain nationalist goals as exceptionally important, the "No big deal" defense is less common than the attempt to specify a good kind of nationalism without becoming a universalist. So far, I have supposed that the principle of nationality supports the use of political force simply as a means of cultivating one's nationality or expressing special concern for fellow-nationals. One promising way to tame the beast is to specify that the sort of political community that one should support, if this is feasible, must express ties of nationality of certain kinds, in certain ways. At least as a first step, a particularist might insist that our fundamental moral interest is in what Dworkin has called "a genuine community" (as opposed to "a bare community"), i.e., a community in which members are expected to be faithful to practices displaying some form of equal concern for all members, practices subject to interpretation and revision in light of the community's shared moral assumptions concerning equality. But the problem with this first refinement (as Dworkin ultimately acknowledges) is that it permits oppression of outsiders (and insiders, as well) when the local assumptions about moral equality are inaccurate.[6] To avoid countenancing disrespect for persons (leading to the arbitrariness I criticized before), humane particularists need to take a further step, reconciling the two aspects of morality, but without absorbing the particular into the universal. Introducing a further refinement into the principle of nationality, they will make it a prescription that further specifies what is left open by a morality of full and equal respect, without conflicting with it.

The more refined principle tells us to seize the opportunity to focus one's concerns and aspirations on one's nationality when this nationality is constituted by a genuine national community whose members try to express, through their practices, full and equal respect for all. If, as presently constituted, these practices are not an adequate expression, one should participate critically, supporting reform and avoiding disrespect, unless participation inevitably contributes to disrespect, on balance. This would still be a form of particularism if it dictates an interest in nationality that is not required, under the circumstances, by every system of rules for social life expressing full and equal respect for all.[7] Although a universalist morality of equal respect does require a substantial bias toward compatriots in tax-financed aid, it usually leaves people otherwise free to devote themselves to cosmopolitan projects. The refined principle of nationality resolves questions left open by this morality, by ruling out some of these remaining options for cosmopolitanism.

The strength of the "Only the good kinds" approach is its capacity to assess conflicts of interest in the same way as a universalism of equal respect. Given the interests in play in a society, political choices should express equal respect, according to the enlightened principle of nationality. This avoids the problem that defeated the "No big deal" approach, namely, the seriousness of imposing burdens on people that are not part of a political expression of full and equal respect for all. The enlightened principle can, nonetheless, introduce an independent, politically-relevant imperative of group-loyalty, by guiding individual nationals in the formation of the personal interests that they bring to bear in respectful political deliberations. However, this retreat to the level of personal development, which avoids troubling harms to others, makes for an extremely implausible moral imperative. The principle of nationality that does not create arbitrariness in the condemnation of ethnic cleansing is too watered-down to do the moral work that particularism requires.

Why suppose that the rejection of a more cosmopolitan way of life in favor of identification with one's nationality is a moral imperative, when this imperative does not rest on the demands of equal respect in one's current personal context? The American (of my acquaintance) who decided to move to Prague because she found life there appealing, the American-born political philosopher who freely moves between London and New York, shedding light on questions of justice while living multinationally, the French doctor who deserts his homeland (and its poor) for the cosmopolitan benevolence of Doctors Without Borders – surely these are not people who have violated a moral duty, for example, an imperative of self-development constituting a duty to oneself. In general, a cosmopolitan outlook gives greater scope for curiosity, wide-ranging empathy, and the unimpeded fitting of life-choices to worthwhile non-nationalist aspirations than a nationalist outlook. If someone's personal cosmopolitanism is combined with whatever interest in nationality her stance of equal respect requires, it seems quite wrong to accuse her of a fundamental moral mistake – even if one accepts that certain nationalist options are no worse, because of their own distinctive virtues of rootedness. Of course, such comparisons will simply be irrelevant in political moralities that refuse to base political choices on judgments of how to live. But in these neutralist liberalisms, there is no room, to begin with, for a politics incorporating a fundamental, independent imperative of concern for one's nationality.

This criticism of the "Only the good kinds" approach might seem to depend on an impoverished, insufficiently political conception of its enlightened principle of nationality. In addition to calling for the cultivation of a personal interest, of the same general sort as some people's interest in opera, philosophy, or medicine, the principle calls on people to be steadfast to this interest in their nationality in certain specifically political ways, and not to cut and run in the face of challenges. As I stated it, the principle explicitly insists that people confront defects in respect for persons in the practices of their nationality as obstacles that they should try to remove, not as excuses for disinterest. Implicitly, the principle requires fellow-nationals to join in collective resistance to attempts to suppress the national culture and to other nationality-based indignities.

I agree that this insistence on abiding commitment sometimes corresponds to plausible moral duties not to cut and run. Up until now, I have ignored these imperatives of steadfastness, not because they are all dubious, but because, when plausible, they are not independent of the demands of a morality of full and equal respect for all. The cause of justice will hardly be served if people fail to address injustices in the practices with which they are at home, using what is just and decent in the shared outlook to reform what is not, with the help of the spontaneous affiliations and easy understanding that are part of shared nationality. I have already argued, on a universalist basis, that the option of humane nationalism can become a duty in time of national oppression. Even the benign cosmopolitan choices that I described before are morally clouded if the cosmopolitan's nation is under attack. Moral criticism of those who left England or France in 1939 for more appealing places (even if they meant to do good works) is certainly intelligible. But the morality of equal respect can explain this: anyone who has full and equal respect for all will want all to be reluctant, at the very least, to desert a community imperilled by unjust attack.

A particularist nationalism must go beyond these diverse and sometimes demanding injunctions, in effect, telling the American who is delighted with life in Prague that she must not abandon her Americanness even though Americanness is not threatened and quite apart from any duty to improve justice. It is hard to see what could sustain such independent imperatives except a view that finding your roots of nationality and remaining steadfastly attached to them is morally superior to all feasible cosmopolitan alternatives. But this judgment does not survive a balanced survey of the gains and losses inherent in each type of life-choice.

If, in contrast, clear duties to rectify and defend one's nationality had no adequate grounding in universalist morality, then the "Only the good kinds" strategy could vindicate humane particularist nationalism. Its extra imperatives would not be excessive, and it does not permit atrocities of ethnic cleansing. Once again, the universalist justifications of nationalist commitments, which exposed the partial falsehood of the claim that ethnic cleansing delegitimates all nationalism, undermine the humane particularist alternative. There is so much basis for humane nationalism in universalism that nationalists should seek no further premises.

Notes

1   See, for example, Charles Taylor, "Why Do Nations Have to Become States?" (1979), in his *Reconciling the Solitudes* (Montreal: McGill University Press, 1994), "The Nature and Scope of Distributive Justice" (written 1976), in his *Philosophy and the Human Sciences* (Cambridge: Cambridge University Press, 1985), "The Politics of Recognition," in Amy Gutmann, ed., *Multiculturalism and "The Politics of Recognition"* (Princeton: Princeton University Press, 1992), and "Can Liberalism be Communitarian?," *Critical Review* 8 (1994): 257–62; Alasdair MacIntyre, *Is Patriotism a Virtue?* (Lawrence: University of Kansas, 1984); David Miller, *On Nationality* (Oxford: Oxford University Press, 1995); Michael Walzer, *Spheres of Justice* (New York: Basic Books, 1983) and *Thick and Thin* (Notre Dame: University of Notre Dame Press, 1994). In *Law's Empire* (Cambridge, MA: Harvard University Press, 1986), esp. pp. 190–215, Ronald Dworkin describes the moral standing of communal obligations in terms that are helpful to the particularist project. However, I take his work as a whole to be neutral as to the ultimate availability of a universalist basis for the various communal obligations that he defends.
2   The crucial distinction, here, is between nationality and citizenship. Someone who regards nationality, in the sense just defined, as devoid of any intrinsic moral importance, might still be deeply concerned to participate in, uphold and

defend her country's political institutions, and might regard fellow-citizens as morally bound to do the same. Citizens of a state most of whose citizens display this purely civic patriotism are not, just by that token, fellow-members of a nationality. So far, what motivates their shared allegiance could be the love of justice, the belief that the local institutions are basically just and contain means to remedy nonbasic defects, and the thought that justice will not thrive unless fellow-citizens can trust one another to pursue justice through commitment to such basically just institutions. One can care about just civic ties, without caring about ties of nationality. And one can have a nationality (Kurdish, for example) without being a citizen of a state with the mission of promoting the distinctive interests of a nationality. Like some Quebecois, one can even yearn for such a state while thinking that one is already a citizen of a state that is just in its treatment of individuals, even though it neglects the collective advancement of one's nationality.

3   See, for example, Will Kymlicka, *Multicultural Citizenship* (Oxford: Oxford University Press, 1995), ch. 5.

4   Note that the diversity that would interfere with a politics of principled consensus need not involve the intrusion of attitudes incompatible with full and equal respect for all. For example, it can be based on conflicts between different national versions of full and equal respect, which are not readily adjudicated through principled argument, the sort of differences that lead many Norwegians to fear that too much European integration would make their politics too Danish or Swedish, removing shared premises about rural life and local culture from the center of Norwegian politics.

5   So I am not just claiming (what is also important) that a datum of moral conscience, the wrongness of ethnic cleansing, is more easily explained by universalists than by particularists. By the same token, the legitimacy of nationalism is more easily explained by particularists, but that does not make it arbitrary for universalists to assert this legitimacy.

6   See Dworkin, *Law's Empire*, pp. 195–206.

7   This strategy of refinement is at least suggested by Walzer's argument, in *Thick and Thin*, that communal practices have moral standing when they are local ways of specifying the vague, "thin" demands of universal morality.

9

Moral Dimensions of Four Ways of Getting Rid of Groups

James W. Nickel

The wars that occurred during the recent disintegration of Yugoslavia illustrate that it is not uncommon for some groups to want to get rid of other groups, to make them disappear permanently. Getting rid of a group may (but usually does not) mean trying to exterminate it. More commonly, it means putting the group outside the borders into some other country or territory, or trying to assimilate its members so that they cease to be a significantly different group. In this paper I explore the moral dimensions of four ways of getting rid of groups. These are genocide, ethnic cleansing, forced assimilation, and expulsive secession. It is an understatment to say that the first two of these ways of getting rid of groups are morally wrong and ought to be prohibited internationally. Nevertheless, there may be a few cases in which forced relocation of peoples is permissible. Harsh coercive measures to promote assimilation are also wrong and worthy of prohibition, I believe, but milder and less coercive measures to the same end are at least sometimes permissible. And unilateral secession, including expulsive secession, has to be judged on a case-by-case basis in relation to several constraints. These conclusions may not find agreement and acceptance, but it is useful and interesting in any case to consider what's wrong with these ways of getting rid of groups, and to ask if any of them are sometimes permissible. In evaluating the moral dimensions of these ways of getting rid of groups I'll appeal both to familiar moral norms such as respect for life and liberty and to specific human rights as found in documents such as the Universal Declaration of Human Rights (1948) and the European Convention on Human Rights (1950).[1]

The motives for trying to get rid of groups are varied. They include hatred and historic grievances, retaliation, fear, disapproval, greed for territory and property, prejudice, nationalism, and the desire to avoid conflict and escape war. These various motives can of course be combined. When a group tries to eliminate another group from the country in which both groups live, the immediate goal is always to avoid living together with the latter group, or with so many of its members. But this immediate goal can be sought for many reasons, as suggested by the long list of generic motives above. Specifically, trying to get rid of a group might be undertaken: (1) to "rectify" historic grievances; (2) to avoid living with a group that is believed to be inferior or depraved; (3) to acquire the territory or property occupied by another group; (4) to realize the nationalist ideal that every large ethnic group should have its own country in which it forms the overwhelming majority of the population; (5) to avoid ethnic conflict and civil war with another group by getting most of them out of the country; and (6) to create a strong military situation in light of actual or feared attacks by another group.

The kinds of groups that other groups have attempted to get rid of are extremely varied. They include the following:

- religious groups such as Jews, Muslims, and Bahais.
- ethnic and racial groups such as African-Americans and Tutsis.
- national groups such as Armenians and Germans.
- despised groups such as homosexuals and Gypsies.
- indigenous peoples such as Cherokees.
- political groups such as Communists and Trotskyites.
- people who are retarded and handicapped.[2]

I Genocide

Not all cases of mass killing aim at exterminating a group or substantially reducing its size. Hatred and retaliation can result in episodes of murderous violence against a group without those episodes having the goal of eliminating it (Hindu–Muslim violence in India has sometimes had this character). This is the distinction between genocide (which is defined by the Genocide Convention as intended to destroy, in whole or in part, a national, ethical, racial, or religious group) and the broader category of mass killing.[3] Genocidal killing usually operates in tandem with other means to eliminate the group, such as driving many of the members of the group into exile. Thus mass killing and ethnic cleansing – which I discuss next – have an intimate connection.

Genocide has been outlawed internationally through the United Nations Genocide Convention of 1949. The Convention prohibits genocide, conspiracy to commit genocide, direct and public incitement to commit genocide, attempts to commit genocide, and complicity in genocide. Genocide can occur in the absence of international or civil war, but is itself a kind of war on a people. Further, genocide is likely to cause war as the victims and their allies engage in self-defense.

Explaining why genocide and mass killing are wrong is easier, and less philosophically interesting, than explaining why ethnic cleansing and forced assimilation are wrong. The wrongfulness of the intentional and malicious killing of innocent people is one of the firmest and most widespread human moral beliefs. In mass killing the horror of murder is multiplied by hundreds or thousands or millions. Further, genocide involves large-scale violations of very important human rights. Rights to life, against torture, and to due process are violated by genocidal attacks on groups. Because the intentional killing of people is generally wrong, we do not need to consider the goals of genocide in order to condemn it. Scrutiny of the legitimacy of the reasons for trying to get rid of a group becomes more important when weaker means are used.

II   Ethnic Cleansing[4]

Ethnic cleansing tries to get rid of a group by killing its members or forcing – or otherwise inducing – it to relocate. It shares with genocide the goal of getting rid of a group. But ethnic cleansing is not necessarily genocidal since it sometimes lacks the goal of destroying the group and sometimes avoids mass killing. As this suggests, there are genocidal and nongenocidal forms of ethnic cleansing. The former has the goal of extermination, but recognizes that it will be difficult or impossible to kill all of the group's members. So the goal in practice becomes killing many and relocating or terrorizing into flight the rest. Nongenocidal ethnic cleansing often uses mass violence and killing to cause a group to leave, but the purpose of this violence is not to destroy the group. It is often difficult to tell whether a case of ethnic cleansing is genocidal or not since those ordering and carrying it out may not agree about its exact purpose.[5]

Forced relocation of a group can be done without the goal of getting rid of it. The relocation may be done, for example, to get the best land and to force the group to live on inferior land within the same country. This was frequently done in the nineteenth century to American Indians. So we need a distinction between ethnic cleansing (which by definition has the goal of getting rid of or reducing the size of a group) and the broader category of forced relocation. We saw earlier that the kinds of groups that may be targeted for elimination are extremely varied, and hence "ethnic" cleansing may be directed at groups that are not ethnic groups. For example, people with certain political or religious loyalties may be targeted for involuntary exile.

In principle, ethnic cleansing could proceed by paying all the members of a group enough money to induce them to emigrate. But murder, violence, terror, and military force are the typical means of ethnic cleansing.

Those who engage in ethnic cleansing try to acquire or keep the territory that is vacated by those killed or exiled. When one group engages in the ethnic cleansing of another group, the cleansers do so to remove the target group from what the cleansers regard as "their" territory. Ethnic cleansing pursues some form of exile for those who are cleansed but not killed; this exile may be in another country or in a different territorial unit of the same country. It is in this respect that ethnic cleansing is different from expulsive secession (discussed below), which moves the border rather than the people and thus abandons territory.

The worst instances of ethnic cleansing have the following five characteristics:

- The desire to get rid of the group is motivated by hatred or prejudice.
- The cleansing is genocidal in the sense that mass killing and large-scale violence are used not only to scarce the group into leaving, but also to destroy as many of its individual members as possible.
- No compensation is provided to the group for its lost territory, membership, and property.
- The means of relocating people is extremely hazardous and causes many injuries and deaths along the way.
- The group has no place to go and no assistance is provided with resettlement and the reestablishment of governance.

These features of the worst cases help us see what's wrong with ethnic cleansing. I'll discuss each feature briefly, identifying the harms and human rights violations in each area.

1 *Goals* We saw earlier that the possible goals of ethnic cleansing are quite diverse. If the ethnic cleansing is genocidal, its goals are of little interest. That sort of thing cannot be done for any reason. But if it is

alleged to be justifiable because it involves low levels of violence or force and is motivated by permissible goals, then the exact character and appeal of those goals may be very important. For example, ethnic cleansing (or perhaps we would now call it forced relocation) carried out to achieve the goal of achieving peace through ethnic partition could, in some circumstances, be justifiable (see below).

2   *Killing and violence as means*   Even when ethnic cleansing is not of the genocidal form it still typically requires high levels of violence, injury, and death. Thus ethnic cleansing typically involves large-scale violations of very important human rights such as life, liberty, and due process. To get people to abandon their historic places of residence it is frequently necessary to kill, torture, and imprison many of them so as to terrorize the others into leaving. It is not just that ethnic cleansing is coercive or forced; it is also that the means of coercion are so severe.

3   *Loss of territory, community, and membership*   When a group is forcibly moved valuable things are likely to be lost or left behind. First, there is the loss of territory and property (e.g., homes and farms). This violates rights to property, to due process in takings of property, and to compensation for property taken. Second, the community that exists between a group of people who lived as neighbors in a town or region is likely to be lost, particularly if many people are killed or dispersed. Third, ethnic cleansing means the loss of nationality or citizenship for those who survive. This loss of citizenship may result in statelessness or having to seek asylum in a foreign country. Loss of community and membership is worse if it is extended or permanent; this links up with the issue of resettlement discussed below.

4   *Going*   The ways in which people are forcibly moved from one place to another are often extremely hazardous. People fleeing violence and terror are often exposed to additional dangers including further violence, hunger, exposure, and sickness. In the former Yugoslavia, busses and trucks carrying refugees were often fired upon.

5   *Resettlement*   When a relocated group arrives at its final destination it faces the arduous task of rebuilding its economy, institutions, and government. Crucial to success in this is not just temporary assistance with food and housing, but also how well the group succeeded in saving and carrying with it some of its assets and its most talented people. If the group does not receive or find a territory on which it could resettle, its members may end up spending long periods in concentration camps and will eventually have to adapt to new countries as immigrants.

These five factors identify injuries and wrongs that result from ethnic cleansing, and thus help us understand what is wrong with it.

Is ethnic cleansing sometimes permissible? Suppose that we had a case of ethnic cleansing that was motivated by an attractive and powerful goal, such as creating ethnic boundaries conducive to stable peace in an area recently plagued by ethnic wars. Suppose also that this cleansing was done in a way that minimized harm and human rights violations in all five of the areas just listed. Could ethnic cleansing in such a case be morally permissible, or at least sometimes tolerable? If the answer were affirmative we might wish to give the permissible cases a different, more neutral name. "Forced relocation" might serve for this purpose.

In this sort of scenario, partition and forced relocation are indispensable means of making possible a stable peace between antagonistic ethnic groups. Further, the relocation is nongenocidal and largely nonviolent, even though force is used to induce people to move. Fair replacements or compensation are provided for lost territory, property, and membership. The mode of transport is sufficiently safe that there are few deaths and injuries as people are moved. And those relocated have places to go and adequate assistance is provided for resettlement.

In this sort of case most of the human rights violations are removed from ethnic cleansing. Might it therefore be permissible in some situations? I'm inclined to think that the answer is affirmative, particularly if partition, together with relocation, are the only ways out of a severely deteriorated situation. If forced relocation of peoples is the only available means to an imperative goal (such as creating a stable peace), I think that it may be used if it does not involve major human rights violations.

Bell-Fialkoff advocates the use of population cleansing or forced relocation as a way of solving a number of irreconcilable ethnic conflicts. "[P]opulation transfers and resettlement are no panacea. But to deny the great advantages of such an ethnic divorce in situations in which it has every chance of success and is the only viable solution is not unlike denying marital divorce to a couple."[6] I agree with this, but generally have a much more cautious view of the permissibility and usefulness of forced relocation in dealing with ethnic conflicts.

III   Forced Assimilation[7]

Forced assimilation is a means of getting rid of a group, but the means are cultural destruction rather than physical. Harsh measures are used to force the group to give up many of its distinctive features and conform better to the dominant culture.[8] Causing the destruction of a group's culture can be done negligently rather than deliberately (particularly in the case of indigenous peoples), but my focus here will be on the forceful and deliberate destruction of a group's culture or some distinctive features of its culture. Attempts to force a group to assimilate are often unsuccessful. Even Stalin's harsh measures against minority groups in the Soviet Union did not succeed in erasing ethnic identities.[9]

Typical ways of destroying a group's culture, identity, and way of life include prohibiting cultural and religious practices, preventing the use of the group's language and historic names, imposing an alien educational regime on the group's children, and dividing and scattering a group.

Note that this means of elimination only applies to groups that have distinctive cultures. But in the case of unpopular political groups, unpopular non-ethnic religious groups (e.g., Bahais), and homosexuals there is an analogous means, namely destroying the group by forcibly "reeducating" its members. Forced assimilation is not always recognized to be wrong. One objection to prohibitions of forced assimilation is based on the fact that the gradual assimilation of distinctive minorities to the culture of a larger surrounding society is a natural and normal phenomenon. It claims that morality and international law should not try to block what is natural and normal. But the fact that cultural change frequently occurs as peoples mingle together does not make forced assimilation or deliberate cultural destruction permissible, any more than the fact that it is natural and normal for humans to die makes murder permissible. Another objection to a prohibition of forced assimilation is that such a prohibition presupposes implausibly strong views about the value of preserving distinctive cultures. It may be alleged that the implausibility lies in assuming that cultural survival is intrinsically valuable, that groups have value independently of their value for their members, or in denying that some members of distinctive cultural groups care little about the survival of their culture and are happy to assimilate to another culture. But none of these assumptions is made in the case I make for a prohibition of forced assimilation. I locate the value of rejecting forced assimilation in the harms and wrongs to individuals that are thereby avoided. And I allow that variations in people's characters and choices lead to differences in how vulnerable they are to harm from the destruction of their group's culture and in how much they gain from its preservation.

1   *Forced Assimilation as Harmful*   One way to defend a prohibition of forced assimilation is to show that such assimilation has very harmful

consequences for the people who lose their original culture, way of life, and group identity. Indigenous peoples are often victims of forced assimilation, and the costs in terms of ruined lives, health problems, and alcoholism have frequently been very high. Imagine a case of forced assimilation in which circumstances have been deliberately created that make it difficult for a group to maintain its culture and way of life. Traditional occupations are made unavailable as an alien economic system is imposed. Children are sent to boarding schools where they are indoctrinated with a different culture. People are required to adopt alien names and learn and function in a foreign language. Traditional religious practices are forbidden. The group attempts to resist, but nothing it is permitted to do is successful in protecting its culture and way of life.

The harmful consequences of forced assimilation are often severe, particularly when imposed on militarily defeated peoples and when the pace of cultural change is very rapid. Many people who are subjected to forced cultural transformation will find the destruction of their culture and way of life to be a major personal loss, one that is costly because it deprives them of things central to their lives and because it is so difficult for them to adapt to a new culture. Hardy individuals may be able to adapt, but the weaker and older members of the group are likely to suffer psychological damage as they try to cope with the destruction of the culture, relationships, institutions, and values with which they built and lived their lives. Some will find that the loss of these things means that there is little that is worth doing, with a consequent inability to choose goals and pursue them effectively. Some will find the destruction of their culture so terrible that they will kill themselves, go crazy, or succumb to alcohol or drugs.

2 *Forced Assimilation as an Invasion of Liberty* Consider the same scenario sketched above, but now from the perspective of liberty. When a group is subjected to forced assimilation its members are deliberately deprived of the liberty to practice and retain their culture and way of life. They are being forced to undergo a process that is analogous to forced religious conversion – that involves the same kind and degree of violation of their autonomy and integrity. (In some cases of forced assimilation, of course, there will be literal violations of freedom of religion.)

The liberty interest in being free to practice and retain one's native culture is a powerful one. These liberties involve matters that are central to one's personal identity – to who one is, to what one most cares about, and to one's most fundamental commitments. One's culture and way of life, like one's religion, is typically part of the core of one's personality, not its margins. Like religion, it penetrates most other areas of life. Further, the liberty interest in being free to practice and retain one's native culture is strong because the harms identified earlier are likely to be suffered when this liberty is violated in a wholesale way. Thus the two explanations work in tandem. The fact that one's culture and way of life are so central to one's identity helps explain why destruction of these things can be so harmful.

There are two possible approaches to prohibiting forced assimilation. One uses a generic prohibition of forced assimilation; the other, which is more narrowly targeted, prohibits only some of the worst and most common means of forcing assimilation.

If a generic prohibition of forced assimilation is used it should contain some qualifications. Legitimate activities of mainstreamers and of the national government may stimulate unwanted cultural change, but should not necessarily be prohibited to protect the cultures of distinctive groups. These activities may include personal and social interaction; requirements of school attendance; military conscription; medical assistance programs; some commercial and business dealings; and reasonable demands for compliance with law and participation in national institutions that national governments can make on distinctive minorities that are willing to remain in the position of semiautonomous nationalities within a larger federal structure.

The United Nations *Draft Declaration on the Rights of Indigenous Peoples*[10] treats forced assimilation in a number of its articles. Article 6 declares: "Indigenous peoples have the collective right to live in freedom, peace and security as distinct peoples and to full guarantees against genocide or any other act of violence, including the removal of indigenous children from their families and communities under any pretext." Article 7 generically prohibits:

> Any form of assimilation or integration by other cultures or ways of life imposed on them by legislative, administrative or other measures.

Article 7 is inadequate because it totally fails to address the problem of separating permissible and impermissible causes of assimilation.

The second approach to regulating forced assimilation, which I prefer, involves prohibiting some of the most familiar means of forced assimilation, such as prohibition of traditional occupations, interference with religious and associational freedoms, taking children away from their families and communities, forbidding the use of a group's native language, and requiring the use of alien names.

IV Expulsive Secession

A larger or more powerful group in an ethnically divided country can get rid of a smaller group by expelling both the people and their territory. The people do not move; the borders do. In contrast to ethnic cleansing, which usually throws out the people and keeps the territory, expulsive secession accepts the loss of territory as the price of getting rid of the other group.

Expulsive secession is uncommon. One possible example of expulsive secession is the exclusion of Singapore from the Malaysian Federation. But expulsion is a possible way of dealing with a rebellious minority where less than half of that minority's population wishes to secede. Objections to "expulsive secession" may be directed to the divorce itself or to the terms of the property settlement.

The desires and intentions of the group expelled and the group doing the expelling are crucial to whether a case of secession is expulsive. If majorities in both parts of the country wish to separate then it is not expulsion. But if most people in the larger, stronger, or richer region want separation, and more than half of the people in the other region do not, secession – if it occurs – will be expulsive.

Expulsive secession is similar to ethnic cleansing in its purposes, but it uses different means. It may be combined with ethnic cleansing in at least two sorts of cases. One is where ethnic cleansing is used to create a sharp boundary during the process of secession. The larger group imposing expulsive secession on the smaller group may use ethnic cleansing to remove members of the smaller group who live on the larger group's side of the boundary that is being created. Another case is where ethnic cleansing is used to minimize the size of the territory that will be lost through the expulsive secession. To achieve this, all or most members of the smaller group will be driven into a territory smaller than the one they originally occupied. Obviously, when expulsive secession is combined with ethnic cleansing its moral assessment will need to take into account both of these elements.

Since expulsive secession does not deprive people of their land or communities perhaps it is less objectionable than ethnic cleansing. What is lost is membership and the benefits – if any – that go with it. This membership may have both social and political dimensions. Politically, the people in the expelled territory lose the citizenship they had and must construct a new polity of their own or acquire that of an adjoining country.

Pure expulsive secession, that is, expulsive secession that does not involve ethnic cleansing, is surely less objectionable than ethnic cleansing because it does not deprive people of their communities, territory, and property. In principle, at least, the people in the expelled territory only lose their membership in the larger polity. How bad this loss is depends in part on whether the expelled territory and people are economically and politically viable as an independent country. Possible annexation by a neighboring country may also be a factor.

Let's say that a political divorce that one side wants and the other side does not is unilateral. It might be objected that any unilateral secession can be seen as expulsive. If Quebec were to secede unilaterally from the rest of Canada one could view this as a case of Quebec expelling the other parts of Canada from union with it. But this view is a stretch because the remaining parts of Canada would be far larger than the new country of Quebec or French Canada. But it is not clear to me that the size of the expelling unit makes any difference morally. The morally relevant dimensions, as far as I can discern them, are (1) the unilateral nature of the separation (the fact that one side does not want it); (2) the risk of war that unilateral secession often creates; (3) the capacity of the expelled area to organize a viable national government; and (4) the equity of the divorce settlement, i.e., the fairness of the division of assets and liabilities between the two groups.

One's moral perspective on expulsive secession is likely to be influenced by one's general views on secession. An advocate of a general and standing right to secede might hold that a majority in one region that decides democratically to secede unilaterally has a right to do so, provided the region it secedes from remains politically and economically viable and provided a fair division of resources and debts occurs.[11] An advocate of this view might see nothing wrong with expulsive secession when these provisions are met.

If one holds instead that the right to secession is only a remedial right, one that arises when a region has been subjected to severe injustice and human rights violations by another region, one would deny that unilateral secession is a matter of right except in those cases where the people of the expelled region have perpetrated significant injustices on the region doing the expelling.[12] A remedial right to secession could be compatible with a prohibition of most cases of expulsive secession.

V   Conclusion

The prohibition of genocide is a settled and absolute norm of international law. A prohibition of ethnic cleansing is also plausible as an international norm. Forced assimilation also merits international prohibition, but perhaps the best way of doing this is by prohibiting some of the harshest and least legitimate means of promoting assimilation. Finally, expulsive secession, like unilateral secession generally, need not be universally prohibited. But it should be subject to substantial constraints that require careful evaluation of each particular case.

Notes

1 On human rights see James W. Nickel, *Making Sense of Human Rights* (Berkeley: University of California Press, 1987).
2 See Andrew Bell-Fialkoff, *Ethnic Cleansing* (New York: St. Martin's Press, 1996), pp. 7–49, for a comprehensive historical survey of cases of population cleansing.
3 Convention on the Prevention and Punishment of the Crime of Genocide, adopted by the United Nations General Assembly, December 9, 1948.
4 This section adapts and develops material from James W. Nickel, "What's Wrong with Ethnic Cleansing?," *Journal of Social Philosophy* 26 (1995): 5–15.
5 Writing about the break-up of Yugoslavia, Aleksandar Pavkovic says the following about the motives for ethnic cleansing:

[E]ach side encouraged or organized forced eviction of hostile populations from the territory under its control (the infamous "ethnic cleansing") for the following reasons. First, and probably most importantly, by removing the populations of their opponent's nationality, the newly established authorities were denying their opponents a source of supplies and recruits in the area. Second, in this way each side was consolidating its authority by removing any source of potential opposition and civil disobedience from persons of an opposing nationality who were, in effect, considered to be citizens of a hostile state. Third, forced eviction of an opposing nationality enabled each side to settle, into the homes of the evicted, refugees of their own nationality who were expelled from enemy-controlled territory. Finally, by eliminating the population of another nationality the new authorities were establishing their claim to the territory in any future settlement. In the process of removing populations, all sides established detention camps in which murder, torture, and sexual abuse were often committed.

Pavkovic here emphasizes the military and political reasons for ethnic cleansing, but in the background there are nationalist ideologies, interethnic hatred and grievances, and desires for territorial expansion. Further, ethnic cleansing does not always occur during wartime. Forced relocation may be a systematic government policy that meets little resistance. Aleksandar Pavkovic, *The Fragmentation of Yugoslavia: Nationalism in a Multinational State* (New York: St. Martin's Press, 1997), pp. 159–60.

6   Bell-Fialkof, *Ethnic Cleansing*, p. 280.

7   This section adapts and develops material from James W. Nickel, "Ethnocide and Indigenous Peoples," Journal of Social Philosophy 25 (1994): 84–98.

8   A 1993 NATO working paper, "The Situation of Minorities in Europe," has this to say about forced assimilation:

> After the Second World War, under Soviet influence, [forced assimilation] became the norm in eastern Europe. As early as 1945, Czechoslovakia officially suggested that all the minorities which had refused to leave its territory should be forcibly assimilated. The policies of Romania, Bulgaria and Albania towards their Hungarian, Turkish and Greek minorities were the harshest in this respect.

9   See Robert Conquest, *Stalin: Breaker of Nations* (New York: Viking, 1991).

10   Available on the World Wide Web at: http://www.hawaiination.org/iitc/decltext.html.

11   See Daniel Philpott, "In Defense of Self-Determination," *Ethics* 105 (1995): 352–85.

12   See Allen Buchanan, "Theories of Secession," *Philosophy and Public Affairs* 26 (1997): 31–61. See also Lea Brilmayer, "Secession and Self-Determination: A Territorial Interpretation," *Yale Journal of International Law* 19 (1991): 177–202.

10

Secession and Self-Determination: A Legal, Moral, and Political Analysis

Alfred P. Rubin

As a matter of positive international law, there seems to be no "right" to self-determination. As a matter of morality, there would be such a "right" only if the benefits of self-rule in the particular circumstances were perceived by the person(s) making the evaluation to be greater than the detriments on the analyst's (analysts') own scale of values. As a matter of political "rights," when the urge for self-determination reaches a point at which people are willing to die and kill for it, it can be said that there is such a "right." But it is a "right" that can be disputed on the basis of legal and moral conclusions and ultimately rests on blood.

A fourth category has been urged, by which the positive agreement of states, that there is an agreed policy to encourage self-determination, has been asserted to create a "right" in the positive law. Since there is no holder of such a "right" and no "standing" in any state to speak for the national or other minority or majority of another, and all states deny such a "right" to their own secessionist movements, it is doubted that this category, although much discussed and asserted loudly, exists.

To many international lawyers there is no clear distinction between the "positive" law and the moral background to "law." Indeed, in the leading legal text on self-determination, resolutions of the United Nations General Assembly, and other statements by statespeople unconcerned with "rules" that do not apply to themselves immediately or, under various rationales to their own countries' minorities or local majorities, are regarded as statements of at least inchoate "natural law," and there seems to be no distinction drawn between this sort of aspirational moral agreement and a legal commitment. That view seems to rest on reading the word "right" in various normative contexts as if defining a legal entitlement but without legal consequences for the obviously widespread violation of the "right."[1] As used in this chapter, however, "positive law" is distinguished from "moral law" and other normative bases of "natural law."[2]

After discussing asserted legal, moral, and political "rights" to secede in Parts I–III, in Part IV we turn to "reconciliation." The assumption is that no "secession" can establish a sable order unless the people losing authority become reconciled to that loss and the people gaining authority understand the legal, moral, and political costs they have incurred in "winning" what they consider to be their "rights." Part V then suggests some ways to approach a stable "resolution" and Part VI sums it all up in a conclusion. Since there are certain to be those unsatisfied that "justice" has been done in any successful secession, there is an irreducible element of instability or forced stability in any "successful" secession. Therefore, I have termed the conclusion "pessimistic."

I The Positive Law

Now, to the positive law.

The positive law is considered to be that promulgated, normally by express or implied "agreement" by the "legislators" of international society. The most sophisticated and simple statement of the sources of that "legislation," considering "states"[3] to be the legislators of the "positive law," is normally taken to be that set out as the sources of "law" to be applied by the International Court of Justice (ICJ). The Statute of the ICJ directs the court to resolve questions of international law by looking to:

a. international conventions, whether general or particular, establishing rules expressly recognized by the contesting states;
b. international custom, as evidence of a general practice accepted as law;
c. the general principles of law recognized by civilized nations;
d. . . . judicial decisions and the teachings of the most highly qualified publicists of the various nations, as subsidiary means for the determination of rules of law.[4]

To authorize the Court to apply its conception of principles of fairness, equity, a special agreement by the parties to a case is necessary.[5]

Underlying these "sources of obligation," there are some "constitutional" rules of the international legal order, such as the rule(s) making the positive law "binding," defining statehood or "sovereignty" and possibly the rules permitting military action in self-defense that seem part of the fundamental concepts of the international legal order that are implicitly accepted by all international persons and cannot be changed by treaty, thus "*jus cogens.*" The subject is too complex for deeper analysis in this chapter.[6]

Aside from these constitutional rules implicit in the basic notion of there being an international legal order, there are discretionary rules. As a matter of national discretion each international "person," indeed, each individual publicist or commentator, can assert to be a rule of international law whatever "rule" she/he likes. But that assertion can never be more than an "autointerpretation." Unless some other rule of "law" can be found to make the "autointerpretation" binding, even those making the initial autointerpretation remain free to change their minds.[7] Thus it is doubtful that any assertion of a rule of substantive law outside of a treaty-creating context, even if given formally, should be considered "binding" on anybody,[8] although arguably viewed as part of a legislative process; a procedure by which action that may be politically determined can contribute to "customary law."

As to second persons, since all "persons" are normally in this context conceived as equal before the law, expressions by anyone to whom the law does not give final law-making authority, even if given most firmly and argued most persuasively, cannot by definition bind a second person equally capable under the law of expressing his/her views as to the law.

In addition to the constitutional rules noted above, to constitute society some fundamental substantive rules are normally accepted without extensive discussion. Some of those rules distribute authority below the level that most Americans conceive to be "constitutional," some relate directly to "rights" enforceable within the existing legal order.[9] Some deal with the legal order itself and might best be considered "constitutional." Some apply directly to ordinary people within that order. Some of those rules define the status of some persons before some aspects of the law. All known municipal societies today and all known municipal societies of the past have treated some people as above, below, or beyond the rules of law considered applicable to others. In early English common law, for example, a "thegn" was apparently considered to have six times the value of a peasant.[10] The King (who at least by American standards is a person as well as a symbol) could do no "wrong" cognizable by "law" in England. Another of these "unequal" rules is the one that makes some (but not all) promises binding in law. In most, if not all, jurisdictions in the United States, for example, in the absence of some special circumstances a child's "promise" is not legally binding, nor is a promise to give a gift or to perform a feat that is known to both promisor and promisee to be impossible.[11]

But the promises contained in the Charter of the United Nations, a treaty, are normally considered "binding" on all the parties to that Charter. And one of the promises contained in the Charter is to "comply with the decision of the International Court of Justice in any case to which it [a Member of the United Nations] is a party."[12] This means that by virtue of the positive law of the Charter, decisions of the ICJ are "binding" in cases to which those parties to the Charter are party. Obviously, each of these words requires legal analysis to see exactly how far each carries, and precisely what "party" to a case means, and what is a "decision" (as distinguished from an "opinion" or dicta given within a "decision") and what circumstances might lessen the apparent legal obligation. All these points and many more are the subject of vigorous discussion and disagreement among scholars.

In practical terms, what this means is that arguments as to a "legal" right to secession must be based on an interpretation of "law" that is disputed. Unless the parties to the dispute agree on a third party arbitrator or judge to resolve the dispute, it is normally resolved instead either by agreement among the parties themselves, which might set a legal "precedent" if so regarded by others, or by bloodshed, or is not resolved but remains a matter of tension and contention among those interested in the situation. Even when the parties agree to third-party settlement, their agreement to abide by the opinion of the third party does not necessarily mean that they agree to the "rule of law" on which the arbitrator or judge rests for his/her opinion of law.[13]

From this point of view, there is no legal "right" to secession or independence. But the lack of legal right does not mean that secession, nearly always illegal (perhaps treasonous) under the municipal law of the preexisting state, is illegal as a matter of international law; that those seeking independence must, as a matter of law, suffer under a legal order they find unacceptable. The problem raised by abominable municipal orders is not resolvable by law, and history has not brought to positions of authority everywhere those whom their subordinates in the legal order in which they have that authority consider kind, merciful, and just people; and if it had, there would remain those who disagree with these evaluations. "Kind," "merciful," and "just" are all terms in the moral order. Whether they are also terms in the legal order of international society, or any other legal order, depends upon evaluations of law by whoever has the authority within that order to attach the words. Those who share in a "state's" governmental authority or benefit from the current distribution of authority in that state or elsewhere might find any particular regime to be morally fine while those who feel the evaluations of the regime's supporters to be biased or otherwise incorrect can certainly disagree. Such disagreements cannot be resolved by appeals to any "objective" standards because there are no objective standards acceptable to all.[14]

As to the international positive law, as noted above the United Nations Charter is a treaty which has been accepted by nearly all members of the international community. It assumes a world community composed of "states."[15] Its obligations run only to its "Members," except for terms more like those of a military alliance than of a center for peaceful cooperation, such as the provision that:

> The Organization shall ensure that states which are not Members of the United Nations act in accordance with these [*previously stated*] Principles so far as may be necessarily for the maintenance of international peace and security.[16]

Another provision forbids interpreting the Charter to authorize the United Nations:

> [T]o intervene in matters which are essentially within the domestic jurisdiction of any state or...require the Members to submit such matters to settlement under the present Charter; but this principle shall not prejudice the application of enforcement measures under Chapter VII.[17]

Enforcement measures under Chapter VII can be taken only after the Security Council of the United Nations "determine[s] the existence of any threat to the peace, breach of the peace, or act of aggression" and "decide[s] what measures shall be taken [including military measures]...to maintain or restore international peace and security."[18]

Now, it is no criticism of the Organization or the drafting of the Charter to point out that rebels or secessionists need not be regarded by anybody as "states," and that in the absence of a Security Council "determination" of a threat to international peace and security, a breach of the peace, or an act of aggression, the Organization has no authority to interpose itself into disputes that seem internal to particular members. This leads to something of an anomaly in the positive law. In the case of secession, opinions will differ as to when, if at all, the seceding entity should be called a "state" for purposes of the United Nations. Until it is considered a "state" in that context, there is little likelihood in fact of a threat to "*international*" peace and security resulting from its fighting for its independence. If that is so, then there can be a bloody conflict internal to a single United Nations Member "state" with no authority in the Organization to act.[19] If the Security Council considers a refugee flow or evidence of atrocities sufficient to "determine" that a "threat to the peace" exists, it can authorize itself to authorize United Nations Members to act militarily. Indeed, even if others disagree, by a vote of nine of its fifteen members and no negative vote by one of the Permanent Five[20] such a determination can be made regardless of the facts as seen by anybody. And once that determination is made, under the positive law of the Charter a "decision" can authorize or even require military action without regard for what others might regard as the facts.

This self-serving authority in the Security Council has been used in the most peculiar circumstances to suit the political convenience of at least one of the Permanent Five when the dissenters have been convinced to abstain rather than veto the proposed action and nine votes total could be mustered to support it.[21] To date, it has not been used to support any "self-determination" or "secessionist" movement although, of course, those interested in establishing a new sovereignty have been free to take advantage of any Security Council or other actions that they can use politically (or militarily) to favor their cause.

In practical terms, this means that neither treaty nor practice, "common-law" precedent, establishes any positive legal "right" to secession or independence of any "people," however grouped.

As to general principles of law recognized by civilized nations, there seem to be two current interpretations of the phrase. One, which is historically correct, is that the formulation is a paraphrase of the Latin notion of "*just gentium*," the municipal law to be found in different "civilized" countries and presumed to exist in all legal orders as a matter of an inborn sense of "justice."[22] The notion that there was an inborn rationality to the positive law demonstrated by concurrent enactments of different legal orders was rejected by Aristotle, among many others, on the ground that the positive law has no relationship to the presumed universality of the conception of "justice" and that a universal conception of "justice" probably does not exist anyhow.[23] Thus, the notion that public international law rests on universal "general principles" expressed in municipal legal orders is rejected by many jurists regardless of the tendency of others to attribute a "legal" bindingness universally to their own and their friends' moral insights.[24]

The second interpretation of this source of "law" for the ICJ that has achieved some currency today as the earlier conceptions are found to be insupportable in fact without an assumption of the analyst's infallibility in perceiving value systems, focuses solely on precedents and statements of governmental officials in the international arena as establishing "general principles" that evidence a view of "law" to be worked out in detail by

the Court. This interpretation of the third "source" of "law" given in the
Statute of the ICJ is very hard to distinguish from the second source of
international law given in that Statute ("custom as evidence of a general
practice accepted as law"). To do so seems to require the analyst to define a
legal precedent, evidence of a "general principle," to include a single
instance – so-called "instant custom" – and to ignore the need for evidence
that the practice is "general" or that the statements indicating that it is
"accepted as law" are not glib, merely politically convenient, or morally
self-exculpatory. The attempt has spawned books.[25]

As with the interpretation of treaty language and the construction of state
behavior and public statements, learned people clearly disagree as to who is
"civilized," what level of generality is required to make a practice "general,"
how that practice is "recognized" by states, and whether the "principles of
law" implied in that recognition can be reduced to specific rules applicable
to some specific situation.[26]

Of course, the practice and statements in actual cases of secession are
hopelessly mixed. Spain waited until the Peace of Westphalia in 1646–8,
some 65 years after the States General of the Netherlands passed their "Act
of Abjuration" in 1581, before accepting the independence of the Dutch
portion of the Habsburg inheritance; the People's Republic of China has
still not accepted the independence of Taiwan after some 50 years of a
separate currency and legal order. There are many other such examples of
metropolitan states and seceding parts of them holding different views as to
the stability and legal effect of formal and informal acts establishing a
"secession."[27] Third states normally do not pronounce on the issue until
they perceive it in their national interest to do so, and then their pronounce-
ment is colored by that interest.[28] It may be concluded that states' "practice
accepted as law" is not to find "objective" criteria of a successful secession,
but to attach the legal labels as a matter of national discretion in national
interest only.

The final "source" of law given by the Statute of the ICJ is the opinions
of learned publicists and tribunals. Since this source of law can be interpreted to give law-making authority to people who represent a single legal
order or, indeed, represent only their own views and possibly those of their
official or unofficial editors, the negotiators who agreed that these opinions
can be a source of "law" made it a "subsidiary" means of ascertaining law,
and restricted the bindingness of even judicial opinions to the particular
parties in the particular case before the particular tribunal.[29]

Again, we are left with the conclusion that the positive law does not give
any guidance to a "right" of "secession" or independence. The general

principles of law under any interpretation do not support the assertion, and the opinions of eminent publicists seem to fall on all sides of the issue and persuade only those already convinced.[30]

II Morality

As to morality, the picture is less clear.

There are those who define the "moral law" as based on one or a few fundamental evaluations and measure the "morality" of all acts by their conformity to those basic evaluations. Thus, those for whom human life is the primary value of society regard abortion under any circumstances as immoral. It is, of course, possible to argue that self-determination is such a primary value. To those accepting the argument, there is a moral "right" to self-determination by definition, and any action inconsistent with the exercise of that "right" is viewed as immoral. To others, "self-determination" might be of little or no value as for some others "human life," or at least the life of human beings outside some religiously or politically defined group, seems of little or no value. Indeed, for some, the infliction of pain on oneself, wearing a hair shirt or even suicide, is considered virtuous. For them, to inflict pain on others might be regarded as a virtuous help to those others too weak (or otherwise immoral) to inflict pain on themselves. To those for whom "self-determination" is not a moral right, again there is simply no argument. The responses have been ruled out of consideration by the basic assumptions of those taking that view.

But to most moralists today, morality involves a broader choice, and the "moral" benefits and "moral" detriments must be weighed before a moral choice can be made. To them, the state is a "moral person" which must constantly make choices both internally and externally; i.e., both as to its municipal laws and actions and its international policies. Which benefits are morally significant and which morally neutral are again matters about which reasonable people can and do disagree. This is not to say that moral argumentation is impossible, only that some understanding of the morally significant factors must be reached before the moral argument can take place, and then the relative weight of the various implied or explicit values must be discussed in an attempt to find a basis for agreement as to "moral" action or inaction.[31]

As applied to secession as a sort of self-determination, the reasons for continued participation in a larger community or legal order must be weighed against the reasons for reducing the political and legal or social horizon to a smaller community. To most Americans, the reasoning given in the American Declaration of Independence of 1776 seems overwhelmingly persuasive; if all men (i.e., all people) have unalienable rights to life, liberty, and the pursuit of happiness, and if governments are instituted among them in order to secure those rights, and if governments can morally justify their authority only by the "consent of the governed," and if the government bequeathed them by history has become destructive of the stated ends of securing life, liberty, and the pursuit of happiness, then it is "the right of the people to alter or abolish" that government.

But there are many logical flaws in this hallowed conception. For example, even at the time the declaration was issued, the asserted right of all men to "liberty" was denied by at least one of the Declaration's principal drafters, Thomas Jefferson, a Virginia slave-holder. It was possible then to deny the hypocrisy that seems obvious to us by denying that persons with a drop of sub-Saharan ancestry were "men" or persons within the contemplation of the moral order, making exceptions for dynastic marriages and the descendants of those whose unions were accepted as proper in the place of their celebration. This obviously led to absurdities that are too wrenching to discuss even today.[32]

To apply these notions of value-defining and value-weighing to self-determination and secession means that the arguments in favor of self-determination and secession must be weighed against the opposing arguments and the analyst must come to his/her own conclusion as to which better serves the values she or he adopts, and has the least detrimental effects on those values. Thus, to those who believe that the government of East Timor by the partially Portuguese-descended majority represents greater good than continued governance by the local agents of the more distant Indonesian authorities, the case for independence might seem sufficient to outweigh the likelihood of atrocities against the Indonesian minority in East Timor. Similar considerations apply to Biafra, Chechnya, the Kurdish areas of Turkey, Iran, Iraq, and Syria, indeed to many "national liberation" secessionist movements. Indeed, I see, as I write, a revenge-seeking ethnic Albanian community in Kosovo making life there intolerable to many of the minority Serbs and Roma (gypsies) of the province, who themselves are blamed (rightly or wrongly) for documented atrocities by yet other ethnic Serbs or Roma against ethnic Albanians in the same area.

There can be no overall solution to particular problems because the evils of one area can be alleviated by means not feasible to apply in others. The weighing of benefits and determinents varies too much from situation to situation for any general rule to apply to all except the usual general rule of moral balancing: that the detriments to accepted values of the proposed solution(s) must be weighed against the benefits perceived by the moralist whose opinion is sought. There is a different moral balancing to be made after the situation is settled by political means, but more of that later.

III   Political "Rights"

Politically, it is undeniable that there are circumstances in which, whether seen by others as morally correct or not, a dissident group feels that the benefits of independence outweigh the detriments – or that the detriments fall on yet others whose well-being is not felt as a responsibility of the acting group. Where there is a relative balance of forces (political, military, economic, and whatever other factors of "power" apply locally) the tensions can go on indefinitely. The receding "sovereign" is usually (but not always) reluctant to accept the secession as a fact.[33]

Assume now that a secession has succeeded politically. But to establish the moral framework for stability, it might be necessary to convince the populace of the seceding unit that a moral order as well as a political and legal order has been established. Revenge for real or imagined atrocities might be sought by both the new authorities and the old. Although political stability can be established by mere force, it is likely nowadays to lead to guerrilla attacks and endless reprisals. A pattern of unending reprisals is obviously inconsistent with stability. It would seem normally to be in the interest of the new "sovereign" to establish its moral position. There is, thus, a moral as well as a political calculation to be made in some cases to find a useful balance between the establishment of political stability by brute force and the establishment of that stability by the widespread acceptance of the new order as "just." Indeed, it is not clear that either pattern, that of stability established by force and that of stability established by "justice," can ever succeed in the long run without some intermixture. There are those who will never concede that any situation is "just" until all those in any way bound to a former "oppressor" are killed, expelled, or otherwise rendered helpless, mere hewers of wood and drawers of water to some dominant party.[34] There are others who will argue to the same ends on the ground of security or the overriding needs of stability as the basis for their conception of wise politics as well as "justice." And it is undeniable that in some societies, force is the glue that holds things together regardless of the considerations that others call "justice." From this point of view, an internal situation might be "stable" but nobody would want to risk his/her capital or moral reputation dealing with or in the society that bases its stability on force whether in the interest of what the dominant members of that society consider "justice" or not. And nobody would want to risk his/her capital or moral reputation dealing with or in a society that does not display some degree of legal and political stability. Again the problem is essentially not solvable in generalities.

But it is predictable that economic and political stability, based on force or not, will encourage investment. When that stability arises, in current international society ways will usually be found to rationalize profitable economic dealing regardless of the moral pain of those whose tender consciences prefer to deal only with or in societies that meet their standards of moral behavior.[35] In general, it can be said that there will be a need for international dealing when a seceding "province" has established that its political situation meets the minimum demands of stability, and that third persons are interested in treating with the now independent "sovereign" as if its legal order acted more or less independently of the legal order of the former metropole. In these circumstances, the international legal order must sooner or later accommodate itself to the new situation, with or without formal "recognition."[36]

From a legal point of view, the problem of transitional "justice" is one of determining which legal order governs the seceding entity. If the order of the receding metropolitan state determines "justice" in the seceding area, then the acts of the officials of the "new" state might be considered treasonous. If the order of the "new" state, then the acts of the soldiery of the receding metropole might equally be considered treasonous. If international law, then there is a "recognition" of at least "belligerency" which might well upset the receding sovereign; which, as noted above, typically denies that the matter involves two international entities. The simplest accommodation (and nobody could call it a "solution" or "resolution") is for third states to abstain from expressing any view until their own interests require attaching labels. It might be supposed that this implies a regime characterized by the international law of belligerency and third party neutrality, and so it does.

The situation gets more complex when the third power has a role in administering at least part of the territory or population involved, as is the case with the forces of five NATO countries plus Russia in Kosovo as this is written. The usual accommodation is for the authorities of the administering power(s) to determine the Constitutional Law of the place on the basis of their political interests and perceptions of politically significant facts, while the "normal" international law of "belligerent occupation" applies to the belligerent forces and nonbelligerent civilians. Under that model, the law of the receding metropole usually continues to apply to normal transactions among noncombatants; private property remains protected by law (although perhaps not very well protected in fact); murder and assault outside the combat remain murder and assault under the law of the receding metropole. The contract, tort, criminal, and other parts of private law are administered by whoever is in control of the levers of authority to administer the law. That control is normally determined not by law, but by the use of force and individuals' accommodations to it.

"Justice" has very little to do with the situation, although in the interest of stability the administering power usually tries to administer rules of law that the private parties will accept as if "just." That is not very different from the normal administration of "justice" in a stable society under its normal legal order.

IV   Reconciliation

A more complex question is that of "reconciliation."

Any major change in the Constitutional order of any state is likely (although not necessarily) to be accompanied by bloodshed. Those losing authority or property usually fancy themselves in a defensive position and interpret the morality and law of self-defense to give them authority to commit whatever atrocities they consider useful to achieving their political goal of retaining either authority or property or both. The laws of war might purport to forbid at least some of those atrocities, but states have been notoriously reluctant to agree to the purview of any third party over the conduct of a struggle they consider internal, especially if involving the secession of part of territory they regard as historically "theirs" to become a new state. Indeed, in all four of the 1949 Geneva Conventions relating to the protection of the victims of armed conflict, the major distinction in rules is based on the categorization of the conflict as an armed conflict "between two or more of the High Contracting Parties" (i.e., states), or an "armed conflict not of an international character occurring in the territory of one of the High Contracting Paries."[37] The 1977 Protocols to those four Conventions repeat this distinction, Protocol I relating only to international armed conflicts, Protocol II only to armed conflicts not of an international character occurring in the territory of one of the High Contracting

Parties.[38] Thus, although some rules have been agreed by positive law to restrict the atrocities committed by a defending government against some of its internal opponents or by some of those opponents against adherents of the defending government, there seems to be no "*jus standi*" in any other party to the Geneva Conventions or their Protocols to raise the issue as a matter of law.

This does not mean that the international community must remain silent in the face of atrocities. There are nongovernmental bodies, like the International Committee of the Red Cross and Amnesty International, whose public statements, even in friend of the court legal briefs, do not require legal "standing" in the sense used here, and forums, like the United Nations General Assembly, at which such questions can be raised even by governments regardless of their lack of "standing." But they are not questions to be resolved by legal means. Instead, they are questions to be discussed as political or moral issues. It can even be suggested that one of the great successes of the "cold war" was the conclusion of the 1975 Helsinki Accords[39] under which the only colorably "legal" obligation any of the parties accepted was an obligation to discuss, at periodical meetings of the Parties, progress made toward achieving the agreed goals of respect for the equal rights of "peoples" and their "right to self-determination."[40] It might be noted that no provision was made for the representatives of those peoples to participate in the meetings, and, of course, no procedures were adopted for assuring that purported representatives had authority to speak for anybody but themselves as individuals. Yet, the ability of one country to call for open discussion of the practices of another in its internal difficulties did exert political pressure on all countries to observe their moral commitments, to live up to their stated aspirations.

V The Resolutions

This experience should point the way to the greatest influence that the non-legal world can apply to those who commit atrocities: exposure and discussion coupled with municipal legislation or policy decisions. Exposure does not involve criminal trials or questions of "standing." It might be institutionalized in municipal or international "truth and reconciliation" commissions, or it might remain in uninstitutionalized news media or other channels for exposure and truth. If nobody is willing to discuss and react to the exposure of an atrocity, then the "conscience of mankind" will have been tested and the purported atrocity held inconsequential. If the opinions of those who hold the atrocity to be more significant than the benefit asserted to result from it prove ineffective to affect behavior, or the detriment asserted to flow from its punishment by whoever does control a legal order with criminal or civil or other jurisdiction over the purported offense proves unable to influence the behavior of those who benefit from the atrocity, then the atrocity will remain uncompensated. In that case there need be no pretense of "justice" and the difficulties of "reconciliation" will be the practical result of this obduracy.

But if the winners of the struggle for authority truly want reconciliation, then exposure of atrocities on all sides of whatever struggle preceded the stability that is to be established seems to be necessary. The moral remedies include isolation; losers and their friends or simply those horrified by the reports of atrocities refusing to deal with those whom they feel are responsible for the atrocities. Other "remedies" might include a sullen and unproductive population, continued murmurings and unquiet, general difficulties in exercising authority without the expensive use of demoralizing force. At best, for those ordering or committing atrocities, their inability to leave their country might be the result: The Waldheim solution – a former Secretary General of the United Nations and President of Austria effectively confined to his lovely country when he had reason to expect an old age of respect and honors abroad. And Kurt Waldheim has never been convicted of anything by any tribunal, international or municipal.

If institutionalized, some weaknesses of the reconciliation process must be recognized. For example, it is patently impossible to "isolate" within their own communities those in a majority who have actually committed atrocities; Israelis who have killed Palestinians, Palestinians who have killed Israelis; Serbs who have killed Kosovar Albanians, Kosovar Albanians who have killed Serbs, and too many etceteras to contemplate. It is patently impossible, e.g. in Rwanda, for all those Tutsi who have killed Hutu, or all those Hutu who have killed Tutsi, to be isolated, as it is also impossible to exact retributive "justice" by punishment. Yet as a practical matter, to expect a person to resume normal intercourse with a neighbor who has tortured or killed relatives of the first is probably unrealistic. And to apply legal or moral sanctions only to the leaders of those who commit atrocities, typically people who have ordered wicked things to be done but who have not killed or tortured anybody themselves, presumes a deterrent effect to those sanctions that has never been shown to work. In my opinion, only time can resolve the issues, and only exposure can allow time to do its healing. In the immediate aftermath of atrocities, no resolution is feasible and the only moral course seems to be to allow people to separate themselves into communities that refuse to deal with those each considers evil.

From this point of view, it is possible to question the moral attitudes of the NATO powers in Kosovo, attempting to create a multi-ethnic community there on the model of the United States, Canada, and Australia; ignoring the difficulties faced with much less immediate cause by the attempts to encourage free movement of labor in Europe. From this point of view, "reconciliation" is the aim ultimately to be reached only by the people themselves involved, and aided by exposure of the atrocities on all sides until people become willing to face the evils done, not only to their ancestors and kin, but by their ancestors and kin.

Legal secession, the creation of a new and independent legal order, is not a resolution of the moral problems; moral secession, the retreat to the narrow community of like-minded fanatics within an existing legal order, seems a fitting, although only partial and not always feasible, resolution for the fanatics in our midst. That retreat need not be physical to be effective and, although only partial, that retreat is not necessarily effective in producing peace and stability. When the retreat to a community of fanatics is physical and accompanied by a legal secession, peace and stability are still not necessarily the outcome.

VI Conclusion

Thus it would seem that, despite various treaties, there is no positive law "right" to secession. The general multilateral treaty terms referring to national self-determination as a "right" represent agreement as to moral or political principle, not legal entitlement.

It would also seem that as a matter of natural law, there is a moral entitlement to secession in some cases but not in all. Generalities assuring such a "right" in the moral order either rest on values accepted a priori which are not necessarily shared by those to whom the argument is addressed, or rest on assumptions of value weighing about which reasonable people certainly differ. For example, if there is universal acceptance of a right to reasonable compensation for work done as well as to self-determination, and the price of self-determination is unemployment until a degree of economic stability is achieved, there are two inconsistent "rights," and which dominates will depend on the analyst's own preferences.

Politically, an asserted "right" to secession represents the replacement of a dominant legislative body or class with another, and the receding body or class can be expected to defend its inherited or acquired status. From this point of view, the political "right" represents only a right to fight for a political goal. The fight involves death and destruction which raises moral problems and, if a legal status of belligerency is achieved, legal problems as well.

In all cases, it seems to be in the interest of the parties to any successful secession to aim at reconciliation. That itself is difficult since there can be no agreement as to the "right" in positive law, therefore no compensation for the mere fact of secession (although compensation for property expropriated by the new legal order has many precedents; but that is another topic that has spawned a vast literature). As to "justice," that is a term in the moral order and definitions of "justice" are inconsistent. Therefore, "justice" cannot be done to universal satisfaction. Politically, the establishment of a stable legal order is probably essential for the establishment of a stable economic order, which is in turn probably essential for the establishment of a stable moral order. Thus it seems to be in the interest of all parties in cases of secession to seek for a way to find stability in whatever distribution of legislative and enforcement authority can be achieved that has some promise of stability. If feelings are high enough, stability might be impossible absent the use of draconian force, which is itself today probably destabilizing in the long run. In any case, absent draconian force, the surest ground rule for stability, appears to be exposure of all relevant facts and freedom of movement.

I am sorry to end on such a pessimistic note, but we are dealing with human beings and real feelings and convictions, so pessimism seems to be in order.

Notes

1 Hurst Hannum, *Autonomy, Sovereignty, and Self-Determination* (University of Pennsylvania Press, 1990), p. 45:

> While General Assembly resolutions do not of themselves make law, the unanimous adoption of Resolutions 1514, 2625, and numerous others reiterating the "right" to self-determination is significant, as is the fact that more than half of the world's states have formally accepted the right of self-determination through their adherence to one or both of the (1966 U.N.) Covenants (on Economic, Social and Cultural rights, and on Civil and Political Rights).

The fact that the "rights" that are embodied in the Covenants are aspirational, and not current rights to be enforced by the legal order, seems irrelevant to those who take this sophisticated "naturalist" view of the international legal order. But see J. Shand Watson, *Theory and Reality in the International Protection of Human Rights* (Transnational Publishers, 1999), for a trenchant rebuttal of this view. It is not proposed to resolve this ages-old dispute as to the "true" meaning of the word or concept of "law." For my own views on the subject and the impossibility of coming to any definitive resolution, see Alfred P. Rubin, *Ethics and Authority in International Law* (Cambridge University Press, 1997).

2   For an introductory description of various normative orders frequently lumped into one as if tributary streams to an overall international legal order, and some reasons why such an ontology seems more confusing than helpful in analyzing international legal questions, see Rubin, "Enforcing the Rules of International Law," *Harvard International Law Journal* 34, 1 (1993); 149–61 slightly revised version also in *Festschrift till Jacob W.F. Sundberg*, (267–83) (Juristförlaget: Stockholm, 1993). The notion that "international law" is comprised of many normative orders is not original in me. By one count Hugo Grotius, publishing in 1625, distinguished among 18 such orders. Y. Onuma, ed., *A Normative Approach to War* (Oxford: Clarendon Press, 1993), fig. 11.1 at pp. 342–3.

3   Or "nations." The two words seem to be used interchangeably in the texts quoted below. The two words are not necessarily synonyms in other contexts.

4   Statute of the ICJ, 59 Stat. 1055, 3 Bevans 1179, article 38.1.

5   Statute of the ICJ, article 38.2:

> This provision (article 38 excerpted above) shall not prejudice the power of the Court to decide a case *ex aequo et bono*, of the parties agree thereto.

To date, no parties have so agreed and the ICJ has never expressly decided a case under this provision. For an argument that the substance of this article is incorporated into article 38.1.c of the Statute of the ICJ, see M. Janis, "The Ambiguity of Equity in International Law," *Brooklyn Journal International Law* 9, 1 (1983): 7–34.

6   See Rubin, "*Jus ad Bellum and Jus Cogens*," in Astrid J. M. Delissen and Gerard J. Tanja, eds., *Humanitarian Law of Armed Conflict Challenges Ahead; Essays in Honour of Frits Kalshoven* (1991), pp. 595–611. For a more complete handling of the issue see Watson, *Theory and Reality, passim.*

7   Leo Gross, "States as Organs of International Law and the Problem of Auto-interpretation," initially published 1953 in G. A. Lipsky, ed., *Law and Politics in the World Community: Essays on Hans Kelsen's Pure Theory and Related Problems in International Law* (University of California Press, 1953), reprinted in Gross, *Collected Essays on International Law and Organization* (Transnational Publishers, 1993), p. 367.

8   Per contra, Nuclear Tests (*Australia v. France*) [1974] ICJ Reports 253, and Nuclear Tests (*New Zealand v. France*) [1974] ICJ Reports 457. There were six dissents; of the nine judges subscribing to the judgment three in separate opinions expressly withheld their concurrences from this part of the rationale. For a fuller analysis of why the "unilateral declarations" part of the judgment seems illogical and insupportable in practice, see Rubin, "The International Legal Effects of Unilateral Declarations," *American Journal of International Law* 71 (1977): 1–30.

9   Wesley Hohfeld, *Fundamental Legal Conceptions* (Yale University Press, 1923). Hohfeld's distinctions between the norms that distribute authority and the norms that create "rights" are now accepted so widely that they might be considered universal.

10 Sir Frederick Pollock and Frederic William Maitland, *The History of English Law* (2nd edn., Cambridge University Press, 1898, 1952), p. 33.

11 See, American Law Institute, *Restatement 2D of the Law of Contracts*, Secs. 18 (capacity to contract); sec. 75 (requirement of "consideration"); sec. (impossibility).

12 UN Charter, article 94.1. Under article 94.2, the Security Council of the United Nations is given authority to decide upon measures to be taken to give effect to the judgment, but it remains within the political discretion of the Security Council whether to exercise that authority. Under article 25 of the Charter, Members of the United Nations promise "to accept and carry out the decisions of the Security Council in accordance with the present Charter." But no legal provisions deal with the failure of a Member to carry out its obligation in this regard; the sanction, if any, is left to the moral and political orders.

13 Cf. the statement by American Secretary of State Charles Evans Hughes after the Norwegian Shipowners Arbitration. *Norwegian Shipowners Claims, 1922* (*Norway v. United States of America*), UN Reports of International Arbitration Awards 1, 309 at 346.

14 An eloquent and revealing example of the sort of "logic" that exalts one's own moral sense to the level of "law" binding on others is Sherard Osborn, *The Blockade of Quedah* (London, 1857, 2nd edn., 1860), p. 193:

> Such are the cruelties perpetrated by these wretched native monarchies...; and yet philanthropists and politicians at home maunder about the unjust invasion of native rights, and preach against the extension of our rule, as if our Government, in its most corrupt form, would not be a blessing in such a region, and as much, if not more, our duty to extend, as a Christian people, than to allow them to remain under native rulers, and then to shoot them for following native habits.

15 Article 3: "The original Members of the United Nations shall be the *states* which...sign the present Charter..." Article 4 says: "Membership in the

United Nations is open to all other peace-loving *states* which accept the obligations contained in the present Charter... " [emphasis added].

16 Article 2.6.

17 Article 2.7.

18 Article 39. The interpretation of the words "determine" and "decide" have been much disputed over the years. See, e.g., the 7–7 split of views among the judges of the ICJ themselves in the Advisory Opinion on the "Legal Consequences for States of Continued Presence of South Africa in Namibia, ICJ Reports 1971," in *International Legal Materials* 10 (1971): 677.

19 See Rubin, "The Status of Rebels under the 1949 Geneva Conventions," *The International and Comparative Quarterly* 21 (1972): 472–96.

20 They are the Republic of China, France, the Union of Soviet Socialist Republics, the United Kingdom of Great Britain and Northern Ireland, and the United States of America, according to article 23 of the United Nations Charter. The Republic of China position was taken by the People's Republic of China, and the Soviet Union's by Russia as a result of various events, but the language of this provision has not been changed. Similarly, various other provisions of the Charter have been amended in practice without the changes in the wording that a strict observance of positive law would seem to have required. One has been the provision that would seem to require an affirmative vote of all the Permanent Five for a "decision" but which has been interpreted since 1950 not to account abstentions as vetoes. See Gross, "Voting in the Security Council; Abstention from Voting and Absence from Meetings," *Yale Law Journal* 60 (1961): 209, reprinted in Gross, *Collected Essays*, p. 201.

21 There are many such examples, but one that comes to hand easily is the use of the Security Council to require Libya to extradite officials accused of complicity in an atrocity. In that case, there was no pertinent extradition treaty and it is almost inconceivable that the great powers involved would have agreed to extradite their own officials accused of similar atrocities in Northern Ireland, Cuba, or elsewhere. See Rubin, "Libya, Lockerbie and the Law," *Diplomacy and Statecraft* 4, 1 (1993): 1–19. None of this is to say that the Libyan officials were not involved in the atrocity of which they were accused; only that the Security Council's response seems notably hypocritical.

22 The usually cited early reference to this conception is Gaius, *Institutes* (165 AD), Part I, paras 1 and 2. For a fuller discussion, see Rubin, *Ethics, passim*. The origins are noted at pp. 12–13.

23 Aristotle, *Nichomachean Ethics*, 1134b18. See Rubin, *Ethics*, pp. 7–8. Possibly the most persuasive of the reasoned early rejections of "*jus gentium*" theory was that of Francisco Suarez first published in 1612. See Rubin, *Ethics*, pp. 50–1.

24 The best-known early advocate of this position is probably Cicero. For an analysis with quotations see Rubin, *Ethics*, pp. 8–9. For a modern attempt to salvage the *jus gentium* under this definition as a source of public international law, see Hersch Lauterpacht, *Private Law Sources and Analogies of International*

Law (London, 1927, 1970), *passim*. In this book, Lauterpacht supports a universalist *"jus gentium"* theory as far as he can, but finds that differences between the "horizontal" international legal order and "vertical" municipal legal orders require major adjustments; that municipal law "general principles" apply in the international legal order principally by analogy.

25 Possibly the most thorough recent work along this line is Michael Byers, *Law, Power and the Power of Law* (Cambridge, 1999). See pp. 160–1 for Byers's discussion of "instant custom." My own "solution" to this conceptual problem has been to argue orally that public statements as to matters of law are not persuasive of a state's view of "law" unless opposed to that state's apparent immediate military, political, or economic interest. Whether the statement is in fact so "opposed" is, of course, again a matter of interpretation about which individual scholars may differ. Until reading Professor Byers's book, I had thought this "solution" so obvious that I have not hitherto put it in writing.

26 As noted above, Sir Hersch Lauterpacht himself, probably the century's pre-eminent spokesman for a moral view of the international legal order, found that the general principles of law "recognized" by states through incorporation of their perceptions into their municipal orders, could not be transferred immediately to the international legal order. See Lauterpacht, *Private Law Sources and Analogies of International Law, passim*.

27 See Rubin, "Recognition Versus Reality in International Law and Policy," *New England Law Review* 32, 3 (1998): 669–74.

28 The most persuasive statement of this view remains that of Chief Justice William Howard Taft of the United States, as Arbitrator in "The Tinoco Arbitration," *Reports of International Arbitral Awards* 1 (1923): 369–99.

29 Statute of the ICJ, article 59. See also *West Rand Central Gold Mining Co., Ltd. v. The King* [1905] 2 K. B. 391. Because tribunals in general do not like to believe that their earlier opinions were ill-conceived, there is a strong tendency to affirm those views, even when they are being distinguished away. See Sir Gerald Fitzmaurice, "Some Problems Regarding the Formal Sources of International Law," in *Symbolae Verzijl* (The Hague, 1958), p. 153 and Fitzmaurice, "Judicial Innovation – Its Uses and Its Perils," in *Cambridge Essays in International Law* (1965), p. 24.

30 See, for example, Grotius's defense of the independence of the Netherlands from Spain, and the equally firm views in the other direction expressed by Grotius's older contemporary Balthasar de Ayala, a native of Antwerp whose father had been a Spanish resident of what is now Belgium for some 16 years before the birth of Balthasar. Sir Henry Maine apparently considered the two publicists both of equal stature as theorists. See Maine, *Ancient Law* (1861, photographic reprint by Dorset Press, 1986), pp. 82, 91. There are too many such examples to cite.

31 An example of the sort of argument involved may be seen in Jacques Baudot, "Follow-Up to the Social Summit and the Spirit of the Time," *UNRISD News*

(Spring/Summer 1999): 1–3. Baudot points out that the assumptions of competitive capitalism that seem to dominate the opinions of the most influential participants in international conferences today are not beyond dispute. The emergence of a "world market society – renders impossible the fulfillment of the social objectives endorsed by most members of the international community: the elimination of poverty, the reduction of inequalities, and the construction or preservation of integrated and harmonious societies." *UNRISD News*, p. 1, col. 3.

32 See, e.g., George W. Cable, *Madame Delphine* (1881). Cable found the anti-miscegenation statutes of his time and place, post-1865 nineteenth-century New Orleans, to be far lower on the moral scale than the course of love; enough so that lying to avoid the effect of the statute is deemed morally acceptable. This short story seems almost pointless today, when opposition to what were then defined as interracial marriages seems immoral or worse. The same point is made in Edna Ferber, *Showboat*.

33 See the text after note 26, the paragraph beginning "Of course...," for one historically influential example. There are many modern examples of continuing tension, like Taiwan/China, as well as examples of peaceful and quick secessions, like the break-up of Yugoslavia into an independent Slovenia and tension-filled Bosnia, Kosovo, Montenegro et al., of peaceful Czechoslovakia into the Czech Republic and Slovakia, or the United Arab Republic back to Egypt and Syria. Each has its own special reasons for the original union and for its breakup via a successful secession. Indeed, it is not clear that "secession" is the right word to use in all cases. But further analysis of the word "secession" leads us to still further complications. The overall picture supports the major thesis that all situations are unique and political as well as moral evaluations of benefits and determents must be made *ad hoc*.

34 Aristotle divided the conception of "justice" into categories that themselves reveal fundamental disagreement about the term: "commutative" justice is not the same as "distributive justice" or "retributive" or "rectificatory justice." See Aristotle, *Nichomachean Ethics*, Bk. V, Chs. 2–5 (1130b–1133b), in Richard McKeon, *An Introduction to Aristotle* (Modern Library, n.d.), pp. 401–10.

35 I do not mean this to be as facetious as it might sound. The United States, for example, enacted a series of embargo measures against South Africa which blocked profitable investment in that tortured society until it had found a path to something approaching the American version of racial equality. See, for example, the Comprehensive Anti-Apartheid Act of 1986, as amended, 22 U.S.C. Sec. 5001 *et seq.*, now happily repealed as South Africa's apartheid laws were repealed. There are many such bits of national legislation expressing individual states' policies based on moral and political evaluations and not resulting from any persuasive international legal argumentation. Of course, it can be argued that the internal situation in South Africa, stable as it might have seemed, still was a capped volcano into whose crater it was foolish to throw

money. But in a democracy like that of the United States, such situations are normally left to individual investors. In this case, the legislation limiting investment in South Africa was passed regardless of the risk-taking penchants of individual investors.

36　"Recognition," attaching legally significant words and their results in the international legal order to the perceived facts, is now normally considered "declaratory" of an existing situation, not "constitutive" of new legal relationships. See Hans Kelsen, "Recognition in International Law," *American Journal of International Law* 35 (1941): 604.

37　Articles 2 and 3 are identical in all four of the Conventions. The Conventions are reproduced in 75 UNTS beginning at pages 32, 85, 135, and 287.

38　Texts reproduced in Dietrich Schindler and Jiri Toman, *The Laws of Armed Conflicts* (2nd revised and completed edition, 1981), pp. 551 and 619. Confusingly, article 1 of Protocol II begins by asserting that it does not modify the existing conditions of application of common article 3 of the 1949 Conventions, but then goes on to fix yet other conditions which seem to restrict even further its application. It might also be noted in passing that there are huge gaps in coverage, e.g., armed conflicts occurring primarily within the territory of a single Party but with incidents outside that territory. But this is not the place for a more thorough analysis of the inconsistencies and lacunae in the 1949/ 1977 texts.

39　The Final Act of the Conference on Security and Co-Operation in Europe, Department of State Publication 8826, General Foreign Policy Series 298 (August 1975); *International Legal Materials* (ILM) 14, 5 (1975): 1292, esp. Principle VIII. The final provisions ("Follow-up to the Conference") make it clear that the Act is not to be regarded as a treaty; "is not eligible for registration under Article 102 of the Charter of the United Nations," but emphasizes their "political significance" and "resolve" to hold future conferences. *International Legal Materials* 14, 5 (1975): 1324–5.

40　Principle VIII.

Afterword to Part Three

The last decade of the second millennium made nationalism appear particularly unattractive (once again). Much of the violence witnessed in this period is generally considered to have been caused by nationalist aspirations. Closely related to this, however, were secessionist movements which successfully engendered support from outside their home country. The internationalization of internal conflicts, in the context of a new geopolitical paradigm of the unipolar world in the aftermath of the cold war, has been the dominant formula in the past ten years for creating some of the most brutal interethnic conflicts. This raises a cluster of issues regarding nationalism, secession, self-determination, nation-state sovereignty, and related questions. The three essays included in Part Three offer new and interesting insights to help us sort out these pressing issues.

Richard W. Miller argues that only an universalist morality, in which fundamental principles are all expressions of equal respect for everyone everywhere, can provide an adequate basis for the moral assessment of atrocities of ethnic cleansing. In contrast, particularist moralities, which include fundamental principles of nationalist loyalty, cannot insist on the profound wrongness of these atrocities without lapsing into arbitrariness or incoherence. This argument against inserting nationalism into the foundations of morality does not, however, support the conclusion that just politics must express cosmopolitan unconcern with the aspirations of one's particular nationality. Miller takes a morality of universal respect to justify a variety of nationalist commitments in specific contexts, while regulating those commitments in ways that provide guidance to humane nationalists who seek to overcome interethnic violence. The proposed mechanism is, therefore, to take into account the ethic cleansing as the test which needs to distinguish the nationalist ethics, which is unacceptable, from those goals which, though nationalistic in their nature, can still be grounded universalistically: the nationalistic ethics is that which would, at least in some cases, demand, i.e. allow, the ethnic cleansing, whereas the universalistic-ally-based nationalism does not allow this. On this view, the ultimate basis for criticizing the unacceptable types of nationalism need not be the cos-mopolitan idea.

The motives a group might have that would make it try to get rid of another group are varied. They include hatred and historic grievances, retaliation, fear, disapproval, greed for territory and property, prejudice, nationalism, preemptive action stemming from the desire to avoid conflict and escape war. These various motives can of course be combined, and the immediate goal is always to avoid living together with a group, or with so many of its members. James Nickel examines the moral issues related to four ways in which one social group can be replaced from the territory that it inhabits by another such group: genocide, ethnic cleansing, forced assimila-tion, and expulsive secession. Closer moral scrutiny of these ways of getting rid of groups shows that while the genocide and the ethnic cleansing are unacceptable, needing to be banned by the international laws, there are rare cases of the morally acceptable separation in the form of the voluntary shifting, nonviolent assimilation or one-sided secession (which at the cost of reducing the size of the relevant territory can *de facto* mean that one group no longer inhabits the given territory). There may be a few cases, Nickel's findings suggest, in which forced relocation of peoples is permissible. Harsh coercive measures to promote assimilation are also wrong and worthy of prohibition, but milder and less coercive measures to the same end are at least sometimes permissible. And unilateral secession, including expulsive secession, has to be judged on a case-by-case basis in relation to several constraints.

Many people speak of a "right" of self-determination including a right to secession. Alfred Rubin examines whether there is such a "right" in the positive law, the "moral law" or the "political" sphere, concluding that there is no such "right" outside of the overblown rhetoric of advocates. He then argues that, since secession inevitably alters all three of the pertinent normative orders, there is a problem with reconciling to the new situation for those who have lost authority or even property as a result of a successful secession. In the end, he concludes, rather pessimistically, that secession cannot by itself create the stability its advocates claim in any of those orders without a high cost in the others.

Careful reading of the chapters in this part of the book reveals that there might exist quite a rift, on the one hand, between the outcome of the academic scrutiny given here to the questions of nationalism, self-determination, and secession, and on the other hand, the popular and simplistic statements that are ubiquitous in the mainstream media and "passionate" pronouncements politicians are likely to make about these matters.

Contemporary predominantly negative assessment of nationalism stands in sharp contrast to its heyday in the mid-twentieth century, when nationalism was highly valued and accepted as leading up to the process of decolonization. This process resulted in a completely new, somewhat fragmented, world of new nations. On the other hand the contemporary, significantly negative, attitude toward nationalism is in stark conflict with the energetic support secessionist movements are currently receiving around the globe. This contradiction may only be an appearance, however, if the world politics is directed toward both a devaluation of nation states (through restrictions on their sovereignty), and, at the same time, a proliferation of such states – making their number as large as possible while the territory they control as insignificant as possible. The questions of sovereignty and authority (or lawfulness) of governments are here necessarily closely connected. Students of the essays from this part of the collection will find many useful insights on such pressing but difficult questions.

Further Reading to Part Three

Andrew Bell-Fialkoff, *Ethnic Cleansing* (New York: St. Martin's Press, 1996).

Robert Goodin, "What Is So Special About Our Fellow Countryman?," *Ethics* 98 (1988): 663–86.

Will Kymlicka, *Multicultural Citizenship* (Oxford: Oxford University Press, 1995).

David Luban, "Just War and Human Rights," *Philosophy & Public Affairs* 9 (1980).

Alasdair MacIntyre, *Is Patriotism a Virtue?* (Lawrence, Kansas: University of Kansas Press, 1984).

Avishai Margalit and Joseph Raz, "National Self-Determination," *Journal of Philosophy* 87 (1990): 439–61.

David Miller, *On Nationality* (Oxford: Oxford University Press, 1995).

Richard W. Miller, "Cosmopolitan Respect and Patriotic Concern," *Philosophy & Public Affairs* 27 (1998): 202–24.

——, "Killing for the Homeland," *Journal of Ethics* 1 (1997): 165–85.

James W. Nickel, "What's Wrong with Ethnic Cleansing?," *Journal of Social Philosophy* 26 (1995): 5–15.

Martha Nussbaum et al., *For Love of a Country* (Boston: Beacon Press, 1996).

Andrew Oldenquist, "Loyalties," *Journal of Philosophy* 79 (1982): 173–93.

Samuel Scheffler, "Liberalism, Nationalism and Egalitarianism" in R. McKim and J. McMahan, eds., *The Morality of Nationalism* (New York: Oxford University Press, 1997.)

Charles Taylor, "The Politics of Recognition" in Amy Gutmann, ed., *Multiculturalism and the Politics of Recognition* (Princeton: Princeton University Press, 1992).

——, "Why Do Nations Have to Become States?" in his *Reconciling the Solitudes* (Montreal: McGill University Press, 1994).

Part Four

The Aftermath of
Collective Wrongdoing

11

Collective Responsibility, "Moral Luck," and Reconciliation

David Cooper

I

Not a few philosophers experience an understandable reluctance toward "being clever" about – as Wittgenstein might have regarded it – "moral gassing" about subjects as sombre as genocide, "ethnic cleansing" and "administrative massacre." This can seem as distasteful as university courses with names like "Holocaust Studies," which subject Auschwitz or Cambodia's "killing fields" to the latest fashions in sociological theory. But perhaps that reluctance is too fastidious, an abdication of responsibility even. For if philosophy has anything, however modest, to contribute to reconciliations that render the occurrence of such evils less likely, it is surely obliged to do so.

It seems to me that it may contribute something, for the following reason. La Rochefoucauld defined "reconciliation with our enemies" as "nothing more than the desire to improve our position, war-weariness, or fear of some unlucky turn of events."[1] But this is a cynic's definition of what is only a charade of reconciliation. It is real reconciliation which is wanted, one which enables men to comport with one another, once more, as men, not as monsters. It is far from clear, however, what real reconciliation requires, what conditions must be met in order to judge. "Now there has been genuine reconciliation, not a bogus truce, a war-weary interlude." In what light must the parties regard one another and their past deeds for us to speak of true reconciliation between them? Such questions invite philosophical reflection.

I shall be suggesting answers to these questions by reflecting on the notions of collective responsibility and so-called "moral luck," on the relations between these notions, and on their bearing on the requirements for reconciliation.

II

The expression "collective responsibility" is variously used. Sometimes it seems to indicate little more than that responsibility or guilt is much more widely spread than is generally assumed – as when one is told that the West or Europe, and not just the warring parties, bear responsibility for the atrocities of the Bosnian war. A more precise sense is indicated in the following remark: "The thrust of the charge of collective guilt is that a person – regardless of that person's actions – is guilty merely by dint of his or her membership in a collectivity," such as a nation.[2] This is close to the sense in which, in British politics, one speaks of the collective responsibility of the Cabinet. Each member of the Cabinet is deemed responsible for a Cabinet decision, even if he or she opposed that decision.

There is a further sense, familiar in the philosophical literature, and the one with which I am primarily concerned. In this sense, unlike the previous one, collective responsibility is not understood as the responsibility of each and every member of some collective (a club, tribe, nation, or whatever). Rather it is a responsibility ascribed to the collective itself, as when, say, the tennis club *itself* is blamed for its closure or bankruptcy – irrespective of the blame, *if any*, attaching to individual members.

I think it is clear that we do operate with a concept of collective responsibility that is not reducible to, or definable in terms of, individual responsibilities.[3] Such a concept was employed at the Nuremburg trials, when the German High Command, and not just individual officers, were charged with planning and waging aggressive war. This concept lurks, too, in Karl Jaspers's famous discussion of German guilt during the Nazi era. Despite denouncing the "crudeness of collective thinking and collective condemnation," Jaspers allows for "a sort of collective moral guilt in a people's way of life," and "a collective morality contained in . . . ways of life and feeling, from which no individual can altogether escape." This collective guilt, he implies, is not the sum or product of each member's individual guilt. If each member, even one who was in opposition to the collective morality, nevertheless accepts "co-responsibility," this will be *because* of belonging to a collective which is *itself* guilty.[4] That is a point I shall return to at the end.

III

So much, for the moment, for the idea of collective guilt. I turn to the topic of "moral luck." This expression, though not the concept it expresses, was introduced by Thomas Nagel and Bernard Williams some twenty years ago. Nagel did so as follows:

> Where a significant aspect of what someone does depends on factors beyond his control, yet we continue to treat him in that respect as an object of moral judgement, it can be called moral luck.[5]

For example, of two drunken drivers one gets home safely, the other runs into a group of schoolchildren. Despite there being no difference between them in terms of degree of negligence, the latter will be condemned – and will probably condemn himself – much more harshly than the former. The latter's "bad luck," therefore, is moral unluck, for it has resulted in a harsher moral judgment.

Moral luck can, as in that example, be a matter of the unintended consequences of actions. But it can arise in other ways, including a way very relevant to our present concerns and one suggested by the following example of Nagel's:

> Ordinary citizens of Nazi Germany had an opportunity to behave heroically ... and most of them are culpable for having failed this test. But it is a test to which the citizens of other countries were not subjected, with the result that even if they ... would have behaved as badly ... they simply did not and therefore are not similarly culpable.[6]

Ordinary Germans, that is, were genuinely culpable while their English contemporaries were not: but there is moral luck here, since those Germans would very likely not have behaved badly, while the Englishmen very likely would have, had their circumstances been reversed.

Why should "circumstantial" moral luck of this kind be germane to issues of wartime atrocities, collective responsibility, and prospects for authentic reconciliation? It certainly will be if, like many writers, one recognizes the pervasiveness of moral luck – the large degree, that is, to which moral judgment is affected by "factors beyond the control" of those being judged – *and* regards the phenomenon of moral luck as a profoundly irrational component in our moral thinking. How, such writers wonder, can it be sensible to regard some people as culpable, other people as not, when the difference in their behaviour is due to context and circumstance?

One way of pressing this argument would be as follows: if we concede that certain people would not have acted wrongly had it not been for their situation and background circumstances, we are implicitly conceding that we – their judges – would likely have acted badly too if we had been similarly placed. But now, to concede that "there, but for the grace of God and the chances of history, go we all,"[7] whilst continuing to condemn those whom grace and chance did not favor, sounds invidious and irrational.

Just such a line of argument has been followed in urging that the culpability of soldiers who have committed atrocities might at the very least be a "diminished" one. Richard Wasserstrom, for instance, argues that we need to bear in mind not only the dire penalties soldiers can face for disobedience, but a whole range of factors – training, "ethos," and so on – which make it understandable why "the ordinary soldier," who you or I might have been, "sometimes regards . . . behaviour as . . . appropriate, even though it is not." "Modern warfare," he maintains, "can be extraordinarily corruptive of the capacity to behave morally," and hence corruptive of the perfectly ordinary soldiers who, but for fortune, might have been us.[8]

A similar argument could be used to question the consistency of the moral position taken by Daniel Jonah Goldhagen in his remarkable book *Hitler's Willing Executioners*, and the similar position of some recent commentators on "ethnic cleansing" in Bosnia. Goldhagen's thesis is that the usual explanations of ordinary Germans' complicity in the Holocaust – economic hardship, fear of punishment, and the like – rest on the "grave error" of assuming that these Germans were "*un*willing executioners" and bystanders. In fact, he argues, "the central causal agent of the Holocaust" was massively shared anti-Semitic beliefs, an "eliminationist anti-Semitism," which led millions of Germans to "conclude that the Jews *ought to die*."[9] Germany, Goldhagen continues, had for centuries been in the grip of a "cognitive model" on which Jews were demonized. So powerful was this grip that "during the Nazi period, and even long before, most Germans could no more emerge with cognitive models foreign to their society . . . than they could speak fluent Romanian without ever having been exposed to it." During that period, children in particular "never had a chance" to reject that model, absorbing anti-Semitic beliefs as "matter-of-factly" as arithmetic lessons.[10]

The problem arises when, in the Foreword to the German Edition of his book, Goldhagen insists that these millions of "willing executioners" are to be "considered guilty" and "criminal." They were, he says, not "will-less cogs in a machine," but "the authors of their own actions."[11] This is problematical since it is not easy to square – according to the line of argument we are presently considering – with the clear cognitive model, of sincere and deep beliefs, which the young at least "never had a chance" to challenge rationally and resist.[12] What business do we have condemning these people if, as the analogy with one's native language suggests, we too would have naturally absorbed those beliefs had we been brought up in their society? As luck would have it, we were not: but luck, on the present argument, should not influence moral judgment.

Similarly problematical, on that argument, is the position taken by some writers towards "ethnic cleansing" in Bosnia, who also combine fierce moral condemnation of the participants with an explanation of their behavior which might suggest a more moderate verdict. In his powerful book *The Bridge Betrayed*, Michael A. Sells rejects what he regards as the flaccid judgment that, in war, "everyone is to blame, of course" and pins responsibility firmly, if not quite exclusively, on the Serbs. Rather in Goldhagen's manner, however, Sells tries to explain the Serbs' actions, not in terms of opportunism, spinelessness, or fear of punishment for nonparticipation, but of an "ideology of genocide" – this time, a "Christoslavism" informed by a demonization of the Turks, a doctrine of the "race betrayal" of those slaves who converted to Islam, and fear of a resurgent, aggressive Islam. Sells concedes that the motives of many Serbs were "deeply religious," and stresses that the component beliefs in Christoslavism constituted a "raging torrent" or "lethal brew" sufficiently powerful or intoxicating to inspire many ordinary people to act as they did.[13] The problem, once more, is that if the ideology was *that* powerful then nearly everyone subjected to it – ourselves included – would have gone along with its dictates.

IV

We have before us, then, the argument that, while the phenomenon of moral luck – of allowing factors outside people's control to influence moral judgments on them – may be a pervasive feature of our moral sensibility, it is also a deeply irrational one. It is irrational, not least, because it requires us to condemn people for behavior in which we too would likely have engaged had we been dealt a different hand in life. If this argument is to be employed in any particular case – like that of the Holocaust or "ethnic cleansing" – so as to preclude or mitigate moral blame, then, of course, various empirical claims would need to be substantiated. It would be necessary, for example, to accept something like Goldhagen's explanation of the behavior of ordinary Germans if these are to be exonerated, in whole or in part, from moral guilt. The validity of such claims or explanations is not in my competence to assess. I take no sides, for instance, on President Chirac's impatient dismissal of the "Christoslavic" factor in the Bosnian war: "Don't speak to me about any religious war," he exclaimed, "these people are without any faith...they are terrorists."[14] I shall be concerned, rather, with a philosophical issue: *if* explanations like Goldhagen's are accepted – *if*, that is, we concede that we too would, under the circumstances, have behaved like those we are tempted to condemn – is that a good reason for resisting the temptation, for witholding or tempering blame?

Before I turn to that issue, however, I want to say a little about the possible connections between moral luck, collective responsibility, and reconciliation. The first thing to say is that if, as charged above, the phenomenon of moral luck is an irrational one, then the reality and importance of collective responsibility (in my primary sense) are confirmed. For what is confirmed is the possibility of holding a collective to blame for its actions without thereby blaming all – or conceivably *any* – of the individual members who participated in those actions. If, for example, it is correct to explain people's vicious behavior in terms of a collective "way of life," the grip of a culture's "cognitive model," or the power of a "raging torrent" of ideology, from which "no individual can altogether escape," then we shall harshly judge that way of life, model, or ideology. But the thought that we too would likely have behaved as many of those people did, had luck placed us in different circumstances, will prevent us from automatically extending our condemnation to them as individuals.

The second thing to say is that, with the notion of collective responsibility thereby vindicated, a certain obstacle to reconciliation might be removed. Many people, I suspect, find it impossible to exonerate, and so to imagine reconciliation with their oppressors because they feel, there would then be nowhere to fix blame for the wrongs committed. And how can wrongs or evils have been done without people being to blame? The notion of collective responsibility suggests an answer: *a* people, a culture, a nation, or whatever can be held responsible and judged in the harshest terms without it being the case that the individual members of such a collective are blamed. (Not, at any rate, all or most of them. Doubtless there will be certain individuals, notably the architects of oppression, who can be singled out for specific responsibility.) And the possibility would thereby be opened up for exoneration, forgiveness, and reconciliation at the level of individual, personal intercourse between the erstwhile victims and oppressors.

That possibility will sound a welcome one to many ears. But whether it is a genuine one depends on finding acceptable the line of argument I was describing earlier – the argument to the effect that moral luck is an irrational phenomenon, that reflection on the truth of "There but for the grace of God . . ." can and, rationally, *ought* to preclude or mitigate moral condemnation of people whose actions were shaped by "factors beyond their control." So, as promised earlier, that line of argument needs to be assessed. Ought "grace of God" considerations temper our moral judgments?

V

With one objection to that argument, I shall be brief. If Goldhagen's explanation of the behavior of ordinary Germans during the Nazi era is right, then there is a problem about asking myself whether I would have behaved in the same way under the circumstances. For the question is not whether I, with my current beliefs and moral commitments, might have so behaved through opportunism or out of fear of punishment for noncompliance. Rather, it is whether I, if brought up in a very different climate of beliefs and values, and subjected to a very different "cognitive model," would have acted as they did. And the problem is that this question seems to lack sense. For in what sense could it be *myself* whose behavior I am then trying to envisage? Is it not crucial to my self-understanding that I am a person with certain beliefs and commitments that lend shape to the life which is mine? The objection to the argument under consideration, then, is that the question it requires each of us to ask himself, "How would I have acted under those circumstances?," is not a question that gets off the ground when "those circumstances" are of the kind emphasized by Goldhagen. Hence, no implications can be drawn from reflection on that question for judgment on those who did act under those circumstances.

This objection is, as far as it goes, well-taken. But perhaps it doesn't go very far. Imagining oneself in the shoes, or circumstances, of other people is, after all, only a heuristic device for attending to the role which chance and contingency play in shaping contexts of action, and indeed the agents themselves. This is something we can still attend to even when those contexts are so different from our actual one that it cannot be we ourselves whom we imagine transplanted into those contexts. Indeed, reflecting that it couldn't be *us* in those contexts forces recognition of the role contingency plays, not only in explaining a person's behavior, but in shaping his or her identity. *Who* people are, not only what they do, owes to "factors beyond their control." And this recognition may seem to reinforce the argument for mitigating or even suspending judgments on people. Interestingly, in the *Bhagavadgita*, Krishna employs this reflection, among others, when persuading the warrior Arjuna to overcome his scruples about killing his own kith and kin in the impending battle.[15]

That very example, however, suggests another objection to the argument under consideration. Whatever the ultimate cogency of Krishna's reasons, it is surely appropriate that Arjuna himself should have scruples. It is appropriate, too, we feel, that he should have regrets, and feel some remorse, after the battle, and not simply shrug off his killing of uncles and cousins as an unfortunate episode for which fate or contingency is alone to blame. To recall an earlier example: however *we* might judge the two drunken drivers, we would be perturbed if the "unlucky" driver were to say "Yes, of course I shouldn't have driven after ten whiskies, but I can't blame myself any more than I would have blamed myself had I got home safely and not run over those schoolchildren."

The problem is this: according to the argument under consideration, detached reflection indicates that it is irrational to base moral judgments on "lucky" factors. But the above examples suggest that we neither expect nor want people to adopt that detached stance toward *themselves*. In other words, it is remarkably hard – and far from obviously desirable – entirely to insulate moral judgment from considerations of luck or contingency. In cool moments, it may seem easy to say, of "an ordinary German" perhaps, "One cannot really blame someone for acting according to beliefs that he never had a chance to resist": but it would be hard to sympathize with the man himself were *he* calmly to say "Yes, I mustn't be too hard on myself for the atrocities I committed. After all, I was brought up in a rampantly anti-Semitic climate, the propaganda was extremely effective, etc. . . . ."

VI

A dilemma seems to have been reached. On the one hand, the claim that recognition of the role of luck or contingency should preclude or temper moral condemnation sounds persuasive. On the other hand, it is important to us that the agents themselves should not, generally, seek to excuse themselves by appealing to such considerations. Put bluntly, it seems that we often want to refrain from blaming people whilst insisting that they blame themselves. And that sounds irrational: a reflection, arguably, of a more general tension between two opposed, yet ineradicable perspectives which, at different moments, we adopt towards human behavior – a detached, "objective" one, where actions are viewed as contingent events in the world, and a more engaged, "reactive" one, where the focus is squarely on the agents and the "quality" of their acts.[16]

The only escape from this dilemma is to argue for an asymmetry between self-ascription of responsibility and ascription of responsibility to others – an asymmetry which would make it intelligible for a person to refrain from holding a second person responsible while nevertheless insisting that the latter holds himself responsible. Some philosophers allow for this asymmetry. Thus, in the case of what he calls the "moral guilt" of Nazis, Jaspers holds that "moral sentence on *the other* is suspended," since such a sentence is a matter of "self-judgement ... up to *the individual alone.*"[17] Nor is it an asymmetry unfamiliar in everyday moral discourse. At any rate, one often reads of people saying things like "No one else can judge you. That's for you alone to do." Still, it is hardly clear how sense can be made of this asymmetry. How, one wants to ask, can it be correct for you alone to judge your actions harshly? Surely the correctness of a verdict cannot depend on who pronounces it.

Here is a possible solution to the dilemma. Perhaps what is required of those who have wronged us is not a *judgment*, an assenting to some proposition, for then it is impossible to see how, if we accept their self-judgment, we can refuse to make the same judgment, assent to the same proposition. Perhaps what is required is an *act* – an apology, an expression of remorse, an owning to the harm they have done, an acknowledgment. (In such trivial cases, certainly, as someone's inadvertently treading on my toes, I expect him to say "I'm sorry," but I am not concerned whether he is passing some internal judgment on his clumsiness.) Why we find it so important that people perform such acts, even in cases where we are willing to withhold or temper condemnation, is a difficult question which I can only touch upon. I suspect that the following remark by a witness to the Truth and Reconciliation Commission in South Africa contains the germ of an answer: "acknowledging responsibility" and "making apology" serve to "confirm one's membership" of the "moral order" and of the social fellowship.[18] (The clumsy man's "I'm sorry," one might say, shows that he regards, and relates to, me as a fellow person, and serves to restore a relation that his clumsiness threatened.) But whatever the explanation, it is undeniable that people do place great weight upon self-ascription of responsibility in the form of public acts of acknowledgement and apology. (Think of the 50-year-old but continuing demand by British prisoners of war for an apology from the Emperor of Japan.)

The above consideration offers a possible escape from our dilemma. In demanding that those who have harmed us accept a responsibility that we ourselves, after due reflection on the role of contingency and "factors beyond their control," are unwilling to ascribe to them, we are not (incoherently) insisting that they judge themselves differently from how we judge them. Rather, we are demanding that they *do* something – something to acknowledge the harm they have done. This acknowledgment is indeed something that they alone can do, and something which does not conflict with the exonerating judgment that we pass.

VII

Such reflections also offer, at long last, an indication of the requirements for genuine reconciliation between peoples, groups, or nations which have inflicted suffering on one another. There are, as I see it, two such requirements which have emerged from my discussion. The first is that the parties to be reconciled hold one another collectively responsible for the sufferings inflicted. That is, they will indeed condemn one another, but without condemning all, or even many, of the individuals who participated or colluded in the wrongs done. They will refrain from such individual condemnations because of their recognition of the role of contingency or luck in shaping people's behavior – of, for example, the terrible power that a distorted "cognitive model" or religious ideology can exert over ordinary people.

But there is a second requirement if members of the erstwhile warring parties are, once more, to comport with one another as fellow human beings. They must acknowledge and apologize for their participation or collusion in the sufferings inflicted, for their unprotesting membership of the guilty collective. For members of one group to take the same "objective" view of their actions as their former enemies are now willing to take, for *them* to "put it all down" to contingency, is a refusal on their part to perform those public acts of restoration which it is essential that people perform if they are to manifest a readiness to engage, once more, in a fellowship of human beings.

Notes

1   Duc de la Rochefoucauld, *Maxims* (Harmondsworth: Penguin, 1959), no. 82.

2   Daniel Jonah Goldhagen, *Hitler's Willing Executioners: Ordinary Germans and the Holocaust* (London: Abacus, 1996), p. 481.

3   See David E. Cooper, "Collective Responsibility," in L. May and S. Hoffman, eds., *Collective Responsibility: Five Decades of Debate in Theoretical and Applied Ethics* (Maryland: Rowman & Littlefield, 1991). This volume contains articles both defending and criticizing the notion of collective responsibility.

4   Karl Jaspers, *The Question of German Guilt*, excerpted in H. Morris, ed., *Guilt and Shame* (Belmont, CA: Wadsworth, 1971), pp. 49 ff.

5   Thomas Nagel, "Moral Luck," in his *Mortal Questions* (Cambridge: Cambridge University Press, 1979), p. 26.

6   Ibid., p. 34.

7   Geoffrey Scarre, "Understanding the Moral Phenomenology of the Third Reich," *Ethical Theory and Moral Practice*, forthcoming.

8   Richard Wasserstrom, "Conduct and Responsibility in War," in May and Hoffman, eds., *Collective Responsibility*, p. 185.

9   Goldhagen, *Hitler's Willing Executioners*, pp. 9 and 14.

10   Ibid., p. 609.

11   Ibid., p. 482.

12   See Geoffrey Scarre, *Ethical Theory and Moral Practice*, for a clear articulation of this problem with Goldhagen's book.

13   Michael A. Sells, *The Bridge Betrayed: Religion and Genocide in Bosnia* (Berkeley, CA: University of California Press, 1996), pp. 63, 69, and 87.

14   Quoted in David Rohde, *A Safe Area – Srebenica: Europe's Worst Massacre Since the Second World War* (London: Pocket Books, 1997), p. 363.

15   *The Bhagavadgita*, trans. W. J. Johnson (Oxford: Oxford University Press, 1994), esp. ch. 2.

16   On this tension, see P. F. Strawson, *Freedom and Resentment and Other Essays*, London: Methuen, 1974, and Thomas Nagel, "Moral Luck."

17   Jaspers, *The Question of German Guilt*, p. 41.

18   Hugo van der Merwe, quoted in Donald W. Shriver, "The International Criminal Court: Its Moral Urgency," Gopher://gopher.igc.apc.org:70/00/orgs/icc/ ngodocs/monitor/seven/shriver.txt, 1997. p. 6.

12

Collective Remorse

Margaret Gilbert

Remorse is an important response to wrongdoing. Among other things, it can be a vital precursor to forgiveness and an important basis for reconciliation. Can a group feel remorse over its wrongful acts? If so, what does group remorse amount to? I consider three accounts of group remorse. Two are aggregative. The first of these takes group remorse to involve an aggregation of cases of personal remorse. Three versions of this account are considered. A crucial problem is that no one, on this account, has to feel remorse over an act of the group. The second aggregative account invokes what I call "membership remorse": a member's remorse over his or her group's act. I argue for the intelligibility of such remorse in light of doubts from Karl Jaspers and others. I propose, however, that generalized membership remorse does not suffice for the remorse of a group. Finally, I present the plural subject account of group remorse that I prefer. I call the phenomenon characterized in the account "collective remorse" and argue for its practical importance.

I   Introduction

As she discovered after the fact, Irene Anhalt's father had been a high-ranking member of the Gestapo in Nazi Germany. In a memoir addressed to him she writes: "I still could not give up my hope that you would feel remorse." Later she describes his deathbed scene: "With infinite effort, as if you already had to call up the words from another world, you spoke: 'It was wrong of the Spaniards to murder the Incas and steal their land.' My throat tightened with tears as I answered you: 'Yes, Daddy – thank you.'"[1]

Moral theory has a tendency to focus on the right and the good rather than on the wrong and the bad. This is not surprising. What we need, it would seem, is instruction as to how to act rightly, not on how to act wrongly.

Yet in the world we live in there is much wrongdoing. Anyone concerned with the right and the good must consider how we should respond to wrongdoing, as perpetrators, victims, and observers.

In this essay I focus on one possible response to wrongdoing. The response in question is remorse. It is not a particularly predictable response.[2] But if and when it does occur it is liable, as Anhalt's story shows, to have significant positive consequences in terms of the feelings of those other than the perpetrator and their relationship to him or her.

Anhalt's father referred not yet to the Nazis or Nazi Germany but rather – as a first step, perhaps – to the Spaniards: "It was wrong of the Spaniards to murder the Incas and to steal their land." This raises the question of wrongdoing by groups and the appropriate responses to that. Insofar as a group can act wrongly, can *it* subsequently feel remorse over its wrongful act?

What could the remorse of a group amount to? This is the question I explore in what follows.

II   Remorse

Remorse in general

To feel remorse over one's act, one must at a minimum judge that one has done something seriously wrong. The term "remorse" suggests that the wrong is definitely more than a mere peccadillo. Regret might suffice for trivial matters. Remorse would be too strong in such a case.

I shall assume that remorse involves a judgment of serious *moral* wrongdoing. That one judges one's act to have been *morally* wrong may or may not be essential to remorse as such. Many instances, however, clearly involve such a judgment.

This does not yet distinguish feeling remorse over one's act from feeling guilt over it. One difference between these two may be that one who feels remorse could always sincerely exclaim, "Would that I had not acted so!" This may not be true of one who feels guilt.[3]

For present purposes I shall assume that we are concerned with altogether *well-founded* remorse. That would mean at least that it is not founded on a mistake about what, if anything, one has done. Nor does it depend on a false judgment to the effect that what one did was seriously morally wrong. It may be that remorse over one's act involves a judgment of one's blameworthiness. In that case well-founded remorse would involve no mistake on that score.

Consequences of remorse

If one truly feels remorse over what one has done, this is liable, when recognized, to find a response in others. There may be a sense that one has undergone a major transformation, a transformation deep enough for something approaching forgiveness to take place.

The reason for this sense of transformation is clear. Remorse is liable to involve a fundamental change of perspective: one did a certain thing without hearkening to any doubts one might have about it. When one feels remorse it is as if, when it is too late to avoid the action, one finally hearkens to such doubts, perhaps *having them* for the first time. Were the original situation to repeat itself now, one is apparently now so disposed that one would not perform the action.

On this account of it, one who experiences true remorse is clearly liable to act differently in the future. Thus it may reasonably provoke not just backward-looking forgiveness but a renewal of forward-looking trust.

Remorse and relationships

Given its connections to forgiveness and the restoration of trust, remorse is clearly of great importance where what is at stake is *a relationship* between a perpetrator and a victim, a relationship that either may or must continue in some form or other.[4] Some such relationships are relationships between groups – for instance, nations, different factions within a nation, and families. Can groups feel remorse over what they have done?

III   Is Group Remorse Possible?

Skepticism about group emotions in general, and an initial response

It may be argued that a group or collectivity cannot feel remorse because remorse is an emotion, and groups cannot have emotions of their own. Their individual human members can, of course, have emotions of *their* own, but *groups* cannot. Why might one think this?

Emotions, it may be argued, essentially involve *feelings*, which are some-what on a par with *sensations*. An example of such feelings would be the so-called pangs of remorse. Let us call feelings with this "sensation-like" quality "feeling-sensations." It may be proposed that nothing that is not a living organism can have feeling-sensations.

One response to this type of argument might be that it is not clear that emotions essentially involve feeling-sensations. It may be questioned, more specifically, whether to feel remorse is essentially to feel anything of the nature of pangs, twinges, and so on. I have supposed that remorse centrally involves a judgment of serious wrongdoing plus a thought of the form "Would that I had not done that!" Such a thought encapsulates, one might say, a desire not to have acted in such a way. Might this judgment and this desire not be the central core and essence of remorse?[5]

The skeptic about collective emotions might respond that even if it is correct, this last proposal requires that emotions are properties of *minds*. And there are no group minds. Hence there can be no group emotions.

Whatever we think of these skeptical arguments, what are we to make of the fact that people often quite comfortably say things like "Our family mourns the loss of a dear friend," "The whole department is in a state of shock," and "The nation views with great remorse what happened in those years"? People ascribe a whole range of emotions to groups, including remorse. What do these ascriptions mean? Alternatively, what are people talking about when they speak this way?

In what follows I shall understand by "a group's remorse" whatever it is that people refer to when they speak in those terms. Let us now pursue the question: What is it for a group to feel remorse over what it has done?[6]

Skepticism about a group's action, and an initial response

The skeptic about group remorse in particular may observe that this raises the question whether a group as such can act. One of the founders of sociology, Max Weber, asserted, indeed, that "there is no such thing as a collective personality which 'acts.'"[7]

Weber may have had in mind the fact that for him action was defined in terms of what he calls "subjective meaning."[8] It may seem to follow that groups as such cannot act. If we take this line, we have a problem similar to that of denying the possibility of group emotion.

There is a problem because people talk all the time as if groups act: "The USSR invaded Afghanistan," "The department elected Jack chair," and so on. Are they referring to some actual situation, and if so, what are the components of that situation? What, in other words, do the group actions of common parlance amount to?

I shall at first proceed on the basis of two rough assumptions about group actions. I take it that many group actions conform to these assumptions. They thus help to define a *standard type* of group action.

I shall assume, first, that when a group acts, one or more members of the group *contribute directly* to the group's action. For example, someone's flying over enemy territory may be a direct contribution to his group's act of war making.

I shall assume, second, that some members of a group that acts may *not* directly contribute to the group's action. Thus a university department may elect Jack Jones chair, though one member of the department, Peg, is on leave abroad and does not know the election is being held. Though Peg did not contribute directly to the group's action, she can properly say *of the department* "We elected Jack."

In relation to a given action of a group, I shall call the members who directly contribute to the action "active" members and the rest "passive" members. The distinction between active and passive members may be hard to characterize precisely, but the examples here fall clearly enough on one or another side.

It is now time to appraise some candidate accounts of group remorse. I shall consider three such accounts.

IV   Group Remorse I:
The Aggregated Personal Remorse Account

The first account is what I call the aggregated personal remorse account. It involves a sum or aggregate of states of personal remorse. By *personal remorse* I mean an individual person's remorse over an act of his or her own.

This account runs roughly as follows:

> *A group G feels remorse over its act A* if and only if each active member of G feels remorse over an act or acts of his or her own and taken together these acts comprise all of the members' acts that contributed directly to the group's act A.

For instance, an officer may feel remorse for having ordered the killing of a group of civilians, and each of his men may feel remorse for following his orders and killing several people. According to the account, the group comprising this officer and his men satisfies the conditions for feeling remorse over the group's act of killing the civilians.

This account has some attractive features. The state of affairs it takes to be a group's remorse is clearly a possible one. No "mysterious" entities, such as a group mind that operates independently of the minds of the group members, are posited. It is clear that only individual human minds are involved. In addition, insofar as some individual members of a group did morally repugnant things, their personally feeling remorse would appear to be desirable. Among other things, it is likely to lead to better things in the future.

In spite of these advantages, several things suggest that this account must be rejected. For one thing, according to the account each of the relevant people must feel remorse over his own action or actions, and that is all. But it is supposed to be saying what it is for a *group* to feel remorse over *its* act. Here no one is even focusing on an action of the group.

In response to this concern, the original account could be amended to run something like this:

> *A group G feels remorse over its act A* if and only if each active member of G personally feels remorse over having directly contributed to the group's act *A*.

In this case there is a sense in which all of the relevant people are, indeed, *focusing on* an action of the group. No one yet, though, feels *remorse over* an action of the group. Each of the relevant members' remorse is over an action of his own, namely, his contribution to the group's action, as such.

This account also shares the following problem with its predecessor. Perhaps very few people directly contributed to the group action in question. Now suppose these people feel remorse over their contributions as such. It would surely seem odd to say, just for that reason, that *the group* felt remorse over its action. Yet if these few do feel remorse, the conditions laid down in the amended account are satisfied.

We could try amending the account again to include remorseful feelings on behalf of the passive members over having acted in such a way as to be associated, *as group members*, with the act in question. Then we would have something along the following lines:

> *A group G feels remorse over its act A* if and only if each member of G feels remorse *either* over his or her direct contribution *or*, for those not directly contributing, over his or her association with the group's act A.

A problem here is that it may not be *reasonable* for the various passive members to feel remorse of this kind. Some may have had little choice, for instance, regarding their membership in this particular group. Some may personally have fought against the performance of the group act as best they could. And so on.

When all or most of the passive members reasonably do *not* feel personal remorse over anything they have done relating to their group membership or to the group's act, can there be no group remorse over the group's act? That is at least not obvious, but the newly amended account makes it true by definition.

Suppose that, as may sometimes be the case, every group member *is* personally remorseful over his or her *contribution to* or *association with* the group act. This situation still involves no remorse over the group's act itself.

It seems, then, that both the original aggregated personal remorse account and two variants on it are problematic. The two variants both require that the personal remorse bear some relation to the group's act, but none involves remorse over the group's act itself. In addition, all seem to give the wrong result for the case in which there are few active members and they are the only group members to feel personal remorse in relation to the group's act. On the first two accounts, which both refer to the active members only, *there will be group remorse* solely by virtue of the personal remorse of these few, which seems wrong. On the third account, which requires all members to feel personal remorse over their participation or association with the group's action, *group remorse is ruled out by definition*. This, too, seems wrong.

V   Group Remorse II: The Aggregated Membership Remorse Account

Is there any other type of account available? In particular, is there an account that does not appeal to the remorse of particular group members over their personal contributions to or association with an act of the group? At this point what I shall call the *aggregated membership remorse account* may suggest itself. It runs roughly as follows:

A group G feels remorse over its act A if and only if the members of G – both active and passive – personally feel remorse over act *A*.

Does it make sense for *any* individual member of a group personally to feel remorse over the *group's* act? Common experience suggests that it does. Reflecting on what her group has done, Sarah may think remorsefully, "We did a terrible thing!" referring precisely to what *her group* did and not to what she personally did. She is not likely to question the intelligibility of her emotional response.

That does not mean its intelligibility cannot be questioned. In *The Question of German Guilt*, philosopher and psychiatrist Karl Jaspers movingly recounts his own similar responses to the acts of his country but worries that in so responding he has "strayed completely into the realm of feeling" without the warrant of reason.[9]

Before pursuing this question, let me give the emotional response at issue a label. I shall call it "membership remorse." It is (more fully) a group member's remorse over the act of a group of which he or she is a member.

What does the present account of group remorse seem to have in its favor? Some of its attractions are as follows.

First, there is here – finally – remorse over the group's act itself. Second, on this account a group could in principle feel remorse even when, reasonably, only a few members felt personal remorse over either personal contributory actions or association with the group. For what is required is that members feel membership remorse, not personal remorse. Precisely which and how many members feel personal remorse – if any – is not relevant to the issue of group remorse on this account.

Third, insofar as membership remorse is intelligible at all, it will apparently be appropriate for all members to feel it in relation to a relevant action of the group's. Its appropriateness, in other words, is not restricted to active members or to any other special category of member. It concerns what the group has done, not what the member has personally done. Hence the conditions postulated by the account are not themselves unfeasible for a group of reasonable people even when most members have no reason for remorse over actions of their own.

Is membership remorse intelligible? Can it indeed be appropriate for both active and passive members in relation to a candidate group action? What of someone who did not know the action was taking place at the time? Or someone who protested the action, or . . . ?

One can argue that there need be no exceptions among group members with respect to the intelligibility of group remorse. The argument I have in mind appeals to a relatively fine-grained model of group action. This will be useful not only in relation to the evaluation of the aggregated membership remorse account but for other purposes of this chapter as well.

VI   Group Action Revisited

I now sketch an account of group action that goes beyond the assumptions I have been operating with so far. It allows us to grant intelligibility to the idea of membership remorse. I first introduced this account of group action in my book *On Social Facts* in 1989.[10] I have been elaborating it since and continue to do so. The core of this account is the following necessary condition on group action:

> For a group to act or (initially) to have its own goal for action, group members must be *jointly committed* to accept the relevant goal *as a body*.

What is it to accept a goal as a body? I understand this somewhat as follows. For two people to accept a goal as a body is for them, *as far as is possible*, to constitute through their several actions (including their utterances) a single "body" or person who accepts that goal. To put it somewhat quaintly, these two people must attempt as best they can to constitute as far as they can a four-handed, two-bodied person who (single-mindedly) has that goal.

The type of commitment appropriate to something like accepting a goal as a body is a *joint* commitment.[11] One way to understand what a joint commitment amounts to is to compare and contrast it with a *personal* commitment. Consider first a personal decision, which is, I take it, a form of personal commitment.

Suppose Mike decides to vote for candidate *C* in the election. One way of thinking about this decision is as embodying a special kind of order or command: a *self-addressed* command. Mike, in effect, commands himself to vote for candidate *C*. He is the sole author of the command; he is also in a position to rescind the command unilaterally by, as we say, "changing his mind." Until he does so, however, the command stands, and if he fails to vote for candidate *C* he can be criticized in light of it.

This "self-addressed" command model of personal commitment can be extended to cover joint commitment also. A joint commitment – as I understand it – is not a sum of personal commitments but a truly joint commitment, the commitment of two or more people. These two or more people constitute the author of the relevant command, and no one is in a position unilaterally to rescind it. The parties must rescind it together.[12]

Given this understanding of joint commitment one can argue that one who defaults on a joint commitment offends against the other parties. They have a clear ground for calling the offender to account, and to rebuke or impose other forms of punitive pressure on him or her.[13]

All joint commitment has the same general form: for some predicate @, people jointly commit *to @ as a body*. People enter joint commitments by mutually expressing their willingness to be jointly committed in the way in question with the relevant others. This is how the relevant joint order is issued. Thus Harry may ask Frank "Shall we meet at six?" If Frank replies "Sure, that'd be great," they now have a joint commitment, indeed, an explicit agreement.[14]

In a large group where people do not know one another personally, they must openly express their willingness to be jointly committed with others of the relevant type. For instance, each might openly express his or her willingness to be jointly committed in some way with others living on a certain island. The commitment in this case might be to abide "as one" by a certain rule of the road or as a body to accept certain people as arbiters in their disputes. It must be apparent that all of the relevant expressions have been made.[15]

The existence of these expressions should, indeed, in all cases be "common knowledge" in roughly the sense introduced by David Lewis in his book *Convention*.[16] Informally speaking, one might say there is common knowledge in a group G that *p* if and only if the fact that *p* is "out in the open" in G.

Going back to group action, we can say:

> *A group G performed an action A* if and only if, roughly, the members of G were jointly committed to accepting as a body the relevant goal X, and *acting in light of this joint commitment*, relevant members of G acted so as to bring X about.

For instance, you and I may be jointly committed to accepting as a body the goal of having the house painted by virtue of the painting activity of each of us. Subsequently we may both act in the light of our commitment, coordinating our behavior in such a way that our goal is reached. It can then be said that we (collectively) painted the house.

Acting in the light of a joint commitment will often involve the parties in a variety of side agreements or in carefully monitoring one another's behavior or both. The initial joint commitment need not specify a procedure for its satisfaction.

For present purposes it is important to note that members of G may be jointly committed to accepting a certain goal as a body without all knowing or even conceiving of the content of the commitment. This can happen if there is a "ground-level" joint commitment allowing some person or body to make decisions, form plans, and so on, on behalf of the jointly committed persons. Thus an established leader and his or her henchmen may formulate and carry out a plan in the group's name, and the members properly say of the group as a whole, "We did it."

VII   Group Blameworthiness

Does remorse over an act imply the blameworthiness of that act? I have not taken a position on this issue here. But if the answer is positive, it seems that feelings of membership remorse can only be fully intelligible if the idea of a blameworthy group makes sense. Many theorists have supposed it does not, or at least they have supposed the unintelligibility of what they refer to as "collective guilt." As they conceive of it, this seems to amount to much the same thing as group blameworthiness.

It is not clear that this skepticism is warranted. Some pertinent points follow.

I take it as a good axiom to respect the intelligibility of common pretheoretical thoughts so far as is possible. Thus if remorse implies blameworthiness, the existence of membership remorse itself suggests the intelligibility of a group's blameworthiness, as it suggests its own intelligibility.

The idea that a group may indeed be blameworthy is also supported by the way people talk outside the context of membership remorse. Outsiders frequently say such things as "Switzerland must take the blame for the current crisis," suggesting that in our everyday conception of things groups can be worthy of blame.

Is there an intelligible basis for speaking of the blameworthiness of a group as such? Insofar as this requires a collective or group agent, I have suggested satisfiable conditions of group action. The framework of analysis I have used in relation to group action can also be applied to such things as group belief, including a group's moral belief. Thus I argued in *On Social Facts* that according to our everyday conception, a group as such believes something if and only if the members are jointly committed to believe that thing as a body.[17]

One can, then, make sense of the idea that a group did something it took to be wrong. It also makes sense to distinguish between the coerced and the uncoerced actions of groups. A group may "cave in" to external pressure – or it may act in disregard of such pressure or in its absence. Thus a group can do something it knows to be wrong without being pressured into it.

If in spite of these things a group for some reason cannot be considered blameworthy for its act, and if membership remorse implies the group's blameworthiness, then membership remorse will be that much less intelligible.[18]

VIII Membership Remorse and the Remorse of a Group

Leaving aside the intelligibility of a group's blameworthiness (in favor of which I have argued), the joint commitment account of group action supports the intelligibility of another aspect of membership remorse. That is its suggestion that the group's members all bear some relevant relation to the act of their group.

The joint commitment underlying a group act, on this analysis, provides such a relation. The remorseful person may be linked to his (or her) group's act not by any directly contributing act of his own but rather by his participation in such a commitment. This provides an intelligible basis for, if you like, his *identification* with the group as agent in this case. It allows him to say, with point, "We did it" – as opposed to "They did it" or "Some of us did it."

Some authors appear to see a person's identification with a group's act as self-justifying. In other words, if I identify with a group's act, there is no issue as to whether this identification is justified.[19] I see such identification as, on the contrary, raising the question of justification.[20] And I see participation in an appropriate joint commitment as sufficient justification. Identification has also been brought forward as a ground of political obligations.[21] Here, too, it remains seriously obscure how identification is supposed to do the necessary work of justification.[22]

If Jane – with justification – feels remorse over an act of her group, she may feel no remorse on her own account. She may know that she has acted honorably in the matter of the group action. She may have attempted to stop it or been ignorant of it without culpability for that ignorance. She is still tied to the group and its action by virtue of her participation in the underlying joint commitment.

She can therefore intelligibly think not only that "We did it" but "We should not have done it!" and "Would that we had not done it!" and "We must never do that again!" And she may feel an accompanying pang of remorse. Given its context, this might reasonably be called "a pang of membership remorse."

Suppose now that we grant that those who express membership remorse are doing something that is fully intelligible and that may be entirely appropriate even for those with no personal culpability. Should we accept the membership model of group remorse? I suggest not.

Note first that this account, like the previous ones, is an aggregative account. What is aggregated here is the (membership) remorse of the individual members. It is not remorse over their own acts, or what I have been calling "personal remorse." Rather it is remorse over the group's act. Still, on the ground, so to speak, we have what is clearly a number of *separate subjects of remorse* rather than one undivided subject of remorse – the group.

Another point, briefly, is that in principle this aggregated membership remorse could be hidden from public view. Each group member may think that he (or she) alone feels remorse. He may therefore not express his remorse openly but suffer it secretly. Once one brings this possibility out, the idea that we should say that the group feels remorse in this case is likely to seem even more suspect.

One could posit common knowledge of the generalized feeling of membership remorse. This, however, does not overcome the first problem. We will then have common knowledge that a set of individuals, the members of group G, feel membership remorse. What of the group as such? There still seems to be a gap between what we have here and something we can with clear aptness refer to as the remorse of a group as such.

It is worth pointing out that this new common knowledge condition can be fulfilled without anyone having publicly expressed remorse. In addition, there may be serious barriers to such public expression. Imagine that in this group the members are jointly committed together to uphold the view that the group can do no wrong. Unless something is done about this joint commitment, it stands as a barrier to anyone's saying that the group has indeed done something wrong.[23]

In this situation group members may constantly speak to one another as if the group's act, A, was perfectly fine, properly justified. This may be the continuing tenor of public discourse. All may realize that they risk rebukes in the name of the joint commitment should they speak otherwise without qualification. And few may wish to risk even the use of the legitimate qualifier "I personally" as in "I personally feel that we acted badly when..."[24] Though this does not amount to outright subversion of the joint commitment, it could be seen as inherently subversive; hence one risks being seen as disloyal to the group even if going only so far.[25]

In the case as it has now been described, it would surely be reasonable to say that *the group* did not yet feel remorse over its act A, though the members individually felt membership remorse over *A*, and this was common knowledge within the group. One might be reluctant to give up the aggregated membership remorse account, perhaps in its common knowledge version, if no alternative was available. There is an alternative, however, to which I now turn.

IX   The Plural Subject Account of Group Remorse

The account

I now come to the account of group remorse that I favor. It is perhaps predictable given all that has gone before. I call it the "plural subject" account. It runs thus:

> *A group G feels remorse over an act A* if and only if the members of G are jointly committed to feeling remorse as a body over act *A*.

Following what was said earlier, the joint commitment of the parties is (more fully) *to constitute as far as possible by their several actions, including utterances, a single body that feels remorse.* I say that people who are jointly committed to doing something as a body constitute the *plural subject* of the "doing" in question. Thus I call this the plural subject account of group remorse.[26]

There is no doubt that the phenomenon characterized by this account is possible. One who takes it to exist is not committed to the existence of any dubious entities. The existence of a joint commitment is a function of the understandings, expressive actions, and common knowledge of the parties.

Pangs of remorse in the context of group remorse

Here is a possible worry about this account. Are what I have been calling "feeling-sensations" part of the phenomenon in question? If not, can it really be remorse?

Let us first consider the case of remorse in general. Can one who does not feel pangs of remorse really feel remorse? Contrary to the drift of the questions, the correct answer may be affirmative.

Consider the case of an individual human being. When I say to you "I feel great remorse" must I be saying something false unless there are pangs or the like in the background? On the face of it, I need not be saying something false. Note that some apparently equivalent expressions do not use the term "feel" at all: "I am full of remorse"; "I am truly remorseful."

If this is right, a joint commitment to constitute with certain others, as far as is possible, a body that feels remorse would not require the production of associated pangs of remorse. Nor would it require that one attempt to produce such pangs.

Be that as it may, pangs of remorse are presumably common accompaniments of remorse in an individual human being. Witness the commonplace nature of the phrase "pang of remorse." Is group remorse, on this account, a type of remorse essentially devoid of these natural accompaniments of remorse in an individual human being?

Against this idea, consider the following. Suppose one is internationally conforming to a joint commitment to constitute with certain others, as far as is possible, a body that feels remorse. One's conformity is likely to involve one in saying such things as "What we did was truly terrible," "Would that we hadn't done that!" and so on. In saying such things and acting accordingly in light of one's joint commitment, one may experience certain associated "pangs."

It is worth considering how best to describe these pangs. Are they associated most directly with one's personal remorse, with one's membership remorse, or with the remorse of the group itself?

By hypothesis, the pangs in question are directly responsive to the group's remorse rather than to any remorse of one's own. Had the group not come to feel remorse, one might never have felt this way. And one's feeling this way may not correspond to any judgments one has made in one's heart with respect to the group's act or to any associated act of one's own.

The pangs in question, then, may best be described as pangs of remorse associated with the group's remorse or, more succinctly, as "pangs of group remorse." That there can be pangs of group remorse in this sense does not fly in the face of common sense, reason, or science. There is no suggestion that there are pangs of remorse experienced within some kind of collective consciousness that exists independent of individual human minds. Pangs of group remorse, in the sense envisaged, exist in and through the experiences of particular group members. Nonetheless, this way of labelling them makes sense.

This is an intriguing line of argument. Whatever one makes of it, for reasons already given the plausibility of the plural subject account of group remorse does not hang on its conclusion – namely, that on that account there is some likelihood of plausibly so-called pangs of group remorse.

I propose that if we are faced with a case of group remorse according to the plural subject account, it is more apt for the title of "group remorse" than the phenomena captured by any of the aggregative or summative accounts considered. It alone brings remorse to the collective level. I propose further that standard everyday claims to the effect that we collectively feel remorse are well interpreted in terms of this account. To make it clear that I am talking about group remorse according to the plural subject account, I shall in what follows refer to it, exclusively, as "collective remorse."

Collective remorse does not rule out personal remorse for one's personal role – and in many cases it will be entirely appropriate to feel such remorse. It does not, however, entail personal remorse for one's personal role – and in many cases it will not be appropriate to feel such remorse.

What I have called "membership remorse" is a person's remorse over the actions of his or her group. This is expressible as "I feel remorse over what my group has done," as opposed to "I feel remorse over what I have done." Evidently, I can feel membership remorse in the absence of collective remorse. Indeed, such membership remorse can be widespread without collective remorse being present, as in the case imagined earlier.

It is possible, too, that there can be collective remorse without membership remorse. In other words, I might be able correctly to avow "We feel remorse over our act" without being able correctly to avow "I personally feel remorse over our act." Perhaps I have not reached my own decision on the matter, though I was willing to be jointly committed with the other members of my group to feel remorse as a body.[27]

Clearly, though, there are likely to be de facto connections between membership remorse and collective remorse. If membership remorse is widespread, it is presumably apt to give rise to collective remorse, though it may not do so in special circumstances. If, by virtue of my participation in the prevailing collective remorse, I regularly allude to the wickedness of what we have done, express the wish that it had not happened, and so on, I may well come to reflect privately on the group act in question. I may myself judge it to be evil, myself wish that we had not acted so. In other words, I may come to experience membership remorse, my own remorse over what we have done.

X   Remorse as a Beginning

Remorse may seem at the end of the day too passive a basis for the reconciliation of victims and persecutors – and of two parties each may have played both roles at some time in their relationship. Yet it is unlikely that without remorse such reconciliation can take place.

Given the existence of remorse, one can expect that perpetrators will go on to perform relevant acts, for instance, to provide restitution or compensation for victims or (in the case of groups) to make relevant changes in their constitution or their laws. Refusal to engage in such acts, when appropriate, will throw doubt on the claim of remorse, if it does not actually refute it.

Thus collective remorse according to the plural subject account is liable to lead to important reconciling actions. When people understand that they are jointly committed as far as is possible together to constitute a single body that feels remorse, they will understand that their remorsefulness (as a body) calls for them to carry out appropriate actions.

I hazard that without collective remorse, where appropriate, intergroup relationships are likely to remain stuck at a level of continuing defensiveness and hostility. Periods of calm are likely to erupt into war over and over again. Collective remorse and collective forgiveness may be required for any genuine reconciliation and any lasting peace.

Notes

Versions of this paper were presented in November 1997 to the Philosophy Department at the University of Connecticut, Storrs; to my undergraduate class in philosophy of social science at the same university; and to an international conference on War Crimes at the University of California, Santa Barbara. I also used some of this material in a presentation at the University of Illinois, Urbana-Champaign, in December 1998. I received many useful and stimulating comments on those occasions. I am particularly grateful to Thomas Fote and Jerry Shaffer. Thanks also to Anthony Ellis for written comments and to James Robertson for lending me the book in which I found Irene Anhalt's essay. The subject is a rich one, and this chapter only begins to explore it. This chapter first appeared in Margaret Gilbert, *Sociality and Responsibility: New Essays in Plural Subject Theory* (Lanham, MD: Rawman and Littlefield, 2000).

1   Irene Anhalt, "Farewell to My Father," in *The Collective Silence: German Identity and the Legacy of Shame*, Barbara Heimannsberg and Christoph J. Schmidt, eds., trans. C. O. Harris and G. Wheeler (San Francisco: Jossey-Bass, 1993), p. 48.
2   People will often remark of someone who has done some dreadful thing, "He showed no remorse." Sometimes they say this with a degree of incredulity, as if they are thinking, "How could he not feel remorse for *that*?" Presumably, though, the more horrible an intentional act, the less one would expect the perpetrator to

feel remorse. The very performance of such an act suggests that the agent lacks moral perspicacity; yet some such perspicacity is necessary for remorse.

3   Thus Herbert Morris: "A person who feels guilty may not be disposed to say, 'I'm sorry' or 'Forgive me'; he may not feel sorry about what he did . . . He may be neither contrite nor repentant . . . We need only think of the young boy who disobeys his father and who, while feeling guilty, also looks upon himself with more respect. He feels guilty but prefers being damned to renouncing his act." Herbert Morris, "Guilt and Suffering," *Philosophy East and West* 21 (1971): 107–8.

4   Irene Anhalt's case and others like it may fall under this rubric in a rather special way. Anhalt would seem to have had several motives for her persisting hope for her father's remorse. She clearly wished her father finally to embrace the values she held dear; this would be a precondition of his remorse and would be liable to give rise to it. She may have felt his remorse would benefit him in that he would at last see true and judge himself accordingly. She evidently also felt it would benefit her in allowing her to experience more positive feelings toward him. Among other things, she would presumably be able both to understand and to respect him more. She seems also to have felt his actions east a shadow on his family, including herself. In that case she may have sought a basis for her own act of forgiveness. As has often been claimed, it is not clear that anyone other than someone's victim can have the standing to *forgive* him or her. Here Anhalt would not be forgiving her father in the name of his primary victims, but she might have a basis for forgiveness nonetheless.

5   Jerome Shaffer has contemplated an analysis of emotion that takes beliefs and desires as essential to emotion in general, though not exclusively so. See his article "An Assessment of Emotion," *American Philosophical Quarterly* (1983): 161–72. The possibility of an analysis purely in terms of beliefs and desires is mooted at p. 171. I thank Professor Shaffer for bringing this article to my attention in the context of this chapter.

6   As will appear from considerations to be advanced later, this is not the only kind of remorse a group might feel. But this question is fine for present purposes.

7   Max Weber, *Economy and Society*, 1, G. Roth and C. Wittich, eds. (Berkeley: University of California Press, 1978) (from the posthumous German original, 1922), p. 14.

8   For discussion of the nature of subjective meanings in Weber's sense see Margaret Gilbert, *On Social Facts* (London: Routledge, 1989), ch. 2.

9   Karl Jaspers, *The Question of German Guilt*, trans. E. B. Ashton (New York: Capricorn, 1947), pp. 80–1. I discuss this passage in more detail in "How to Feel Guilt: Three Different Ways," presented at the conference Guilt, Shame, and Punishment at Columbia University School of Law, March 8, 1998, in honor of Herbert Morris.

10 See especially Gilbert, *On Social Facts*, pp. 154–67. See also chapter 8, *Sociality and Responsibility* (2000).

11 For relatively extensive discussions of joint commitment see Margaret Gilbert, *Living Together: Rationality, Sociality, and Obligation* (Lanham, MD: Rowman and Littlefield, 1996), introduction, and chapter 1, *Sociality and Responsibility* (2000).

12 I elaborate on the "self-addressed command" interpretation of commitment and joint commitment in chapter 4, *Sociality and Responsibility* (2000).

13 In chapter 4, *Sociality and Responsibility* (2000), there is a related argument that those who are party to a joint commitment have inextricably associated obligations toward and rights against the other parties.

14 An explicit agreement is not required for the formation of a joint commitment; see chapter 1, *Sociality and Responsibility* (2000), and elsewhere. I take it, though, that everyday agreements are joint commitment phenomena. An agreement may be characterized as a joint decision, a joint decision as constituted by a joint commitment to uphold a certain decision as a body. See Margaret Gilbert, "Is an Agreement an Exchange of Promises?" *Journal of Philosophy* 90, 12 (1993): 627–49.

15 For further discussion of the large-group case see, for instance, chapter 6, this volume.

16 David Lewis, *Convention: A Philosophical Study* (Cambridge, Mass: Harvard University Press, 1969); reprinted by Basil Blackwell. For further discussion and references on common knowledge see Gilbert, *On Social Facts*, chapter 4. See also chapter 1, *Sociality and Responsibility* (2000).

17 I have discussed collective belief in a number of places; see Gilbert, *Living Together*, 7–8, for a brief overview of these discussions. See also chapter 3, *Sociality and Responsibility* (2000).

18 See chapter 8, *Sociality and Responsibility* (2000), for a discussion of philosophical skepticism about collective guilt and the relationship of such skepticism to an account of collective guilt along the lines sketched here.

19 See, for instance, Herbert Morris, "Nonmoral Guilt," in *Responsibility, Character, and the Emotions: New Essays in Moral Psychology*, Ferdinand Schoeman, ed. (Cambridge: Cambridge University Press, 1987), pp. 239–40; John Horton, *Political Obligation* (Atlantic Highlands, NJ: Humanities Press International, 1992), pp. 151–4.

20 For further remarks on the appeal to identification see Margaret Gilbert, "Group Wrongs and Guilt Feelings," *Journal of Ethics* 1, 1 (1997): 65–84.

21 See, for instance, Yael Tamir, *Liberal Nationalism* (Princeton: Princeton University Press, 1993): "Our obligation to help fellow members derives from a shared sense of membership." On the need for some grounding to a "shared sense of membership" (in a distributive sense of "shared") see the discussion in Gilbert, *On Social Facts*, pp. 146–52.

22 Cf. A. John Simmons, "Associative Political Obligations," *Ethics* 106 (1996): 247–73: "Identification with a political community or with the role of member within it is not sufficient for possessing political obligations" (264). Simmons

goes on to envisage that one might "cast identification as a sort of consent," rightly seeing this as an additional move, wrongly (I would say) seeing it as tantamount to a reassertion of the "voluntarism that the identity thesis was originally advanced to replace" (265). For some explanation of why I say "wrongly" here, see Gilbert, *Living Together*, chapter 12 and chapter 6, *Sociality and Responsibility* (2000).

23 See the discussion of collective belief in Chapter 3, *Sociality and Responsibility* (2000).

24 On the permissibility of the use of such qualifiers in the context of an established group belief see Gilbert, *On Social Facts*, chapter 5, especially 288–292, or the similar discussion in Gilbert, *Living Together*, 200–203.

25 Cf. Chapter 3, *Sociality and Responsibility* (2000).

26 I introduced the phrase "plural subject" with the meaning I am giving it here in Gilbert, *On Social Facts*, chapter 4.

27 Compare the discussion in Gilbert, *Living Together*, pp. 206–7, of reasons why one might be willing to participate in one's group's belief that such-and-such though not personally believing that such-and-such.

13

Reparations to Native Americans?

J. Angelo Corlett

North American history is replete with accounts of atrocities being inflicted by members of one group on members of another. Some such examples include: the seizure by the French, the British, the Spanish, the Dutch, and later by the United States and Canadian governments, respectively, of millions of acres of land inhabited by Native Americans; the genocide (or attempt therein) of certain Native (North) Americans[1] by the US military at the order of, among others, former US President Andrew Jackson; the enslavement of several Native Americans in the US, etc.[2] These and other significant harms have found little justice in the form of reparations. This paper seeks to clarify the nature of reparations and analyzes arguments against reparations to historically and seriously wronged groups with the primary focus being on the Native American experiences in the US.[3]

It is an embarrassing fact that major western political philosophies by and large ignore (or, at best, give short shrift to) the claims of Native (North) Americans[4] to property.[5] And given the importance of the concept of private property rights in historic and contemporary western political philosophy, it is vital to delve into problems which, among other things, question who ought to be seen as having the overriding moral claim or right to, say, the lands on which entire countries and their citizenry's reside, such as with the United States. For the moral legitimacy of a country, it is assumed, is contingent on at least the extent to which that country acquires *justly* the land on which it and its citizens reside. The problem of reparations to Native Americans raises queries concerning the fundamental moral legitimacy of the US. For it challenges the moral basis of putative US rights to lands which, it is assumed, are necessary for its economic and political survival.

What *are* reparations? And are reparations to Native Americans morally justified? This chapter seeks to answer these and related questions as they concern how Native American lives and lands were lost to the US by means of war crimes committed against various Native American nations by the US Government and its military. It is assumed herein that the concept of property rights itself is an important part of a plausible political philosophy.

Reparations, according to *Black's Law Dictionary*, involve "payment for an injury: redress for a wrong done." They are payments "made by one country to another for damages done during war." Reparations involve restitution, which is the "act of restoring . . . anything to its rightful owner; the act of making good or giving equivalent for any loss, damage or injury; and indemnification. . . . A person who has been unjustly enriched at the expense of another is required to make restitution to the other."[6] Those receiving reparations are typically groups, though there seems to be no moral or logical preclusion to individuals receiving them. Often the evils perpetrated are such that there is no "just" or genuinely sufficient manner by which to rectify matters between the wrongdoer (or her descendants) and the party wronged (or her descendants). *Reparative compensation* is the main form of reparations. It seeks to rectify severe wrongs of the distant past by providing the wronged parties or their descendants a sum of money, property, etc., which might be (roughly) proportional to the harms experienced by them. *Reparative punishment*, if it is ever morally justified, should be reserved for those who are themselves guilty of intentionally not paying substantial compensatory reparations. Moreover, reparative compensation/ punishment must always conform to the Principle of Proportional Compensation and/or Punishment: *Compensation and/or punishment for significant wrongdoing is always to be meted out in (albeit rough) proportion to the wrongdoing(s) committed.*

Although reparations are for the most part a compensatory matter, they share much in common with some of the "expressive functions" of punishment articulated by Joel Feinberg.[7] Feinberg describes four expressive functions of punishment ("hard treatment"). Punishment involves "authoritative disavowal" of a society of a criminal act. It says publicly that the criminal had no right to act as she did, that she did not truly represent society's best aims and aspirations in committing the criminal deed. Punishment also involves a society's "symbolic non-acquiescence" or it's speaking in the name of the people (when it is a democratic society) against the criminal's wrongful deed. Punishment involves "vindication of the law" as a society goes on record by way of its statutes to reinforce the genuine standards of law. Finally, punishment "absolves the innocent" of blame for what a criminal does. Reparations, I argue, share with punishment these expressive features. Like punishment, reparations disavow the wrong(s) committed, and charges that the wrongdoers had no right to perform such evil(s). Reparations, like punishment, say publicly that wrongdoings do not represent society's highest aims and aspirations. In democratic regimes, reparations speak in the name of the people against the wrongdoings in question, and they uphold the genuine standards of law in the face of past failures of the legal system to carry out true justice. In addition, reparations alienate a reasonably just society from its corrupt past, absolving society of its historic evils. These are some of the specific expressive functions of reparations.

More generally, the expressive feature of reparations is to make public society's *own* liability concerning the wrongs *it* has wrought upon a group or individuals. It is to offer an unqualified and unambiguous *apology* to the wronged parties (or their successors) without presumption of forgiveness or mercy. Moreover, it is to acknowledge, in a public way, the moral wrongness of the act(s) in question, and to never forget the act(s). For as George Santayana encourages, those who do not remember the errors of the past are doomed to repeat them. The expressive feature of reparations is articulated by Jeremy Waldron when he writes: "Quite apart from any attempt genuinely to compensate victims or offset their losses, reparations may symbolize a society's understanding not to forget or deny that a particular injustice took place, and to respect and help sustain a dignified sense of identity-in-memory for the people affected."[8] Insofar as reparations have their expressive functions, they send messages to citizens (and to others, for that matter) which seek to build and strengthen social solidarity toward justice and fairness. In this way, the justification of reparations is forward-looking.

Briefly, reparations can be supported on the grounds that they truly respect the actions (or inactions, as the case may be) of history in the sense that they attempt to correct significant imbalances of power or fortune which result from undue force or intrusion, fraud, or other gross forms of wrongdoing. Moreover, reparations disrespect as being morally arbitrary any statute of limitations on cases of the kind in question. This is especially true where the extent of the facts of guilt, fault, harm, and identity of the perpetrators and victims are unambiguous. Whether it is a crime occurring 40 or 400 years ago, justice requires that evils be compensated in manners which would do justice to the idea of proportional compensation for damages in cases where the perpetrator(s), victim(s) and damages are provable by current legal standards (beyond reasonable doubt, for example, in criminal cases, and by the preponderance of evidence in tort cases). With reparations, then, both objectively true morality (i.e., the balance of human reason) and history must be our twin and primary guides to the truth of whom owes what to whom, and why. For purposes of this chapter, it is assumed that the law ought to follow these guides. The argument for reparations to Native Americans assumes that reparations ought to be made when a right has been infringed by way of significant injustice.[9] (In assessing the plausibility of precisely this sort of argument, David Lyons points out that it relies on the ideas of original acquisition and legitimate transfer of land.)[10] Thus, the justification for reparations is essentially backward-looking as well as forward-looking.

I   Arguments Against Reparations to Native Americans

It is assumed, herein, that wherever there is significant injustice there is at least a prima facie reason to believe that such injustice deserves compensation or rectification. Moreover, where the facts of the guilt, fault, harm, and identity of the perpetrators and victims are clear, reparations ought to be pursued for the sake of corrective justice. Hence, there is a presumptive case in favor of reparations to Native Americans by the US Government, given the evil many Native Americans have experienced at the hands of the US military.

Precisely what is/was the harm perpetrated against Native (North) Americans? At the very least, it is the following. To the extent that Will Kymlicka is correct when he argues that cultural membership is crucial for self-respect,[11] and to the extent that a Rawlsian liberalism is correct in arguing that cultural membership is a primary good,[12] the *particular* cultural membership which is crucial to *their* self-respect is/was undermined for Native Americans by force and fraud. The campaigns against various Native American nations by the US military serve as examples here. One specific instance of US war crimes against the Lakota Sioux was the massacre at Wounded Knee, which in turn culminated in the retaliatory violence against the US military at Little Big Horn. Yet for all of the several instances of unjustified violence and other crimes committed by the US military against various Native Americans, few, if any, apologies or reparations have been issued by the US Government. This is one reason that forms the presumptive case for reparations to Native Americans. But such a presumption can be overridden if it can be shown that considerations against such reparations outweigh the strength of the prima facie case for them where the instances in question are not "hard cases."[13] Hence it is important to consider the plausibility of various of the strongest objections to reparations to Native Americans: the Argument from Historical Complexity, the Argument from Collective

Responsibility, the Argument from Inter-Nation Conquests, the Argument from Historical Progress, the Argument from Normative Progress, the Argument from Affirmative Action, the No Native American Concept of Moral Rights Argument, the Argument from the Indeterminacy of Native American Identity, the Historical Reparations Argument, the Argument from Social Utility, the Counterfactual Argument, the Acquired Rights Trumping Original Lands Rights Argument, and the Supersession of Historic Injustice Argument. To the extent that such arguments are defeasible, the presumptive case for such reparations gains strength.

II   The Argument from Historical Complexity

Given the above understanding of the nature of reparations, are reparations to Native Americans by the US Government morally justified? A number of arguments can be marshaled against the imposition of reparations, and they require close scrutiny. First, there is the *Argument from Historical Complexity*. This argument says that history contains far too many complex situations of conflict, such that it would be impossible to figure out all of the injustices that would putatively justify reparations. Where the perpetrators of the evils are dead, and cannot be punished for their horrors, it would be sheer dogmatic idealism to think that respecting rights requires or even permits the kind of complex legal casework that would rectify all past wrongs. To award reparations to the wronged party or her descendants would end up forcing innocent parties (perhaps the descendants of the wrongdoer(s)) to pay for what they themselves did not do.[14]

The Principle of Morally Just Acquisitions and Transfers. In response to this argument, it might be pointed out that the inability to figure out with precise accuracy *all there is to know* about a case which putatively involves reparations hardly prohibits a judicial system from awarding some measure of significant reparations where cases are clear (based on unambiguous historical records, for example). Moreover, though the parties to a putative case of reparations would involve those who themselves did no harm to the victims in question, such "innocent" parties who currently reside on or "own" lands that were once resided on by Native Americans are in violation of the Principle of Morally Just Acquisitions and Transfers:

> Whatever is acquired or transferred by morally just means is itself morally just; whatever is acquired or transferred by morally unjust means is itself morally unjust.[15]

Basically, the intended meaning of this principle is that: to the extent that property is acquired or transferred in a morally justified way (i.e., without force, fraud, etc.), the acquisition or transfer of that property carries with it a genuine moral claim or entitlement to occupy it without interference from others. To the extent that the Principle of Morally Just Acquisitions and Transfers is violated, there is no legitimate claim or entitlement to occupy the property being acquired or transferred. Thus the principle need not specify ownership rights to property. In this way, then, it is neutral concerning the matter of property rights of ownership between liberals and Marxists. This point of clarification precludes a Marxist-style objection that reparations to Native Americans are not morally justified in that they are contingent on Native Americans having original land rights, which themselves are dubious on moral grounds. For the Principle of Morally Just Acquisitions and Transfers does not support reparations to Native Americans by the US because Native Americans had property *ownership* rights to the lands, but because Native Americans had property *occupancy* rights therein.

Although the locutions "morally just" and "morally unjust" are somewhat vague, relatively clear cases of unjust acquisition or transfer, for instance, exist: when such acquisitions or transfers occur as the result of significant non-voluntariness (the violent use of force, for example) on the part of those relinquishing property,[16] when acquisitions or transfers involve fraud,[17] or severe misunderstanding between principal parties.[18] In the case of Native American lands (then a part of the US), most of which were taken from them forcibly by the US military at the direction of Jackson and other US officials (many of which lands were encroached upon illegally by US citizens or civilians), there is no question who the wrongdoer was (the US Government, along with its citizen trespassers) and who the harmed parties were (Native Americans of various nations). In other cases, Native Americans were believed to have "given away" their land to invaders, interpreted as such, presumably, because of the hospitality of the Native peoples toward the invaders. In such cases, the questions are not who is the guilty party and who was the victim, but precisely how ought the victims to be reparated for the wrongdoings. In still other instances, such as our own, US citizens have purchased in good faith lands to which they may not in fact have an overriding moral right. That a person purchased in good faith a stolen item in no way entitles her to that item, as even the law stipulates. She who is truly entitled to the item has a right to it, and that right must be respected by all who take seriously what morality requires.

III The Argument from Collective Responsibility[19]

This raises the issue of collective moral retrospective liability responsibility of, say, the US Government for severe wrongs committed in *it's* name or on *it's* behalf against Native Americans. The *Argument from Collective Responsibility* challenges the morality of reparations to Native Americans on the grounds that it is problematic to hold the current US Government and it's citizenry morally accountable for wrongs committed by previous generations of people who acted or failed to act, as the case may be, to harm Native Americans and on behalf of the US Government, its agencies, and/or on behalf of themselves as actual or putative US citizens.

However, the Argument from Collective Responsibility falls prey to at least two weaknesses. First, the fundamental documents which form at least the basis of US Government are still those which govern the US. Even though the atrocities committed against Native Americans generations ago were not the direct responsibility of today's US citizens, the fact is that the US Government has persisted over time. Furthermore, it is plausible to think that when the US Army and the US Government acted in committing genocidal acts of violence against various Native American nations that they did so in such ways that they were, collectively, guilty, at fault, acting knowingly, intentionally, and voluntarily to such extents that we are justified in inferring that they were both causally responsible and morally liable (culpable) for those harms committed by them against the Native American nations. Additionally, though legally speaking it is not required that a guilty party apologize to the victim(s) of its wrongdoing(s), the extent of the harms committed by the US Government against various Native American nations would seem to suggest one. If this is true, then it would appear that both US Governmental (collective) feelings and expressions of guilt and remorse are suggested. That is, we would expect that the US Government would, in some official manner, express its genuine feelings of guilt and remorse to Native Americans, publicly renouncing its history of racially motivated oppression and holocaust against Native Americans and vowing that it never occur again. Of course, a clear record of governmental policies must reflect a support for such genuine feelings of guilt and remorse.

It is reasonable, then, to hold *it* (the US Government) accountable for *it's* past wrongdoings, pending some adequate argumentation in support of the morality of a statute of limitations on trying and punishing/compensating such crimes. If it was just "discovered" that a corporation committed a gross wrongdoing in 1900, would not justice dictate that the courts seek rectification in such a case, especially if that corporation is still in operation? The reasoning behind this might be either that the putatively guilty corporation is simply deserving of being forced to compensate some parties for the wrongdoing in question (a retributivist rationale) or that the corporation has gained an unfair advantage in committing such acts (a non-retributivist rationale). In either case, where matters are clear, past wrongs of such magnitude as happened to many Native Americans require that justice be realized, and there appears to be no adequate reason why past wrongs against Native Americans by US governmental representatives should not be treated in a similar manner as those in which we treat gross corporate wrongdoings that result from corporate representatives' actions or inactions.[20] As for the individuals or aggregate mobs who committed theft, violent crimes, etc., against Native Americans, in some cases some criminals' transfers of assets/fortunes can be traced to current US citizens or institutions, thereby providing a source of reparations.

A second problem with the Argument from Collective Responsibility is that the Principle of Morally Just Acquisitions and Transfers renders irrelevant the issue of whether or not the current US Government and it's citizenry can legitimately be held accountable for the past evils committed against Native Americans. And the principle does this in the following way: If, say, most or all of the lands currently occupied by the US Government and it's citizens are in fact occupied in violation of the principle, then it matters not whether current occupants of those lands are actually liable for the illegitimate transfer of the lands. What truly matters here is whether or not the lands in question have indeed been transferred legitimately. Since most or all of them have not been legitimately transferred to current occupants, then no such occupants can have a legitimate and overriding moral claim to the lands they occupy. The problem of collective responsibility simply does not effect this fact. It is a red herring given the plausibility of the Principle of Morally Just Acquisitions and Transfers.

IV The Argument from Inter-Nation Conquests

Related to the Argument from Historical Complexity is what I shall refer to as the *Argument from Inter-Nation Conquests*. This argument states that reparations to Native Americans are not warranted because some such peoples themselves are guilty of violating the Principle of Morally Just Acquisitions and Transfers, and against other Native Americans! A case in point, it might be argued, is the Lakota's driving-off several Crow, Kiowa, and other

Native American nations from land which was then considered to belong to or to be justifiably inhabited by the latter nations, respectively. Thus, the historical complexity of the violations of the Principle of Morally Just Acquisitions and Transfers is of such a magnitude that it is unclear, historically speaking, who is genuinely and morally entitled to the lands in question.

However, there are at least two replies to the Argument from Inter-Nation Conquests. First, only a minority number of Native American nations engaged in conquest behavior.[21] Even when the Lakota did engage in conquest of Native American lands, it did so *after* the European invaders had long since succeeded in pitting several Native American nations against each other as a way of eventually fulfilling manifest destiny.[22] The majority of Native American nations were peaceful, and when some did engage in inter-nation violence, it was not, arguably, for purposes of conquering, but rather for reasons of retributive justice or in self-defense.[23] Thus, the most that can be said for the Argument from Inter-Nation Conquests is that where history is clear about which Native Americans violated the Principle of Morally Just Acquisitions and Transfers, only those Native peoples who did not violate this principle in their acquisition or transfer of land are plausible candidates for reparations. Of course, most Native Americans would qualify for reparations by this standard.

Secondly, even *if* no existing Native Americans did qualify for reparations because of their violating the Principle of Morally Just Acquisitions and Transfers, it would not logically follow that anyone *else would* have a genuine and overriding moral claim to the lands of North America. This is true due to the widespread violation of the moral principle in question by the governments and explorers who preceded those of us who currently reside on the lands. Either some Native Americans have valid moral claims/ interests sufficient to ground their respective moral rights to North American lands, or no subsequent non–Native American residents do, except for a possible *few* cases where a *genuine* transfer of land transpired between Native Americans and others.

V   The Argument from Historical Progress

The *Argument from Historical Progress* states that groups experiencing harms at the hands (or weaponry) of others have in many cases triumphed over such problems. Examples here include several African-Americans. There is, then, no need for reparations to Native Americans. As history progresses, so will the well-being of Native Americans.

However, the Argument from Historical Progress suffers from the error of supposing that those who deserve reparations are somehow beyond the pale of reparative justice in that history itself "compensates," in one way or another, even severely wronged groups. This sort of fatalism runs counter to our moral intuitions about rights and justice. Justice should not wait for the wheels of historical inevitability to turn, especially since the doctrine of historical inevitability is in itself morally odious and unconvincing.

VI   The Argument from Normative Progress

A more sophisticated version of the Argument from Historical Progress is the *Argument from Normative Progress*. This argument holds that victims of severe wrongdoings of the distant past *should* simply rise above their respective circumstances which, though caused by others unjustly, can be overcome. The lives and messages of Gandhi and Martin Luther King, Jr., respectively, serve as grist for the mill of this argument, which sees reparations as a crutch for those who are too slothful to make their own ways in life, perhaps blaming others for their own shortcomings. So even if history is clear about many cases of injustice toward Native Americans, and even if it is untrue that those who experience evil at the hands of others do not succeed, reparations are not morally justified in that a genuinely good life can and should be attained by such persons nonetheless.

In reply to the Argument from Normative Progress, it must be pointed out it's rather excessive insensitivity concerning the ways in which history influences humans as individuals and as groups. For the injustices experienced in the past clearly have some significant bearing on a person or group's ability to realize virtue in the present and in the future. It is certainly important for the victims of wrongdoing to attempt to "get on with their lives" and not be *overly* concerned about the injustices they or their ancestors have experienced in the past. But this is a social psychological consideration; it hardly defeats any moral claim or entitlement to reparations. Furthermore, the abilities of members from different ethnic groups victimized by oppression might differ remarkably. For instance, while it may be true that African-Americans have, as a group, made continual and rather impressive strides toward flourishing, Native Americans as an ethnic group (more precisely, as a set of sub-ethnic groups) have languished.[24]

The Argument from Normative Progress rather naïvely assumes that those who have experienced the most horrible forms of oppression ought to rise above it and get on with their lives, just as many African-Americans have flourished in areas such as medicine, politics, business, education, athletics, music, entertainment, and so forth. However, there are good reasons that explain why African-Americans can and do flourish in US society, while Native Americans find it rather difficult to do so. While African-Americans have had much or all of their original African heritage stripped from them during slavery, they were nonetheless able to create their own new heritage based on their experience as African-Americans. As displaced people, African-Americans were forced through acculturation to give up their former heritage as they were forced to become slaves on US soil. But Native Americans still reside on (albeit small) sections of what was once *their* territory, and many see no need, nor do they have the desire, to adopt the ways of a people whose very values included the inflicting of evil on Native Americans. While African Americans found themselves being a part of a newly developing heritage of displaced survivors bent on succeeding in a new environment as unwilling foreigners, Native Americans as a class see themselves as having the greatest moral claim to the lands of North America as it was theirs in the first place. For African-Americans, liberation from slavery, and later on, equal rights, were ways of gaining an "improved" lifestyle that was in accord with the way they were acculturated into the Christian religion. Moreover, slaves were often valued rather highly, even if as mere means to the end of a slaveholder's profit, and they never had reason to think of themselves as having a legitimate moral claim to the land on which they resided either as slaves or as African-Americans. For Native Americans, however, there was a genuine sense that they were invaded by hostile forces that sought to displace them in the name of European religion, values, etc., Native Americans were not deemed as being useful to the European invaders, especially given that Native Americans cherished, above all, their land and culture. Most Native Americans do not believe it would be honorable to concede their great cultures to those who took the land illegitimately, and who had values which would do to that land irreparable damage. Had the Native Americans been enslaved *as* were many Africans and stripped of their original culture,[25] then one might expect that Native Americans "flourish" in US society. For an ethnic group that has been deprogrammed of its original culture and successfully reprogrammed into the culture of the dominant group is in general in a better sociological and psychological position to "succeed" in terms of what the dominant group deems valuable. But instead of "merely" being enslaved by the European invaders, which would have been evil enough, those Native Americans who were enslaved or deprogrammed and acculturated in "Indian Schools" were hunted like buffalo, the basic goal of which was, rather ironically, to make room for a society which declared that it respected the rights of all humans.[26] Native American economic structures, many of which took centuries to build and stabilize, were destroyed by the effects of the European invaders. It is no wonder that native peoples as a class languish, and that despite US material "prosperity."[27] The Argument from Normative Progress hardly counts as a good reason to reject as morally unjustified reparations to Native Americans.

VII   The Argument from Affirmative Action

There is another objection to reparations: the *Argument from Affirmative Action*. This argument states that reparations are otiose given the existence of affirmative action in the hiring of underrepresented groups, typically, those which have been victimized by racial discrimination. Such legal support of historically wronged/underrepresented groups takes the form of affirmative action programs. With affirmative action programs in place, there is no need for reparations policies to Native Americans since Native Americans qualify for affirmative action programs.

However, affirmative action legislation is designed to assist in the providing of equal opportunities in employment, education, etc., for Native Americans, African-Americans, etc. Yet in the case of employment opportunities, it would seem that affirmative action serves as a cruel form of mockery when construed as compensation for the numerous and harsh civil rights violations of these groups by the US Government and its citizens. Moreover, if distributive justice is the reason for the grounding of affirmative action, then affirmative action cannot serve as a challenge to reparations. For the recipients of such programs *earn* the wages or salaries they receive. This can hardly be seen as a legitimate form of compensation for damages. Affirmative action programs, whatever their legitimacy status, cannot and should not be construed as a form of reparations.[28]

VIII   The No Native American Concept of Moral Rights Argument

Yet another objection to reparations, especially in the cases of Native American nations, is that the Native Americans had no conception of rights as entitlements to the lands in question. As John Locke argues, Native Americans lived in a state of nature and had no government that would adjudicate rights claims to land and other property.[29] I shall refer to this as the *No Native American Concept of Moral Rights Argument*. It follows, according to this argument, that reparations to Native Americans are unjustified because lands were acquired from those who did not even believe in rights, not to mention land rights. Moreover, the objection continues, invaders acquired moral rights to at least some of the lands, though such rights may not have justified the violent and evil ways in which such lands were taken (this part of the objection is developed below in the "Acquired Rights Trumping Original Land Rights Argument"). The No Native American Concept of Moral Rights Argument is a complex one, and is aimed at specific kinds of cases of putative reparations, such as those said to accrue to Native Americans.

In reply to this objection, it must be pointed out that it is a fallacy of reason to think that simply because someone does not believe that they possess X that they in fact do not have X. Many persons who do not enjoy the privilege (right?) of a good education often do not understand that they have certain rights. But it is hardly true that such persons do not have such rights, morally speaking. For they might simply be ignorant or fearful of claiming such rights, especially in the face of coercive force, propaganda, etc. Thus, the argument that Native Americans should not be awarded reparations for past injustices due to the claim that Native Americans had no notion of rights is beside the point. The real issue here is whether or not objectively true morality requires that reparations be awarded to Native Americans.

But even if it was true that the moral justification of reparations to Native Americans was contingent on Native Americans, many of whom held some concept of rights, one must ask which rights concept is required? Given that philosophers have not themselves settled on a singular notion of rights[30] (indeed, many doubt the very sense of rights talk itself!),[31] it can hardly be argued that reparations to Native Americans are justified if there is a singular notion of rights among Native Americans. So it appears that the question here is whether or not Native Americans, or at least many of them, had some working idea of rights, especially rights to the lands on which they resided and that which, in most cases, was subsequently and forcibly taken from them. On this score, E. Pauline Wilson, a Mohawkan poet, writes:

> Starved with a hollow hunger, we owe to you and your race.
> What have you left to us of land, what have you left of game,
> What have you brought but evil, and curses since you came?
> How have you paid us for *our* game? how paid us for *our* land?..

You say the cattle are not ours, your meat is not our meat;
When *you* pay for the land you live in, *we'll* pay for the meat we eat.
Give back *our* land and *our* country, give back *our* herds of game;
Give back the furs and the forests that were *ours* before you came;..[32]
But they forget we Indians *owned* the land
From ocean unto ocean; that they stand
Upon a soil that centuries agone
Was *our* sole kingdom and *our* right alone . . .
By *right*, by birth we Indians *own* these lands. . .[33]

Other Native Americans expressed notions of rights, in particular, rights held against invaders of their lands. Sitting Bull states that "What treaty that the whites have kept has the red man broken? Not one. What treaty that the white man ever made with us have they kept? Not one. Where are *our* lands? Where are *our* waters? Who owns them now? Is it wrong for me to love my own?"[34] Old Tassel, in a letter to the South Carolina Governor (1776) stated that "We are the first people that ever lived on this land; it is ours."[35] In a letter to John Ross, Aitooweyah, The Stud and Knock Down wrote: "We the great mass of the people think only of the love of our land . . . where we were brought up . . . for we say to you that our father who sits in Heaven gave it to us . . ."[36] In 1860, Ross advised the Cherokee council that "Our duty is to stand by *our rights*, . . ." and he wrote to Ben McCulloch that "Our country and our institutions are our own. . . . They are sacred and valuable to us as are those of your own . . . I am determined to do no act that shall furnish any pretext to either of the contending parties to overrun *our country* and destroy *our rights*. . . ."[37] Isaac Warrior of the Senecas once said that " . . . Then we always thought . . . when we ran away we did nothing, and *always consider the land we have as ours yet*, and we want to stand there yet."[38] Ten Bears of the Comanches once said that "I want no blood upon *my land* to stain the grass. I want it clear and pure, and I want it so that all who go through among my people may find peace when they come in and leave it when they go out."[39] Satanta added: "A long time ago *this land belonged to our fathers*; but when I go up the [Arkansas] river I see camps of soldiers on its banks. These soldiers cut down *my timber*; they kill *my buffalo*; and when I see that it feels as if my heart would burst with sorrow."[40] Towaconie Jim of the Wichitas once said that "We have always thought *our lands would remain ours*, and never be divided in severalty; and *it can never be done with our consent*. The Government treats us as if we had no *rights*, but we have always lived at our present place, and that is *our home*."[41] Certainly these words contain at least a pre-reflective notion of rights as entitlements to ownership of natural resources, for those, that is, who acquire them legitimately and care for them responsibly. So it is simply false, and perhaps even unusually insulting, to think that rights are indicative of a civilized society and that Native Americans were too barbaric to have and understand some notion of rights which would be recognizable today.

Moreover, as James Tully insightfully points out, various Native American nations indeed had governments which recognized equality and trust in negotiations and treaties between parties, and European invaders themselves (at least many colonists) recognized Native Americans as being sovereign nations with whom treaties could and should be negotiated and signed.[42] Hence, the baselessness of Locke's rather naïve analysis of Native American peoples as having no governments which articulate and protect property rights, including land rights.

It is false, then, to claim that the moral justification of reparations is contingent on the wronged party having a sense or conception of rights which would ground the reparations, and it is also false of many Native Americans in particular that they had nothing akin to a contemporary notion of rights, broadly construed. One wonders why the constant cries for Native American rights to be respected were ignored by the majority of the European invaders and especially by the US Government and its citizenry, each of whom proclaimed to respect the rights of all humans.

IX   The Argument from the Indeterminacy of Native American Identity

Another objection to the awarding of reparations to Native Americans is the *Argument from the Indeterminacy of Native American Identity*. This argument states that, even if the statute of limitations has not expired on legitimate Native American claims to reparations, such reparations are unwarranted because of the overly difficult task of determining the boundaries of ethnic group membership in general, and of Native American tribal affiliations in particular.[43] For example, does it make moral sense to provide reparations to those who are, say, 10 percent Cherokee and 90 percent Anglo? What are the boundaries of ethnic group identity for purposes of reparations in particular and corrective justice more generally?

However, the Argument from the Indeterminacy of Native American Identity is too pessimistic concerning the abilities of history, the law, and Native Americans themselves to trace ethnic ties within and between Native peoples. Today's Native American nations (such as the Navajo Nation in Window Rock, Arizona, USA, or Six Nations in Brantfort,

Ontario, Canada) keep track of membership within their respective nations. Thus, to the extent that a person is able to be clearly identified as someone belonging to a particular Native American nation (or to more than one nation, for that matter), and to the extent that that nation (or members of it) are owed reparations, that is the extent to which each member of the nation, as a descendant of the victims of gross forms of wrongdoing, are deserving of reparations. It is irrelevant to the moral status of reparations (or the moral desert notion of reparations) that such reparations might impinge on the privacy of persons in regards to their ethnicities, or that a "Balkanization" of ethnic groups might ensue. Insofar as the boundaries of Native American identity are concerned, perhaps these possible problems are, in the end, insoluable in any precise or uncontroversial sense. But these factors hardly render unjustified reparations to Native Americans. For many Native Americans are 50 percent or greater Native Americans of one or more such nations. And the fact that some people's Native American identity is dubious in no way serves as a reasonable consideration to refuse reparations to those who are clearly of substantially Native American ethnicity and who are otherwise deserving of them. Furthermore, the difficulties in defining precisely the boundaries of Native American identity hardly justifies the current occupation of lands, once used and settled by Native Americans, by non-Native Americans, where such land possession violates the Principle of Morally Just Acquisitions and Transfers. To the extent that this principle is violated in the chain of transfers of lands which have a trail to Native Americans and the taking of their lands and lives by, say, the US military, then it is in no way justified for current non-Native American residents of the lands to claim anything more than a mere prima facie right to the lands.

X The Historical Reparations Argument

Yet another objection to reparations to Native Americans is that reparations have been paid to Native American nations in the past for wrongs committed by the US Government. I shall refer to this objection as the *Historical Reparations Argument*. In the case of those awarded to Native Americans by the US, there are the examples of the State of Georgia's restoration of many Cherokee landmarks, a newspaper plant and other buildings in New Echota, and Georgia's repealing of its repressive anti-Native American laws of 1830 (it took until 1962 for this to occur, however). Moreover, in 1956 the Pawnees were awarded over $1,000,000 in a suit they brought before the Indian Claims Commission for land taken from them in Iowa, Kansas, and

Missouri. In 1881, the Poncas were compensated by Congress for their ill-treatment by the Court of Omaha, Kansas. For the illegal seizure of the Black Hills in 1876, then owned by the Sioux, compensation was paid. In 1927, the Shoshonis were paid over $6,000,000 for land illegally seized from them (the amount was for the appraised value of *half* of their land, however). There are a few other instances of reparations to Native Americans, as history tells us.[44]

However, the Historical Reparations Argument is based on evidence of reparations to a few Native American nations for property rights violations. There is a three-fold difficulty here. First, such reparations were hardly sufficient to serve as anywhere close to adequate compensations for the property, "maltransfers," damages, etc., in question. Furthermore, the objection ignores completely the question of reparations for undeserved violence against the Native Americans, much of such violence was inflicted on various Native Americans by the US military. Finally, it ignores the fact that the far majority of property rights violations and civil rights violations against Native Americans in general are as of yet *un*compensated. Not unlike the Argument from Historical Progress, the Historical Reparations Argument, then, seems to be more of a *non sequitur* than a genuine concern.

XI   The Argument from Social Utility

There is another objection to the argument for reparations to Native Americans, and it concerns whether or not the awarding of reparations to Native Americans by the US would significantly decrease overall social utility. It would render the US and its citizens – not to mention Native Americans themselves – worse-off. For, as Locke argues, the European-based commercial system makes life far better-off for everyone than the primitive hunting and gathering ways of life enjoyed by the Native American nations.[45] I shall refer to this as the *Argument from Social Utility*. This utilitarian-based concern is that, strictly speaking, the awarding to Native Americans of the lands that were acquired from them in violation of the Principle of Morally Just Acquisitions and Transfers would surely mean the dissolution of the US as we know it, as mostly each US citizen resides on land which would, presumably, be relinquished to Native peoples should reparations be enforced. The economic, political, and social implications of this action would be unthinkable, even if the awarding of reparations in this fashion were permitted by objectively valid moral rules. So, social utility requires that reparations not be awarded because of the undue disruption that would certainly be experienced by the majority of citizens of each of the countries in question. Where would such citizens go if forced by, say, international law, to vacate the premises? Which countries would be in economic and political positions to admit these newly homeless persons? Thus reparations to Native Americans are morally unjustified, it is argued, because they would violate some acceptable principle of social utility.

However, the Argument from Social Utility does not take seriously what people deserve and what retributive justice requires. For even if, strictly speaking, objectively true morality permitted or required reparations which would then force US citizens from the land on which they reside, this would not mean that the moral prerogative of the reparations in question would lead to the disbandment of the current citizens of the US. For Native peoples might very well settle for ownership and control of the existing lands, yet lease such lands to the rest of the inhabitants. This mode of reparations would most likely dissolve the US as we know it. But perhaps the US, insofar as it was founded on the clear and intentional violation of the content of the Principle of Morally Just Acquisitions and Transfers, deserves to be dissolved in favor of taking seriously morality and justice. Nonetheless, the ownership and leasing out of certain lands by Native Americans to others satisfies the concern for morality and justice in that it gives back to Native peoples the lands to which they had and have ultimate ("trumping") moral rights. But it also does not unduly effect those currently living on those lands in violation of the Principle of Morally Just Acquisitions and Transfers. For they are not left without a place of residence, evading the aforementioned concern. Thus, the Argument from Social Utility does not pose an insoluble problem for reparations to Native Americans, though at least one strict form of reparations to Native Americans does imply the dissolution of the US as we know it. The citizens of the US would become highly dependent on the goodness of the Native tribes. Of course, history shows that most, if not all, Native peoples are not the kinds of people with whom one has to worry regarding good will and cooperation. A lengthy history of upheld treaties with the US speaks loudly to this effect.

Furthermore, there is something misleading about the Argument from Social Utility as it applies to reparations to Native Americans. The objection is that the majority of persons now residing in the US would be significantly and adversely affected by the awarding of such reparations to a minority of persons, all in the name of some "ideal" of retribution. Yet the argument fails to recall that upon the invasion of such lands centuries ago by Europeans, the clear majority of residents were Native Americans! The

Argument from Social Utility seeks to argue that reparations to Native Americans would pose social utility problems for current US citizens. This argument, at least in some contexts, represents a rather insensitive attitude toward the war crimes committed by the US military against various Native Americans. Moreover, if the same argument is indexed to the times in which Native American lives and lands were improperly acquired by the US Government, then considerations of social utility might well favor a policy of reparations to Native Americans as a (then) numerical majority whose rights were violated by certain (then) numerical minority of invaders. Thus, we cannot without independent and plausible argumentation simply assume that current US citizens, say, count as the primary index of social utility maximization. For when social utility maximization is indexed to the times in which Native American lands and lives were lost to, say, former US President Andrew Jackson's military campaign to fulfill manifest destiny, then Native Americans are the ones who (cumulatively speaking) count as the index of social utility maximization. After all, if the Argument from Social Utility works against the awarding of reparations to Native Americans by indexing what counts as social utility maximization to what maximizes happiness for today's residents of the lands in question, then by parity of reasoning it works against attempts to compensate US citizens should, say, a more populous China succeed in conquering North America by way of genocide. After all, if what is most important is the maximization of social happiness or such for the greatest number of persons, then what truly maximizes a majority group of conquerors will always trump the rights of those of the conquered minority groups. The difference between this sort of "ethic" appears indistinguishable from a policy of "might makes right," hardly to be taken seriously by a serious moral philosopher. If it demonstrated anything at all, the Argument from Social Utility shows the futility of an act utilitarian standpoint in taking serious the rights of minority members of society. This point about act utilitarianism is hardly novel.

Closely related to the Argument from Social Utility is the *Argument from Religious Freedom*, one which objects that reparations to Native Americans is morally unjustified because it would lead to the dissolution of the US, which was founded on the principle of religious liberty for all. Since this principle is sound, whatever would pose a significant problem for it must be rejected. Since the dissolution of the US would spell the demise of its protection of liberties of various religious groups within US borders, substantial reparations to Native Americans are unjustified.

But the Argument from Religious Freedom fails to see the bitter irony in what it claims to support. For the US was established, among other things, to secure religious liberty, yet in the process it ran roughshod over the religious freedom of hundreds of Native American nations! Moreover, as if that were not sufficient, the US still engages in such duplicity.[46] Thus the Argument from Religious Freedom cannot be used to thwart reparations to Native Americans without exposing the crudest form of hypocrisy. Furthermore, even if the Argument from Religious Freedom works, it works so as to *support* Native American reparations, as such reparations would surely serve to secure religious freedom for the descendants of native peoples.

XII The Counterfactual Argument

There are further concerns with policies of reparations to Native Americans. Waldron notes a counterfactual difficulty regarding reparations:

> The present surely looks different now from the way the present would look if a given injustice of the past had not occurred. Why not therefore change the present so that it looks more like the present that would have obtained in the absence of the injustice?.... The trouble with this approach is the difficulty we have in saying what would have happened if some event (which did occur) had not taken place.[47]

Waldron adds that the problem of reparations becomes even fuzzier when we factor into the rectificatory scheme the matter of human choice. For given the fact that humans do have some choices, this makes it quite problematic to figure out how the present situation might be readjusted to best approximate the scheme of things had a particular injustice not taken place. Besides the matter of whether or not such human choices can rightly have normative import and to be nonarbitrary, argues Waldron, "Ultimately, what is raised here is the question of whether it is possible to rectify particular injustices without undertaking a comprehensive redistribution that addresses all claims of justice that may be made...."[48] I shall refer to this as the *Counterfactual Argument*.

In reply to Waldron's concerns about counterfactual aspects of reparations, it might be argued that it hardly counts against the moral justifiability of reparations to, say, Native Americans that the subsequent redistributive scheme of compensatory justice would lead to a proliferation of rights claims to historic injustices pertaining to the settlement and development of North America. Even if it were true that few such claims could or would be settled adequately, this does nothing to count against the claim that reparations are morally justified as a matter of moral principle. Nor does it somehow render senseless the multidimensional aspects of the expressive functions of reparations to Native American nations. Furthermore, in the case of Native American nations, there are records of leaders of such nations declaring their unambiguous aversion to and despising of most anything to do with "manifest destiny," and other social, political, and cultural features of the "American experiment." Historical records provide a keen understanding of the culture and beliefs of Native American peoples, and we can be sure that what is important to them is at least the returning of their land to them, even though the land is hardly in the condition in which it was seized from them. That it is impossible to return to Native American nations what was once theirs and in the same condition as it was when it was taken from them by force and fraud is not a good enough reason to think that it is morally unjustified to return such lands to them. For there is nothing in Native American history to suggest that Native Americans would have freely chosen to give up their lands to anyone who would do to the lands what European settlers by and large did to it.

Although the counterfactual approach to reparations is indeed a problem for reparations policies, it says nothing about the moral justifiedness of reparations themselves, except that, like matters of punishment and compensation in general, rectificatory justice is at best imprecise. The Counterfactual Argument against reparations to Native Americans would seem to imply that punishment and compensation are too problematic even for most contemporary courts to handle, as evidence and argumentation is rarely unambiguous in interpretation. Yet this is surely an implication few would find plausible. Imprecision and Herculean cases are hardly excuses for the law's turning its head from the need for justice. So the Counterfactual Argument against reparations to Native Americans hardly shows that reparations are morally unjustified, or that they are not feasible as a legal means of compensating (to some significant extent) those who deserve them.

XIII The Acquired Rights Trumping Original Land Rights Argument

Some would argue that certain rights can be acquired where previously there were no such rights. In particular, some would object to the moral justification of reparations to Native Americans on the grounds that the US descendants of the European invaders are not themselves morally accountable for the evils inflicted on earlier Native peoples in America, thus escaping the pale of moral retrospective liability responsibility on which such reparations are said to be based. Those who currently reside on putatively US soil and who are not Native Americans did not secure the land illicitly. Furthermore, it is argued, recent generations of US citizens have actually acquired moral rights to the lands on which they reside.[49] What grounds such rights? To be sure, many US citizens have mixed their labor with the land in the forms of building/purchasing homes, working the land, etc.[50] This Lockean point regarding what one has a right to is said to ground the moral rights of contemporary US citizens to "their" land. In addition, one might argue that what the supporters of reparations to Native Americans neglect to see is that there is more to this matter than mere original land acquisition rights. There are also the issues of merit and desert. Arguments for reparations to Native Americans based on original land acquisition are implausible given that they ignore the fact that current non-Native peoples have since acquired rights to the lands based on their acquiring such lands legitimately.[51] I shall refer to this as the *Acquired Rights Trumping Original Land Rights Argument*.

But the Acquired Rights Trumping Original Land Rights Argument is flawed, and for several reasons. First, it ignores the fact that reparations do not require that those who pay them are morally accountable for the wrongdoing that justifies – even requires – them. Secondly, a ruthless invader can steal land and then mix her labor with it and thereby, according to the argument, gain rights to the stolen land. Yet this is hardly morally justified. Furthermore, that invader may sell her ill-gotten land to an "innocent" party, yet this is a clear violation of the Principle of Morally Just Acquisitions and Transfers. In a similar way, then, the mixing of one's labor with the land is insufficient to ground a moral right had by US citizens to the lands in question. Furthermore, as Waldron argues,

> the Lockean image of labor (whether it is individual or cooperative) being literally embedded or mixed in an object is incoherent. . . . For it would be impossible to explain how property rights thus acquired could be alienable – how they could be transferred, through sale or gift, from one person to another – without offense to the personality of the original acquirer.[52]

So, something else must be true to make plausible the claim that current US citizens have overriding moral rights to the lands on which they reside. But what would that be, except that one must inherit or acquire land *without* it being the case that the Principle of Morally Just Acquisitions and Transfers is violated? One cannot legitimately inherit or deserve what has been acquired or transferred by way of immorality or injustice. Finally, if some US citizens have moral rights to "their" lands by "just" inheritance, then why would we not think that original land rights of Native peoples in turn accrue to current Native Americans? This would mean that the real question of which set of rights "trumps" another's boils down to, among other things, whether or not there was a violation of the Principle of Morally Just Acquisitions and Transfers concerning what is now deemed by many to be US territory.

It might be argued that there is a statute of limitations on rights claims, and that the statute of limitations has expired for Native Americans to justly claim their rights to the lands. In US law, this is referred to as the "Laches Doctrine": If there is a significant amount of time that passes without a wronged party's attempting to claim it's right to something, then the claimant loses her right to that thing. Or, at the very least, the right "fades" over time.[53]

But this line of reasoning neglects the historical reality that at several points in time various Native American nations have publicly claimed their land rights – even to the US government! That such claims were made repeatedly and not respected is a matter of historical fact, and that the claims of many Native Americans were not respected hardly counts as evidence for the claim that the statute of limitations has truly expired. For many Native Americans satisfied the condition in question. But their pleas were simply ignored or turned away. We must bear in mind that an unjust legal system's failure to uphold Native American claims to lands (and compensation for war crimes constituting violence to persons, among other things) hardly serves as a rational foundation for a statute of limitations on Native American claims concerning what they deserve as compensation for wrongdoings. Reparations to Native Americans in the US are either morally justified or they are not, regardless of the fact that morally corrupted legislative and judicial systems were put in place to (among other things) bias decisions against Native American claims, thus supporting the idea of the expiration of the statue of limitations on Native American land claims. Furthermore, that contemporary US citizens are not causally responsible for the past wrongs committed against Native Americans in no way nullifies the fact that today's lands are, in the main, occupied by those who have acquired them through a chain of possessions which is in clear violation of the Principle of Morally Just Acquisitions and Transfers. That one has not wronged Native Americans in some direct way hardly justifies ones being in the possession of stolen or ill-gotten property. Thus, there needs to be a reason other than the one provided by the statute of limitations advocates that would ground the acquisition of moral rights to lands now occupied by US citizens.

Some might argue that the Lockean Proviso grounds the rights of current US citizens to the lands on which they reside in that Native Americans in the distant past had more land than they could use, and that the Native Americans had no right to deprive European "invaders" of their settlement of North American lands that were not in use by Native Americans.

However, this line of reasoning is problematic for the following reasons. First, most of the land acquired by the European invaders (including the US Government) was by way of force and fraud against Native Americans (not to mention, non-Native Americans!). So even if Native Americans had an obligation (based on the Lockean Proviso) to share some of the North American lands with others, it does not follow that the lands had to be shared with those who dealt Native Americans injustices of the harshest orders. This holds whether the invaders were conquering "explorers," or "mere settlers." The possible difference between these two groups in terms of their putative collective moral liability for harms against Native Americans does not diminish the fact that each group played a crucial role in the unjust acquisitions and transfers of lands that were inhabited by Native Americans.

Secondly, the Lockean Proviso states that one has a right to X to the extent that there is enough and as good of X for others.[54] However, US history is replete with examples of Native Americans *welcoming with open arms* European invaders, under the assumption, no doubt, that something like the Principle of Morally Just Acquisitions and Transfers would not be violated in the course of the latter groups' settling the lands. So Native Americans, by and large and from the outset of the invasion of the Americans, acted in congruence with the Lockean Proviso both in terms of their dealings with non-Native Americans and in terms of their dealings with most other Native Americans. Yet history tells the complicated and dismal stories of injustices Native Americans experienced in losing their lands to European invaders, hardly a moral foundation for current US claims to North American lands.[55]

XIV The Supersession of Historic Injustice Argument

Finally, there is the *Supersession of Historic Injustice Argument* against reparations, articulated by Waldron. The basic idea here is that "changing circumstances can have an effect on ownership rights notwithstanding the moral legitimacy of original appropriation."[56] Applied to the Native American experience, the argument runs as follows. There have been historic injustices committed against Native Americans, as we all know. But historical circumstances have changed, and situations where resources are scarce, such as now, are those in which the future generations of those who themselves wronged Native American are morally *entitled* to share resources (including land) with Native Americans. Thus, the initial injustices by past generations of European invaders and the US military (among others) against Native Americans is superseded by changing circumstances. "Claims about justice and injustice, must be responsive to changes in circumstances," as Waldron argues.[57] So the issue of historic injustice, though an important one, is superseded by the fact that inhabitants of lands are entitled to share it with others under conditions of scarcity of resources. After all, "the aboriginal inhabitants would have had to share their lands, whether the original injustice had taken place or not."[58] Waldron writes.

> If circumstances make a difference to what counts as a just acquisition, then it must make a difference also to what counts as an unjust incursion. And if they make a difference to that, then in principle we must concede that a change in circumstances can effect whether a particular continuation of adverse possession remains an injustice or not. . . .
> . . . It may be that some of the historic injustices that concern us have not been superseded, and that, even under modern circumstances, the possession of certain aboriginal lands by the descendants of those who expropriated their original owners remains a crying injustice. My argument is not intended to rule that out. But there have been huge changes since North America and Australasia were settled by white colonists. . . . We cannot be sure that these changes in circumstances supersede the injustice of their continued possession of aboriginal lands, but it would not be surprising if they did.[59]

There are problems, however, with the Supersession of Historic Injustice Argument against reparations to Native Americans. Although the argument admist that European invaders (and the US Government, more specifically) had no rightful claims to lands that they expropriated from Native Americans, the argument seems to say that later generations of at least some of those European invaders gained land rights based on the premise that under conditions of scarcity, resources must be shared by all occupants of a territory. Yet the fact is that such conditions of scarcity would, so far as history informs us, not likely have existed if not for the doings of the European invaders themselves! There was certainly significant land and resources (Buffalo, for instance, and other food sources) for the millions of

Native Americans prior to the invasion of North America by Europeans and prior to the massacres of various Native Americans by the US military. Nor is there uncontroversial evidence to suggest that there is a high probability that there would have been a scarcity of such resources among Native Americans absent natural disasters and European invaders. So the argument, in effect, seeks to ground the future generations of European invaders' putative moral claims to the lands on which they reside on the fact that those, whose ancestors by and large created a problem of resource scarcity, have a moral claim on the lands over and above those who once possessed the land without scarcity of resources. But why not infer from history and morality a rather different conclusion, namely, that at best current non-Native Americans possess trumping or overriding moral claims to whatever property they legitimately own which is *on* the land belonging to the descendants of those from whom the European invaders expropriated it? Is this not the more intuitively sensible inference, given historical circumstances? How, then, can we say that the violations against Native Americans are superseded? Simply because such evils occurred long ago? Hardly. For neither the Laches Defense nor statutes of limitations seem plausible, morally speaking. Would we dare infer that a thief who breaks into my home, takes me hostage and residers there for months on end, eating my food, making herself "at home" in various other ways in turn, somehow gains a right to the home, even if she should assume some of the household chores (after all, she is a rather tidy thief, and doesn't like to live in a messy place)? Would we not say that she is a thief, and that no matter how much she makes herself at home, that she has made herself at home in *my* home, and that she is to be arrested, tried, and if found guilty by way of a fair trial, then she is to be punished and made to compensate me for damages? Why, then, do we not conclude similarly in the case of reparations to Native Americans? I say "similarly" in that those who currently reside on US lands do so while they themselves are not causally responsible for the war and other crimes perpetrated against Native Americans by the US military. Thus compensation, not punishment, is what is at issue regarding reparations to Native Americans. The Supersession of Historic Injustice Argument, then, surely has little to recommend it.

The previous discussion pertained to the matter of whether or not reparations by the US Government to Native Americans are morally justified. However, there is a line of argument that would challenge the very basis of the discussion, it would appear. It is that the fundamental flaw in the previous discussion, especially as concerns the Principle of Morally Just Acquisitions and Transfers, is that it wrongly assumes the plausibility of the notion of property rights, something that Karl Marx, among others, refuted (especially in terms of original acquisition of land rights). Thus, to the extent that the concept of property rights (whether ownership or occupancy rights) is problematic, so is the entire line of reasoning of the previous discussion supporting reparations by the US Government to Native Americans.

In reply to this concern, several points might be made in order to neutralize its argumentative force. First, even if sound, this criticism is not open to a defender of US capitalism in that US capitalism is contingent on the plausibility of the notion of property rights. So if it turns out, for example, that Marx is correct in his call for "the abolition of landed property" (1869), then it would follow that no US citizen (or the US Government, for that matter!) has a moral right to *any* land, in particular, to the land on which she (or it) currently resides. Thus, this Marxist-style concern about the morally problematic nature of property (land) rights and of the original acquisition of it is *not* open to the defender of the US or its citizens from paying reparations to Native Americans.

Secondly, even if it turns out that the concept of property rights is null and void, especially as it pertains to land, it would not follow that reparations by the US Government are not owed to Native Americans. For though the arguments for land-based reparations might become problematic, such reparations might be justified on the basis of the Native American holocaust itself. It is hard to imagine that Marx would object to the victims of racist oppression in the form of a holocaust holding that they ought not to receive their compensation from the capitalist aggressors. So even if Marxist arguments against the ownership of land are plausible and win the day, it hardly follows that they in turn defeat the claim that reparations by the US Government to Native Americans are morally justified on the basis of severe *civil* rights violations. One need not argue, by the way, that property rights, or rights more generally, are the core of an adequate moral and political philosophy. For rights (and their correlating duties) are at best merely part of what is needed and desired for a plausible moral and political economy. Nothing that I have argued in this paper assumes a solely rights-based morality or political economy, though my defense of reparations (in terms of land) against various objections to them assumes the significance of property (land) rights.

Thirdly, *to the extent that* the concept of property (land) rights is plausible, it would appear that this same concept both supports the moral viability of US capitalism (if it does at all) and condemns it on moral grounds in that US capitalism is founded on the Native American holocaust. What the Principle of Morally Just Acquisitions and Transfers and the preceding discussion of various arguments against reparations to Native Americans show is that the concept of property rights condemns (not supports) US capitalism, morally speaking. To the extent that the US was established on the intended and voluntary genocide of various Native American nations, US capitalism is condemned on moral grounds. And this moral condemnation hardly, except on the crudest of act-utilitarian grounds, can be rescued by an appeal to the relative economic productivity experienced by the US in recent years. Nor can the moral evils of the US be somehow erased or neutralized by the ignoring of the Native American holocaust in favor of appeals to alleged or actual progress that the US has made in terms of democratic civil rights reforms. For no amount of reform can itself serve as compensation for the degrees and kinds of physical harms of a holocaust.

The argument of this paper has concerned the moral *justifiedness* of reparations to Native Americans by the US Government. Yet one might argue that it hardly follows from this claim, if true, that such reparations are morally *required*. Thus, the argument for the moral justification of reparations of Native Americans falls short of its desired goal of showing that the US Government ought to pay such reparations to Native Americans.

However, the step from reparations to Native Americans by the US Government being morally justified to such reparations being morally required is not as daunting as it might seem. Although arguments in favor of a policy's being morally justified are not identical with those that show that such a policy is required by objectively true morality, moral intuition would suggest that, if it is true that those who harm others ought to be forced (i.e., are morally required) to compensate those whom they harm in proportion (roughly) to the harm caused, then reparations, as a matter of corrective or retributive justice, are morally required. Thus it is both morally justified and required that the US Government pay reparations (i.e., compensate) Native Americans for harms of the Native American holocaust.

If the arguments against reparations to Native Americans are specious for at least the reasons noted, and if the Principle of Morally Just Acquisitions and Transfers is plausible and applicable to the Native American experiences, then the balance of reason suggests at least the prima facie plausibility of some policy of reparations to Native Americans. Moreover, it is incumbent on the supporter of such reparations to devise a plausible policy of reparations. However, a fully-fledged theory and policy of reparations to Native Americans is beyond the scope of this chapter.

XV Conclusion

If the arguments against reparations to Native (North) Americans in the US are defeasible for the reasons given herein, then the presumptive case in favor of reparations to Native Americans gains strength. Barring further argumentation that would render morally problematic such reparations, then a case for such reparations has been made along the following lines. To the extent that history is unambiguous concerning the extent of guilt, fault, wrongdoing, and the identities of perpetrators and victims of historic injustices, policies of reparations should be enacted according to some fundamentally sound principle of proportional compensation.

If the foregoing analysis is sound, then one hope that the US has of dragging itself out of the mire of its own perpetration of historic injustices against Native Americans is for it to institute adequate policies of reparations to Native Americans. Even so, such policies must receive far more commitment by the US Government than the treaties made by the US Government with Native American nations had received in the past, and it cannot be assumed that even the most far-reaching of reparations policies would satisfy the strict demands of objectively true morality. What is also needed is a national sense of shame-based guilt[60] and collective remorse[61] for the roles that the US and it's citizenry played in founding the US. Yet if such shame requires a higher-level self-consciousness,[62] this might well be precisely what US society lacks, providing its critics with ammunition for claims of the fundamental immorality of the US in general. For a society that is based on unrectified injustice is itself unjust. But a society that simply refuses to admit its unjust history toward others not only remains unjust on balance, but serves as a stark reminder of the unabashed arrogance of its unspeakable badness.[63]

Notes

I am grateful to Robert Audi, John Bishop, Bernard Boxill, Anthony Ellis, Margaret Gilbert, Howard McGary, Richard W. Miller, Jan Narveson, James Nickel, Michael Slote, Burleigh Wilkins, and Clark Wolf for incisive comments on an earlier draft of this chapter. Parts of this chapter in earlier draft forms were presented at the Canadian Society for the Study of Practical Ethics, Canadian Learneds Society, 1997, and at the Conference on War Crimes: Legal and Moral Issues, University of California, Santa Barbara, 1997.

1 Similar points might well apply to Native Americans in Central and South America.

2 William L. Anderson, ed., *Cherokee Removal* (Athens: University of Georgia Press, 1991); Garrick Bailey and Roberta Glenn Bailey, *A History of the Navajos* (Santa Fe: School of American Research Press, 1986); Robert Berkhofer, Jr., *Salvation and the Savage* (New York: Atheneum, 1965); Dee Brown, *Bury My Heart at Wounded Knee* (New York: Henry Holt and Company, 1970); Angie Debo, *A History of the Indians of the United States* (Norman: University of Oklahoma Press, 1970), *And Still the Waters Run* (Norman: University of Oklahoma Press, 1989); John Ehle, *Trail of Tears* (New York: Anchor Books, 1988); Grant Foreman, *Indian Removal* (Norman: University of Oklahoma Press, 1932); Michael D. Green, *The Politics of Indian Removal* (Lincoln: University of Nebraska Press, 1982); Robert V. Remini, *The Legacy of Andrew Jackson* (Baton Rouge: Louisiana State University Press, 1988); David E. Stannard, *American Holocaust: The Conquest of the New World* (Oxford: Oxford University Press, 1992); Ian K. Steele, *Warpaths* (Oxford: Oxford University Press, 1994); Clifford E. Trafzer, *The Kit Carsen Campaign* (Norman: University of Oklahoma Press, 1982); Peter H. Wood, Gregory A. Waselkov, and M. Thomas Hatley, eds., *Powhatan's Mantle* (Lincoln: University of Nebraska Press, 1989); Grace Steele Woodward. *The Cherokees* (Norman: University of Oklahoma Press, 1963).

3 Other philosophers who have written on reparations, but concerning the African-American experience, include J. L. Cowan, "Inverse Discrimination," *Analysis* 33 (1972); Alan H. Goldman, "Reparations to Individuals or Groups?" *Analysis* 35 (1975); Howard McGary, "Morality and Collective Liability," *Journal of Value Inquiry*, 20 (1986), pp. 157–65; Howard McGary, "Justice and Reparations," *The Philosophical Forum* (1978): 250–63; James W. Nickel, "Discrimination and Morally Relevant Characteristics," *Analysis* 34 (1973), "Should Reparations Be Made to Individuals or to Groups?," *Analysis* 34 (1974); Roger A. Shiner, "Individuals, Groups, and Inverse Discrimination," *Analysis* 33 (1973); Philip Silvestri, "The Justification of Inverse Discrimination," *Analysis* 34 (1973); Paul W. Taylor, "Reverse Discrimination and Compensatory Justice," *Analysis* 33 (1973). The main philosophical work which focuses on reparations to Native Americans is David Lyons, "The New Indian Claims and Original Rights to Land," *Social Theory & Practice* 6 (1977): 249–72.

4 I assume that Native Americans are indigenous and aboriginal peoples to North America, and that even if they are not so indigenous or aboriginal, that they acquired the lands on which they resided in North America in ways that did not violate the Principle of Morally Just Acquisitions and Transfers, discussed below.

5 James Tully, "Aboriginal Property and Western Theory: Recovering a Middle Ground." *Social Philosophy & Policy* 11 (1994): 153.

6 Note that nothing in this conception of reparations requires that the reparations be "paid" or rendered by the perpetrators of wrongdoing only. Compare the

conception of reparations set forth in D. N. MacCormick. "The Obligation of Reparations," *Proceedings of the Aristotelian Society* 78 (1977–8): 175. Contrast this notion of reparations with one articulated by Bernard Boxill: "Part of what is part of the transgressor that what he is doing is required of him because of his prior error." See Bernard Boxill, "The Morality of Reparations," in Bary R. Gross, ed., *Reverse Discrimination*, (New York: Prometheus, 1977), p. 274.

7   Joel Feinberg, *Doing and Deserving* (Princeton: Princeton University Press, 1970), ch. 5.

8   Jeremy Waldron, "Superseding Historic Injustice," *Ethics* 103 (1992): 6.

9   MacCormick, "The Obligation of Reparations," p. 179.

10 Lyons, "The New Indian Claims and Original Rights to Land," p. 252.

11 Will Kymlicka, *Liberalism, Community, and Culture* (Oxford: Oxford University Press, 1989), p. 165.

12 John R. Danley, "Liberalism, Aboriginal Rights, and Culture Minorities," *Philosophy & Public Affairs* 20 (1991): 172.

13 For a discussion of hard cases in the context of law, see Ronald Dworkin, *Taking Rights Seriously* (Cambridge, MA: Harvard University Press, 1978), ch. 4.

14 A version of the Argument From Historical Complexity seems to be articulated by Loren Lomasky when he writes: "It is undeniably the case that virtually all current holdings of property descend from a historical chain involving the usurpation of rights. It does not follow that those holdings are thereby rendered illegitimate, morally null and void." See Loren Lomasky, *Persons, Rights, and the Moral Community* (Oxford: Oxford University Press, 1987), p. 145. A similar view is articulated, but not endorsed, in A. John Simmons, "Original Acquisition Justifications of property," *Social Philosophy & Policy* 11 (1994): 74–5.

15 This principle bears a keen resemblance to the principle of just acquisitions, transfers and rectification found in Robert Nozick, *Anarchy, State, and Utopia* (New York: Basic Books, 1974), p. 150.

16 For examples of the taking of Native American lands by force and violence, see Debo, *A History of the Indians of the United States*, pp. 47, 87, 96, 118, 297, 304–5, 317, and 320.

17 For examples of the taking of Native American lands by fraud, see Debo, *A History of the Indians of the United States*, pp. 89, 106, 118, 207, 261, 320–1, and 379.

18 For examples of the taking of Native American lands by misunderstanding, deliberate or otherwise, see Debo, *A History of the Indians of the United States*, pp. 76, 190–91.

19 For discussions of the concept of collective responsibility, see J. Angelo Corlett, "Collective Responsibility," in Patricia Werhane and Edward Freeman, eds., *Encyclopedic Dictionary of Business Ethics* (Oxford: Blackwell, 1997), pp. 117–20; Joel Feinberg, *Doing and Deserving* (Princeton: Princeton University Press,

1970), ch. 8; Peter French, *Corporate and Collective Responsibility* (New York: Columbia University Press, 1984), *Responsibility Matters* (Lawrence: University of Kansas Press, 1990); Larry May, *The Morality of Groups* (Notre Dame: Notre Dame University Press, 1987), *Sharing Responsibility* (Chicago: University of Chicago Press, 1992).

20 For discussions of corporate responsibility, see J. Angelo Corlett, "Corporate responsibility and Punishment," *Public Affairs Quarterly* 2 (1988): 1–16; "Corporate Punishment and Responsibility," *Journal of Social Philosophy*, forthcoming.

21 Debo, *A History of the Indians of the United States*, ch. 1.

22 Ibid., pp. 67, 74.

23 Ibid., ch. 1.

24 I say "flourished" and "languished" because some might argue plausibly that African-Americans have sold their souls to succeed in a society that stripped them of what is most valuable in life and hence cannot truly be said to flourish, while Native Americans, many of them, have decided to remain alienated from the society which is substantially responsible for the evils perpetrated against what is most important to Native Americans: their culture. For what profits someone if they should gain material prosperity while losing one's own soul? For a discussion of why African-Americans as a group have flourished while Native Americans have, by comparison, languished in US society, see J. Angelo Corlett, "Surviving Evil: Jewish, African, and Native Americans," *Journal of Social Philosophy*, forthcoming.

25 Many Native Americans were enslaved as such, as we read in Brown, *Bury My Heart at Wounded Knee*, pp. 2, 4, 14, 204; Debo, *A History of the Indians in the United States*, pp. 43, 47, 49–50, 67, 74, 77, 119, 162, 165, 269.

26 One of the most disappointing ironies of US history is that the class of people who most boldly declared equality for all humans acted so inhumanely toward some of the most noble of humans. Moreover, the fact that the US has *yet* to even apologize for such inhumane behavior sets it apart as being, in a genuine way, significantly more evil than most nations in history.

27 Let us also not forget the significance of linguistic complications which go toward explaining the difficulty of the Native American voices to be heard and respected by invaders. As N. Scott Momaday argues, "One of the most perplexing ironies of American history is the fact that the Indian has been effectively silenced by the intricacies of his own speech, as it were. Linguistic diversity has been a formidable barrier to Indian-white diplomacy." See N. Scott Momaday, "Personal Reflections," in Calvin Martin, ed., *The American Indian and the Problem of History* (Oxford: Oxford University Press, 1987), p. 160.

28 A similar point is made in Boxill, "The Morality of Reparation," p. 271.

29 John Locke, *The Second Treatise of Government* (Indianapolis: Bobbs-Merrill, 1952), sections 14, 28, 30, 34, 36, 37, 41–3, 48–9, 108–9. For a helpful

assessment of Locke's views on the political status of Native Americans, see Tully, "Aboriginal Property and Western Theory," p. 158 f.

30   For a sample of some of the leading contemporary thinking about the nature, value, and function of rights, see Joel Feinberg, *Social Philosophy* (Englewood Cliffs: Prentice-Hall, 1973); *Freedom and Fulfillment: Philosophical Essays* (Princeton: Princeton University Press, 1992); Will Kymlicka, ed., *The Rights of Minority Cultures* (Oxford: Oxford University Press, 1995); Lomasky, *Persons, Rights, and the Moral Community*, p. 145; L. W. Sumner, *The Moral Foundations of Rights* (Oxford: Oxford University Press, 1987); Judith J. Thomson, *The Realm of Rights* (Cambridge: Harvard University Press, 1990); Carl Wellman, *A Theory of Rights* (Totowa: Rowman & Littlefield, 1988), *Real Rights* (Oxford: Oxford University Press, 1955).

31   J. Waldron, *Nonsense Upon Stilts: Bentham, Burke, and Marx on the Rights of Man* (London: Methuen, 1987), p. 44.

32   From "The Cattle Thief," in E. Pauline Johnson, *Flint and Feather: The Complete Poems of E. Pauline Johnson (TEKAHIONWAKE)* (Ontario: Paper-Jacks, 1972), pp. 13–14. Emphasis mine on the use of "our" and "ours."

33   From "A Cry From an Indian Wife," ibid., pp. 15–17. Emphasis mine.

34   Quoted in Corlett, "Moral Compatibilism: Rights Responsibility, Punishment and Compensation." Emphasis added.

35   Debo, *A History of the Indians in the United States*, p. 86.

36   Ibid., p. 124.

37   Ibid., p. 171.

38   Ibid., p. 181.

39   Ibid., p. 219.

40   Ibid., p. 220.

41   Ibid., p. 302.

42   Tully, "Aboriginal Property and Western Theory," pp. 169–79.

43   This issue is raised in relation to reparations to African-Americans. See Boris Bittker, "Identifying the Beneficiaries," in Bary R. Gross, ed., *Reverse Discrimination* (New York: Prometheus Books, 1977), p. 279 f. A philosophical analysis of the conditions of ethnic group membership is found in J. Angelo Corlett, "Latino Identity," presented to the American Philosophical Association, Eastern Division, Atlanta, GA, 1996; "Parallels of Ethnicity and Gender" in Naomi Zack, ed., *Race/Sex* (London: Routledge, 1996), pp. 83–93.

44   Debo, *A History of the Indians in the United States*.

45   Locke, *The Second Treatise of Government*, sections 34, 37, 40–3. For an assessment of Locke's view, see Tully, "Aboriginal Property and Western Theory," 161 f.

46   See Burleigh T. Wilkins, "A Third Principle of Justice," *The Journal of Ethics* 1 (1997): 355–74.

47   Waldron, "Superseding Historic Injustice," pp. 7–8.

48   Waldron, "Superseding Historic Injustice," p. 13.

49   This argument is set forth and defended in Lyons, "The New Indian Claims and Original Rights to Land," p. 252f.

50   See Locke, *The Second Treatise of Government*. For a helpful discussion of Locke's positions on rights and other political concepts, see A. John Simmons, *The Lockean Theory of Rights* (Princeton: Princeton University Press, 1992), *The Edge of Anarchy* (Princeton: Princeton University Press, 1993). Locke's line of reasoning has been plausibly refuted in Robert Nozick. "Distributive Justice," *Philosophy & Public Affairs* 3 (1973): 70 f. See also Jeremy Waldron, *The Right to Private Property* (Oxford: Oxford University Press, 1988), chs. 6–7; "Two Worries About Mixing One's Labor," *The Philosophical Quarterly* 33 (1983): 37–44.

51   Lyons, "The New Indian Claims and Original Rights to Land," p. 254.

52   Waldron, "Superseding Historic Injustice," p. 17.

53   A similar point is found in Waldron, "Superseding Historic Injustice," p. 15.

54   See John Locke, *Second Treatise on Government*, Sections 34, 37, 40–3; Robert Nozick, *Anarchy, State and Utopia* (New York: Basic Books, 1974); A. John Simmons, *The Lockean Theory of Rights* (Princeton: Princeton University Press, 1992).

55   Furthermore, it has been argued that it is reasonable to hold that the Iroquois indeed acquired rights to some North American lands, and on a Lockean basis! See John D. Bishop, "Locke's Theory of Original Appropriation and the Right of Settlement in Iroquois Territory," *Canadian Journal of Philosophy* 27 (1997): 311–38.

56   Waldron, "Superseding Historic Injustice," p. 24.

57   Ibid., p. 25.

58   Ibid., p. 25.

59   Ibid., pp. 25–6.

60   For an account of collective feelings of guilt, see Margaret Gilbert, "Group Wrongs, Guilt Feelings," *The Journal of Ethics* 1 (1997): 65–84.

61   For an account of collective remorse, see Margaret Gilbert, "Collective Remorse," chapter 12 in this volume.

62   Gabrielle Taylor, *Pride, Shame, and Guilt* (Oxford: Oxford University Press, 1985), p. 67.

63   For a delineation of what Marx has in mind here, see G. A. Cohen, *Self-Ownership, Freedom, and Equality* (Cambridge: Cambridge University Press, 1996), p. 168.

14

Transitional Justice and International Civil Society

David A. Crocker

The term "transitional justice" is increasingly used to address the question of how emerging democracies should deal with past human rights abuses perpetrated or permitted by former authoritarian regimes. This chapter has two sections. In the first section I discuss the challenge of transitional justice and argue that there are at least eight objectives that such transitions should strive to accomplish. I also identify and evaluate briefly an array of tools – from trials, through truth commissions, to amnesty – that societies have employed to accomplish transitional justice. In the second part I bring together the usually separate discussions of transitional justice and civil society and argue that a nation's civil society is often well suited to prioritize the ends and implement the means of transitional justice.[1] Then I investigate what role *international* civil society can and should play in a society's transition to justice. I argue that, despite some dangers and limitations, and depending on the context, international civil society may play a helpful and even indispensable role. One overall conclusion is that the most promising approaches to both transitional justice and civil society – whether domestic or international – involve the ideals of the public sphere, discursive democracy, and public deliberation.

Although philosophers have not entirely ignored the topics of transitional justice and civil society, it is legal scholars, social scientists, policy analysis, and activists who have made the most helpful contributions.[2] It is understandable that much of the work on transitional justice has been of an empirical and practical nature. Fledgling democracies need effective institutions and strategies for addressing prior human rights violations. Legal and historical studies have been helpful in comparing how various societies have in fact coped with prior human rights abuses. However, there are also large and pressing ethical questions. How should "success" with respect to transitional justice be conceived? Are the ends that societies seek to achieve and the means they adopt to achieve them *morally justified?* Questions such as these should not be overlooked or swamped by legal or practical considerations.

I Transitional Justice

The challenge

The late Carlos Nino, an Argentine legal theorist and human rights advisor to Argentine President Raúl Alfonsín, put the question of transitional justice this way: "How shall we live with evil? How shall we respond to massive human rights violations committed either by state actors or by others with the consent and tolerance of their governments?"[3] What ethical and practical considerations should guide answers to these questions and who should try to answer them? What national and international institutions should implement transitional justice, however conceived, and how should they do so?

These questions have emerged in many and diverse contexts. After the Second World War, the question was debated and answered in relation to the international war crimes trials in Nuremberg and Tokyo. More recently, emerging or renovated democracies in Latin America (Argentina, Chile, and El Salvador) and the former East bloc countries have addressed the issue. Currently, Bosnia, France, Guatemala, Rwanda, South Korea, and South Africa are responding in very different ways to atrocities committed by earlier governments or their opponents. Chinese human rights exiles and others hope that a more liberal China someday will face the events of Tiananmen Square.

There have been a variety of ends and means that societies have pursued in responding to human rights violations committed by a prior regime. Candidate fundamental objectives include revenge (victor's justice), retribution, social amnesia, truth about the past, reconciliation, forgiveness, and economic and democratic development. The means or tools embrace international war crimes tribunals and national criminal or civil proceedings, lustration (purging or banning perpetrators from public office), investigatory or truth commissions, public acknowledgment and apology, compensation of victims or their families, public monuments commemorating victims, social stigmatization, general amnesty, individual pardon, and impunity (exemption from punishment).

Three warnings

Before assessing candidates for morally justifiable ends, three warnings are in
order. First, we must guard against a rigid and overly specific universalism
and recognize that local peculiarities rule out a "one size fits all" blueprint.
The particularities of each situation are enormously important in determining what ought to be done in a given context. Even if there are – as I believe
– transcultural ethical principles, each society and region has more or less
idiosyncratic features to be taken into account as it decides how to respond
to prior human rights violations. For instance, what transitional justice
requires will depend to some extent on what the transition is *from*. Is the
prior situation one of a government's military defeat in a war between
nations (the Second World War); a government's collaboration with an
occupying military (Vichy France, the Ustashe regime in Croatia); a civil
war in which one side is victorious (Rwanda, Democratic Republic of the
Congo); a stalemated civil war (El Salvador, Guatemala); a military dictatorship (Argentina, Uruguay, Chile); two distinct nations (West and East
Germany); a unified nation (Yugoslavia or Czechoslovakia); or apartheid
(South Africa)? or collaboration in a war between nations (the Second
World War), a civil war in which one side is victorious (Chile, Rwanda),
a stalemated civil war (El Salvador, Guatemala), a military dictatorship
(Argentina), or apartheid (South Africa)? Does the country have a prior
history of democratic institutions (Chile and Uruguay), colonialism
(Rwanda), ethnic conflict (Rwanda and South Africa), or military repression (Guatemala)? How long did the human rights violations last? What
percentage of the population was directly or indirectly responsible for
human rights violations? More than half, as in the former East Germany,
or a much smaller proportion, as in Honduras?

Equally important is what the transition is *to*. Does the successor, more
democratic society perpetuate, perhaps in a new guise, the ruling party,
judicial system, and military of the old regime? Or have one or more of
these been replaced with (more) democratic institutions? What is the
strength and progressive potential of the government, market, and civil
society? How poor or prosperous is the society and what internal or external
resources might be made available for reckoning with past human rights
crimes? To what extent has civil strife been eliminated and relative stability
established, and to what extent are these conditions dependent on occupying forces or other international institutions?

Second, we must also guard against what Whitehead called "the fallacy of misplaced concreteness."[4] The fallacy occurs when one phenomenon, in this case transitional justice, is artificially delinked from other phenomena with which it is importantly connected. The challenge of transitional justice is linked to the importance of protecting, legitimating, and strengthening the transition to a (more) democratic government. The issue of transitional justice, as we are using the term, does not emerge when there is no transition or the transition is from one dictator to another. There are certain things that a fragile democracy should not do and other things that it must do if it is to distinguish itself from a prior repressive regime and if it is not to imperil its own existence.

There are other facts and values, however, to which a country's navigation of transitional justice should be linked in order that this issue not be addressed in an artificial vacuum. Among these are the causes and cures of past conflicts and rights abuses, the relation between transitional justice and both peacemaking and peacekeeping, and the possible links between transitional justice and other social goals, such as poverty alleviation, demilitarization, multiculturalism, and further democratization. A society's handling of transitional justice may undermine or advance its efforts to bring about good development, however conceived.

Third, my framing of the question of transitional justice does not presuppose that the United States and other countries are guiltless with respect to human rights violations in their own or other societies. Double standards must be avoided. The United States, arguably, must reckon with its own past human rights violations if it is to deepen its democratic institutions. Nor am I suggesting that Americans are specially qualified to solve the many moral quandaries connected to transitional justice. In my view some of the most illuminating work on the ethics and politics of transitional justice is being done by academics, policy-makers, and citizens in societies in transition. I do want to argue, however, that a society's deliberation on these matters can benefit from international dialogue and that philosophers, from a variety of origins, may contribute (as well as benefit).

II Ends and Means

When a society makes a transition from an authoritarian regime, such as a military dictatorship, or reaches a negotiated settlement to a civil war, it must also decide what, if anything, it will do with respect to the human rights violations committed by the prior government or its opponents. What should be an emerging democracy's basic purposes in this choice?

Two extreme and opposite goals are, it seems to me, morally defective and should be ruled out: revenge, and "forgetting and moving on." Revenge can be either private or public. In Ariel Dorfman's play and film "Death and the Maiden," Paulina gains some measure of revenge over the doctor she believes to have been her torturer during the earlier dictatorship. In the play/film, we are not unsympathetic to Paulina's taking justice into her own hands because the truth commission, to which her husband has been appointed head, is responsible for disclosure and then only with respect to those killed or "disappeared," not those "merely" tortured. Yet, as Paulina's case shows, private revenge is beset by problems. There is some possibility that she may have the wrong man. Her private settling of scores is contemptuous of due process and the rule of law.[5]

Revenge, in the form of "victor's justice," can also function with public trappings. In "kangaroo courts" or "show trials" the winning side subjects alleged rights violators from the losing side to a judicial proceeding or official investigation bereft of due process. Mere membership on the losing side is a sufficient basis for legal and moral guilt. However, it is unjust to convict someone, without good evidence that they committed a crime. It is unfair to punish violations by the losing side and ignore or "whitewash" violations by the winning side.

The goal of "forget and move on" is also morally defective. A society adopts this aim when, facing current and future challenges, it denies that past atrocities ever happened, extinguished social memory of abuses, or lets bygones be bygones.[6] Concerning past atrocities, public silence reigns. The obvious problem with the goal of "forget and move on" is that it is difficult if not impossible to execute, at least in the long run and in a reasonably democratic society. The question of the guilt of everyday Germans with respect to the Holocaust was more or less contained if not silenced for more than fifty years. But a recent provocative and arguably flawed book on the subject stirred German intellectuals and the public to confront issues that many had relegated to oblivion.[7] As the fall 1997 trial of a French collaborator with the Nazis showed, historians, journalists, and younger generations have their ways of opening old wounds and awakening repressed memories. Even if forgetting were possible, it would be morally undesirable. Social amnesia fails to give either the perpetrators or victims of atrocities their due.[8]

Repressed emotions of rage, humiliation, and fear can be expressed in uncontrolled and harmful ways. Justified indignation gets transformed into irrational vengeance. Public virtue becomes private vice. The goal of forgetting turns into the goal of revenge.

Assuming that these two ends – revenge and oblivion – should not be the goals of societies seeking transitional justice, what are some morally defensible goals that might guide these transitions? There are many. A pluralist approach would make a place for all of them, although they would be specified, weighted, and combined in different ways in different contexts. The choice of a package of tools and methods to achieve transitional justice, as well as the design of the most appropriate version of a particular measure, should be made in the light of at least the following objectives:[9]

1 An authoritative investigation and disclosure of the known facts with respect to human rights victims and their violations and at least a general picture of the violators and their institutional chain of command. This is an important goal, for without reasonably complete truth with respect to the past, none of the other goals in transitional justice are likely to be realized.

2 A platform for the victims or their families to tell their stories publicly and receive public redress in the form of acknowledgment or compensation. Achieving this goal both expresses respect for victims and is a means to getting at the truth.

3 The fair ascription to individuals and groups of responsibility for past abuses and the meting out of appropriate sanctions.

4 Compliance with the rule of law and due process. This is an especially important goal for a new and fragile government bent on distinguishing itself from prior authoritarianism.

5 Promotion and elevation of public deliberation about what happened, who was responsible, and how society should respond, permitting all sides a fair hearing rather than requiring unanimity or consensus.

6 Recommendations for changes in the law and governmental institutions, including the judiciary, the police, and the military, to remove the causes of past abuses and ensure that they will not be repeated.

7 Reconciliation of former enemies at least in the sense that, while they may continue to disagree and even be adversaries, they live together nonviolently and as fellow citizens ("liberal social solidarity").[10]

8 Promotion of good long-term changes such as further democratization and just economic development.[11]

Several comments about these eight objectives are called for. First, each of these goals calls for further clarification and defense. Take the third objective, for example. How should accountability be understood and assigned? How should we understand the degrees and kinds of responsibility with respect to the planning, execution, material support for, and covering up of atrocities? To what extent is one responsible for omissions as well as commissions? Nino vividly identifies the many questions that call out for answers:

> Massive human rights violations could not be committed without the acquiescence of many people. There are those who planed [sic] the deeds and those who committed them. There are those who informed on neighbors or friends or who lent material resources to those who actually commit the atrocities. Some victims even helped to victimize others. There are also hosts of people who may have cooperated by omission. Judges, for example, may have refrained from conducting proceedings that could have stopped the violations. Journalists may have failed to publicize the atrocities and helped contain reactions from within and without. Diplomats may have helped conceal what was occurring or even actively justified the actions of their governments. Even common people – like those who lived near concentration camps – often turned a blind eye to what was happening close to them. Some may have refrained from passing along knowledge to others and may even have mildly justified the deeds to themselves and each other. "It must be for something" was the common saying when they learned that a neighbor or acquaintance had been kidnapped by security forces and made to "disappear." And if almost everybody is guilty, there is a feeling that nobody really is.[12]

Without a suitably nuanced view of accountability, a society falls into the morally objectionable options of whitewash or oblivion. Likewise with the issue of sanctions, whether criminal, civil, or non-legal. What types of sanctions are appropriate for what violations and on what bases? Should a theory of criminal punishment include a retributive element and, if so, how should it be understood and institutionalized? Who should decide?

Second, although it is important to try to get a wide agreement on the meaning and justification of each of these eight goals, in a liberal society we should accept the fact of fundamental dispenses. Hence, a liberal society's response to prior human rights violations need not issue from or yield a consensus about the specific meanings of or foundations for the eight objectives.

Third, the various tools mentioned above – ranging from war tribunals through impunity – should be chosen and fashioned in order to achieve these objectives. All of these goals should be considered with respect to their relevance for a particular transition. Unless the result is likely to be disastrous, none of these goals should be completely sacrificed – at least in the long run – to obtain one or more of the others. The practical demands of a concrete case, however, might require that some of the goals be given significantly less emphasis or postponed. In extreme cases, one or more goals may have to be ignored, for the best should not become an enemy of the good.

Suppose, for instance, that someone proposes that transitional justice should select its tools in relation to only two ends: first, full disclosure of past truth, and second, whatever promotes economic development.[13] Undeniably such a view is much simpler than the ethical pluralism adumbrated above. But the proposed maxim completely leaves out *direct* concern about and consideration of sanctions, compensation, accountability, the rule of law, public deliberation, accommodation of differences, and recommendations for change. As W. D. Ross said in defending – in contrast to far simpler theories – his ethical theory of seven prima facie duties, "it is more important that our theory fit the facts than that it be simple, and the account we have given . . . corresponds (it seems to me) better than either of the simpler theories [Kant's categorical imperative and the utilitarian principle of beneficence] with what we think."[14]

Fourth, each of the proposed eight ends may also be a means contributing to the attainment of one or more of the other ends. Determining accountability and sanctions sometimes contributes to truth about the past. Truth about the past is necessary for allocating responsibility, sanctions, and compensation, as well as for making recommendations about removing the causes of the human rights abuses.[15] Public deliberation about transitional justice both contributes to and benefits from reconciliation and democratic development.

It is not that all good things always go together, for sometimes achieving one end will be at the expense of (full) achievement of another. Legal sanctions against former human rights perpetrators can imperil a fragile democracy in which the military responsible for the earlier abuses still wields social and political power. Obedience to law can protect human rights abusers if prior governments passed laws that prohibit investigations or prosecution. Perhaps a trial determining the past guilt or innocence of an individual accused of human rights violations is not a very good means of achieving *general* truth about past atrocities. Consider, for example, France's Papon case, in which Maurice Papon, an official in the Vichy government, was charged with signing deportation orders for more than 1,500 French Jews in roundups of victims destined for Auschwitz. French Prime Minister Lionel Jospin may have been right in arguing that the trial of one man cannot yield truth about an era: "Justice does not establish history. History is not made in the dock."[16] Sometimes, however, tools can be chosen that contribute to a good end, such as determination of individual accountability, that in turn promote other good objectives, such as general truth and public deliberation about the past atrocities.

Fifth, in any transitional context, we should expect that more than one tool will be needed, that no one tool will by itself achieve or best approximate the plural objectives. No matter how well fashioned, any one tool may have limitations or defects that can best be compensated for by the use of another tool, for instance, trials and punishment, rightly conceived and utilized. What is needed is the best package of tools in a particular context where "best" is a function of the fullest possible realization of the eight ends. For instance, in a society with nonfunctioning corrupt, or ideologically tainted judicial institutions, transitional justice may have to depend more on a truth commission than it would in a society with a basically healthy court system.

Sixth, each of the tools mentioned earlier can be designed in a variety of ways and a measure's particular shape should take into account both the eight goals and the unique demands of the particular society. For instance, criminal trials should respect due process, presume innocence, and assign guilt or innocence on the basis of the evidence rather than the mere group affiliation of either the accused or the judge.[17] Trials should guard against white-washing and different standards for winners and losers. In the use of the adversary attorey system, the selection of juries, and the protection of defendant's rights, conflicting viewpoints may have their day both in and outside of court.[18] Osiel comments:

> The least we might fairly expect from [liberal criminal] courts, at such trying times [of a divided national community] is a stimulus to democratic dialogue between those who wish us to remember very different things. A courtroom may not be the optimal place for such a dialogue to occur, still less be resolved. But a courtroom is one place where it might fruitfully begin... Public memory can be constructed publicly if the law advances social solidarity by ventilating and addressing disagreement, rather than concealing it – by acknowledging and confronting interpretive controversy, not suppressing it.[19] Osiel's remarks accurately describe the debate stirred up in France by the Papon trial where, as explained in the subtitle of the article cited above, "[the] nation debates more than one man's wartime role:"
>
> What kind of responsibility do the French bear for the extermination of 75,000 French Jews? How representative of occupied France's collective spirit was Vichy, the Nazi's French Puppet government? How representative was Papon, the loyal civil servant who claims he was, while a Vichy official in Bordeaux, also an active undercover member of the anti-Nazi Resistance?[20]

Similarly, there are many options open to truth commissions with respect to their institutional origin, composition, scope, resources, duration, procedural tools, legal powers, and so forth.[21] Truth commissions may gain legitimacy when composed of persons representative of the winners, the losers, and those in between and who are known to be fair. In a polarized national context, such as El Slavador at the close of its tumultuous civil war, it may be necessary to have investigatory bodies composed of representatives of foreign countries or international bodies. Yet outsider participants risk delegitimizing a commission's findings. The South African Truth and Reconciliation Commission was the first investigatory body to give individualized amnesty – or better pardon – to those who provide full disclosure; in this case greater truth may be gained but at the price of foregoing criminal or tort proceedings.

Seven, although all eight objectives are important, the fifth objective – public deliberation – has a certain priority. It is a sort of metaprinciple relevant to the choice, specification, weighting, and implementation of each of the other objectives. It concerns the other objectives for, as noted earlier, each of the other objectives requires society-wide debate and democratic decision-making as to whether each is publicy justified, as well as to how each should be specified and weighted. Similarly, public deliberation can play an important role in designing various transitional tools and combining them into an integrated and complementary set. Public deliberation is also uniquely justified because it contributes to, is a component of, and is strengthened by societal democratization. In a society aspiring to be (more) liberal and democratic, public deliberation expresses the commitment to respect one's fellow citizens and to enter into give and take with them so as to arrive at a democratic decision that all can live with, even though all do not agree with it.[22]

Given the challenge, ends, and tools for transitional justice, what roles can and should civil society play? Before pursuing an answer to this question, however, we must get some purchase on the concept of civil society, both domestic and international.

III   The Role of Civil Society in Transitional Justice

A nation's civil society is often well suited to specify and prioritize the ends of transitional justice as well as choose and implement the means. To defend this claim, as well as argue for a role for *international* civil society, requires some clarification of the term "civil society." For civil society is a fashionable and contested concept. Its multiple meanings permit people of almost every political stripe to employ it, usually in a celebratory way, as a beneficial institution to be protected or an ideal to be aimed for. The various civil society debates, however, have a special hue in the context of societies undergoing democratization and reckoning with prior human rights abuses.

Three models of civil society

Michael Ignatieff, writing about the aspirations of East European intellectuals in the 1970s and 1980s, tried to capture their ideal of civil society: "the kind of place where you do not change the street signs every time you change the regime."[23] This one-liner nicely captures the antigovernmental approach to civil society, made popular after the fall of the Berlin Wall. "Civil society," on this interpretation, is a rallying cry for individuals and groups, such as churches and capitalist enterprises, to get governmental spies, police, economic planners, and bureaucrats out of their affairs. The banner of privatization, waved in different ways by the 1994 Republican "revolution" in the United States and by the World Bank around the world, echoes this approach. Civil society exists if, and only if, people and their groups are free from government interference to pursue their own conceptions of the good, especially their economic self-interest.

This model usefully provides a basis to undermine state authoritarianism and corporatism, for it envisions a zone of life free of government control. When a government has violated human rights or permitted their violation, the antigovernment approach to civil society opens space to criticize and undermine state oppression and to build a different kind of society. Nongovernmental groups, often working underground, help people survive repression or civil war and then begin the onerous process of democratization. The antigovernmental model is illuminating to the extent that its civil ferment is composed of a variety of groups, sometimes in alliance with each other – church groups, self-help and mutual support groups, and human rights organizations as well as the mass media and other business and professional groups.

But this model of civil society in a transitional justice context is also misleading. Whatever legitimate role nongovernmental groups may play, when a society in the process of democratization grapples with prior human rights violation, that society's national *government* has important and often unique democratic responsibilities. These duties include protecting its citizens' present democratic rights and promoting their future economic opportunity. Government obligation also extends to reckoning with the rights violations perpetrated by the prior nondemocratic regime. One of the three branches of government is often best situated to employ certain tools – such as prosecution, investigation, compensation, commemoration – designed to achieve transitional justice.

Furthermore, what democratization and transitional justice often require is not a rejection of government but a reform of some branch of government, for example, bringing the military and police under ("civilian") control of elected officials, or ensuring that the judiciary becomes more independent of executive or private pressures. An antigovernmental approach to civil society in a context of transitional justice neglects the myriad ways in which the government and nongovernmental groups can work together and supplement each other's efforts. Honduras's Human Rights Commissioner, Leo Valladares, uses the resources of his office to help strengthen that part of civil society that is playing an important role in transitional justice. Government and civil society need not be at odds, and each can contribute something important to democratization and transitional justice.

A narrower approach to civil society, which in the US debate has been termed the *associational* model, excludes for-profit groups and commercial organizations and emphasizes private voluntary associations such as churches, self-help groups, amateur sports leagues, and groups pursuing common hobbies. On this view, civil society is a "third sector," differing from both state and market. The state coercively protects or promotes the public good. In the market, private producers and consumers freely exchange goods and services. In civil society, private individuals freely join together to pursue some noneconomic common passion or project.[24]

Inspired by the nineteenth-century social critic Alexis de Tocqueville, Robert Putnam has recently employed this associational model to describe and explain an alleged increase in America of distrust of others, social isolation ("bowling alone"), and political apathy.[25] Whether or not Putnam is correct, to what extent is this model of civil society relevant to societies confronting the challenge of transitional justice? One problem with this model is that it includes such a heterogeneous list of groups. Some, such as certain church groups or the Argentine Madres de la Plaza del Mayo, have played an important role in ending government repression, promoting democratization, and advancing transitional justice. These beneficial groups may themselves be quite diverse. Some may be primarily inwardly oriented, such as the Madres self-help group, while others, such as human rights groups, may see their basic mission as that of promoting transitional justice.

The associational model, however, also covers other voluntary groups that are either indifferent to, or have limited consequences for, transitional justice (for example, amateur soccer teams), or are opposed to, and detrimental for, transitional justice (for instance, paramilitary associations or the right wing Catholic organization, Opus Dei). Enemies of democratization, these groups may be bent on either private revenge or public forgetting.

While the first model emphasizes civil society's freedom from state invasion, and the second emphasizes the variety of associations within civil society, their diversity of objectives, and their capacity for stimulating social trust and other valuable products, a third model emphasizes a different aspect of civil society. It focuses on the communicative activity generated by civil society's groups and upon its potential to strength democracy. The continual public conversation generated by civic improvement associations, religious groups, political and social movements, advocacy groups, and the like, filtered through media organs such as newspapers and television, constitutes a public sphere that supports the formation of public opinion, a necessary ingredient in democratic politics. This third model has been worked out most fully by Jürgen Habermas, Jean Cohen, and James Bohman. Cohen contends that "the concept of the public sphere . . . [is] the normative core of the idea of civil society and the heart of any conception of democracy."[26] Explicitly indicating her indebtedness to Habermas, Cohen defines the "civil public sphere" as

> a juridically private (non-state) "space" where individuals without official status can communicate and attempt to persuade one another through argumentation and criticism about matters of general concern. Ideally participation in discussion is universally accessible, inclusive, and freed from deformations due to wealth, power, or social status. Argumentation and critique involve the principles of individual autonomy, parity of discussants, and the free and open problematization of any issue that is of common concern, including the procedural principles guiding discussion.[27]

Given this idealization of the public sphere, the third model is especially interested in civil society associations whose internal structure mirrors the structure of the public sphere itself: they are egalitarian, democratic, and inclusive. The public sphere model highlights those inwardly democratic, outwardly oriented nonstate, nonmarket groups that deliberate about and try to protect and extend democratic forms. Included would be democratically-organized unions, human rights and other advocacy groups, think tanks, and so forth. Cohen remarks that "the political role of civil society [in the sense of the civil public sphere] is not directly related to the conquest of power, but to the generation of influence, through the life of democratic associations and unconstrained discussion in a variety of cultural and informal public spheres."[28] One effect of this public deliberation in the context of transitional justice has been – *pace* Ignatieff and sometimes with state help – to *change* the names of streets and buildings to commemorate the memory of human rights victims.

Yet, while this third model in effect highlights groups that are internally democratic and egalitarian, its main point seems to be that civil society is constituted by groups, often dissimilar in internal structures and missions, which accept each other as partners in a public conversation about societal concerns. Civil society breaks down when public debate ceases and violence begins (again).

IV National Civil Society

Our conclusion, then, is that each model of civil society alerts us to the positive and negative roles civil society organizations can play in transitional justice. Let us consider civil society's contributions, limitations, and dangers.

First, with respect to the challenge of transitional justice, civil society can play an important role in deliberating about, formulating, and prioritizing goals and in forgoing measures to realize them. A particularly important occasion for such public deliberation is during peace negotiations between the two opposing sides.

A crucial element in negotiating the end of military conflict is an accord about how past human rights violations will be treated once peace is achieved. For instance, in the difficult and drawn-out peace negotiations between the Guatemalan government and the 20-year-old guerilla movement, the Guatemalan National Revolutionary Union (URNG), civil society played a strong and increasingly formalized role. The UN brokered Framework Agreement signed in January 1994 "recognized the role played [in earlier negotiations] . . . by the various sectors of organized civil society and gave them a legitimate place within the negotiating process in an Assembly of Civil Society (ACS)."[29] Charied by the highly respected cleric Monsignor Quezada, the ASC comes closest to the first model of civil society discussed above, for it was composed of representatives not only of grassroots nongovernmental organizations but also of political parties, universities, and small and medium business associations. It should be noted, however, that the assembly, while representing many business groups, did not include the most powerful one, the Comitet Coordinador de Asociaciones Agrícolas, Comerciales, Industriales y Financieras (Chamber of Agricultural, Commercial, Industrial, and Financial Associations).

The Guatemalan ASC formulated and transmitted to the negotiating parties and the UN mediator its consensus positions on the various topics being negotiated, including the formation of a truth commission, an agreement on indigenous rights, and an agreement on socio-economic goals. According to Teresa Whitfield, the ASC helped broaden the peace negotiations to address the original sources of a conflict that had cost over 150,000 lives since 1960.[30] Moreover, the opposing parties also presented to the ASC each negotiated accord for the ASC's consideration and endorsement. Whitfield remarks that this consultation both "fueled public discussion and enhanced the validity of the peace process within Guatemalan society at large."[31]

Here we see civil society engaged in public deliberation, achieving consensus on some basic policies and disagreement on others, stimulating further public discussion, and lending democratic legitimation to the peace process and transitional justice. James Bohman articulates the ideal:

> [P]olitical decision making is legitimate insofar as its policies are produced in a process of public discussion and debate in which citizens and their representatives, going beyond mere self-interest and limited points of view, reflect on the general interest or on their common good.[32]

It is not that the ASC was the only embodiment of civil society, let alone of public deliberation about transitional justice. After all, the peace negotiations, initially brokered by the Catholic prelate, were themselves a form of public deliberation, and such deliberation also occurred – albeit unevenly and with much narrower representativeness – within the Guatemalan parliament. Nor should it be thought that the mere existence of an Assembly of Civil Society guarantees that diverse citizens will do more than rubber stamp the decisions of the political or military leadership. Sometimes, especially following years of brutal repression, civil society is too weak to advance and widen public deliberation. In the Guatemalan case, however, the ASC was uniquely responsible for getting the peace negotiators to tackle the root causes of the conflict and the outlines, at least, of some remedies.

Second, in societies making a democratic transition, civil society can play an important role in assisting the victims of human rights violations. In Chile and other countries, various civil society groups – especially families, religious groups, human rights groups, legal and medical clinics, and neighborhood support groups – provide often crucial assistance in rehabilitating victims of human rights abuses and helping them reintegrate into the larger society. This activity often is a continuation of the work of clandestine neighborhood and professional groups that emerged during the Pinochet dictatorship and played an important role in aiding victims of official oppression and their families. One worry is that aid-giving nongovernmental organizations (NGOs) flourish only under repressive conditions, and that they will decline if not altogether disappear during democratization.

It may be, however, that the change that occurs is only that different types of NGOs have emerged to perform the same beneficial function. Sometimes, however, a new democratic government can and should take over the task of rehabilitating and compensating victims, especially when it recognizes that it has a responsibility to restore certain basic opportunities as compensation for past governmental abuses.

Third, civil society groups can be enormously helpful and even indispensable in obtaining the truth about the past. During the 17-year Pinochet dictatorship, two religious organizations – the ecumenical Comité de Cooperación Para la Paz en Chile (1974–5) and the Roman Catholic Church's Vicaría de la Solidaridad (1976–92) – collected thousands of judicial transcripts concerning disappearances. Such records were invaluable for the investigations of the presidentially-appointed National Commission for Truth and Reconciliation, which had to complete its work in only 18 months.

In Guatemala, prior to the peace accords and the founding of Guatemala's official truth commission, the Historical Clarification Commission (CEH), the Guatemala City archdiocese's human rights office launched an unofficial Project for the Recovery of Historical Memory (REMHI). Increasingly dissatisfied with CEH's limited mandate, resources, and initially slow progress, REMHI undertook a comprehensive investigation of Guatemala's past atrocities. Local citizens, whom REMHI trained as "ambassadors of reconciliation," recorded more than 6,000 testimonies, which communal leaders, elected by their villages, gave in their native (Indian) language. On April 24, 1998, REMHI released its report, "Guatemala: Nunca Mas." A press release and public lecture charged that the army and so-called civilian self-defense patrols were responsible for about 80 percent of the 150,000 deaths and 50,000 disappearances in the war, while the leftist rebels were cited for about 9 percent of the deaths. Because Guatemalan illiteracy is so high, diffusion of the report employed theater, radio, videos, public workshops, and ceremonies. REMHI, like other Guatemalan human rights groups and the CEH itself, has directly contributed to truth about the past and manifested respect for victims by providing them a platform in their own language. The challenges and dangers involved in uncovering truth about past evil were tragically underscored two days after the release of REMHI report: Auxiliary Bishop Juan Gerardi Conedera, the director of the archdiocese's human rights office and coordinator of the report, was brutally bludgeoned to death in his home in Guatemala City.

Although usually appointed by a government's executive or legislature, official truth commissions can be viewed either as parts of civil society or as hybrid entities that mediate between the state and civil society. Truth commissions are normally composed of prestigious and respected citizens not holding public office, and often these citizens represent important NGOs, a spectrum of political outlooks, and commercial groups. Desmond Tutu, for example, is a cleric who heads South Africa's Truth and Reconciliation Commission.

Compared with judicial proceedings, truth commissions usually lack subpoena and plea-bargaining powers. Moreover, adversarial defense and cross-examination of witnesses do not occur. Still, public deliberation occurs if and when truth commissions publicly deliberate about the focus of their investigation and make their proceedings accessible to a live audience or through the mass media. Public acknowledgment occurs when victims of human rights abuses admit their guilt. In South Africa, a mixture of pardon and social stigmatization occurs when perpetrators exchange disclosure, acknowledgment, and sometimes confessions of guilt for pardon. Investigatory commissions also engage the wider public sphere when they defend their aims, procedures, and costs in public debate and in response to public criticism.

Fourth, some organizations in a nation's civil society adopt as one of their main goals the monitoring and evaluation of the government's (and wider society's) actual steps toward achieving peace, democratization, and ways of handling past human rights violations. One role of civil society is to constitute an independent site to assess whether promises are kept and rhetoric becomes reality. Such monitoring and assessment is part of what Jean Dreze and Amartya Sen calls public action – action of NGOs designed to advance the public good.[33] Possible actions include public petitions, protests and marches, strikes, press conferences, public fora, and complaints addressed to public officials.

Each of these activities helps undermine what Leo Valladares, the Human Rights Commissioner of Honduras, calls the "culture of impunity." In such a culture, government officials, the police and military, and ordinary citizens break the law without fear of punishment, for there is a shared understanding that each person will be silent about the other's abuses as long as the favor is returned. Many NGOs in transitional societies are seeking to replace such a culture of impunity with a "culture of responsibility" or a "culture of rights" in which citizens respect human and legal rights and publicly protest their violation. As the 1996 report of Honduras's National Commission of Human Rights puts it:

> Civil Society ought to join forces so that judicial reform is a reality, and this requires the strengthening of a democratic and human rights culture in order to halt the epidemic of corruption and be able to save our democratic institutions. As the Commissioner has expressed it: "Democracy is shown not only at the ballot box but also by accusations, by opposition to official abuse and corruption, and by the system of justice. Hence, democracy ought to fight so that injustice is the exception and justice the rule."

Not only do such advocacy groups fight impunity and advance citizenship in the wider culture, but also groups within civil society, especially internally democratic ones, are schools for democratic citizenship.

Three such organizations struggling to promote transitional justice in Guatemala are REMHI, discussed above, the Myrna Mack Foundation, and the Center for Human Rights Legal Action. The Foundation has been described as "generating public debate and legislative change on key issues such as judicial, police and intelligence reform in Guatemala."[34] In particular, this group is attempting to bring to trial the military intelligence officers accused of the 1990 murder of Myrna Mack. Mack, an internationally renowned anthropologist who had been investigating the forced displacement of indigenous peoples, was savagely killed in the streets of downtown Guatemala City. The Center for Human Rights Legal Action aims to end impunity for Guatemala's human rights abusers, implement human rights in the Guatemalan peace process, and promote "the involvement of a broad cross-section of civil society representatives in the process."[35] These three Guatemalan NGOs are among those keeping public pressure on the Guatemalan Truth Commission to name perpetrators and not merely profile the general pattern of human rights abuses.

The civil public sphere clearly functions in countries undergoing transitional justice insofar as the mass media occasion a society-wide debate that evaluates and seeks to improve the ends and means of transitional justice. For instance, South African newspapers and television report daily on the Truth and Reconciliation Commission's work. They also provide fora for a spectrum of critics and defenders of the Commission. The mass media covered in detail the acrimonious dispute between Commission chair Tutu and former South African President de Klerk concerning whether the latter's testimony to the Commission omitted confession of government compliance with apartheid's worst rights violations. Likewise, since the mid-eighties, many Guatemalan newspapers have enlarged and invigorated the public sphere by reporting and commenting on the peace process and by opening their pages to a variety of public opinions.

The foregoing examples illustrate what a country's civil society in general and its civil public sphere in particular may do to advance the aims of transitional justice. Civil society, however, is not without some limitations, and there are some dangers in putting undue (and the wrong kind of) emphasis on civil society. First, groups in civil society may be very weak and disunited, thereby limiting their potential impact on transitional justice. Just as civil society groups can differ considerably within a given national society so too the civil societies of particular nations or regions exhibit much variety. Civic groups and a nation's civil society as a whole differ with respect to longevity, vitality, formality, resources and sustainability, orientation (inward or outward), internal structure (democratic vs. hierarchical), and external relations (grass roots, regionally/nationally federated, or internationally linked). Depending on their type and social context, many groups and networks are limited in what they can contribute to transitional justice, for they often have scant resources, outreach, and staying power. They may rise and fall before they are able to make much of a difference in the lives of their members or the larger society. Their knowledge of similar groups or networks also may be limited, so that they are unable to learn from each other. Their scope may be entirely at the "grass roots," preventing them from influencing national institutions. National governments may be indifferent or hostile to their activities. Due to these deficiencies, national governments or international institutions may have important roles in helping create, strengthen, and form alliances among various civic groups.

Societies undergoing transitional justice should beware of certain dangers with respect to thinking about the potential roles of civil society in meeting the challenges of transitional justice and democratic development. First, civil society must not be absolutized as the new source of salvation, permanently replacing roles that other actors, including national and local governments, should play. As innovator, facilitator, critic, educator, and (temporary) substitute, there is much that civil society can contribute to transitional justice. Yet, here as in other areas, the state must be "brought back in."[36] For government has an indispensable role with respect to some forms of prosecution, punishment, compensation, and commemoration. And just as civil society can supplement and correct the state, a democratizing state may fortify and help unify a weak, timid, and fragmented civil society.

A second peril is the opposite of the first, namely, that civil society will *narrow its scope* and function as exclusively inward-oriented voluntary associations and thereby fail to assess and influence other institutions that affect transitional justice. Although Putnam is concerned with the decline of civic culture, Cohen correctly sees that his conceptual framework prevents him from sufficiently emphasizing the activist and deliberative potential of civil society. A self-help group of human rights victims or perpetrators, while important in a free and pluralistic society, is not all that civil society can be in relation to the challenge of transitional justice.

Third, a civil society that is neither absolutized nor isolated and diminished may still fail to give citizens in a transitional society what they need, for civil society can easily be *coopted by either state or market*. Strong, pervasive governments can dangle funds or power in front of voluntary associations and turn them into parastatal flunkies. Leaders of social movements or citizen members of truth commissions can use their positions to line their own pockets rather than advance the group's mandate. Military or corporate financial support may coopt critics into hired guns who sell slick arguments to promote revenge or forgetfulness.

Inflexibility is a fourth danger for civil society and its advocates. This is because, depending on historical developments and what the state and market in that society are currently doing or failing to do, civil societies in diverse social formations have diverse roles to play. The role of civil society in Chile, where – prior to Pinochet – there was a long and rich democratic history, is quite different from the potential role of civil society in Guatemala, in which repression lasted longer and democracy had shallower roots. The challenges to civil society and the public sphere vary with the circumstances.

V   International Civil Society

It is in relation to the strengths, limitations, and weaknesses of domestic civil societies and national governments that we can best understand the ways in which international civil society may contribute to a nation's approximating the goals of transitional justice. International civil society (ICS), I argue, can fortify, supplement, and correct domestic civil society, strengthen the hand of local democrats, and reinforce or (temporarily) substitute for a society's own institutions, including its government and civil society.

A domestic civil society (DCS) consists of groups whose members are (predominately) citizens of that nation and whose concerns, if they go beyond the group itself, (predominately) are contained within the borders of the nation-state. The weasel word "predominately" is used to acknowledge that the concepts of domestic and international civil society are fuzzy. A paradigm case of ICS, as I shall use the term, would be a group whose membership consists of citizens from many countries, and whose activities or concerns extend to many countries and to international structures and issues. The Roman Catholic Church, Physicians without Borders, the International Campaign to Ban Landmines, and the International Soccer Federation would be clear cases of ICS. However, a group whose members were all citizens in one country, such as Costa Ricans for World Peace, could be part of ICS if its members had global concerns or activities.

Let us distinguish two types of ICSs and a closely related kind of international institution: civil society groups from one country that aid the efforts of civil society groups in a country undergoing transitional justice; international not-for-profit organizations and movements; and transnational institutions such as the Organization of American States and institutions within the United Nations system.

The first type, the internationally oriented DCS, is illustrated by the Washington Office on Latin America (WOLA). Composed largely of US citizens, this US advocacy group supplies moral and financial support and US speaking opportunities to representatives of NGOs from countries such as Guatemala. Moreover, WOLA may transmit lessons that DCSs learn about transitional justice in one country to DCSs confronting the challenge of transitional justice in their own country.

The second type of ICS is illustrated by a profusion of heterogeneous international NGOs and movements. The term "globalization" is often used to denote global capital flows and transnational economic institutions. There is, however, another kind of globalization – movements and NGOs that investigate, debate, and help implement policies that affect transitional justice in particular nations and regions. This network is constantly changing and often lacks formal institutional definition; sometimes an ICS is little more than a "virtual community" committed to a common cause and linked by email, fax, and list servers. Still the contributions to transitional justice by groups of this second type should not be underestimated. Let me indicate a few of these ICSs and what they are providing.

Consider the global scholarly community concerned with issues of transitional justice in the context of democratic transitions.[37] It generates conferences, often subsidized by private philanthropic organizations such as the

Aspen Institute, the New York-based Charter 77 Foundation, the Friedrich Ebert Foundation (Germany), and the Instituto de Defensa Legal (Peru), that bring together scholars, policymakers, and policy analysts to understand, compare, and improve approaches to transitional justice.[38] A notable achievement in this area is the important three volume study entitled *Transitional Justice: How Emerging Democracies Reckon with Former Regimes*.[39] Emphasizing both national and international assessments of the ends and means of transitional justice, these three volumes include general essays, which evaluate different aims and tools in diverse contexts; 21 country studies, ranging from Germany after Nazism to Lithuania after the fall of communism; and a collection of laws, rulings, and reports that have emerged in the last 50 years. Thanks to these and similar studies, when a country embarks on a path to transitional justice its government and DCS will have intellectual resources and practical models on which to draw. They will not, as President Raúl Alfonsín said about Argentina's efforts in the eighties, have to invent "their approach from nothing." Although each country's experience is unique, Argentina's "having material regarding the Greek experience [1974–5] on the table would have been extremely valuable in helping them [the Argentines] to frame the issues and the options."[40]

Also noteworthy are the international investigatory/advocacy groups that conduct inquiries into human rights violations, monitor human rights compliance, and make recommendations as to how past abuses should be treated and future violations prevented. By providing international attention and support, these international groups can also lend legitimacy to, and strengthen the hand of, domestic civil groups and democratically elected governments in pursuing the goals of transitional justice.[41] Funded by a variety of private and national sources, these ICSs include Amnesty International, Human Rights Watch, the NGO Coalition for an International Criminal Court, and the Joint Evaluation of Emergency Assistance to Rwanda, an international team that investigated the international response to the Rwandan massacres.[42] Through their published documents and press conferences, these sorts of groups can inform domestic and world opinion and contribute to public deliberation about what should be done.

Organizations of the United Nations system play a variety of roles in national transitional justice. It is, of course, debatable whether the UN is best viewed as a quasi-world government, an international regime, or a part of global civil society. The category of civil society is used chiefly in relation to nation-states and national social formations. But, just as the increasing power of transnational corporations and decreasing power of national governments require a reconceptualization of international relations, law, and political economy, so the roles of the UN system require a rethinking of civil society and its relation to states, markets, and international forces and institutions. Not a superstate with coercive power, the UN seems to be best understood as an international body interacting with national and international civil societies. Although the UN has been beset with financial problems (largely due to the United States), waste, and inefficiencies, it has contributed to transitional justice in several significant ways.

In Guatemala, the United Nations Human Rights Observer Mission in Guatemala (MINUGUA) facilitated the peace negotiations, including agreements between the contending parties with respect to truth commissions and other measures of transitional justice.[43]

The UN established and funds the International Criminal Tribunal for the Former Yugoslavia (ICTY) in the Hague and the International Criminal Tribunal for Rwanda (ICTR). ICTY was established to "prosecute persons responsible for serious violation of international humanitarian law committed in the territory of the former Yugoslavia since 1991." ICTY has the authority to prosecute four clusters of offenses: (1) grave breaches of the 1949 Geneva Conventions, (2) violations of the laws or customs of war, (3) genocide, and (4) crimes against humanity. The ICTY has accused and issued arrest warrants for 74 people, indicted 20, 20 are in custody, 2 have been tried and sentenced, and (as of May 1, 1998) 5 trials are in process.[44]

Building upon the ICTY, the UN in late 1994 belatedly set up an International Criminal Tribunal for Rwanda (ICTR) as an international response to genocidal massacres in Rwanda. It is estimated that between April and June 1994, 120,00 Hutus killed as many as 500,000 Tutsis and their Hutu sympathizers. The ICTR's trial chamber is in Arusha, Tanzania; its Prosecutor and appeals chamber, shared with the ICTY, are in the Hague; and its investigatory and prosecutorial units are located in Kigali, Rwanda. The Rwandan case is not (yet) one of transitional justice in our sense since the predominantly Tutsi government in Rwanda is far from democratic. In any case, in its first two and a half years, the ICTR had achieved little: it had indicted just 35 people, had only 25 in custody (although some were Hutus accused of playing major roles in planning or ordering the massacres), had one trial in progress but had convicted no one. The ICTR's maximum penalty, like that of the ICTY, is life imprisonment.

Perhaps, due to this meager international judicial response to past evil, Tutsi-dominated Rwandan authorities are holding as many as 130,000 Hutus in custody, have tried 350 people and found all but 26 guilty. Of those found guilty, about a third have been sentenced to death, the domestic

Rwandan supreme punishment. On April 14, 1998, 22 Hutus were exe-cuted by firing squads in 4 sites throughout the country. While thousands of Tutsis cheered and talked about both retribution and the deterrence of Hutu guerrillas in the countryside, international observers had grave worries. Not only were there clear signs of victor's justice – for instance, many of those executed had neither legal consul nor sufficient time to prepare their cases – but the perceived lack of justice could result in Hutu reprisals rather than reconciliation. Given the sheer numbers of accused, the condition of the Rwandan judicial and governmental system, the lack of democratic tradi-tions and institutions, the continuing ethnic hostilities, and the multitude of Tutsis bent on revenge, transitional justice in Rwanda – through either domestic courts or ICTR – will be extraordinarily difficult.

An institution that likely would reduce these problems and substantially advance (eventual) transitional justice in Rwanda and Bosnia as well as in other countries would be the kind of UN sponsored *permanent* international criminal court that many countries agreed to in July 1998.

In El Salvador, the UN established and funded the truth commission and contributed personnel. In the Republic of the Congo, the UN funded a team to investigate human rights violations. When the Congolese officials refused to allow the team to begin its inquiry and arrested a UN investi-gator, the UN withdrew its team.

In sum, the UN has tried to influence and assist states in transition to forego morally untenable approaches, such as private revenge, victor's justice, and impunity, and to adopt mechanisms likely to realize the multiple aims of transitional justice spelled out earlier. In these efforts the UN has a mixed record ranging from important – if not unqualified – successes in El Salvador, to slow progress in Guatemala and Bosnia, to – up to May 1998 – the dismal failures in the Rwandan tribunal, to an agreement for an Inter-national Criminal Court.

Further work on this topic should assess the strengths and weaknesses of the two types of international civil society and UN institutions with respect to the roles they may play in transitional justice. Let us conclude, however, by suggesting the peculiar merits and limitations of ICS as such.

We have seen that international civil societies (and international regimes) can promote transitional justice by providing for domestic civic groups and democratically elected governments such things as material resources, rele-vant tools, international legitimacy, and moral support. Such assistance may be indispensable as domestic civil groups and fledgling democracies face the forces of revenge or impunity. ICS can also criticize and be a backup or substitute for domestic civic groups and national governments when there is good reason to believe that these have succumbed to anti-democratic forces.

In these various activities ICS groups often apply or appeal to international (human rights) law and promote a culture of universal human rights. Naomi Roht-Arriaza describes the situation:

> Over the last ten years or so, the insistency by human rights lawyers and institutions on the legal limits to government choices in this area [of transitional justice] has had an impact, albeit an indirect one. That impact has come through norm creation and diffusion, the creation of an authoritative vision of what is right.[45]

This "authoritative vision" takes two forms. First, it is embodied in international human rights conventions, treaties, and interpretations. These norms prescribe a nation's ignoring past violations and set forth that states have a duty to investigate and punish human rights violations, especially torture and genocide.[46] Second, the normative vision is an ethical outlook, the result of attempts to clarify and defend a global or world ethic, whose principles are used to assess international law as well as individual and institutional conduct that transcends national boundaries.[47]

Of course, in a world of putatively sovereign nation-states and powerful global economic forces, many national governments and some international bodies have routinely ignored these norms. Moreover, international norms can be used as smokescreens by which powerful countries dominate weaker countries. But newly democratic governments often ratify human rights treaties and conventions, and human rights proponents in domestic civil society advance transitional justice in their own countries by insisting on compliance with these international norms:

Before the 1980s, it was widely believed that decisions about prosecutions, investigations, amnesties, and the like were entirely within the sphere of each country's domestic jurisdiction. That has now changed; both governments and nongovernmental organizations now compile information, issue protests, rate government performance, and condition aid and trade on the treatment of past human rights violations as well as on the prevention of current abuses.[48] Yet, we must be wary here, not just due to political realism but also on moral grounds. For, as Carlos Nino rightly insists, too much or the wrong kind of international response to a country's past rights violations can do more harm than good for democratization and transitional justice.[49] International involvement and appeals to universal human rights can give some factions – for instance, the military – in a nation the pretext to reject, as an "outside job," international recommendations or pressure. In El Salvador, the fact that three non-Salvadorans composed the Salvadoran Truth Commission was used as justification for the government to declare – the week after the Commission's report was released – a general amnesty for all those individuals charged with violating rights during the civil war. Furthermore, international aid for domestic transitional justice can backfire. Instead of nurturing robust domestic civil societies, public deliberation, and responsive governments, international support for a nation's democratic transition in fact may insulate governmental efforts from domestic criticism. In turn this insulation may reduce public deliberation, narrow the national consensus, and, thereby, weaken popular support for the government's efforts.

To mitigate such risks, groups in ICS must stress, not only a nation's duty to investigate and prosecute rights violations, but also the right of citizens to be governed democratically. This right, however, would cut two ways. On the one hand, it would caution national and international actors alike not to push so hard for investigation and prosecution of a fragile democracy that was itself jeopardized. On the other hand, Roht-Arriaza is probably right that if a right to democracy were accepted, then "mere inconvenience or cowardice (or connivance) of [a] new government" would not excuse a government's failure to investigate and prosecute rights violations.[50] More-over, with a right to democracy internationally accepted, then there could be a variety of international sanctions against "attempts to disable or over-throw a democratically installed transitional regime in order to avoid legit-imate prosecutions or investigations."[51]

One role of democratic governments, as well as both domestic and international civil society, is to promote the acceptance of and compliance with universal human rights that include both a right to democratic govern-ance and a nation's duty to reckon with prior human rights atrocities. We should not underestimate the ways in which such international law, itself informed by a global moral consensus, can guide both international and national actors. Michael Walzer remarks: "There is today an international civil society, the very existence of which raises questions about the useful-ness of the state."[52] Walzer is correct in recognizing that ICS exists and raises issues about the role of the state. He is incorrect, at least in relation to the challenge of transitional justice, when he assumes or implies that the state has no role. Rather than seeing civil society at odds with or replacing the nation-state, I have argued that national and international civil societies can and often should play various roles in enabling emerging democratic governments to reckon with prior human rights violations. National governments are not obsolete if and when their sovereignty is limited, corrected, and supplemented by global norms generated, diffused, and implemented by domestic and international civil societies.

Notes

1 Transitional justice and civil society have attracted a recent flurry of academic and policy interest. The best collections on transitional justice are Neil J. Kritz, ed., *Transitional Justice: How Emerging Democracies Reckon with Former Regimes*, vol. I, *General Considerations*; vol. II, *Transitional Country Studies*; vol. III, *Laws, Rulings, and Reports* (Washington, D.C.: United States Institute of Peace Press, 1995); and Naomi Roht-Arriaza, ed., *Impunity and Human Rights in International Law and Practice* (New York: Oxford University Press, 1995). The *locus classicus* for the historical and analytic treatment of civil society is Jean L. Cohen and Andrew Arato, *Civil Society and Political Theory* (Cambridge, MA: MIT Press, 1992). An international discussion appears in Michael Walzer, ed., *Toward a Global Civil Society* (Providence, RI: Berghahn Books, 1995). For an accessible sample of the American debate, see *Brookings Review* 15, 4 (Fall 1997).

2 In the eighties, moral and legal philosophers Ronald Dworkin, Owen Fiss, Thomas Nagel, and Thomas Scanlon attended hearings in Argentina and conferences in the United States on transitional justice. Argentine philosopher Eduardo Rabossi drafted much of *Nunca Mas* (Buenos Aires: Editorial Universitaria de Buenos Aires, 1985), the report of Argentina's National Commission for the Disappearance of Persons. Another Argentine philosopher, Gregory Klimovsky advised Argentine president Raúl Alfonsín. In December 1996, the International Development Ethics Association and the Committee on International Cooperation of the American Philosophical Association sponsored a panel entitled "Justice, Amnesty, and Truth-telling: Options for Societies in Transition." Participants included philosophers Kenneth Aman, David A. Crocker, Pablo De Greiff, David Luban, William McBride as well as legal scholars Ruti Teitel and Gisela von Muhlenbrock. See also Kenneth Aman, "Amnesty vs. Justice: Latin America's Ethical Dilemma," a paper presented in the conference "Nuevo Orden Económico y Desarrollo: Desafíos Eticos para el Siglo XXI," Centro de Realidad Contemporánea, Santiago, Chile, Oct. 25–8, 1995; Pablo De Greiff, "Trial and Punishment: Pardon and Oblivion: On Two Inadequate Policies for the Treatment of Former Human Rights Abusers," *Philosophy and Social Criticism* 22 (1996): 93–111; Wilhelm Verwoerd, "Justice after Apartheid? Reflections on the South African Truth and Reconciliation Commission," a paper presented at the Fifth International IDEA Conference on Ethics and Development, Centre for Research on the New International Economic Order, Madras, India, Jan. 2–9, 1997.

3   Carlos Santiago Nino, *Radical Evil on Trial* (New Haven, Connecticut: Yale University Press, 1996), vii. In this quotation, although not in the rest of his book, Nino puts the question without indicating that the society deciding on its response is in the process of democratization. Mark J. Osiel, although he is centrally concerned with the special problems that what he calls "administrative massacre" poses for "new democratic rulers," also frames the question in this more general way:

> Administrative massacre, as I shall use the term, entails large-scale violation of basic human rights to life and liberty by the central state in a systematic and organized fashion, often against its own citizens, generally in a climate of war – civil or international, real or imagined.

Osiel, *Mass Atrocity, Collective Memory, and the Law* (New Brunswick, New Jersey: Transaction, 1997), p. 9.

4   Alfred North Whitehead, *Science and the Modern World* (New York: Macmillan, 1925), p. 200.

5   Ariel Dorfman, *Death and the Maiden* (New York: Penguin, 1991). For a penetrating analysis of the moral and legal questions that the play raises, see David Luban, "On Dorfman's *Death and the Maiden*," *Yale Journal of Law & the Humanities* 10, 1 (1998): 115–34. Luban disturbingly suggests that public prosecution and investigation is not (always?) the best way to deal with state-sanctioned human rights abuses.

6   See Pablo De Greiff, "Trial and Punishment: Pardon and Oblivion: On Two Inadequate Policies for the Treatment of Former Human Rights Abusers," *Philosophy and Social Criticism* 22 (1996): 93–111.

7   Daniel Goldhagen, *Hitler's Willing Executioners: Ordinary Germans and the Holocaust* (Cambridge, MA: Harvard University Press, 1996). For the reception of Goldhagen's book in Germany and evaluations, see James Joffe, "Goldhagen in Germany," *New York Review of Books* 28 (November 1996): 18–21; and Fritz Stern, "The Goldhagen Controversy: One Nation, One People, One Theory," *Foreign Affairs* 75 (November/December 1996): 128–38. Goldhagen responds to Stern in "Germans vs. The Critics," *Foreign Affairs* 76 (January/February 1997): 163–6.

8   This is not to say that any particular way of opening old wounds is justified. Victims who testified in hearings of South Africa's Truth Commission report suffered from flashback, sleeplessness, and depression following their testimony. Not receiving material or other compensation that they believed they were promised or due, these victims insisted that they had become expendable means to the end of the Commission's work. See Suzanne Daly, "In Apartheid Inquiry, Agony is Relieved but Not Put to Rest," *New York Times*, July 17, 1997, A1, A10.

9   For the first four of these objectives, see Margaret Popkin and Naomi Roht-Arriaza, "Truth as Justice: Investigatory Commissions in Latin America," *Law and Social Inquiry* 20 (Winter 1995): 79–116.

10 Mark Osiel argues that what he calls "liberal" or "discursive social solidarity" can be promoted "through public deliberation over continuing disagreement, a process by which rules constrain conflict within nonlethal bounds and often inspire increasing mutual respect among adversaries" (*Mass Atrocity*, p. 17, n. 22; see also pp. 47–51, 204, n. 136, 263–5).

11 For ethically-based approaches to good political and economic development, see David A. Crocker, "The Hope for Just, Participatory Ecodevelopment in Costa Rica," in J. Ronald Engel and Joan Gibb Engel, eds., *Ethics of Environment and Development: Global Challenge, International Response* (Tucson, Arizona: University of Arizona Press, 1990), pp. 150–63; Martha C. Nussbaum and Jonathan Glover, eds., *Women, Culture and Development* (Oxford: Clarendon Press, 1995); and Jean Dreze and Amartya Sen, *India: Economic Development and Social Opportunity* (Oxford: Clarendon Press, 1995).

12 Nino, *Radical Evil on Trial*, p. xi.

13 A proposal that Jack Upper made following my presentation of an earlier version of this paper to the Values and Development Group, World Bank, October 3, 1997.

14 W. D. Ross, *The Right and the Good* (Oxford: Clarendon Press, 1930), p. 19.

15 Osiel, *Mass Atrocity*, pp. 54–5.

16 Charles Trueheart, "France's Papon Case Puts an Era on Trial," *Washington Post*, October 22, 1997, A 23. See also Charles Trueheart, "Letter from France," *Washington Post Book World*, November 2, 1997, 15.

17 For the strengths as well as the dangers and weaknesses of employing criminal prosecution as a tool in transitional justice and especially as a way "to influence a nation's collective memory of state-sponsored mass murder," see Osiel, *Mass Atrocity*, p. 7. For an argument against trial and punishment, see De Grief, "Trial and Punishment: International Courts and Transitions to Democracy," *Public Affairs Quarterly* (forthcoming).

18 Osiel, *Mass Atrocity*, p. 43; see also pp. 68, 174–8.

19 Ibid., pp. 282–3.

20 Trueheart, "France's Papon Case," A 23.

21 Priscilla B. Hayner, "Fifteen Truth Commissions – 1974–1993: A Comparative Study," in Kritz, ed., *Transitional Justice*, I., pp. 225–61.

22 For a thorough clarification of this concept of public deliberation, in contrast to rational consensus, political bargaining, and aggregation of given preferences, see James Bohman, *Public Deliberation: Pluralism, Complexity, and Democracy* (Cambridge, MA: MIT Press, 1996).

23 Michael Ignatieff, "On Civil Society: Why Eastern Europe's Revolutions Could Succeed," *Foreign Affairs* 74 (March/April 1995): 128.

24   See Benjamin R. Barber, "Clansmen, Consumers and Citizens: Three Takes on Civil Society," Civil Society Working Paper #4 (College Park, Maryland: National Commission on Civic Renewal, 1997), p. 21.

25   See Robert D. Putnam, "Bowling Alone: America's Declining Social Capital," *Journal of Democracy* 6 (January 1995): 65–78; Robert Putnam, "Bowling Alone Revisited," *The Responsive Community* 5 (1995): 18–33; Robert Putnam, "The Strange Disappearance of Civic America," *American Prospect* 24 (Winter 1996): 34–48; Robert Putnam, "Robert Putnam Responds," *American Prospect* 25 (March–April 1996): 26–8.

26   Jean L. Cohen, "American Civil Society Talk," Civil Society Working Paper #6 (College Park, Maryland: National Commission on Civic Renewal, 1997), p. 7.

27   Ibid., p. 27.

28   Jean L. Cohen, "Interpreting Civil Society," in Walzer, *Toward a Global Civil Society*, p. 38.

29   Teresa Whitfield, "The Role of the United Nations in El Salvador and Guatemala: A Preliminary Comparison," paper presented at the conference "Comparative Peace Processes in Latin America," Woodrow Wilson International Center for Scholars (March 13–14, 1997), pp. 16–17.

30   Ibid., p. 17.

31   Ibid.

32   Bohman, *Public Deliberation*, pp. 4–5 (footnote omitted).

33   Dreze and Sen, *Hunger and Public Action* (Oxford: Clarendon Press, 1989), pp. 275–9.

34   Announcement of briefing, "Guatemala After the Peace Accords," Washington Office on Latin America and Center for Human Rights Legal Action, Washington D.C., March 6, 1997.

35   Ibid.

36   See Theda Scocpol, et al., *Bringing the State Back In* (Cambridge: Cambridge University Press, 1985) and Michael Schudson, "The 'Public Sphere' and Its Problems: Bringing the State (Back) In," *Notre Dame Journal of Law, Ethics and Public Policy* 8 (1994): 529–46.

37   See Naomi Roht-Arriaza, "Conclusion: Combating Impunity," in Roht-Arriaza, *Impunity and Human Rights*, p. 295.

38   Notable recent conferences include "Deliberative Democracy and Human Rights: A Conference in Memory of Carlos Santiago Nino," Yale Law School, September 23–4, 1994; and "Comparative Peace Processes In Latin America," Woodrow Wilson Center, March 13–14, 1997.

39   See note 1, above.

40   Kritz, *Transitional Justice* I, p. xxi. Kritz is reporting a conversation with Alfonsín during the conference whose proceedings resulted in the book.

41   Roht-Arriaza, "Conclusion: Combating Impunity," p. 302. See also Osiel, pp. 235–6.

42 See *The International Response to Conflict and Genocide: Lessons from the Rwanda Experience* (Odense, Denmark: Steering Committee of the Joint Evaluation of Emergency Assistance to Rwanda, 1996), 5 vols. See especially, John Erickson, ed., *Synthesis Report*, ch. 4, 37–9, and *Study 4: Rebuilding Post-War Rwanda*, ch. 9.

43 Whitfield, "The Role of the United Nations."

44 See David Rieff, "The Case Against the Serb War Criminals," *Washington Post*, September 8, 1996, C1–C2; and the World Wide Web site of the NGO Coalition for an International Criminal Court <http://www.un.org/icty/facts2.htm>.

45 Roht-Arriaza, "Conclusion: Combating Impunity," p. 294.

46 Diane Orentlicher, "Settling Accounts: The Duty to Prosecute Human Rights Violations of a Prior Regime," in Kritz, *Transitional Justice*, I, pp. 375–416.

47 See David A. Crocker, "Insiders and Outsiders in International Development Ethics," *Ethics and International Affairs* 5 (1991): 170–3, "A New Global Ethics," in *Our Creative Diversity: Report of the World Commission on Culture and Development* (New York: UNESCO, 1995): 34–51; and Charles Taylor, "A World Consensus on Human Rights?," *Dissent* (Summer 1996): 15–19.

48 Ibid., footnote omitted.

49 Carlos Santiago Nino, "Response: The Duty to Punish Past Abuses of Human Rights Put into Context: The Case of Argentina," in Kritz, *Transitional Justice*, I, pp. 417–36. See also Diane F. Orentlicher, "A Reply to Professor Nino," in ibid., pp. 437–8.

50 Roht-Arriaza, "Conclusion: Combating Impunity," p. 296.

51 Ibid.

52 Michael Walzer, "Introduction," in Michael Walzer, ed., *Toward a Global Civil Society* (Providence and Oxford: Berghahn Books, 1995), p. 3.

Afterword to Part Four

"Time cures all wounds," goes an old saying. When a war is over, however, the groups involved must face prospects of living together once again (or, if not together, then side by side in the state of new peace). And one would like to think procedures exist that can make healing and reconciliation likely while not too slow in coming. Leaving everything simply to the factor of time is unsatisfactory and unattractive, but we must recognize that different goals and corresponding processes may require different time frames for their prudent implementation. What, then, could be done in the aftermath of conflict to promote not only peace and security but also a sense of justice? These are difficult questions, and progress can be made only by achieving better understanding of the necessary conceptual tools for thinking these matters through. The goal of the articles in this final section of the book was, in large part, to help achieve just that. Concepts such as collective responsibility, transitional justice, "collective remorse" for wrongs committed by groups such as nations, and reparations for past injustices are among those that received closer scrutiny.

David Cooper explores the relationship between collective responsibility and reconciliation. He argues that there are two requirements for reconciliation among groups or peoples that have committed wartime atrocities: (a) While the groups are held "collectively responsible" for the atrocities, individual members – many of them, at least – are not themselves blamed, since considerations of "moral luck" (the ideology they were subject to, the "corruptive" circumstances of war, etc.) may exonerate them from moral blame; (b) While individual members are not morally judged by their enemies, they must themselves exhibit remorse for their actions. In arguing for (a) and (b), Cooper attempts to establish the cogency of the notion of collective responsibility, and to resolve the apparent paradox of how we can expect people to blame themselves for actions which we, the judges, do not blame them for on grounds of "moral luck."

But, can a group feel remorse over its morally bad actions, asks Margaret Gilbert? Or is it only individual group members who can feel remorse of any kind? Drawing on her previous work on the nature of social phenomena, Gilbert argues for an account of group remorse that does not reduce it to the remorseful feelings of individual group members. The phenomenon captured by the account is labeled "collective remorse." In short collective remorse in this sense exists when members of a given population are *jointly committed* to feel remorse *as a body*. Two other accounts of group remorse are considered: an account in terms of the remorse of group members over acts of their own that associate them in some way with their group's action, and an account in terms of the remorse of group members over their group's act. With respect to the last Gilbert argues that, contrary to what has been assumed, such "membership remorse" is indeed intelligible. Nonetheless, an account of group remorse as widespread membership remorse appears not to be adequate, as is also the case with accounts in terms of members remorse over relevant acts of their own.

Angelo Corlett sets out to outline and carefully consider several important objections to the claim that Native Americans in the United states are owed (deserve) reparations due to historical and contemporary injustices perpetrated against them by the US Government and its citizens. Corlett rebuts each objection to reparations, and then he offers and considers an array of possible methods of reparations to Native Americans.

Finally, David Crocker attends to discussing the role on national and international civil society in transitional justice. The so-called transitional societies face the specific problem in relation to their attitude towards the violation of human rights occurring within the society from which they stem. Crocker first takes a look at this problem by relating the goals that the transitional societies ought to achieve to various means of implementing justice, in view of both forming truth commissions as well as holding trials and granting amnesty. He then offers an argument in favor of the view that in a good many cases the national civil society itself ought to specify its goals and implement the means of "transitional justice," whereas the international civil society would only play an auxiliary role. The principles necessary for this process would have to be the principles of publicity and the principle of "discursive democracy."

The essays of this section take seriously the fact that there always will be wars and atrocities that come with them. They attempt to clarify and formulate a set of procedures for dealing with this reality from the perspective of sound moral and legal insight with an eye on what is practically feasible.

Further Reading to Part Four

Collective Action and Responsibility

Brenda Almond and Donald Hill eds, *Applied Philosophy: Morals and Metaphysics in Contemporary Debate, Part III* (London: Routledge, 1991).

Geoffrey Best, *War and Law Since 1945* (Oxford: Clarendon Press, 1994).

Margaret Gilbert, *Living Together: Rationality, Sociality, and Obligation* (Rowman and Littlefield, 1996), esp. chs. 1, 6, 7, 14, and 16.

——, *On Social Facts* (Princeton University Press, 1989), esp. chs. 1, 4, 5, and 7.

L. May and S. Hofman eds., *Collective Responsibility: Five Decade of Debate in Theoretical and Applied Ethics* (Rowman and Littlefield, 1991).

Thomas Nagel, "Moral Luck," in his *Moral Questions* (Cambridge University Press, 1979).

Morality and Reparations

John Bigelow, Robert Pargetter, and Robert Young, "Land, Well-Being and Compensation," *Australasian Journal of Philosophy* 68 (1990): 330–46.

Bernard Boxill, "The Morality of Reparations," in Barry R. Gross, ed., *Reverse Discrimination* (New York: Prometheus, 1977).

Joel Feinberg, *Doing and Deserving* (Princeton: Princeton University Press, 1970).

David Lyons, "The New Indian Claims and Original Rights to Land," *Social Theory & Practice* 6 (1977): 249–72.

Janna Thompson, "Land Rights and Aboriginal Sovereignty," *Australasian Journal of Philosophy* 68 (1990): 313–29.

James Tully, "Aboriginal Property and Western Theory: Recovering a Middle Ground," *Social Philosophy & Policy* 11 (1994): 153–80.

Jeremy Waldron, "Superseding Historic Injustice," *Ethics* 103 (1992): 4–28.

Ethics and Transitional Justice

Timothy Garton Ash, "The Truth About Dictatorship," *New York Review of Books* 45 (February 19, 1998).

Belinda Cooper, ed., *War Crimes: The Legacy of Nuremberg* (New York: TV Books, 1999).

David A. Crocker, "Reckoning with Past Wrongs: A Normative Framework," *Ethics & International Affairs* 13 (1999): 43–64.

Pablo De Greiff, "Trial and Punishment, Pardon and Oblivion: On Two Inadequate Policies for the Treatment of Former Human Rights Abusers," *Philosophy and Social Criticism* 12 (1996): 93–111.

——, "International Criminal Courts and Transitions to Democracy," *Public Affairs Quarterly* 12 (1998): 79–99.

Priscilla B. Hayner, "In Pursuit of Justice and Reconciliation: Contributions of Truth Telling," in Cynthia Arnson, ed., *Comparative Peace Processes in Latin America* (Washington, D.C.: Woodrow Wilson Center Press; Stanford: Stanford University Press, 1999), pp. 363–84.

Neil J. Kritz, ed., *Transitional Justice: How Emerging Democracies Reckon with Former Regimes*, 3 vols. (Washington, D.C.: United States Institute of Peace Press, 1995).

A. James, McAdams, ed., *Transitional Justice and the Rule of Law in New Democracies* (Notre Dame: University of Notre Dame Press, 1997).

Martha Minow, *Between Vengeance and Forgiveness: Facing History after Genocide and Mass Violence* (Boston: Beacon Press, 1998).

Aryeh Neier, *War Crimes: Brutality, Genocide, Terror and the Struggle for Justice* (New York: Times Books, 1998).

Mark Osiel, *Mass Atrocity, Collective Memory, and the Law* (New Brunswick, NJ and London: Transaction, 1997).

Steven R. Ratner and Jason S. Abrams, *Accountability for Human Rights and Atrocities in International Law: Beyond the Nuremberg Legacy* (Oxford: Clarendon Press, 1997).

Tina, Rosenberg, "Confronting the Painful Past." Afterword in Martin Meredith, *Coming to Terms: South Africa's Search for Truth* (New York: Public Affairs, 2000).

Robert I. Rotberg and Dennis Thompson, eds., *Truth v. Justice: The Moral Efficacy of Truth Commissions in South Africa and Beyond* (Princeton, NJ: Princeton University Press, 2000).

Ruti Teitel, *Transitional Justice* (Oxford: Oxford University Press, 2000).

Wilhelm Verwoerd, "Toward a Recognition of Our Past Injustices," in Charles Villa-Vicencio and Wilhelm Verwoerd, eds., *Looking Back, Reaching Forward: Reflections on the South African Truth and Reconciliation Commission* (Cape Town: UCT Press/London: Zed Books, 2000), pp. 155–65.

Index

Page numbers in bold type indicate a main or detailed reference.